SQL FOR SQL
SERVER

SQL FOR SQL SERVER

Bijoy Bordoloi

Southern Illinois University
Edwardsville

Douglas Bock

Southern Illinois University
Edwardsville

PEARSON

Prentice
Hall

UPPER SADDLE RIVER, NEW JERSEY 07458

Library of Congress Cataloging-in-Publication Data

Bordoloi, Bijoy
    SQL for SQL server / Bijoy Bordoloi, Douglas Bock
      p. cm.
    Includes bibliographical references and index.
    ISBN 0-13-113299-7 (pbk)
      1. SQL (Computer program language) 2. SQL server. 3. Client/server computing.
    I.Bock, Douglas Brian [date] II. Title.

    QA76.73.S58 2003
    005.75′85—dc22   2003058248

Executive Editor: Bob Horan
Publisher: Natalie E. Anderson
Project Manager: Lori Cerreto
Editorial Assistant: Robyn Goldenberg
Media Project Manager: Joan Waxman
Marketing Manager: Sharon M. Koch
Marketing Assistant: Danielle Torio
Managing Editor (Production): John Roberts
Production Editor: Maureen Wilson
Permissions Supervisor: Suzanne Grappi
Manufacturing Buyer: Michelle Klein
Cover Design: Bruce Kenselaar
Cover Illustration/Photo: Gettyimages/Photodisc
Composition/Full-Service Project Management: Progressive Publishing Alternatives
Printer/Binder: Courier–Westford

Credits and acknowledgments borrowed from other sources and reproduced, with permission, in this textbook appear on appropriate page within text.

Pearson Education LTD.
Pearson Education Singapore, Pte. Ltd
Pearson Education, Canada, Ltd
Pearson Education-Japan
Pearson Education Australia PTY, Limited
Pearson Education North Asia Ltd
Pearson Educación de Mexico, S.A. de C.V.
Pearson Education Malaysia, Pte. Ltd

10 9 8 7 6 5 4 3 2 1
ISBN 0-13-113299-7

BRIEF CONTENTS

CONTENTS

PREFACE

The Structured Query Language (SQL) is one of the foundation building blocks of relational database technology. SQL is taught within Schools of Business and Computer Science Departments in 2-year, 4-year, and graduate degree programs. Regardless of the level of instruction, as a student studying the computing field, you need to acquire SQL programming skills.

Our book teaches fundamental skills in SQL with additional coverage of Microsoft's Transact-SQL (T-SQL). T-SQL is Microsoft's implementation of SQL for its SQL Server relational database management system (DBMS). Although this book uses SQL Server as a DBMS platform for teaching the material, you will find that each chapter's concept questions and coding exercises, especially Chapters 3 through 9 cover the core SQL statements used for data retrieval and manipulation, and are applicable to the American National Standards Institute and International Standards Organization-92 (ANSI/ISO-92) standard for SQL implementation.

THE COURSE

SQL is taught using many different approaches depending on the collegiate level of the students. This book can serve as a main text for a stand-alone course on SQL or as a supplemental text for either an introductory DBMS course or an advanced course on information systems (IS) implementation.

USING OUR BOOK AS MAIN TEXT

Our book is an excellent primary instructional text for a course that focuses exclusively on learning about SQL and Microsoft's T-SQL procedural extensions to the language. The material in this book easily fits into a single term. We suggest covering the chapters in the order in which they are presented, especially Chapters 1 through 9, which comprise the core subject matter. You may alternatively reverse the order of Chapters 6 and 7.

Chapters 10, 11, and 12 are *overview* chapters. Chapter 10 surveys procedural aspects of T-SQL in terms of how the language can be used to write stored procedures and database triggers. Chapter 11 covers SQL Server database administration including the graphic user interface available in Enterprise Manager, database creation, database account creation and management, establishing roles, and granting permissions. Chapter 12 explains how SQL statements can be embedded in Microsoft Visual Basic programs. Hence, these chapters can be optionally covered.

USING OUR BOOK AS SUPPLEMENTAL TEXT

Many baccalaureate (BA, BS) and masters programs (MS, MBA) within business schools (management information systems) and science and engineering schools (computer science) offer a single introductory DBMS course, and include coverage of SQL as a topic within the course. The database textbooks used most often for these courses provide limited coverage of SQL—usually a single chapter. This text provides the additional supplementary material needed to add to the depth of coverage of SQL in such a course. Depending on the desired technical orientation of the course, instructors may wish to allocate considerable time to SQL, ranging from one-fifth to even one-third of the course duration. When the instructional focus is on *data retrieval,* Chapters 3 through 9 provide a focus on writing SQL queries. The database creation process described in Chapter 2 can be accomplished by having students download the SQL scripts necessary to create the databases used in the end-of-chapter exercises.

This text can also meet the needs of those seeking a supplementary SQL book that supports "self-study" for IS implementation and "capstone" IS project courses. Our book provides an approach that facilitates self-study complete with exercises and solutions to the exercises, while requiring minimal tutorial assistance.

PEDAGOGY

This book focuses on teaching standard ANSI/ISO-92 SQL; however, the textbook is "flavored" with additional examples of the supplemental statements provided in Microsoft's SQL Server and T-SQL. Hence, most of the SQL concepts and statements covered in the book are applicable to any DBMS software that follows the ANSI/ISO-92 SQL standard including DB2, Oracle, and MySQL, among others. Chapters 10 and 11 are the exception. These chapters are specific to Microsoft's SQL Server and highlight some of the procedural capabilities of T-SQL. This material is important because of the wide adoption of SQL Server as a relational DBMS product by industry and academic institutions.

SHORT CHAPTERS

Pedagogically, you will find that you can learn complex technical materials better when the material is presented in "bite-size" chunks. This enables you to assimilate the material better. Consequently, we have divided the various topics into short chapters. The typical chapter can be completed in one or two settings, depending on the length of a class period.

FEATURES AND USAGE (PROBLEM-SOLVING) APPROACH

You probably notice that you learn more by *doing* than by *listening.* This book emphasizes a *doing* approach. At first the text focuses on teaching the *features* of SQL commands. This approach is necessary to build your basic SQL knowledge if the topic is new to you. Following this, we emphasize the *usage* of SQL commands. Beginning with Chapter 3, each chapter follows this *features-usage* approach.

You can learn how SQL provides the information needed to answer management questions that typically arise as part of the management decision-making process. The chapters present typical management questions, and then show how different SQL coding techniques can provide the data needed to support the decision-making task. This pedagogical approach teaches you to match SQL coding techniques to different types of management questions. Hence, relevant management questions precede most of the query examples in the text.

EXAMPLES, EXERCISES, AND DATABASES

Each chapter provides numerous examples that initially present and then reinforce the concepts through the use of repetition. The book provides two sets of end-of-chapter exercises for each chapter. The exercises are based on two different databases. The *Company* database provides the majority of the coding examples provided within each chapter. This database is also used for the first set of end-of-chapter exercises. The Company database consists of seven entities and nine relationships. The database can be created by running an SQL script that is included in the text. The database creation process is explained in Chapter 2. The script can also be downloaded from the book's website.

The *Riverbend Hospital* database is a more complex database. It has 14 tables and 14 relationships. This database is used for the second set of end-of-chapter exercises that accompany each chapter. This enables you to complete additional work in a self-taught mode.

The inclusion of two sets of SQL coding exercises with each chapter provides instructors additional exercises to assess your learning of topics covered in the chapters. The SQL script for the Riverbend Hospital database is quite large (over 1,000 lines of SQL code) and can be downloaded from the book's website.

Solutions to the odd-numbered end-of-chapter exercises are provided to facilitate self-study and self-assessment of your learning. The solutions to the remaining exercises are available only to the instructor through the book's website.

OVERVIEW OF EACH CHAPTER

Chapter 1 reviews some basic relational database and DBMS concepts. It covers use of the SQL Query Analyzer as a graphic user interface software package for executing SQL statements. We assume that you have learned or will learn to design databases through the study of other textbooks and courses; thus, part of this chapter reviews fundamental relational database concepts including how tables are related to one another. For those of you who have not completed a course in relational data modeling, this chapter provides sufficient knowledge of relational databases for you to learn SQL as a programming language. Chapter 1 also introduces the Company database case that provides all the tables and data used for in-chapter and part of the end-of-chapter exercises throughout the book.

Chapter 2 teaches you how to define and create your own database and tables for data storage. Step-by-step instructions are detailed. The chapter teaches the use of data definition language (DDL) statements to define and create the critical elements of a database such as tables, columns within tables, primary keys, foreign keys, integrity constraints, and indexes. It also teaches the use of data manipulation language (DML) to insert, update, and delete rows in a table. This chapter reinforces your understanding of the relational database structures.

Chapters 3 through 9 cover all the primary components of SQL. The topics covered include querying single tables, querying multiple tables (joins), coding nested and correlated subqueries, using common functions, defining views, using autonumbering for surrogate key definition, and other topics.

The last three chapters focus on additional topics. Chapter 10 is an overview of procedural coding techniques provided through Microsoft's T-SQL for defining stored procedures and database triggers. Chapter 11 teaches you principles of database administration for Microsoft's SQL Server relational DBMS. Chapter 12 covers the use of embedded SQL statements within the Microsoft Visual Basic and Visual Basic.NET languages. This chapter does not teach embedded SQL coding; instead, it provides students with familiarity about how SQL is incorporated within procedural logic in database applications.

SUPPLEMENTS

This book is supplemented by a MyCompanion Website (www.prenhall.com/bordoloi) that provides the following supplementary materials to facilitate instruction. Note that instructors may need to first register at this Website to receive access to the Faculty area. Please choose the "Faculty Registration" link to complete the registration form. If you are already a registered instructor and have a MyCW account, choose the "Faculty Login" link and proceed to your account. You can then choose the "Add Book" link on your home page and locate the Bordoloi text from the management information systems (MIS) menu under the "Add MyCompanion Website Textbook Support" link. There you find the following:

1. Suggested syllabi for 2-year, 4-year, and graduate level programs;
2. PowerPoint slides for all chapters;
3. Complete SQL scripts for generating both sample databases;
4. Solutions to all end-of-chapter exercises;
5. Test Item File in Microsoft Word containing True/False, Multiple Choice, and short Essay questions.

ACKNOWLEDGMENTS

The origin of this book is our SQL class notes that we have modified over many years based on student feedback. This feedback shaped the contents, structure, and pedagogy of this book. Although we are thankful to all our students, we are specifically thankful to Nathan Boehler, Osman Hyder, and Susan Briner. We are also grateful for the insights and detailed comments and suggestions from the following reviewers:

Carolyn W. Carter, Milligan College
Steve Conger, Seattle Central Community College
James R. Engebretson, Cerritos College

Sarah A. Jones, Santa Fe Community College
Edd Joyner, The University of Tennessee at Martin
John M. Kiener, William Rainey Harper College

We extend our special thanks to the staff and associates of Prentice Hall for their support and guidance throughout this project. In particular, we would like to thank Robert F. Horan, Executive Editor of Prentice-Hall, who guided us through this project. We also extend special thanks to Mary Ellen Bock, R.N., for her support and guidance in creating the Riverbend Hospital database used for end-of-chapter exercises.

This book is dedicated to our parents, Dr. Nobin C. and Tilottoma Bordoloi, and Loren V. and Dorothy F. Bock.

SQL FOR SQL SERVER

CHAPTER 1

INTRODUCTION

Welcome to the study of the *Structured Query Language* or SQL (pronounced sequel or S-Q-L) as it is more commonly known. SQL is the worldwide language of choice for accessing and manipulating the information stored in relational databases. Why? Now and for the foreseeable future relational databases will play a dominant role in the design and development of information systems. They are the repositories of choice for the storage of all types of business and organizational information. This information includes both text data (such as customer names and addresses) and product identifiers and descriptions, as well as graphical image data, voice and sound data, and other types of data. Further, SQL is the language that is most often used to store and retrieve all types of information from relational databases. This makes SQL a very important language for you to understand as you work toward your goal of becoming an information systems professional.

At this point in your computing career, you may not have a complete understanding of what a relational database is. This chapter teaches you some basic concepts about relational databases so that you can learn the fundamentals of SQL.

This book focuses on learning Transact-SQL (T-SQL)—Microsoft's implementation of the SQL language. T-SQL is used with Microsoft's SQL Server database management system software. SQL Server is software that is used to create and manage relational databases whereas T-SQL is the language used to manipulate the data stored in a SQL Server databases.

OBJECTIVES

You can master the fundamentals of T-SQL and build your skill set one chapter at a time so let us get started! This chapter has the following learning objectives:

- Develop a basic understanding of what a relational database is.
- Learn the general capabilities of a relational database management system.
- Become familiar with the features of the SQL Server relational database management system.
- Learn to use the SQL Query Analyzer.

- Become familiar with the basic relational operations including the selection, projection, and join operations.
- Become familiar with the basic syntax of the SELECT statement.
- Learn the T-SQL naming conventions.

DATA AND INFORMATION

As you have no doubt learned in your earlier computer courses, companies and organizations, both large and small, create and manage large quantities of data. Raw data alone is generally not very useful—it has to be manipulated or processed in some fashion in order to convert the data into useful information. Often the manipulation of data is done by, or with assistance of, an information systems professional. A common task for an SQL programmer is to support the needs of an organizational manager. In other instances, the organizational managers may have sufficient computer knowledge and skill to manipulate data on their own.

You may ask, "What does the phrase *manipulation of data* mean?" This question is best answered by some examples. Suppose that a product manager needs to know the total sales quantity of a specific set of products that have been sold over a certain period of time by salespersons within a particular marketing region. This need is met by the aggregation (totaling) of data based on specific criteria including product identifiers, salespersons identifiers, and marketing region identifiers. The aggregated data is information.

Consider another example—a product manager needs to have a report that sorts the total dollar sales figures by salespersons from largest to smallest. This type of sorted information can enable managers to make decisions about which salespersons are meeting sales quotas and performing best. This same information can enable managers to determine which salespersons may need additional training in order to improve their sales performance. You may find that SQL is an excellent language for manipulating data.

RELATIONAL DATABASES

As organizations and businesses generate data, the data is collected and stored in a database. A database is an integrated unit of collected data. In this book we focus on the storage of data in relational databases through the use of Microsoft's SQL Server software.

Relational database technology dominates the current information systems world. Relational databases are designed and developed based on guidelines provided by the relational data model—a database modeling approach first described by E. F. Codd in 1970. Relational databases are complex structures that are actually composed of different types of objects, each object type having different purposes. Table 1.1 lists some of the more typical relational database objects. The primary object type of interest to us is the *table* because tables are used to store data in a relational database. You may or may not recognize the other objects that

TABLE 1.1	
Object Type	*Definition and Usage*
Table	An object that stores data including both user data and system data; conceptually, a table is usually depicted as a two-dimensional object with rows and columns where the rows represent data records and the columns represent data fields.
Index	An object that stores internal database information that is used to retrieve rows from a table as rapidly as possible.
View	An object that stores an internal definition of how a particular class of system user "views" logically organized information—usually a view defines how to combine data from one or more tables into a meaningful, logical organization that is meaningful to a particular class of user.
Stored Procedure	An object that stores programming code that is executed in order to complete a specific type of business transaction such as updating a table.
Trigger	An object that stores programming code that is executed in order to enforce business rules about the maintenance of data within tables.

are described—if not, do not worry about them at this point because each of these objects will be covered in detail in later chapters.

TABLES

Conceptually, a relational database stores data in the form of tables, such as that shown in Figure 1.1. This figure shows output produced by using the SQL Query Analyzer software. Specifically, an SQL SELECT statement was used to retrieve information from the *employee* table of the Company database. The information retrieved is known as a *result table* or *result set*. Do not worry about understanding the SELECT statement at this point. It is covered in detail later in this and future chapters.

A *table* is defined as a collection of rows and columns such as those you see in Figure 1.1. Tables are formally known as *relations* although it is actually fairly rare these days to hear someone refer to tables as relations. Most often, we simply use the term *tables*.

As you can see in Figure 1.1, rows represent records and columns represent fields in a file-processing sense. Each row has information about an individual employee. Each column displays information about a specific attribute that all employees have in common such as the social security number attribute or the employee last name attribute.

Each table has one and only one *primary key*. The primary key can be a simple key composed of a single column or a composite key composed of more than one column. Composite keys are covered later in this chapter. The primary key value uniquely identifies rows in a table. The *emp_ssn* column that stores each employee's social security number is the primary key column for the *employee* table.

Each column has a unique *column name* within the table. Column names may be reused in other tables and this is often done within a relational database. When a column name is awkward to use, it is possible to specify a *column alias name* that may be more meaningful to the system user than the actual column name allocated within

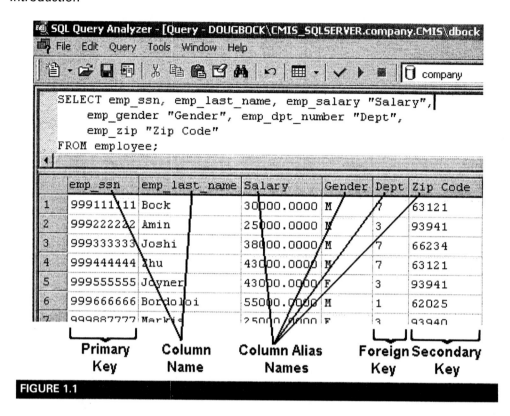

FIGURE 1.1

the table. In Figure 1.1, four column alias names are given. It is obviously easier to refer to an employee's *Salary* and *Gender* than it is to use the *emp_salary* and *emp_gender* column names.

One or more *secondary key* columns may exist that can be used to retrieve groups of rows that have a common value, such as employees who live within a specific zip code. A column may also store *foreign key* data. Foreign key columns are used to link rows in one table to rows in related tables. If you are not already familiar with these terms, you will become quite conversant with them as you study later chapters in this textbook. In fact, the next section explains foreign keys.

RELATING TABLES

Earlier we emphasized that relational databases are composed of tables (plural)! Figure 1.2 depicts what is termed an entity-relationship diagram that shows several tables and how they are related. This is, in fact, part of one of the sample databases used in this book called the Company database that you will learn throughout your studies of this and the chapters that follow. Appendix A describes the Company database in detail.

One of the primary tables in the Company database is the *employee* table. Employees have dependents and dependent data is stored in the *dependent* table. The relationship between these two tables is named *Has Dependent* as shown in Figure 1.2. The line connecting the two tables uses what is termed "crow's foot" notation to depict

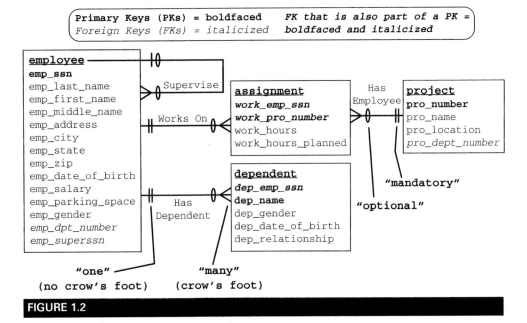

> Primary Keys (PKs) = boldfaced   *FK that is also part of a PK =*
> *Foreign Keys (FKs) = italicized*   **boldfaced and italicized**

FIGURE 1.2

the nature of the relationship. This is termed a *one-to-many relationship* meaning that each employee may have many dependents, but a dependent belongs to only one employee. The use of a crow's foot indicates many whereas the absence of a crow's foot means one.

So, how is it that the rows in the *employee* and *dependent* tables are linked? They are linked because the *dep_emp_ssn* column in the *dependent* table only stores Social Security number values that are found in the *emp_ssn column* of the *employee* table. The *dep_emp_ssn* column of *dependent* is a foreign key linked to the primary key column of *emp_ssn* in the *employee* table. Thus, foreign key columns in one table always link to primary key columns in either that same table or another table. For example, the foreign key link in the *dependent* table enables you to produce a listing of employees and their related dependents. You will learn to do this in Chapter 6.

You may also note that the lines connecting the various tables have lines and circles across them—these define whether or not the relationship is mandatory or optional in a particular direction. For example, the *Has Dependent* relationship is optional from employee to dependent. This simply indicates that some employees may have dependents whereas others may not—the Company does not require employees to have dependents! However, the relationship is mandatory from dependent to employee meaning each dependent must belong to an employee. This just makes sense if you think about it because the Company would not gather information about dependents that belonged to some other firm's employees.

The two relationships named *Works On* and *Has Employee* relate the *assignment* table to the *employee* and *project* tables. Normally the relationship between employees and projects is a *many-to-many* relationship. This means that an individual employee can be assigned to work on many projects and an individual project may have many employees assigned to it. When relational databases are implemented, these many-to-many relationships are decomposed into two one-to-many relationships as was done here by the creation of the *Works On* and *Has Employee* one-to-many relationships, and by the creation of what is termed an *intersection* or *association* table—here the association table is named *assignment*.

The *assignment* table links rows from the *employee* and *project* tables through the use of *foreign keys*. The employee social security number (primary key of employee) for each employee that is assigned to a project is stored in the *assignment* table. The corresponding project number (primary key of project) from the *project* table for the project to which the employee is assigned is also stored in the *assignment* table. Although this may be confusing now, it clears up completely when you study how to join tables through the use of foreign keys in Chapter 6.

Figure 1.2 has one additional relationship named *Supervise*. This is termed a *unary* or *recursive* relationship and simply means that an employee row may be related to other employee rows by virtue of the fact that some employees supervise other employees. The relationship is optional in each direction because the top-level employee has no supervisor and employees at the very bottom of the supervisory hierarchy do not supervise anyone. This type of relationship is also covered in detail in Chapter 6.

RELATIONAL DATABASE CHARACTERISTICS

As you learned earlier in this chapter, a relational database provides the ability to store and access data in a manner consistent with a defined data model known as the *relational model*. This model consists of a number of guidelines for storing data in a relational database, together with a number of operators that are used to manipulate the information. The characteristics of a relational database are:

- *It is data driven, not design driven.* This means that the design of a database tends to be stable over a long time period because the types of data that an organization stores over time are very stable. Also, a database designed with a data-driven approach minimizes the storage of duplicate data. Older, design-driven approaches often caused organizations to build information systems that could not easily communicate among themselves because of data definition inconsistencies.
- *The data are self-describing.* This means that table and column names are meaningful.
- *Consistency of data values is maintained among all applications.* With older technologies, a customer's address might be stored by an organization in two different data files. If the customer address is changed in one file but not the other, the data values become inconsistent. Relational databases minimize the duplicate storage of data so that customer addresses are stored in only a single table. This helps ensure data consistency.
- *Rules are defined and enforced concerning how data values are stored.* This means that the data stored in a database is valid. This is termed *data integrity*. As an example, an organization may have a rule that no hourly wage can exceed $75/hour. Another example of data integrity is the enforcement of a restriction that states that no customer sales order can exist in the database without a corresponding customer record.

The advantage of relational databases is that they are generally easier to use and have a higher degree of data independence than older database technologies. Data independence is the ability to make changes in a database structure without having to make changes in the computer application programs that access a database. Examples of computer application programs include programs that enable a system user to store new sales order information or information about new customer accounts.

DATABASE MANAGEMENT SYSTEMS

A database management system (DBMS) is a software package used to manage the data in a database. Figure 1.3 shows that a DBMS is a layer of software that enables information system users to interact with a database. A DBMS is a general-purpose software system that facilitates the processes of defining, constructing, and maintaining databases for various applications. Without a DBMS, it is impossible to retrieve or look at data, update data, or delete obsolete data in a database. The DBMS alone knows how and where the data are stored on an organization's permanent disk storage devices. A DBMS also enables data to be shared; information system users and managers can get more information value from the same amount of data when data sharing occurs.

DATA TYPES

Two types of data are stored within a database:

- *User data.* Business-related data stored by an organization. User data includes all information relevant to an organization's computer software applications that aid in running and managing the organization's various business operations.
- *System data.* Data the DBMS needs to manage user data and to manage a database. This is also termed *metadata*, or data about data. System data include information such as the maximum allowable characters that can be entered when storing an employee's name, as well as the fact that the name is stored as CHARACTER data. System data are covered in detail in Chapter 11.

DBMS SERVICES

A relational database is implemented through the use of a relational database management system (RDBMS). An RDBMS performs all the basic services of DBMS

FIGURE 1.3

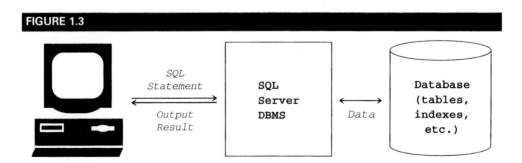

software mentioned above along with a multitude of other services that make the relational model easier to understand and to implement. These services include:

- Data definition for defining and storing all the objects that comprise a database such as tables and indexes.
- Data maintenance for maintaining rows (records) for each table in a database.
- Data manipulation for inserting, updating, deleting, and sorting data in a database.
- Data display for optionally providing a method of displaying data for information system users.
- Data integrity for ensuring the accuracy of the data.
- Data security for ensuring that only authorized information system users can access specific pieces of data.
- Database backup and recovery to automate the backup of important organizational data and to support recovery operations in the event of some type of systems failure.

SQL SERVER RELATIONAL DBMS VERSIONS

Microsoft's SQL Server is one of the most widely used RDBMS products. It is popular because it is a powerful data management product, and because SQL Server runs on Microsoft's popular Windows operating system. At the time of writing this book, SQL

TABLE 1.2

Edition	Description
SQL Server 2000 Standard Edition	Small- and medium-sized businesses without large data center applications will find this edition best fits their budget; it supports up to four central processing units (CPUs) and 2 GB of random access memory.
SQL Server 2000 Enterprise Edition	Aimed at large companies including multinational conglomerates that are moving into e-commerce; this version provides high availability and scalability; it can support up to 32 CPUs and 64 GB of random access memory; this package includes all management tools for managing multiple large databases; an Enterprise Evaluation Edition is also available for evaluation; the Evaluation Edition cannot be licensed for use in a production environment.
SQL Server 2000 Developer Edition	This is like the Enterprise Edition, but for system developers; it cannot be licensed for use in a production environment.
SQL Server Desktop Edition	This Edition has the SQL Server 2000 database engine, but not all of the management tools or analysis services; database size for this edition is limited to 2 GB; it supports full application development and deployment for small business applications.
SQL Server 2000 Personal Edition	This version has much of the functionality of the Standard Edition; it can service small groups of concurrent access users; it runs on desktop Windows operating systems from Windows 98 to Windows 2000 Professional Edition.
SQL Server 2000 Windows CE Edition	This runs on the Windows CE operating system for pocket personal computer (PC) devices.

TABLE 1.3	
Feature	**Description**
Internet standard support	SQL Server uses Microsoft's new .NET technology to support data exchange across the Internet including new detailed support for the extensible-markup language or XML.
Scalability	SQL Server can be used to build very large, multiprocessor systems.
Security mechanisms	SQL Server's sophisticated security mechanisms control access to sensitive data through an assortment of privileges, for example, the privilege to read or write specific information within a database.
Backup and recovery	SQL Server's sophisticated backup and recovery programs minimize data loss and downtime if problems arise.
Space management	SQL Server's automated space management capability makes it easy for a database administrator to manage disk space for storage; these capabilities also include the ability to specify subsequent allocations on how much disk space to set aside for future requirements.
Open connectivity	SQL Server's open connectivity functionality provides uninterrupted access to the database throughout the day; it also provides open connectivity to and from other vendors' software.
Tools and applications	SQL Server provides a wide range of development tools, end-user query tools, and support for third-party software applications that are used to model business processes and data and to generate program language code automatically.

Server 2000 is Microsoft's latest release of SQL Server. Earlier versions of SQL Server exist and are still in use including the successful Version 7.0. There are also different editions of SQL Server 2000 that support specific user needs and budgets. Table 1.2 provides a summary of these different editions. We will focus on the use of SQL Server 2000 Standard Edition in this textbook, and subsequently we will generally simply refer to this RDBMS product as SQL Server.

SQL SERVER FEATURES

SQL Server functions almost identically on all of the editions that are available. Therefore, an information system professional or system user who learns skills using one type of Microsoft Windows operating system can easily transfer these skills to the use of a different version of SQL Server on a different Windows operating system. The wide adoption of the Windows operating system makes knowledgeable SQL Server designers and programmers very much in demand. Table 1.3 outlines the significant features of SQL Server.

WHAT IS SQL?

SQL as a language is standardized by the American National Standards Institute (ANSI) and the International Standards Organization (ISO). SQL is a comprehensive database language. Prior to SQL, there were no standard data access languages.

IBM developed an SQL relational database interface in the late 1970s. The ANSI and the ISO both adopted SQL as the standard language for relational database management access. The current standard for SQL is the ANSI/ISO-92 version that was published in 1992.

In the introduction to this chapter, you learned that SQL is a computer programming language used to query relational databases to retrieve information from them. Actually, as a comprehensive database language, SQL goes beyond simply querying a database. You have already learned that SQL has capabilities to store data to a database. It also has the capability to define a database. These SQL capabilities are divided into *data manipulation language* (DML) and *data definition language* (DDL) statements.

DML AND DDL

The users of relational database management systems manipulate data with special (DML) statements. Database objects such as tables are defined with (DDL) statements. Both DML and DDL statements can be executed through use of SQL Server's SQL Query Analyzer. You saw part of an SQL Query Analyzer screen earlier in Figure 1.1. You will learn more about using SQL Query Analyzer later in this chapter.

DML primarily involves the use of four different statements: SELECT, INSERT, UPDATE, and DELETE. You will learn the basic syntax of the SELECT statement, which is used for information retrieval, later in this chapter. The INSERT statement is used to insert data into a table whereas the UPDATE statement is used to modify existing table rows. The DELETE statement removes rows from tables storing data that is out of date and no longer needed. You will study the INSERT, UPDATE, and DELETE statements in Chapter 2.

The CREATE TABLE statement is one of the primary DDL statements. Obviously the statement is used to create tables by defining the structure of tables. Other DDL statements are used to create indexes to facilitate rapid row retrieval from tables, as well as the creation of other database objects. DDL statements also allow database objects to be altered and dropped. DDL is the focus of the first half of Chapter 2 and the topic is revisited in Chapter 11 where you will learn about DDL statements that will enable you to administer an SQL Server database.

T-SQL

Transaction-SQL or Transact-SQL, or simply T-SQL for short, as we noted earlier, is Microsoft's version of the current ANSI standard for SQL. T-SQL has been in use for well over a decade and is popular because it provides many additional capabilities not found in the ANSI/ISO-92 SQL standard; however, all SQL Server's data access and manipulation tools are firmly based on the current ANSI/ISO-92 version of SQL.

T-SQL is used by SQL Server for almost all interactions with a database. T-SQL includes both DDL and DML statements. Further, T-SQL is basically a free format language. This means that there are no particular spacing rules that must be followed when typing a T-SQL statement. In addition, the nonprocedural portion of T-SQL's vocabulary is rather limited. Because of the limited vocabulary, T-SQL is relatively easy to learn for nonprocedural programming. The next section provides you a more detailed explanation of procedural versus nonprocedural programming.

PROCEDURAL AND NONPROCEDURAL

SQL is primarily a nonprocedural language. The term *nonprocedural* means that you can extract information from a database by simply telling the DBMS what information you need *without* telling the DBMS how to perform the data retrieval. Procedural programming, on the other hand, requires you to specify the logic needed to retrieve data from a database. Table 1.4 shows two different sets of programming statements that contrast the nature of nonprocedural versus procedural data retrieval. The SELECT statement on the left is nonprocedural—SQL Server retrieves the employee information requested without the system user explaining in a programming language how to retrieve the data.

The programming script shown on the right side of Table 1.4 specifies procedural pseudo code to accomplish the same task accomplished by the nonprocedural SELECT statement. This pseudo code may represent any procedural programming language and processes the rows in the *employee* table one row at a time. This procedure searches row-by-row for rows that satisfy the condition that the *emp_last_name* column stores name BOCK.

As you can see, a nonprocedural language requires you to specify only the task for the DBMS to complete—you do not have to write detailed programming instructions. Nonprocedural programs tend to be very short—not necessarily programs at all, but instead statements or commands. You also do not need to know how data are physically stored in terms of the storage format in order to use nonprocedural languages, such as SQL. Procedural languages, on the other hand, provide tremendous flexibility in terms of processing data; otherwise they would not exist at all.

T-SQL is both a nonprocedural and procedural language. It includes numerous *procedural* extensions and capabilities that are not part of the ANSI/ISO-92 SQL standard. As such, T-SQL provides the best of both the nonprocedural and procedural world. In this text, although we focus primarily on learning to write nonprocedural statements, we do cover basic procedural aspects of T-SQL such as Stored Procedures and Triggers. You will learn more about Stored Procedures and Triggers in Chapter 10.

TABLE 1.4

Nonprocedural	*Procedural*

SELECT emp_last_name,
emp_first_name
FROM employee
WHERE emp_last_name = 'BOCK';
	intIndex = 1
	DO WHILE intIndex <= Count_Of_Rows
	  If emp_last_name = 'BOCK' Then
	    DISPLAY emp_last_name,
	      emp_first_name
	  End If
	  intIndex += 1
	LOOP

SQL QUERY ANALYZER

The SQL Query Analyzer provides an excellent graphical user interface (GUI) for writing T-SQL statements. It processes both DDL and DML statements. You can use the SQL Query Analyzer to write T-SQL statements to define table and column structures; query a table; and manipulate data by inserting, updating, and deleting table rows. Extensive on-line help is also available through the SQL Server Books Online feature available from the Help menu.

QUERY ANALYZER CAPABILITIES

You will soon discover that the SQL Query Analyzer does much more than just process T-SQL statements. It also provides a GUI that can be used to:

- Create databases.
- Develop, test, and debug stored procedures once you learn to write procedural code using T-SQL.
- Run SQL scripts—these are miniature programs that contain either DDL or DML commands or a combination of these commands. An example would be a script to create a database, and then populate the tables in the database with data.
- Optimize system performance.
- Analyze query plans—these are the plans that the DBMS generates for processing a query.
- Maintain and manage statistics concerning database performance.
- Tune table indexes—the indexes are supposed to improve system performance for data retrieval, but sometimes adjustments are necessary in order to optimize system performance.

USING THE QUERY ANALYZER

Figure 1.4 displays a Microsoft Windows 2000 operating system screen where a system user has selected the *Start* button and *Programs* menu option to locate the Microsoft SQL Server tools menu options. As you can see, this menu allows you to start up the SQL Query Analyzer (simply called Query Analyzer on the menu) and other GUI tools such as the Enterprise Manager.

Figure 1.5 displays the log-in screen for SQL Query Analyzer. There are two methods by which you can be authenticated for log-in to SQL Server GUI tools. The first is Windows authentication. The Windows authentication approach confirms you as an authorized user based on the fact that you have a user account and password to connect to the Windows 2000 operating system. The second authentication method is SQL Server authentication and is based on the allocation of a user account and password for SQL Server by your system administrator.

Figure 1.6 displays the start-up SQL Query Analyzer window. Take time now to examine the figure. SQL Query Analyzer has many of the standard Microsoft menu options. The options here include File, Edit, Query, Tools, Window, and Help. Below the menu bar you can find the button toolbar that has many different buttons that make it easy to carry out common tasks quickly.

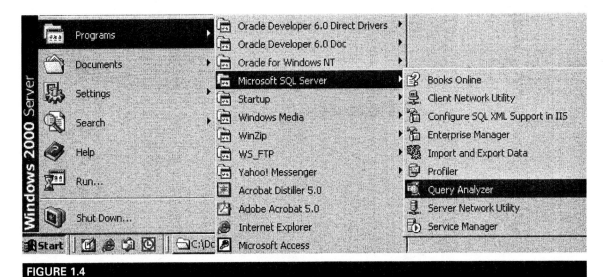

FIGURE 1.4

One of the main components of the SQL Query Analyzer is the Object Browser. The Object Browser in Figure 1.6 shows the server computer to which you are connected and lists the various databases available on the server. The database currently in use is the *Company* database that is expanded to show the available User Tables. The tables belong to the user *dbo* and are named *assignment, department, dependent,* and so forth.

Figure 1.7 displays the Query window of the SQL Query Analyzer. A SELECT statement has been typed into the window and executed. The Query window provides an Editor pane for use as a text editor. You can use the Editor pane to enter, edit, and execute T-SQL commands. After typing a statement into the Editor pane, you can click

FIGURE 1.5

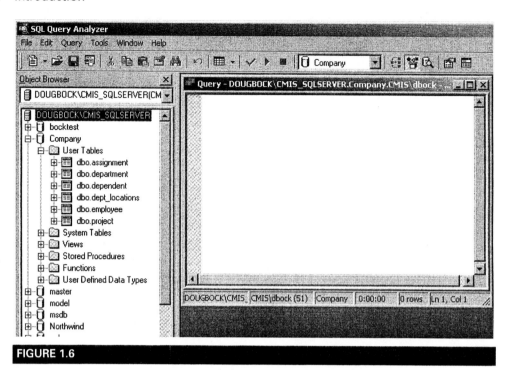

FIGURE 1.6

the Parse Query button (or Ctrl + F5 keys) shown in Figure 1.7 to check the syntax of the statement. Clicking the Execute Query button (or F5 key) causes the statement to execute and the Results pane displays the result of the statement.

You can change the relative size of the Editor and Results panes by using the mouse to drag the splitter bar up and down. The results can be displayed in a grid format as shown in Figure 1.7, or in a plain text format. You can also send the results to a file.

You can cut and paste, copy, and select all text just as you would with any other text editor. You can also do 'find and replace' text operations. A really nice use is to copy example code from the SQL Server Books Online help to assist you in writing T-SQL commands.

CREATING A DATABASE

When SQL Server is initially installed, five system databases are generated. These are named: (1) master, (2) model, (3) msdb, (4) distribution, and (5) tempdb. When you create a new database in SQL Server, the DBMS uses the model database as a template to create a new database. That is all you need to understand about the system databases or the actual files that are created as part of the database creation process at this point in your study of SQL Server and T-SQL. The actual command used to create a database is CREATE DATABASE. The simplest form of the command is:

```
CREATE DATABASE <database_name>
```

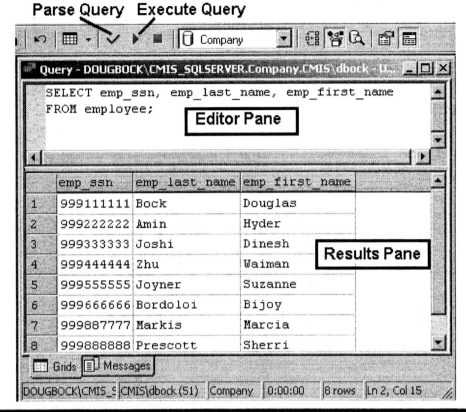

FIGURE 1.7

Normally only a system administrator has the authorization to execute a CREATE DATABASE command. The system administrator can grant you authorization with the GRANT CREATE DATABASE command. Assuming you have been granted authorization, let us create a database named Company. The command is shown here along with SQL Server's response in the Results pane:

```
CREATE DATABASE Company;
The CREATE DATABASE process is allocating 0.63 MB on disk 'company'.
The CREATE DATABASE process is allocating 0.49 MB on disk 'company_log'.
```

Simply type the command in the Editor pane of the Query window and click the Execute Query button (or press the F5 key). SQL Server then generates the system files needed to store your database. This may take a few moments or even a minute or two depending on the power of your computer. Once the Company database has been created, you will see it listed in the Object Browser. If you do not see it in the Object Browser, simply right-mouse click and select the Refresh option to refresh the screen. The USE command selects a database as the database to use for future processing. You can type the USE command into the Editor pane and execute it also.

```
USE Company
The command(s) completed successfully.
```

THE COMPANY DATABASE

Throughout this textbook you will study SQL commands against the backdrop of a sample database called the Company database which is described in Appendix A. You may wish to familiarize yourself with Appendix A at this time. At this point you do not need to worry about whether or not you understand everything you read in Appendix A. By the time you finish this textbook, you should be able to understand all the material in Appendix A.

The Company database consists of seven tables: *employee, dependent, assignment, project, department,* and *dept_locations,* and *equipment.* This does not include the practice *product* table that you will learn to create later in this chapter. Appendix A also lists the sample data stored in each of these seven tables. The number of data rows for each table is kept small intentionally. This should aid you in determining whether or not a query that you are writing works properly. It is very important that you verify that queries execute correctly with a small data set before using the query in a production environment on a much larger data set.

Note that the Company database that you just created does not contain any data yet. Chapter 2 explains the commands to populate a database through creation of tables and insertion of rows in much more detail. You will create the Company database in entirety as part of your study of Chapter 2. You will also learn more about the SQL Query Analyzer as you study future chapters in this textbook.

EXECUTING SCRIPTS

Sometimes you need to execute a script that contains a series of T-SQL commands or statements. The Editor pane can be used to create and save a script, as shown in Figure 1.8. Simply select the Editor pane to make it the active window; then use the toolbar Save option and specify the location, file name, and file format when the Save Query dialog box displays. You should use the default filename extension of *.sql* when naming a script file.

You can also open scripts and execute them, even if they were created with another text editor, such as Microsoft Notepad or Word. Figure 1.9 shows this operation. Select the Load SQL Script toolbar button and when the Open Query File dialog box displays, locate and select the name of the file to be opened. You also have the option to execute only a portion of a script. This is accomplished by highlighting the commands to be executed in the Editor pane; then use the F5 key or toolbar's Execute button to "run" the selected commands.

If a long-running query needs to be canceled, which may be the case if you suspect that the T-SQL code has caused an infinite programming loop of some sort, you can select the Cancel Executing Query from the Query menu. You can also cancel a query by pressing the ALT + BREAK keys simultaneously. Sometimes it takes a minute or more for a long-running query to actually cancel.

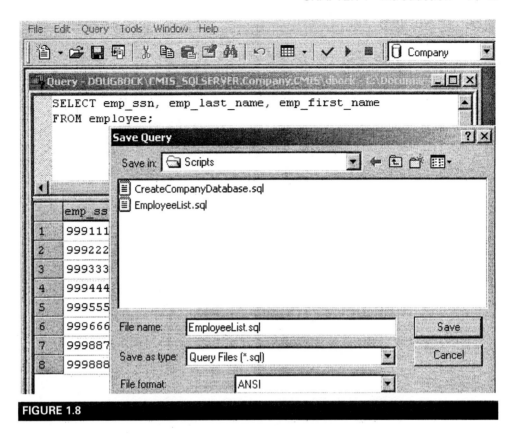

FIGURE 1.8

Creating, Saving, and Running a Sample Script

Now let us practice creating, saving, and running a sample script file. Create a script file by typing the statements shown in SQL Example 1.1 into the Editor pane of the Query window. This set of statements creates a table named *product* in the Company database; inserts three rows of data into the table; and, finally, displays the data rows from the *product* table.

```
/* SQL Example 1.1 */
/* Product.sql script - creates a Product table */
/*  in the Company database.            */
USE Company;
CREATE TABLE product (
  pro_id        SMALLINT PRIMARY KEY,
  pro_description  VARCHAR(25),
  pro_cost      MONEY );
GO
INSERT INTO product VALUES (4, 'Kitchen Table', 879.95);
INSERT INTO product VALUES (6, 'Kitchen Chair', 170.59);
INSERT INTO product VALUES (12,'Brass Lamp', 85.98);
GO
SELECT *
```

```
FROM product;
/* end of script file */

/* Result table output produced by the script. */
pro_id pro_description        pro_cost
------ ---------------------- ----------------
4   Kitchen Table          879.9500
6   Kitchen Chair          170.5900
12  Brass Lamp              85.9800

(3 row(s) affected)
```

Note the use of the GO statement in the script. The GO statement is used in a script where multiple statements are executed—here the multiple statements are the CREATE TABLE, INSERT, and SELECT statements. The GO statement is used to group a set of statements into a batch and execute the batch at one time. Do not worry about your level of understanding of the statements at this point. You are to be taught the details of each of these statements in the chapters that follow.

Save the script file as ***Product.sql***. Practice loading it and executing it. Note that after you have created the *product* table once, you cannot create it again without first dropping it. The statement to drop (delete) the table is shown in SQL Example 1.2. The DROP statement is covered in detail in Chapter 2.

```
/* SQL Example 1.2 */
DROP TABLE product;
```

FIGURE 1.9

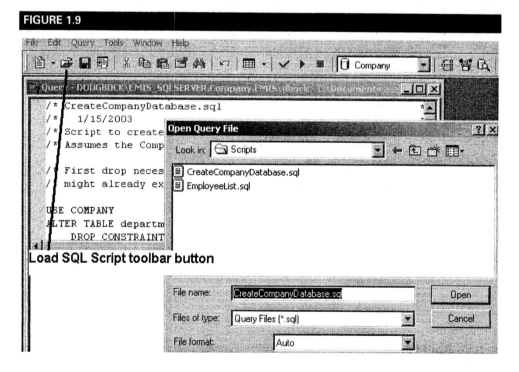

Load SQL Script toolbar button

INSERTING REMARKS IN A FILE

You may wish to include remarks within a script file in order to provide programming documentation. The ***Product.sql*** script file described earlier has several remarks. SQL Example 1.3 highlights the use of remarks with another script file. These remarks will help you remember what tasks the T-SQL statements in a script file accomplish at some later date. We have used the standard approach of enclosing remarks within "/*" and "*/" delimiters, as shown in SQL Example 1.2. Another method is to use the ANSI/ISO comment notation of two dash marks at the beginning of a remark line.

```
/* SQL Example 1.3 */
/*-- Employee Info Report lists SSN and last name. */
-- The Employee table is a master, base table.
SELECT emp_ssn, emp_last_name
FROM employee;
```

RELATIONAL OPERATIONS

As you have already learned, SQL statements can create tables, insert data rows into tables, update table rows, delete table rows, and query tables to display data rows. The remainder of this chapter focuses on the concept of querying tables and provides an introduction to writing simple SQL SELECT queries.

The SELECT statement is used primarily to write query statements that retrieve information from database tables. Remember that a database is a collection of related tables, with each table composed of rows and columns. The power of the SELECT statement comes from its ability to combine data from many tables to produce output in the form of a *result table*. Consider the SELECT statement shown in SQL Example 1.4 and the result table that is produced. Here, the SELECT statement queries the *employee* table and selects values from two columns named *emp_ssn* and *emp_last_name*.

```
/* SQL Example 1.4 */
SELECT emp_ssn, emp_last_name
FROM employee;

emp_ssn    emp_last_name
---------  --------------------
999666666  Bordoloi
999888888  Prescott
999111111  Bock
more rows will display...
```

For now, you do not need to worry about the syntax or format for the SELECT statement. Note that the *result table* is in tabular format with columns and rows. Each column has the column name as the heading. SQL Server dutifully displays each row in the table. Later, you learn how to limit the display to a subset of the rows from a table. You also learn to write SELECT statements that can include columns from more than one table. The ability to select specific rows and columns from one or more tables is referred to as the fundamental relational operations, and there are three of these operations: *select*, *project*, and *join*.

SELECT OPERATION

A select operation selects a subset of rows (records) in a table (relation) that satisfies a selection condition. The subset can range from no rows, if none of the rows satisfy the selection condition, to all rows in a table. The SELECT statement in SQL Example 1.5 selects a subset of rows through use of a WHERE clause. The result table displays only rows that satisfy the condition of the WHERE clause. Chapter 3 covers the WHERE clause in detail.

```
/* SQL Example 1.5 */
SELECT emp_ssn, emp_last_name, emp_first_name
FROM employee
WHERE emp_ssn = '999111111';

emp_ssn   emp_last_name            emp_first_name
--------- ------------------------ ----------------
999111111 Bock                     Douglas
```

Because each employee has a unique Social Security number (*emp_ssn*), SQL Example 1.5 selects a subset of exactly one row. Of course, if none of the employees has a Social Security number matching that specified in the WHERE clause, then the result table does not display any rows.

PROJECT OPERATION

A project operation selects only certain columns (fields) from a table. The result table has a subset of the available columns and can include anything from a single column to all available columns. SQL Example 1.6 selects a subset of columns from the *employee* table, specifically each employee's Social Security number, first name, and last name. Chapter 3 covers project operations in detail.

```
/* SQL Example 1.6 */
SELECT emp_ssn, emp_first_name, emp_last_name
FROM employee;

emp_ssn   emp_first_name           emp_last_name
--------- ------------------------ ---------------
999111111 Douglas                  Bock
999222222 Hyder                    Amin
999333333 Dinesh                   Joshi
more rows will display...
```

JOIN OPERATION

A join operation combines data from two or more tables based on one or more ***common column values***. Consider the *employee* and *department* tables depicted in Figure 1.10.

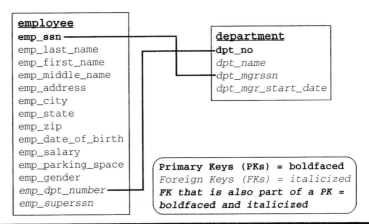

FIGURE 1.10

We know that a typical company may be organized into departments. Employees are assigned to work in a single department, and each department may have more than one employee.

The *employee* table has the *emp_ssn* column as the primary key column. Recall that a primary key column uniquely identifies rows in a table. The *department* table has the *dpt_no* column as the primary key column. Follow the line that links the *department* table's *dpt_no* column to the *employee* table's *emp_dpt_number* column. The *dpt_no* and *emp_dep_number* columns share common values, and rows from the two tables can be joined based on the values stored in these columns. The *emp_dpt_number* column in the *employee* table is a *foreign key* column. Chapter 2 covers primary and foreign keys in detail.

A join operation enables an information system user to process the relationships that exist between tables. The SELECT statement in SQL Example 1.7 displays column information from both the *employee* and *department* tables. Note that this SELECT statement also completes both select and project operations. The tables are joined based on values stored in the department number columns named *emp_dpt_number* in the *employee* table and *dpt_no* in the *department* table. The result table enables a system user to determine the name of the department to which each employee is assigned. The join operation is very powerful because it allows system users to investigate relationships among data elements that might not be anticipated at the time that a database is designed.

```
/* SQL Example 1.7 */
SELECT emp_ssn, emp_first_name, emp_last_name, dpt_name
FROM employee, department
WHERE emp_dpt_number = dpt_no;

emp_ssn    emp_first_name emp_last_name dpt_name
---------  -------------- ------------- ----------------
999111111  Douglas        Bock          Production
999222222  Hyder          Amin          Admin and Records
999333333  Dinesh         Joshi         Production
more rows will display...
```

The SELECT statement in SQL Example 1.7 is termed a *legacy inner join* statement because it represents an older form of the join operation. The newer ANSI/ISO SQL-92 version of the join operation is shown in SQL Example 1.8. Chapter 6 covers join operations in detail.

```
/* SQL Example 1.8 */
SELECT emp_ssn, emp_first_name, emp_last_name, dpt_name
FROM employee JOIN department ON (emp_dpt_number = dpt_no);

emp_ssn    emp_first_name emp_last_name dpt_name
---------- -------------- ------------- ---------------------
999111111 Douglas        Bock          Production
999222222 Hyder          Amin          Admin and Records
999333333 Dinesh         Joshi         Production
more rows will display...
```

SQL SYNTAX

Now that you have learned some basic T-SQL statements, you may have noticed that SQL requires you to follow certain syntax rules; otherwise, an error message is returned by the system and your statements fail to execute. This section formally defines the syntax conventions that you must follow in writing SQL statements. These rules are expanded on throughout the remaining chapters of the text. We begin with the SELECT statement.

SYNTAX CONVENTIONS AND RULES

Each SELECT statement must follow precise syntactical and structural rules. The following is the minimum structure and syntax required for an SQL SELECT statement.

```
SELECT [DISTINCT | ALL] {* | select_list}
FROM {table_name [alias] | view_name}
  [{table_name [alias] | view_name}]...
```

You may find syntax and structure examples such as the one above confusing. In the following paragraphs you learn how to interpret the brackets ([ ]), braces ({ }), vertical bars (|), and ellipses (**...**) used to define syntax and structure for commands. With a little bit of reading and work the conventions become second nature.

BRACES ({ }) surround mandatory options. In the example above, braces surround the second row. This indicates that either a table name or a view name must be specified. In fact, the specification of a table name only applies if the select_list contains columns from database tables and the FROM clause is used—as you will learn later, the FROM clause is optional.

```
{table_name [alias] | view_name}
```

A VERTICAL BAR (|) indicates that one and only one option must be chosen. Refer again to the second row.

```
{table_name [alias] | view_name}
```

The ({ }) indicate that a table_name or view_name must be chosen. The (|) specifies that either a table_name or a view_name must be chosen—not both.

When options are separated by a comma (,), both a table name and a view name can be chosen. See the command line below. If more than one option is chosen, the options must be separated by commas in the SELECT statement.

```
{table_name [alias], view_name}
```

BRACKETS ([ ]) surround optional keywords or identifiers. When more than one option is presented, it is separated by either a vertical bar (|) or a comma (,). In the following example, DISTINCT and ALL are optional keywords. You may use either DISTINCT or ALL, but not both.

```
[DISTINCT | ALL]
```

The square brackets ([ ]) indicate that a keyword can be chosen. The vertical bar specifies that one and only one option should be chosen. If a comma had separated the optional items, you could choose none, one, or more than one of the items enclosed in brackets ([ ]).

ELLIPSES (**...**) mean that you can repeat the last unit as many times as you like.

```
[{table_name [alias] | view_name}]... ]
```

PARENTHESES (**( )**), when encountered, are to be included in your SQL statements when indicated.

> *NOTE:* Brackets, braces, vertical bars, and ellipses are never included in an SQL statement. They are guides to usage and are not part of an SQL statement.

SQL KEYWORDS

Keywords are words that have a predefined meaning in SQL. Keywords must be spelled as shown. Uppercase letters are used above to depict keywords. In practice, keywords may be entered in upper or lowercase letters; however, most information system professionals follow the practice of always entering keywords in uppercase. Because this is an accepted naming convention, you should follow it. You should understand, though, that SQL statements entered in both upper and lowercase letters are exactly the same as would be the case for the SELECT statements shown as SQL Examples 1.9 and 1.10.

```
/* SQL Example 1.9 */
SELECT *
FROM employee;

/* SQL Example 1.10 */
select *
from employee;
```

In some cases, keywords can be abbreviated. The allowed abbreviation is shown in uppercase letters with the remainder shown in lowercase. This means you can use either the full word or only the uppercase part.

Lowercase letters denote user-supplied identifiers, expressions, constants, etc. The use of expressions and constants are covered in later chapters. For now, we focus on creating identifiers.

T-SQL NAMING RULES

The rules for creating identifiers in T-SQL differ slightly from those in the ANSI/ISO-92 SQL standard. Identifiers are the names given by information system developers and system users to database objects such as tables, columns, indexes, and other objects as well as the database itself. There are several rules for naming database objects that must be followed:

- Identifiers must be no more than 128 characters.
- Identifiers can consist of letters, digits, or the symbols #, @, $, and _ (underscore).
- The first character of an identifier must be either a letter (a-z, A-Z) or the #, @, or _ (underscore) symbol. After the first character, you may use digits, letters, or the symbols $, #, or _ (underscore).
- Temporary objects are named by using the # symbol as the first character of the identifier. Avoid using this symbol as the leading character when naming permanent database objects.
- The @ symbol as the first character of an indentifier denotes a variable name. Avoid using this symbol as the leading character when naming other database objects.
- SQL keywords such as SELECT and WHERE cannot be used as an identifier.

Delimited identifiers can be identified as those that are enclosed in quotation marks (double-quotes) or the use of square brackets. Single quote marks delimit character strings. Delimited identifiers can enable you to use identifiers that would otherwise be illegal, for example, you can use a blank space within a delimited identifier; for example,—[Product Code] is a delimited identifier. The best practice is to avoid the use of blank spaces in identifiers.

OVERVIEW OF SELECT STATEMENT SYNTAX

The basic syntax for a SELECT statement is presented opposite. We have intentionally limited the discussion to a description of the main clauses of the SELECT statement because you learn the various clauses throughout your study of this text. All of the clauses are optional except for the SELECT clause. However, you need to understand that when optional clauses are included, they must be placed in the order as shown below.

```
SELECT [DISTINCT | ALL] [TOP n [PERCENT][WITH TIES]] {* | select_list}
  [INTO {table_name} ]
[FROM {table_name [alias] | view_name}
  [{table_name [alias] | view_name}]]...
  [WHERE condition | JOIN_type table_name ON (join_condition) ]
[GROUP BY condition_list]
[HAVING condition]
[ORDER BY {column_name | column_# [ ASC | DESC ] } ...
```

As you have already seen, the SELECT clause is mandatory and carries out the relational project operation. It "selects" the *columns* to be included in the result table. The simplest SELECT statement has only the SELECT clause. SQL Example 1.11 returns today's date and time from the system by using the GETDATE function. The DISTINCT, ALL, TOP, and INTO keywords are explained in later chapters.

```
/* SQL Example 1.11 */
SELECT getdate() "Today's Date/Time";


Today's Date/Time
------------------------------------------
2003-01-28 18:56:13.450
(1 row(s) affected)
```

The FROM clause is optional providing you are not selecting from a table. SQL Example 1.11 shows a SELECT statement that does not select from a table. However, most of the time you will use the FROM clause anyway because it identifies one or more tables or views from which to retrieve the column data displayed in a result table.

The optional JOIN clause specifies the manner by which rows from two or more tables are to be linked. It is also used for linking rows within a single table.

The WHERE clause is optional and can optionally be used in place of a JOIN to link two or more tables. Much of the time the WHERE clause carries out the relational select operation. It specifies which *rows* are to be selected.

The GROUP BY clause is optional. It organizes data into groups by one or more column names listed in the SELECT clause.

The optional HAVING clause sets conditions concerning which groups to include in a result table. The groups are specified by the GROUP BY clause. As you can see in studying later chapters, the HAVING and GROUP BY clauses tend to go hand in hand.

The ORDER BY clause is optional. It sorts query results by one or more columns in ascending or descending order. The maximum number of columns allowed in ORDER BY is 16 columns, which is a very large number of columns by which to sort any type of data!

SUMMARY

Information is raw data that has been manipulated, and SQL is the language of choice for manipulating data stored in relational databases. The primary database object with which you work is the table. It stores business and organizational data as well as system data about a database. Each table has a primary key column that uniquely identifies rows and each column has a unique column name within the table. Tables are related or linked through the use of foreign key column values.

A relational DBMS is a software package that is used to manage data in a relational database. SQL Server is Microsoft's multi-user relational DBMS software package. It comes in different editions and has numerous features including SQL Query Analyzer, a graphical user interface (GUI) that supports the execution of both data manipulation language (DML) and data definition language (DDL) SQL statements.

T-SQL is Microsoft's implementation of SQL for use with SQL Server. T-SQL supports both procedural and nonprocedural programming practices. SQL Query Analyzer enables you to build and execute script files that contain related sets of SQL statements. SQL statements perform three fundamental relational operations: select, project, and join. Each of these operations is performed through the use of various SELECT statement clauses. As you can see, a SELECT statement can be very complex. This is reasonable considering that the SELECT statement is the primary tool used to query a database. In the chapters that follow, you learn about the different clauses of the SELECT statement. In each chapter, the minimum SELECT syntax to query a database is explained and demonstrated.

REVIEW EXERCISES

LEARN THESE TERMS

ANSI/ISO-92. The current standard version of SQL.

Column and **Column Name.** Terms used to refer to a *column* of data in a relational database table. These terms are analogous to *field* in a file-processing sense. Each column has a unique column name within a table.

Column Alias Name. A meaningful name that refers to a column name that may be awkward to use.

Data. Raw facts.

Data Definition Language (DDL). A set of SQL commands used to create and define objects in a database.

Data Independence. The ability to make changes in the database structure without having to make changes in the programs that access the database.

Data Manipulation Language (DML). A set of SQL commands that allow users to manipulate the data in a database.

Database. An integrated unit of collected data.

Database Management System (DBMS). Manages the data in a database.

Foreign Key. A column that is used to link rows in one table to rows in a related table or table(s).

Information. Data organized in a logical and meaningful way.

Join. An operation that combines data from two or more tables.

Metadata. Data about data; also termed *system data*.

Nonprocedural. Means that you can extract information from a database by simply telling the DBMS what information you need *without* telling the DBMS how to perform the data retrieval.

Procedural. Means that you must specify the logic needed to retrieve data from a database.

One-to-Many Relationship. Rows in one table may be related to zero, one, or more than one rows in another table.

Primary Key. Uniquely identifies rows in a table.

Project.   An operation that selects only certain columns of a table or a subset of all available columns.

Query.   An SQL command that retrieves information (data rows) from database tables.

Relation.   The formal term for table in the relational model.

Relational Database.   A collection of tables (relations).

Relational Database Management System (RDBMS).   A DBMS based on the relational model.

Relational Model.   A set of guidelines for designing and storing data in a relational database.

Result table.   Also termed a *result set*, this is the subset of data retrieved by an SQL SELECT statement.

Row.   A term that refers to a *row* of data in a relational database table. This term is analogous to a *record* in a file-processing sense.

Secondary Key.   A column that can be used to retrieve groups of rows with a common value.

Select.   An operation that selects a subset of rows in a relation that satisfies a selection condition. Also, SELECT is a command within SQL.

SQL.   An acronym for Structured Query Language.

SQL Query Analyzer.   A graphical user interface component of SQL Server that enables you to perform various DML and DDL tasks.

System Data.   Data the DBMS needs to manage user data and to manage a database.

Table.   A database object that stores organizational information. Conceptually, a table stores information in rows, one row per record, and columns, one column per data field.

Transact-Structured Query Language (T-SQL).   Microsoft SQL Server's database language for the manipulation and definition of relational databases.

User Data.   Business-related data stored by an organization.

CONCEPTS QUIZ

1. Differentiate between User data and System data.
2. What is another term for System data?
3. Conceptually, how are data stored in a relational DBMS?
4. What are some of the characteristics of a relational DBMS?
5. List and describe four of the seven services provided by a DBMS for the management of a database.
6. List and describe three of the significant features of SQL Server as a DBMS.
7. One of your colleagues has proposed using the names listed below as column names for an SQL Server database table. Explain whether the names proposed are suitable for column names.

   - First Name
   - &Salary
   - Weekly_4
   - Select

8. What type of activities can be accomplished with a data definition language?
9. What type of activities can be accomplished with a data manipulation language?
10. SQL is described as a *nonprocedural language*. T-SQL is described as both a nonprocedural and a *procedural language*. What do these two terms mean?

SQL CODING EXERCISES AND QUESTIONS: COMPANY DATABASE

1. What is the purpose of the SQL SELECT statement?
2. What is the purpose of the WHERE clause in a SELECT statement?
3. How do you specify which columns from a table are displayed by a SELECT statement? How do you specify the order in which columns are displayed by a SELECT statement?

4. What type of operation is used to combine data from two or more tables based on common table column values?
5. What syntactical operator is used to separate column names and table names in a SELECT statement?
6. Complete the following paragraph by filling in all spaces: It is important to learn how to interpret syntax and structure examples. It is essential to understand that _____ surround mandatory options. In addition, a _____ indicates that only one option must be chosen, whereas a _____ indicates that one or both options can be chosen. _____ surround optional keywords or identifiers.
7. What effect does typing a command in either uppercase or lowercase letters have on execution by SQL Server?
8. What are the rules for naming a database object?
9. Which clause in a SELECT statement is used to sort query results?
10. Invoke the SQL Query Analyzer. Create a database called *Company,* if you did not already do so while studying this current chapter.

SQL Coding Exercises and Questions: Riverbend Database

Appendix B describes the Riverbend Hospital Database case. Chapter 2 provides details on the creation of this database. Complete the questions in this section as pencil-and-paper exercises. Beginning with Chapter 2, you will complete similar exercises using SQL Query Analyzer.

1. Study the *patient* and *patient_note* tables in Appendix B. Is the relationship between these two tables one-to-one, one-to-many, or many-to-many? Explain why.
2. Write a SELECT statement to display the patient identifier (*pat_id*) and patient last name (*pat_last_name*) for all patients with a last name of 'Young'.
3. Write a SELECT statement to display all columns for a patient with the ID of 100306.
4. Study the patient, bed, room, and bed_type tables in Appendix B. What are the relationships between these tables? Explain why.
5. Write a SELECT statement to display all rows and all columns from the *bed_type* table.
6. The Riverbend Hospital has many different wards and departments. Information about these areas of the hospital is stored to a table named *ward_dept.* Study the relationship between the *ward_dept* and *staff* tables in Appendix B. Is the relationship between these two tables one-to-one, one-to-many, or many-to-many? Explain why.
7. Write a SELECT statement to display the *ward_id* and *ward_dept_name* columns from the *ward_dept* table (all rows).
8. Based on your study of Appendix B, how is the relationship between the *staff* and *medical_specialty* tables implemented?
9. Write a SELECT statement to display the *staff_id* and *specialty_code* columns for all staff members with a specialty code of 'RN1' — the code for registered nurse.
10. The Riverbend Hospital provides various medical services to patients. These services are categorized for purposes of insurance reporting. Information about these service

categories is stored in the *service_cat* table. Write a SELECT statement to list all columns and rows from this table.

11. Staff members provide services to patients. Based on your study of Appendix B, what is the name of this relationship? What are the names of the tables that implement this relationship?

12. Rows stored to the treatment table are identified by a combination of the *treatment_number* and *treatment_date* columns. Write a SELECT statement to the *treatment_number*, *treatment_date*, and *treatment_comments* columns from the *treatment* table where the *treatment_number* = 10.

13. Prescriptions are provided by staff members for medicine to be given to patients. What is the name of the table used to store information about prescriptions, and what are the names of the tables that participate in relationships with the table used to store prescription information?

14. Write a SELECT statement to list the *medicine_code*, *med_name_sci* (scientific name), and *med_name_common* (common name) columns from the *medicine* table. Your query should list all of the rows, but you only need to submit output for grading that lists the first eight rows.

REFERENCES

Codd, E. F., 1970. A relational model of data for large shared data banks. *Communications of the ACM*, 13 (June), 377–387.

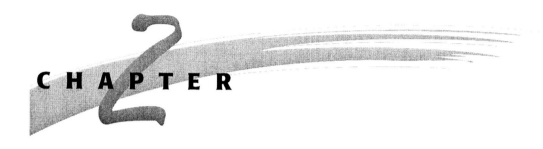
CREATING TABLES AND INDEXES

Databases vary in complexity. To a great extent, this complexity depends on the organizational environment. Some databases, like those used by government agencies or large corporations are very large and are distributed across wide-area networks (WANs). Distributed databases provide database access for thousands of system users and enable the storage of millions and millions of rows of data in hundreds of tables. At the other extreme are small, personal databases that run on desktop computers. Most databases fall somewhere between these extremes.

Database design involves identifying system user requirements for various organizational systems such as order entry, inventory management, and accounts receivable. Databases grow and evolve over time. A single information system, such as that associated with processing customer orders, can interface with a number of tables, and often these tables can be accessed by many different, yet related information systems. A typical corporate organization may have several hundred tables within the enterprise-wide database.

OBJECTIVES

Regardless of database size and complexity, each database is composed of *tables*. One of the first steps in creating a database is to create the tables that will store an organization's data. In this chapter, you will learn to create tables and store data in tables. You will also learn how to define a relationship between rows in one table to rows in another table by using the concept of *foreign keys (FKs)*. Additionally, you will learn to define different types of *integrity constraints* for database tables to maintain the validity of the data that are stored. The latter part of this chapter teaches you how to modify tables and how to create indexes that enable the rapid retrieval of data based on data characteristics. In later chapters, you will study the creation of other physical components of a database. Your learning objectives for this chapter are:

- Learn how to name tables, columns, and constraints.
- Select appropriate data types for data storage (includes understanding the different characteristics of SQL Server data types).

- Create and drop tables (includes understanding data integrity and table constraints).
- Rename and modify tables.
- Specify and maintain referential integrity among tables.
- Specify primary and foreign keys .
- Insert rows into and update rows in tables.
- Delete rows from tables.
- Create and drop indexes.

> *NOTE:* Completion of the exercises in this and subsequent chapters assumes that you created a database named Company during your study of Chapter 1. Use the Company database to store the tables that you create during your study of this chapter.

TABLE CREATION

To create a table, four pieces of information must be determined: (1) table name, (2) column (field) names, (3) column data types, and (4) column sizes.

NAMING TABLES AND COLUMNS

Naming tables and columns is a type of physical design task. You may work as a database designer or a systems analyst, or may, in fact, fill both roles by developing or following written system specifications for the logical design of an information system. The logical design documentation usually specifies table names, column names, and type of data to be stored in each column. As a database designer, you will translate the logical system specifications into physical specifications.

When you build a new information system, you do not build it in a vacuum. The typical firm that exists in todays business environment already has existing databases with defined tables storing data that are in use for automated systems. In fact, in the vast majority of cases, new information systems access database tables that already exist. Additionally, a new information system may require the creation of new tables or the modification of existing tables.

For example, if a firm has an existing automated inventory system that stores product information to a database, the *product* table already exists. If you are building a new, automated order entry system that needs to access product information, then the existing *product* table used by the inventory system can also be accessed by the order entry system. You would not build two separate *product* tables because the duplicate storage of product data would be costly and could result in data inconsistencies, that is, data values such as product descriptions that are different in two separate tables. In larger firms, an experienced database administrator (DBA) can assist you with the table creation task. In smaller firms, you may be responsible for completing both logical and physical design tasks.

Table and column names should be meaningful and reflect the nature of the data that is to be stored. If you are storing data about products that a firm sells, then the table should probably be named *product* or some similar name. Similarly, if products are identified by a string of eight characters, then the column that stores product identification data should be named *product_number, product_code,* or a similar meaningful name. You may also use prefixes as we do in Chapter 1. For example, *pro_number* would be meaningful in such a setting.

SELECTING A DATA TYPE

The data type you choose for a column determines the nature of the data that can be stored in the column. This is termed the *domain* of valid column values. For example, if you declare a column to be DATETIME type data, then any date value stored to the column can only be accepted by the database management system (DBMS) if the date is valid. Attempting to store March 32 will not work because there is no day 32 in March. Likewise, attempting to store the value 182 or the value Tom to a DATE column will not work because data types provide rudimentary error checking. This reduces the probability that incorrect values are assigned to a column. Data types also allow disk storage space to be used efficiently. SQL Server provides a number of predefined data types as well as the ability to declare your own data types. We focus on the predefined data types.

Transact-SQL (T-SQL) provides numerous data types categorized as follows:

- Numeric data types;
- String or Character data types—including binary data (bit strings);
- Date or time data types;
- Derived data types;
- Special, new data types.

We restrict our focus in this chapter to the data types that can be used to declare the type of data to be stored in columns of a data table.

NUMERIC DATA

The numeric data types encompass both integer, fixed-point, floating-point, and monetary numeric values. You should choose a numeric data type when a column stores numeric data that can be used in mathematical calculations. The numeric data types are summarized in Tables 2.1 through 2.3. These data types store numbers using varying quantities of disk space.

The four integer data types are BIGINT, INT, SMALLINT, and TINYINT. BIGINT is a new numeric data type in SQL Server 2000. Table 2.1 shows that the difference between these four data types is the amount of data storage needed to store values, and the range of values that can be stored. BIGINT can store both very large

TABLE 2.1   Integer Numeric Data Types

Integer Numeric Data Types	*Description*
BIGINT	Integer values requiring 8 bytes of storage; values stored range from -2^{63} to $2^{63} - 1$
INTEGER or INT	Integer values requiring 4 bytes of storage; INT is short for INTEGER
SMALLINT	Integer values requiring 2 bytes of storage; values stored range from -32768 to 32767
TINYINT	Integer values (nonnegative only) that can be stored in 1 byte; values stored range from 0 to 255

TABLE 2.2 Real Numeric Data Types	
Real Numeric Data Types	*Description*
DECIMAL(p,[s]) or DEC	Fixed point values with precision *p* that specifies the total number of digits, with assumed decimal point of scale *s* to the right of the decimal; memory requirements vary from 2 to 17 bytes depending on the value of *p;* the specification of a value for *s* is optional
NUMERIC(p,[s])	Same as DECIMAL
REAL	Floating point values; positive values stored range from 2.23E—308 to 1.79E + 308; negative values stored range from −2.23E − 308 to −1.79E + 308
FLOAT[(p)]	Floating point values like REAL where the parameter *p* specifies the precision; when *p* < 25, the number is stored using 4 bytes and is single precision; when *p* >= 25, the number is stored using 8 bytes and is double precision

TABLE 2.3 Monetary Numeric Data Types	
Monetary Numeric Data Types	*Description*
MONEY	Monetary values requiring 8 bytes of storage; this corresponds to 8-byte DECIMAL values rounded to four digits to the right of the decimal point
SMALLMONEY	Monetary values requiring 4 bytes of storage

and very small integer values, but requires 8 bytes of storage whereas TINYINT uses a single byte, but can only store an integer in the range from 0 to 255.

Fixed-point numeric values are stored as either DECIMAL or NUMERIC data types. These two types are equivalent. The amount of memory varies depending on the degree of precision, that is, the total number of digits to be stored. Note the scale that is the number of digits stored to the right of the decimal point is also specified and optionally defaults to zero. For example, the specification needed to store the value 7543.648 is DECIMAL(7,3).

Floating point values can be stored as REAL or FLOAT. The advantage of FLOAT is that the precision can be specified and this affects the amount of storage space required for the column. REAL data columns store very large positive and negative numbers with over 300 digits of precision.

The MONEY and SMALLMONEY data types store data for monetary values. The MONEY data type provides automatic rounding of decimal values to four digits to the right of the decimal point. This helps avoid rounding errors in financial and accounting applications.

STRING OR CHARACTER DATA

The term *string* data is synonymous with *character* data. Other DBMS or programming languages use the term *alphanumeric* data. We use the term *character data* throughout the remainder of the text. It may be obvious that basic character data include letters in the alphabet; however, numbers that are not used for calculations are also stored as character data. Character data also includes special characters such as the $, #, and % symbols.

TABLE 2.4 Character (String) Data Types

Character (String) Data Types	*Description*
CHAR[(n)] or CHARACTER(n)	Fixed-length string values where *n* is the number of characters in the string; the parameter *n* cannot be greater than 8,000; the default length when *n* is omitted is 1 character
NCHAR[(n)]	Fixed-length string values storing Unicode character data; each NCHAR character requires 2 bytes of storage whereas CHAR data requires 1 byte of storage per character; the parameter *n* cannot be greater than 4,000
VARCHAR[(n)]	Variable-length string values where *n* is the maximum number of characters in the string; the parameter *n* cannot be greater than 8,000; also termed CHAR VARYING and CHARACTER VARYING
NVARCHAR[(n)]	Variable-length string values storing Unicode characters; this data type has the same characteristics of storage as NCHAR
TEXT[(n)]	Fixed-length string up to $2^{31} - 1$ (2,147,483,647) characters
NTEXT[(n)]	Stores large string values of varying lengths with a maximum length of $2^{30} - 1$ (1,073,741,823) characters; NTEXT data characters are stored using the Unicode scheme of 2 bytes per character whereas TEXT data requires 1 byte of storage per character

Examples of character data include customer name, customer address, customer zip code, customer telephone number, product number, and product description. Have you noticed that some alphanumeric data consist strictly of numbers such as a zip code or telephone number? In general, strings of numbers are stored as character data as opposed to numeric data if they are not to be used in mathematical calculations.

Character data types also store binary strings and bit strings. The character (string) data types are summarized in Tables 2.4 and 2.5. Like the numeric data types, character data types provide you with the ability to select a type that optimizes the use of disk storage space.

TABLE 2.5 Binary (and Bit) String Data Types

Binary (and Bit) String Data Types	*Description*
BINARY[(n)]	Fixed-length bit string of exactly *n* bytes where the maximum value of the parameter *n* is 8,000
VARBINARY[(n)]	Variable-length bit string where *n* is the maximum number of bytes stored; the maximum value of the parameter *n* is 8,000
IMAGE[(n)]	Fixed-length bit strings of nearly unlimited values; the limit is approximately 2^{31} bytes
BIT	Stores Boolean data; each value requires only a single bit of storage; the values stored are limited to TRUE, FALSE, or NULL

The CHAR (or CHARACTER) data type stores fixed-length character columns. When a data value is stored in a CHAR location and the data value is smaller than the specified value of the parameter n, the string of characters is padded with blanks so that each value stored is the same fixed length. The maximum length of a CHAR column is 8,000 characters or bytes. CHAR is a good choice for columns that store fixed-length coded fields or values that are all about the same size such as the two-character abbreviations for state names or telephone numbers. For example, a Social Security number (SSN) in the United States is assigned to every citizen and is always nine characters in size. Even though an SSN is strictly composed of digits, the digits are treated as characters, and would be specified as CHAR(9).

VARCHAR, on the other hand, stores strings that are variable length. The strings can contain both printable and nonprintable characters. The string can also be NULL. For this data type, the parameter n specifies the maximum length of the column. This is a good choice for columns storing data that can vary considerably such as customer names, street addresses, and city names. A *CustomerLastName* column might be specified as VARCHAR(50), but the customer name *Bock* would only require four bytes of storage space for the actual data. Space would not be wasted because a VARCHAR column is not blank padded.

NCHAR and NVARCHAR data types are used to store data following the Unicode encoding scheme. The Unicode scheme is used for almost all characters that are widely used around the world in the various fields of business. This ensures that data, in terms of the bit pattern, is always converted to the same character set on all computers. The Unicode scheme allocates two bytes to encode each character. The requirement for two bytes means that the maximum size of NCHAR and NVARCHAR columns is 4,000 characters of storage.

TEXT and NTEXT data types store very large character data that typically consists of documents (.txt, .doc). The use of TEXT and NTEXT is discussed in additional detail below.

Binary Large Objects (BLOBs) consist of large variable binary or character data. Large binary objects include pictures (.jpeg, .bmp, .gif, .tif) as well as audio (.wav) and video data (.mpeg). Binary data types are used to store data objects in the internal format of the system. The previously mentioned TEXT data type, when combined with the IMAGE data type specified below constitutes the TEXT/IMAGE or BLOB data type. BLOB data are normally not stored with other values in the database. Instead, these data values are stored in 8-KB data pages separately from the other data pages that comprise a table. These 8-KB pages are stored using b-tree structures that contain pointer values pointing to the various text and image data pages. The exceptions are very small binary objects that may be stored in the same data pages as the other data values. IMAGE data can store any kind of data such as audio and video data whereas TEXT stores any kind of printable text data.

If the data to be stored can never be larger than 8 KB, use VARBINARY or VARCHAR to store binary or text data. If the data object to be stored may be larger than 8 KB, use TEXT, NTEXT, or IMAGE data types.

DATETIME DATA

Quite simply, a DATETIME column is used to store valid date and time information. For example, businesses and organizations may store the date and time when a customer order is processed, the date and time of birth of a newborn child in a hospital database, or even the date (perhaps ignoring the time) on which you complete your college degree. The storage of data and time data is summarized in Table 2.6. These data types actually have their values stored as numeric values. The value stored represents a date from a specific reference point.

The DATETIME data type uses the first 4 bytes of storage to store the number of days from the reference date January 1, 1753; thus, the value is stored as an integer number. The largest date that can be stored in a DATETIME location is December 31, 9999—obviously a date that few of us are ever likely to experience.

Likewise, the SMALLDATETIME data type uses the first 2 bytes of storage to store the number of days from the reference date January 1, 1900. The largest date that can be stored in a SMALLDATE location is June 6, 2079.

The time value of a DATETIME location is stored in the second 4 bytes of storage as the number of three-hundredths-of-a-second increments since midnight. Note that storage to the nearest hundredth of a second is not possible. The time value of a SMALLDATETIME location is stored in the second 2 bytes of storage as the number of minutes since midnight. The default value for the time, if the time is not stored, is midnight.

By default, dates in Transact-SQL are specified as a string of format 'mmm dd yyyy' where mmm = the month abbreviation, dd = the day of the month, and yyyy = the 4-digit year. An example date specification is 'Dec 14 2004'. Dates may be stored inside either single or double quotation marks. You also have the option of using the forward slash (/) or dash (-) characters as delimiters in dates. If you store a time value without specifying a date, the date defaults to January 1, 1900. It is also a common practice to insert date values into a DATETIME column by specifying the month, day, and year using a format like the one shown here: '1–15–2003' which is January 15, 2003.

SQL Server does not allow you to store invalid dates into a DATETIME or SMALLDATETIME column. For example, attempting to store the value '13–15–2003' in a row causes the error message, *The conversion of a char data type to a datetime data type resulted in an out-of-range datetime value* to display.

Time values are specified, by default, in the format 'hh:mm AM' and 'hh:mm PM' depending on whether the time is before or after noon. Here hh = the hour and mm = the minutes. However, the internal storage of time is 'hh:mm:ss.mil' where ss = seconds and mil = milliseconds rounded to the nearest three-hundredths of a second. An example date and time could be: '20030704 00:00:00.000' which reads July 4, 2003 at precisely midnight.

What about the Year-2000 (Y2K) problems we heard about several years ago? What date is displayed for a Transact-SQL statement that attempts to display

TABLE 2.6   Date and Time Data Types

Date and Time Data Types	*Description*
DATETIME	Date and time data requiring 4 bytes of storage for the date and 4 bytes of storage for the time
SMALLDATETIME	Date and time data requiring 2 bytes of storage for the date and 2 bytes of storage for the time

TABLE 2.7 Derived Data Types	
Derived Data Types	*Description*
SYSNAME	Columns defined as NVARCHAR(128) that store the names of database objects in the system catalog
TIMESTAMP	Columns defined as VARBINARY(8) or BINARY(8) that store the current value for each database used to timestamp rows that are inserted or updated, and contain a TIMESTAMP column

'07–04–03'? The answer is July 4, 2003. SQL Server maintains an internal century value that controls the interpretation of two-digit years. All two-digit years are interpreted as falling betweens the years 1950 and 2049. You should develop systems that use four-digit years to avoid any ambiguity.

DERIVED DATA

Two derived data types are supported—TIMESTAMP and SYSNAME. These are summarized in Table 2.7.

The system catalog uses the SYSNAME data type for columns that store the names of database objects. The TIMESTAMP data type is used to determine the relative time when a data row was last modified or when a data row was initially created. The system timestamp value is an 8-byte binary value that is unique within a database. Any time a row containing a TIMESTAMP column is created (inserted) or modified (updated), the value in the TIMESTAMP column is updated by the system.

SPECIAL DATA TYPES

There are two fairly new data types (beginning with SQL Server 7) available with SQL Server 2000. The CURSOR data type enables the creation of cursor variables that are used in stored procedures for processing data in a row-by-row fashion. You cannot specify a column of a table as type CURSOR, and because the focus of this text is not on writing storage procedures, we do not use this data type in our examples.

The UNIQUEIDENTIFIER data type stores unique identification numbers as 16-byte binary strings. The storage of data to this type of column is described later in this text.

DATA DEFINITION LANGUAGE

As we learned in Chapter 1, T-SQL has a subset of statements that comprise its *data definition language (DDL)*. Recall that DDL statements define, that is, create objects such as tables, indexes, and the like. This section focuses on basic DDL for table and index creation. We assume that you are using the SQL Query Analyzer that you learned in Chapter 1 to execute the various DDL statements shown throughout the remainder of this chapter. We also assume that you are using the Company database that you started in Chapter 1. Later in this chapter you will learn how to create the remaining tables and other objects required to complete the Company database.

CREATING A TABLE

Now that you understand how to choose appropriate data types, we can begin creating a table. Let us create a very simple table that stores five items of information about employees for an organization. We name the table *employee* and store information about each employees' social security number (SSN), last name, first name, date hired, and annual salary. The CREATE TABLE statement shown in SQL Example 2.1 creates this simple table.

```
/* SQL Example 2.1 */
CREATE TABLE employee (
emp_ssn                CHAR(9),
emp_last_name          VARCHAR(25),
emp_first_name         VARCHAR(25),
emp_date_of_birth      DATETIME,
emp_salary             MONEY
);
```

Examine the syntax of the CREATE TABLE statement. The table name *employee* is specified along with five data columns. Each column has a name that is unique within the table. Some information systems departments require system developers to follow specific naming conventions when naming columns. The convention is to use a prefix abbreviation of the table name (our abbreviation is *emp*) as part of the column name. This is optional and is not always followed although the practice may make it simpler to work with tables and column names.

Each column is specified to store a specific type of data. The specification of column names begins with a left parenthesis before the first column name, and ends with a closing right parenthesis after the last column specification. Each column name specification is separated from the previous column specification by a comma. For clarity, each column name and associated data-type specification are entered on a separate command line. Also, the American National Standards Institute (ANSI) standard for all statements including the CREATE TABLE statement is to end the statement with a semicolon. T-SQL allows individual statements to be executed with the SQL Query Analyzer without ending them with a semicolon. There are numerous additional options for the CREATE TABLE statement. We cover some of those options later in this chapter. Other options are beyond the scope of this book.

The first column is *emp_ssn* (SSN). Later in this chapter, we designate this column as the primary key (PK) for the table. This column stores a unique, nine-digit SSN for each employee in the database; however, we have specified that the column is CHAR because we do not intend to perform any mathematical operations with SSN data. Also each SSN is a fixed length in terms of the number of characters required to store the value.

When the CREATE TABLE statement executes, the SQL Query Analyzer processes the statement. If there are no syntactical errors, the message *The command(s) completed successfully* displays to confirm that the table definition was successfully stored to the database.

DATA INTEGRITY AND TABLE CONSTRAINTS

The simple *employee* table shown on the opposite page has some very severe limitations. It lacks the specifications needed to aid in maintaining the integrity of data that are stored in the table. The term *data integrity* simply means that the data stored in the table is valid. There are different types of data integrity, and we often refer to these as *constraints*. In fact, the specification of different data types aids in maintaining certain aspects of the data stored for employees. For example, specifying the *emp_date_of_birth* column as DATETIME prevents the storage of invalid dates and nondate data. However, there are additional integrity constraints that can be used to aid in maintaining data integrity.

NOT NULL CONSTRAINT

A NOT NULL constraint means that a data row must have a value for the column specified as NOT NULL. The code in SQL Example 2.2 specifies that every employee must have a first and last name. If a column is specified as NOT NULL, SQL Server does not allow rows to be stored to the *employee* table that violate this constraint. To allow a column to store a NULL value (really, the absence of a value), you simply do not specify an integrity constraint for that column. Optionally, you can specify the integrity constraint NULL. This also allows the column to store NULL values. For example, this means that the *emp_middle_name* column is allowed to be NULL, as shown in SQL Example 2.2.

```
/* SQL Example 2.2 */
emp_last_name      VARCHAR(25)
    CONSTRAINT nn_emp_last_name NOT NULL,
emp_first_name     VARCHAR(25)
    CONSTRAINT nn_emp_first_name NOT NULL,
emp_middle_name    VARCHAR(25) NULL,
```

A fairly standard practice is to assign each constraint a *unique constraint name*. In selecting a constraint name, it is common to use either a prefix or suffix to denote the type of constraint. In this text, we use prefixes. The prefix for a NOT NULL constraint is *'nn,'* and it is common to combine this prefix with the table name or column name to make it easy to determine the nature of an error whenever a constraint violation is reported by SQL Server. If you do not name constraints, then SQL Server automatically assigns a system-generated constraint name. Unfortunately, these system-generated constraint names are fairly meaningless so it is always a better practice to assign a meaningful constraint name.

PRIMARY KEY CONSTRAINT

Each table must normally contain a column or set of columns that uniquely identifies rows of data that are stored in the table. This column or set of columns is referred to as the *primary key*. Most tables have a single column as the PK. This is the case for the *employee* table where the *emp_ssn* column is unique and, thus, qualifies to serve as the PK. If a table requires two or more columns to identify each row uniquely, the PK is termed a *composite* PK. We cover examples of composite PKs later in the chapter.

By assigning a PRIMARY KEY constraint to the *emp_ssn* column, you can automatically give the column two properties. First, the *emp_ssn* column must be NOT NULL for each row by default—this constraint is built into the PRIMARY KEY constraint specification. Second, an *emp_ssn* value may not occur twice within the *employee* table; that is, each *emp_ssn* value must be unique within the table. If you attempt to enter the same value for the *emp_ssn* for two employees, SQL Server stores the first row of data; however, SQL Server generates an error message and refuses to store the second data row. The PRIMARY KEY constraint shown in SQL Example 2.3 is essential to maintaining the integrity of a database. Imagine the tax reporting and pay problems that would result if two employees were accidentally assigned identical SSNs.

```
/* SQL Example 2.3 */
emp_ssn CHAR(9)
    CONSTRAINT pk_employee PRIMARY KEY,
```

Note that the PRIMARY KEY constraint is assigned a constraint name of *pk_employee*. In naming a PRIMARY KEY constraint, the standard practice is to use a two-character prefix of *'pk'* combined with an underscore and the name of the table. Later in this chapter, you learn how to specify a PRIMARY KEY constraint for a composite PK.

CHECK CONSTRAINT

Sometimes the data values stored in a specific column must fall within some acceptable range of values. For example, the organization owning our *employee* table may specify that employee salary figures stored to the database represent the annual salary of each employee, and that annual salary cannot exceed $85,000. SQL Example 2.4 shows how to write a CHECK constraint to enforce this data limit.

```
/* SQL Example 2.4 */
emp_salary MONEY
    CONSTRAINT ck_emp_salary
        CHECK (emp_salary <= 85000),
```

The CHECK constraint is named *ck_emp_salary,* and uses a two-character prefix of *'ck'* to denote that it is a CHECK constraint. A CHECK constraint requires that the specified check condition is either true or unknown for each row stored in the table. The constraint specification must evaluate to a Boolean value. A condition is classified as unknown if the *emp_salary* value for a given row is NULL. If it is desirable to require that the monthly salary value be stored for every row in the table, then both CHECK and NOT NULL constraints can be specified as shown in SQL Example 2.5.

```
/* SQL Example 2.5 */
emp_salary MONEY
    CONSTRAINT ck_emp_salary
        CHECK (emp_salary <= 85000)
    CONSTRAINT nn_emp_salary NOT NULL,
```

If a computer application or an information system user attempts to store a row to the *employee* table that violates either constraint, SQL Server returns an error message and the row is not stored to the table. Violations of the NOT NULL constraint generates the error message: *Cannot insert the value NULL into column 'emp_salary', table 'company.dbock.employee'; column does not allow nulls.* Violations of the CHECK constraint generates the error message: *INSERT fails* and *INSERT statement conflicted with COLUMN CHECK constraint 'ck_emp_salary'. The conflict occurred in database 'company', table 'employee', column 'emp_salary'. The statement has been terminated.* Thus you can see, each error message includes details that let you determine exactly which constraint has been violated. In the case of the second error message, the *ck_emp_salary* constraint name is used to reference the specific constraint that is violated.

UNIQUE CONSTRAINT

Sometimes it is necessary to enforce uniqueness for a column value that is not a PK column. Let us add another column to the *employee* table that stores information about the parking space that is assigned to each employee. Assume that each parking space for the organization is numbered with a unique, integer number, and that no two employees can be assigned the same parking space. The UNIQUE constraint can be used to enforce this rule and SQL Server rejects any rows that violate the constraint. The SQL code is shown in SQL Example 2.6.

```
/* SQL Example 2.6 */
emp_parking_space INT
    CONSTRAINT un_emp_parking_space UNIQUE,
```

The *un_emp_parking_space* constraint has a two-character prefix of *'un'* to denote that it is a UNIQUE constraint. The updated CREATE TABLE statement for the *employee* table is shown in SQL Example 2.7.

```
/* SQL Example 2.7 */
-- Drop the employee table first if it has already been created.
create table employee (
    emp_ssn CHAR(9)
        constraint pk_employee primary key,
    emp_last_name varchar(25)
        constraint nn_emp_last_name NOT NULL,
    emp_first_name VARCHAR(25)
        CONSTRAINT nn_emp_first_name NOT NULL,
    emp_middle_name    VARCHAR(25) NULL,
    emp_date_of_birth DATETIME NULL,
    emp_salary MONEY
        CONSTRAINT ck_emp_salary
            CHECK (emp_salary <= 85000)
        CONSTRAINT nn_emp_salary NOT NULL,
    emp_parking_space          INT
        CONSTRAINT un_emp_parking_space UNIQUE,
);
```

Additional constraints that enforce data integrity for rows that are stored in related tables are discussed later in this chapter.

VIEWING A TABLE DESCRIPTION WITH THE OBJECT BROWSER

Database administrators and application programmers must be able to view table descriptions as part of the system development process. The SQL Query Analyzer provides you with the ability to examine the columns that comprise a table through the *object browser* facility shown in Figure 2.1. You select the database of interest, and then select the *user tables* folder and the name of the table within that folder to be examined. Figure 2.1 shows the columns of the *employee* table. The columns folder for each table lists the columns including each column name, data type, and NULL/NOT NULL specification. For example, the *emp_ssn* column is shown as defined as a fixed length of CHAR(9) with a NOT NULL specification, whereas the *emp_date_of_birth* is defined to store DATETIME data; however, if an employee's date of birth is unknown, the column is allowed to be NULL.

FIGURE 2.1

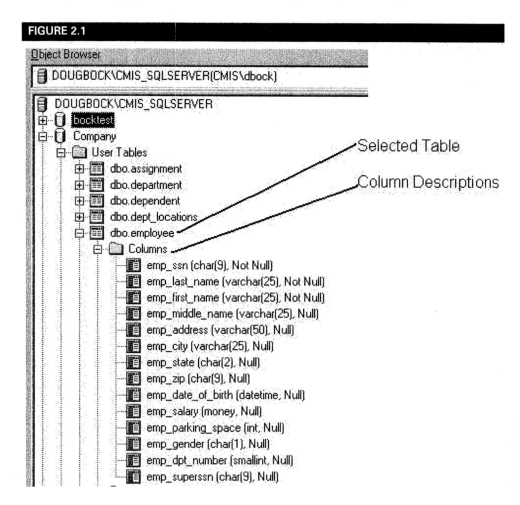

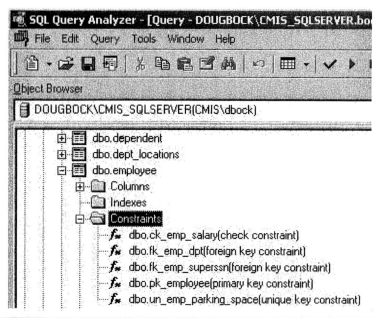

FIGURE 2.2

Figure 2.2 shows the object browser for the *employee* table with the *constraints* folder opened. This enables you to identify existing constraints such as the PRIMARY KEY, CHECK, and UNIQUE constraints. For example, there exists a PRIMARY KEY constraint named *pk_employee*.

The figure also lists FK constraints. You learn about FK constraints later in this chapter.

ALTERING TABLES

Over time it is fairly common to modify tables to either alter existing columns or to add new columns to a table. Without this capability, it would be necessary to delete and then recreate tables. This would be a very time-consuming task when a table may already have thousands of data rows stored in it.

Altering existing columns and adding new columns are tasks that can both be accomplished by use of the ALTER TABLE statement. There are many formats for the ALTER TABLE statement and these are explained in detail in the SQL Server Books Online Help. We examine several of these formats.

ALTERING EXISTING COLUMNS

Suppose, for example, that you have identified the need to modify the data type used to store information in the *emp_parking_space* column. The current data type of the *emp_parking_space* column is INT (INTEGER). Due to growth in the availability of employee parking spaces, you have determined that it is necessary to modify the definition of this column to specify a BIGINT data type. The ALTER TABLE statement shown in SQL Example 2.8 modifies the *emp_parking_space* column to specify the BIGINT data type.

```
/* SQL Example 2.8 */
ALTER TABLE employee DROP CONSTRAINT un_emp_parking_space;
ALTER TABLE employee ALTER COLUMN emp_parking_space BIGINT;
ALTER TABLE employee
    ADD CONSTRAINT un_emp_parking_space
        UNIQUE (emp_parking_space);
```

Because the *emp_parking_space* column already has a specified UNIQUE constraint, it is necessary to first drop this constraint. The first ALTER TABLE statement in SQL Example 2.8 accomplishes this task. The second ALTER TABLE statement alters the column to specify BIGINT as the new data type. The third ALTER TABLE statement restores the UNIQUE constraint for the column.

If a table already has data rows, then it is possible for problems with data storage to arise when you change the data type that is defined for a column. Suppose, for example, that you decide to modify a column from an INT to the SMALLINT data type. The SMALLINT data type is not capable of storing values that are as large as those that can be stored in an INT column. SQL Server returns an error message if data rows already exist such that their data cannot fit into the new specified column size. In this case, the ALTER TABLE statement fails to execute.

ADDING NEW COLUMNS

Suppose that the manager of human resources notifies you that the Company must begin tracking the gender of employees to meet a governmental reporting requirement. This requires the addition of a new column to the *employee* table. An *emp_gender* column can be added to the *employee* table as shown in SQL Example 2.9. The *emp_gender* column is a single-character column used to store a coded value, where M = male and F = female.

```
/* SQL Example 2.9 */
ALTER TABLE employee ADD emp_gender CHAR(1);
```

The ALTER TABLE statement has many additional capabilities including the ability to set default column values, disable and re-enable column constraints, and drop a column from a table. You may wish to explore these capabilities by examining the SQL Server Books Online documentation.

RELATING TABLES: IDENTIFYING FOREIGN KEYS

Tables in a database rarely exist alone. Normally, data rows in one table are related to data rows in other tables. Let us build a second table named *department*. The *department* table stores information about departments within our organization.

Each department has a unique, two-digit, department number. Each department also has a department name, location, and primary telephone number for contacting the department manager, although you are more likely to reach an administrative assistant. The CREATE TABLE statement is shown in SQL Example 2.10.

```
/* SQL Example 2.10 */
CREATE TABLE department (
    dpt_no SMALLINT
        CONSTRAINT pk_department PRIMARY KEY,
    dpt_name VARCHAR(20)
        CONSTRAINT nn_dpt_name NOT NULL
);
```

Employees are generally assigned to work in departments. In our organization, an employee is usually hired into a department and, at any given time, is only assigned to a single department. Employees can be reassigned to another department depending on departmental workloads. Of course, a department may have many different employees assigned to it. To link rows in the *employee* table to rows in the *department* table we need to introduce a new type of constraint, the FOREIGN KEY constraint.

Figure 2.3 depicts the *employee* and *department* tables. The PK column *dpt_no* of the *department* table is shown in boldface. Note the line leading from the *dpt_no* column of the *department* table to the *emp_dpt_number* column of the *employee* table. The *emp_dpt_number* column is a FK in the *employee* table.

FKs are columns in one table that reference PK values in another table or in the same table. In this situation we need to relate *employee* rows to the PK column named *dpt_no* in the *department* table. We can do this by specifying a FOREIGN KEY constraint as part of the CREATE TABLE statement. If this was a new database, we would most likely first create the *department* table, and then create the *employee* table. This would facilitate creating the FOREIGN KEY constraint because it would be impossible to reference a column in the *department* table if the table has not yet

FIGURE 2.3

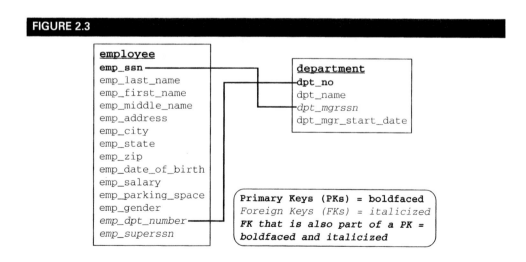

been created. The new *employee* table CREATE TABLE statement shown in SQL Example 2.11 includes a column to store the department number to which each employee is assigned. The new *emp_dpt_number* column and FOREIGN KEY constraint are shown here:

```
/* SQL Example 2.11 */
-- Drop the employee table first if it has already been created.
CREATE TABLE employee (
    emp_ssn                     CHAR(9)
        CONSTRAINT pk_employee PRIMARY KEY,
    emp_last_name               VARCHAR(25)
        CONSTRAINT nn_emp_last_name NOT NULL,
    emp_first_name              VARCHAR(25)
        CONSTRAINT nn_emp_first_name NOT NULL,
    emp_middle_name             VARCHAR(25) NULL,
    emp_address                 VARCHAR(50) NULL,
    emp_city                    VARCHAR(25) NULL,
    emp_state                   CHAR(2) NULL,
    emp_zip                     CHAR(9) NULL,
    emp_date_of_birth           DATETIME NULL,
    emp_salary MONEY
        CONSTRAINT ck_emp_salary
            CHECK (emp_salary <= 85000)
        CONSTRAINT nn_emp_salary NOT NULL,
    emp_parking_space           INT
        CONSTRAINT un_emp_parking_space UNIQUE,
    emp_gender                  CHAR(1) NULL,
    emp_dpt_number              SMALLINT,
CONSTRAINT fk_emp_dpt FOREIGN KEY (emp_dpt_number)
    REFERENCES department,
);
```

The value stored to the *emp_dpt_number* column for any given *employee* row must match a value stored in the *dpt_no* column of one of the rows of the *department* table. Note that we did not specify a NOT NULL constraint for the *emp_dpt_number* column. This enables the organization to hire a new employee who has not yet been assigned to a specific department. In this case, the value of the *emp_dpt_number* column would be NULL for the new employee.

If the *employee* table already exists and the *department* table is subsequently added to the database, then we must use the ALTER TABLE statement to modify the *employee* table. In this situation, we would be adding the *emp_dpt_number* column and the associated FOREIGN KEY constraint shown in SQL Example 2.12.

```
/* SQL Example 2.12 */
ALTER TABLE employee ADD emp_dpt_number SMALLINT;
ALTER TABLE employee ADD CONSTRAINT fk_emp_dpt
    FOREIGN KEY (emp_dpt_number) REFERENCES department;
```

Maintaining Referential Integrity

FOREIGN KEY constraints are also referred to as *referential integrity* constraints, and assist in maintaining database integrity. Referential integrity stipulates that values of an FK must correspond to values of a PK in the table that it references. As you continue your study of the Company database, you will discover additional tables. One of these is the *dependent* table that stores information about employee dependents, that is, spouses, sons, and daughters. Figure 2.4 depicts these two tables and the relationship between them.

The *dependent* table's column named *dep_emp_ssn* is an FK column linking to the *emp_ssn* column in the *employee* table. If you examine the data in Appendix A, you find, for example, that employee Waiman Zhu with SSN 999-44-4444 has as dependents Susan, Andrew, and Jo Ellen. The SSN 999-44-4444 is stored in both the *emp_ssn* and *dep_emp_ssn* column to link the rows of the two tables.

What if Waiman Zhu decides to seek employment elsewhere and leaves the Company? If Zhu's row is deleted from the *employee* table, the *dependent* table has three rows (dependents) that do not belong to an employee row. A special clause for the FOREIGN KEY constraint enables the maintenance of referential integrity to prevent this type of problem. This is the ON DELETE CASCADE clause.

SQL Example 2.13 shows the CREATE TABLE statement for the *dependent* table. Note the location of the ON DELETE CASCADE clause. If Zhu's row is deleted from the *employee* table, this special clause in the *dependent* table causes Zhu's dependents to be deleted automatically from the *dependent* table, thereby maintaining referential integrity between the two tables. You need to exercise discretion in using the ON DELETE CASCADE clause so that you do not cause the database to delete data rows that store information that the firm needs to maintain.

```
/* SQL Example 2.13 */
CREATE TABLE dependent (
    dep_emp_ssn             CHAR(9),
    dep_name                VARCHAR(50),
    dep_gender              CHAR(1) NULL,
    dep_date_of_birth       DATETIME NULL,
    dep_relationship        VARCHAR(10) NULL,
CONSTRAINT pk_dependent PRIMARY KEY (dep_emp_ssn, dep_name),
CONSTRAINT fk_dep_emp_ssn
    FOREIGN KEY (dep_emp_ssn) REFERENCES employee
        ON DELETE CASCADE
);
```

The other ON DELETE clause option is to specify NO ACTION as the object of the clause. When NO ACTION is the option, any attempted deletion of an employee row that has associated dependent rows fails with an error from SQL Server.

SQL Server also supports the ON UPDATE CASCADE option. With this option, if a referenced employee row has the PK value changed, that is, a change in the employee SSN (an unlikely occurrence, but then the Social Security Administration has been known to make this type of mistake), then the associated dependent rows would have the FK value updated at the same time.

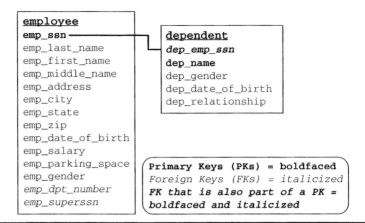

FIGURE 2.4

Other relational DBMS products, such as Oracle, support the ON DELETE SET NULL option. This enables setting the FK value to NULL if the referenced row is deleted; however, SQL Server does not support this option.

COMPOSITE PRIMARY KEYS AND MULTIPLE FOREIGN KEYS

You often encounter situations where you need to create an association table that represents a many-to-many relationship between two base tables or entities. A many-to-many relationship is one where a row in table 1 may be related to many rows in table 2; and, similarly, a row in table 2 may be related to many rows in table 1. As an example, consider the relationship between rows in the *employee* table and rows in the *project* table. Each employee can be assigned to work on more than one project. Further, each project can have many employees assigned to work on the project. We can extend our database by creating a table to store information about projects. The statement to create the *project* table is shown in SQL Example 2.14.

```
/* SQL Example 2.14 */
CREATE TABLE project (
    pro_number                SMALLINT
        CONSTRAINT pk_project PRIMARY KEY,
    pro_name                  VARCHAR(25)
        CONSTRAINT nn_pro_name NOT NULL,
    pro_location              VARCHAR(25) NULL,
    pro_dept_number           SMALLINT,
CONSTRAINT fk_pro_dept_number FOREIGN KEY (pro_dept_number)
    REFERENCES department
);
```

The column *pro_number* stores the project number for each project. It also serves as the PK. Each project also has a project name and location. A specific department controls each project. This relationship is enforced through the *pro_dept_number*

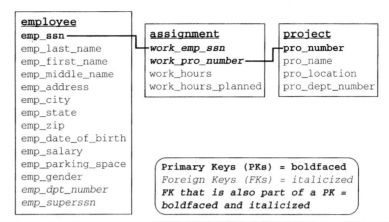

FIGURE 2.5

column and associated FOREIGN KEY constraint that references back to the *department* table. We only mention the *department* table so that you can understand the CONSTRAINT clause shown in SQL Example 2.14. We ignore the *department* table for the time being because it is not our focus.

We are concerned with the fact that employees can be assigned to work on many different projects at the same time, and a project can have many different employees assigned to complete various project tasks. This *Works-On* relationship between employees and projects is implemented by creating an association table named *assignment* as shown in Figure 2.5.

The CREATE TABLE statement for the *assignment* table is shown in SQL Example 2.15.

```
/* SQL Example 2.15 */
CREATE TABLE assignment (
    work_emp_ssn            CHAR(9),
    work_pro_number         SMALLINT,
    work_hours              DECIMAL(5,1) NULL,
    work_hours_planned      DECIMAL(5,1) NULL,
CONSTRAINT pk_assignment
    PRIMARY KEY (work_emp_ssn, work_pro_number),
CONSTRAINT fk_work_emp
    FOREIGN KEY (work_emp_ssn) REFERENCES employee
        ON DELETE CASCADE,
CONSTRAINT fk_work_pro_number
    FOREIGN KEY (work_pro_number) REFERENCES project
        ON DELETE CASCADE
);
```

The PK for the *assignment* table is a composite key consisting of both the *work_emp_ssn* and *work_pro_number* columns. Study the syntax of the PRIMARY KEY constraint declaration. The constraint declaration shown in SQL Example 2.15 is different syntactically than the DDL shown in earlier SQL Examples such as 2.14. SQL Example 2.15 shows how to specify a PRIMARY KEY constraint for a composite key.

It is also necessary to enforce FOREIGN KEY constraints between the *assignment* table and the *employee* and *project* tables. Values stored in the *assignment* table's *work_emp_ssn* column reference values in the *emp_ssn* column of the *employee* table, whereas values stored in the *assignment* table's *work_pro_number* column reference values in the *pro_number* column of the *project* table. Thus, there are two FOREIGN KEY constraints specified. This enforces the following rule: We cannot have a row in the *assignment* table for a nonexistent employee or nonexistent project. You may also note that the total hours an employee works on a project are accumulated in the *work_hours* column whereas the total planned hours an employee is to work on a project is stored in the *work_hours_planned* column. The placement of commas after each column and constraint specification is important to avoid syntax errors.

DROPPING TABLES

Sometimes tables are no longer needed. At other times a DBA may need to delete a table to reorganize a database due to the installation of new computer hardware. The database statement used to delete a table is the DROP TABLE statement. SQL Example 2.16 shows the *assignment* table to be dropped. This statement deletes both the table structure, its data, related constraints, and indexes.

```
/* SQL Example 2.16 */
DROP TABLE assignment;
```

If you attempt to drop a table that is referenced through FOREIGN KEY constraint by another table, then the DROP TABLE statement fails. For example, the *project* table is referenced by a FOREIGN KEY constraint defined for the *assignment* table. As earlier, this means that *assignment* data rows are existence dependent on *project* data rows. SQL Example 2.17 demonstrates an attempt to drop the *project* table and the system error message that is generated. It is not legal to drop the *project* table without first either dropping the *assignment* table or altering the FOREIGN KEY constraint for the *assignment* table — normally the constraint must be dropped if the *assignment* table is not dropped.

```
/* SQL Example 2.17 */
DROP TABLE project;

Server: Msg 3726, Level 16, State 1, Line 1
Could not drop object 'project' because it is referenced
by a FOREIGN KEY constraint.
```

POPULATING TABLES WITH DATA

The task of populating tables with data as systems are converted from one type of database to another generally can be handled by using special utility programs.

However, application programs use the statements described in this section to manage table data, including row insertions, row updates, and row deletions.

INSERT STATEMENT

We have created several tables, but have yet to store data in any of them. The INSERT statement is used to store data in tables. The INSERT statement is often used in higher level programming languages such as Visual Basic.NET or C++ as an embedded SQL statement; however, this statement can also be executed within SQL Server's Query Analyzer. The INSERT statement has several options. We focus on two different syntaxes for the INSERT statement.

The first form of INSERT is used if a new row has a value inserted into each column of the row. The general form of the INSERT statement is:

```
INSERT INTO table VALUES (column1 value, column2 value, ...);
```

For example, the INSERT statements in SQL Example 2.18 insert three rows of data into the *department* table, and three rows of data into the *employee* table.

```
/* SQL Example 2.18 */
INSERT INTO department VALUES (7, 'Production');
INSERT INTO department VALUES (3, 'Admin and Records');
INSERT INTO department VALUES (1, 'Headquarters');
INSERT INTO employee VALUES ('999666666', 'Bordoloi', 'Bijoy',
    NULL, 'South Main #12', 'Edwardsville', 'IL', 62025,
    '11-10-67', 55000, 1, 'M', 1);
INSERT INTO employee VALUES ('999555555', 'Joyner', 'Suzanne',
    'A', '202 Burns Farm', 'Marina', 'CA', 93941,
    '06-20-1971', 43000, 3, 'F', 3);
INSERT INTO employee VALUES ('999444444', 'Zhu', 'Waiman',
    'Z', '303 Lindbergh', 'St. Louis', 'MO', 63121,
    '12-08-1975', 43000, 32, 'M', 7);
```

Character data values are enclosed in single quotes, whereas numeric data are not. Data stored to DATETIME columns can be enclosed as strings of characters in single quotes because SQL Server automatically converts the characters to the DATETIME data type.

The second form of the INSERT statement shown below is used to insert rows where some of the column data is unknown (NULL). This form of the INSERT statement requires that you specify column names for which data are stored.

```
INSERT INTO table (column1 name, column2 name, . . .)
    VALUES (column1 value, column2 value, . . .);
```

The INSERT statement in SQL Example 2.19 stores information to the columns listed for a new data row in the *employee* table. Note the specification of the column names for which data are to be inserted.

```
/* SQL Example 2.19 */
INSERT INTO employee (emp_ssn, emp_last_name, emp_first_name,
    emp_salary) VALUES ('999111111', 'Bock', 'Douglas', 30000);
```

DELETE Statement

The DELETE statement is one of the simplest of the SQL statements. It removes one or more rows from a table. Multiple table delete operations are not allowed in SQL. The syntax of the DELETE statement is:

```
DELETE FROM table_name
[WHERE <condition>];
```

The DELETE statement deletes all rows in a table that satisfy the *condition* in the optional WHERE clause. BE CAREFUL. The WHERE clause is optional. This means that you can easily delete all rows from a table by accident by omitting a WHERE clause because the WHERE clause limits the scope of the DELETE operation. For example, the DELETE FROM statement in SQL Example 2.20 removes all rows in the *assignment* table. (Note: This example fails to execute if you drop the *assignment* table earlier in SQL Example 2.16.)

```
/* SQL Example 2.20 */
DELETE FROM assignment;
```

UPDATE Statement

You can modify (update) values stored in individual columns of selected rows with the UPDATE statement. *Updating* columns is different from *altering* columns. Earlier in this chapter, you studied the ALTER statement. The ALTER statement changes the table structure, but leaves the table data unaffected. The UPDATE statement changes data in the table, not the table structure. The general syntax of the UPDATE statement is:

```
UPDATE table SET column = expression [,column = expression] . . .
    [WHERE condition];
```

The *SET column = expression* enables any combination of characters, formulas, or functions that can update data in the specified column name to serve as the expression. The WHERE clause is optional; but if it is included, it specifies which rows are to be updated. Only one table can be updated at a time with an UPDATE statement.

Suppose you wish to update the salary of Waiman Zhu who is presently paid $43,000 annually. He has been given a raise of $2,000, which results in a new salary of $45,000 annually. SQL Example 2.21 gives the statement to update Zhu's row in the *employee* table.

```
/* SQL Example 2.21 */
UPDATE employee SET emp_salary = 45000
    WHERE emp_ssn = '999444444';
```

Again, you must BE CAREFUL. Because the WHERE clause is optional for the UPDATE statement, you can easily update all rows from a table by accident by omitting a WHERE clause just as you were able to delete all rows in a table accidentally with the DELETE statement.

COMMITTING TRANSACTIONS

In other relational DBMS products such as Oracle, statements such as INSERT, DELETE, and UPDATE do not cause data insertions, deletions, or updates to affect the database until the transaction is committed via a COMMIT statement. SQL Server does NOT work in this fashion. Instead, SQL Server automatically commits after every INSERT, DELETE, or UPDATE operation. If you make an error in an INSERT, DELETE, or UPDATE operation, you cannot easily undo the damage to the database tables that are affected.

One option for controlling when transactions commit is to use explicit transaction specifications by grouping SQL statements within transaction delimiters. The transaction delimiter statements are BEGIN TRANSACTION and COMMIT TRANSACTION. SQL Example 2.22 shows the use of these delimiter statements.

```
/* SQL Example 2.22 */
BEGIN TRANSACTION
DELETE FROM employee
    WHERE emp_ssn = '999111111';
DELETE FROM employee
    WHERE emp_ssn = '999444444';
COMMIT TRANSACTION;
```

The BEGIN TRANSACTION statement begins an explicit transaction. Two employee rows are deleted, but the change to the database does not take place until the COMMIT TRANSACTION statement processes. At any point prior to execution of COMMIT TRANSACTION, the ROLLBACK TRANSACTION statement can be used to cancel the deletions that are in process. In fact, ROLLBACK TRANSACTION can reverse the effect of any data manipulation statement.

COMPUTED (DERIVED) COLUMNS

Sometimes you may want to store information in a column that is derived from other information stored in the table. Examine the CREATE TABLE statement shown in SQL Example 2.23 that creates the *equipment* table. The column *eqp_total_value* (equipment total value) is a *computed* column (sometimes termed *derived* column). The value stored in *eqp_total_value* is computed by multiplying the values stored in the columns named *eqp_value* and *eqp_qty_on_hand* (equipment value and equipment quantity on hand).

```
/* SQL Example 2.23 */
CREATE TABLE equipment (
    eqp_no                      CHAR(4)
        CONSTRAINT pk_equipment PRIMARY KEY,
    eqp_description             VARCHAR(15),
    eqp_value                   MONEY,
    eqp_qty_on_hand             SMALLINT,
    eqp_total_value AS eqp_value * eqp_qty_on_hand,
    eqp_pro_number              SMALLINT,
CONSTRAINT fk_eqp_pro_number FOREIGN KEY (eqp_pro_number)
    REFERENCES project
        ON DELETE CASCADE );
```

When values are inserted into the table, it is not necessary to insert a value for the *eqp_total_value* derived column. In fact, data for a computed column is not actually stored, it is computed by SQL Server at the time that data for the column is selected. Likewise, if a value stored in a row for either the *eqp_value* or *eqp_qty_on_hand* column or columns change, the value displayed for the corresponding *eqp_total_value* computed column during a SELECT operation is automatically updated.

Limitations for computed columns must be observed. Columns used to compute a value stored to a computed column must be from the same table. Computed columns cannot contain a subquery (see Chapter 7). You cannot use the DEFAULT constraint for a computed column. You cannot compute a value for a computed column that is of the TEXT/IMAGE data type.

INDEXES

Indexes are optional structures associated with tables. Indexes facilitate the rapid retrieval of information from tables much like the index of a book enables you to find specific topics in the book rapidly. Without indexes, SQL Server sequentially accesses data rows—this means that every data row in a table must be scanned to determine whether it should be returned in the result set. Indexes, quite simply, speed up the retrieval of data. There is a downside to indexes; indexes must be maintained by the DBMS and so any time that new rows are inserted or rows are updated, indexes probably need to be modified. As more indexes are created for a table, insert and update processing will require additional time to complete.

There are different types of indexes. Some enforce PRIMARY KEY constraints. Others are simply unique indexes that support the retrieval of individual rows based on column values that are not PKs. You may also create composite indexes and other index types covered later in your course of study.

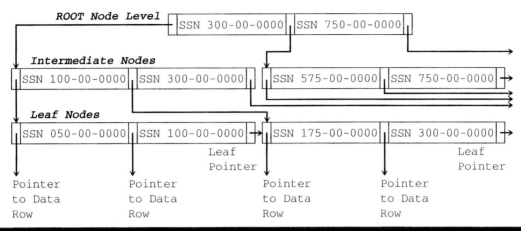

FIGURE 2.6

Indexes also have limitations. The maximum size of an index entry is 900 bytes. Also, if an index is a composite of two or more columns, there is a maximum limit of 16 columns in the index. Composite indexes are explained in detail later in this chapter. SQL Server allows a maximum of 249 nonclustered and 1 clustered index per table. Nonclustered indexes do not change the actual physical location of data rows in a table whereas clustered indexes do. Thus, only one clustered index can be supported because rows can only be physically stored in a single arrangement. Both the maximum number of columns and the maximum number of indexes are really not limitations because it would be exceedingly rare for you to need such large numbers of columns or indexes in a real-world application.

Figure 2.6 illustrates an index. As you can see, indexes are tree structures. SQL Server uses tree structures of the *b-tree* type as do most relational DBMS products. Index searches proceed at the root node in the tree and the search filters down the tree structure to the leaf node.

The actual information stored at each node includes logical key values, for example, employee SSNs for an employee PK index, as well as the information needed by SQL Server to locate the next node as the search proceeds. The leaf nodes store information that can be used to locate the data block on disk within which a specific data row is stored. The information used to traverse the tree and to point to specific data blocks is generally termed pointer information. At the leaf nodes, there are also pointers that connect the nodes. This enables SELECT statements to specify the display of data rows in either ascending or descending order.

PRIMARY KEY INDEXES

When you specify a PRIMARY KEY constraint, SQL Server automatically creates a unique index to support rapid data retrieval for the specified table. As we note above, without an index, a SELECT statement that retrieves data can cause SQL Server to completely scan a table for rows that satisfy the retrieval condition. For example, consider the SELECT statement in SQL Example 2.24 that displays a list of employees assigned to a specific department:

```
/* SQL Example 2.24 */
SELECT emp_last_name, emp_first_name, emp_dpt_number
FROM employee
WHERE emp_dpt_number = 3;
```

If the *employee* table is not indexed on the *emp_dpt_number* column, SQL Server has to scan the entire table to satisfy the query. If you review the DDL used to create the *employee* table, you may recall that the *emp_ssn* column is specified with the PRIMARY KEY constraint. Thus, it is very likely that SQL Example 2.24 will cause an entire table scan to find rows for employees assigned to department 3. SQL Example 2.25 retrieves data for a specific employee. This SELECT statement uses the PK index to find the desired employee row rapidly.

```
/* SQL Example 2.25 */
SELECT emp_last_name, emp_first_name, emp_dpt_number, emp_ssn
FROM employee
WHERE emp_ssn = '999555555';
```

A DBA usually supervises the creation of indexes. This is necessary because although indexes can speed the retrieval of data, they also slow down data storage. When new rows are added to a table, any indexes created must also be updated.

Indexes are logically and physically independent of the data in the associated table. Indexes that you explicitly create can be dropped at anytime without affecting the base tables or other indexes; however, PRIMARY KEY indexes created by SQL Server can only be dropped by dropping the PRIMARY KEY constraint. This is another good reason for explicitly naming the PRIMARY KEY constraints. If we drop an index that we create or one that is created by SQL Server, all applications that access the associated table continue to work; however, access to previously indexed data probably slows down considerably. You also need to understand that indexes are database objects and, as such, require storage space.

CREATING INDEXES

The general form of the CREATE INDEX statement is:

```
CREATE INDEX <index_name>
    ON <table_name> (column1, column2...);
```

Let us create an index on the *emp_dpt_number* column of the *employee* table. The statement is shown in SQL Example 2.26. This is an example of a *nonunique* index because many different employees can be assigned to each department.

```
/* SQL Example 2.26 */
CREATE INDEX employee_emp_dpt_number
    ON employee (emp_dpt_number);
```

CREATING UNIQUE INDEXES

The Riverbend Hospital Case described in Appendix B stores data in numerous tables. One of the most important tables is the *patient* table that stores information about hospital patients. The Riverbend Hospital assigns each patient a patient identification number (*patient_id*), and this serves as the PK for the *patient* table. Additionally, each patient has an assigned SSN (*pat_ssn*). Management at the hospital has identified the need to retrieve patient records by the SSN. To facilitate efficient row retrieval, you need to create a unique index based on the *pat_ssn* column. The general form of the CREATE UNIQUE INDEX statement is:

```
CREATE UNIQUE INDEX <index_name>
    ON <table_name> (column1, column2...);
```

SQL Example 2.27 shows the statement to create the *patient_pat_ssn* unique index.

```
/* SQL Example 2.27 */
CREATE UNIQUE INDEX patient_pat_ssn
    ON patient (pat_ssn);
```

CREATING COMPOSITE INDEXES

A *composite index* (also called a *concatenated index*) is an index created on multiple columns of a table. Columns in a composite index can appear in any order and do not need to be adjacent columns in the table. Composite indexes enhance row retrieval speed for queries in which the WHERE clause references all or the leading portion of the columns in the composite index. Generally, the most commonly accessed or most selective columns are listed first when creating the index.

The *treatment* table in the Riverbend Hospital database stores data about treatment services. These services are provided by various staff members to hospital patients. It may be desirable to create a composite index on this table based on the staff identification (*staff_id*) and patient identification (*pat_id*) columns to support the preparation of a weekly staff-to-patient load report. The CREATE INDEX statement shown in SQL Example 2.28 is appropriate because this index is not unique.

```
/* SQL Example 2.28 */
CREATE INDEX treatment_staff_id_pat_id
    ON treatment (staff_id, pat_id);
```

DROPPING INDEXES

An index should not be retained unless it improves system processing in some fashion. This is because all indexes on a table must be updated whenever row data is changed that is referenced by an index. This updating or maintenance of indexes adds overhead to database processing. Useless indexes burden the system by adding unnecessary maintenance and by needlessly occupying disk space. You also need to understand that you cannot modify indexes. To change an index, you must drop it, and then create a replacement index. The syntax of the DROP INDEX statement is simple, but requires you to reference both the table and index name using the "dot" notation shown here.

```
DROP INDEX table_name.index_name;
```

The DROP INDEX statement in SQL Example 2.29 drops the index named *employee_emp_dpt_number* for the *employee* table.

```
/* SQL Example 2.29 */
DROP INDEX employee.employee_emp_dpt_number;
```

SQL Server provides for additional types of indexes and index usage. For a complete treatment of indexes, refer to the SQL Server Books Online documentation.

PRACTICING WHAT YOU HAVE LEARNED ABOUT THE COMPANY DATABASE

Now you are ready to create all the tables of the Company database that you are to use in the remaining chapters. This is easily accomplished by opening and executing the script file named **CreateCompanyDatabase.sql**. The script file is given in Appendix A. It is also available for downloading from the textbook website. Remember, the "**sql**" file name extension means that the script file stores T-SQL statements. Creating the Company database is Exercise 14 at the end of this chapter—you should first complete Exercises 1 through 13.

NOTE: Your instructor needs to give you permission to create the database and tables for the Company database on your institution's SQL Server installation. Your instructor can provide you with an account on your institution's server. See Chapter 11 for details on SQL Server permissions and account validation.

You may need to review the material in Chapter 1 that discusses executing script files using the SQL Query Analyzer. Remember, you open the script file to load it into the Editor pane of the Query window; then you execute (run) the script file by pressing the F5 key or selecting the Execute button on the toolbar. If you have already created the *employee, department, dependent*, or other tables, you need to first drop these tables before running the script; otherwise, the script generates an error message and fails to execute properly.

As the CreateCompanyDatabase.sql script file executes, a series of messages *(1 row(s) affected)* flash across your computer screen. You can scroll down the Results pane to the last set of messages. The last set of messages tells you whether the number of rows of data created in the various tables matches that expected from running the script file. An example message for the *department* table as a T-SQL result table is:

```
Department Count should be 3
-----------------------------
3
```

If you have previously created the Company database and wish to recreate it, you should run a different script file named **RecreateCompanyDatabase.sql**. The statements stored in this file delete the existing tables and then recreate them. If this is the first time you have created the Company database or if you have not created ALL the Company database tables, the **RecreateCompanyDatabase.sql** script file cannot execute properly in SQL Query Analyzer.

SUMMARY

In this chapter you learned the basics of table creation including table modification. You also learned how to modify individual columns of a table and to insert data into tables. The most common data types are covered and examples of the use of these data types are provided. In addition, you learned how to link various tables (as per the Entity-Relationship definitions) using the concept of FKs and define various types of *integrity constraints* for each of the tables in the database.

The chapter also covers basic data manipulation statements including INSERT, DELETE, and UPDATE. In addition, you learned some basic concepts about creating and dropping indexes. After completing the review exercises provided in the next section, you will have the skills needed to work with tables and to understand the material that follows in later chapters.

REVIEW EXERCISES

LEARN THESE TERMS

ALTER.   A statement used to alter the structure of a database object such as a table.

BEGIN TRANSACTION.   A statement used to mark the explicit beginning of a set of data manipulation statements.

CHAR.   A type of column data used to store fixed length character data.

Check constraint.   A constraint that forces data values stored in a specific column to fall within some acceptable range of values.

COMMIT TRANSACTION.   A statement used to irrevocably commit data manipulation transactions to a database.

Composite index.   An index created on multiple columns of a table.

Composite primary key (PK).   When a PK consists of two or more columns to identify each row uniquely.

CREATE INDEX.   A statement used to create an index for a table.

CREATE TABLE.   A statement used to create a table in a database.

Data integrity.   Simply means that the data stored in a column is valid.

DATETIME.   A type of column data that can only store valid dates and times.

DECIMAL (NUMERIC).   A type of column data used to store numeric data values.

Derived Column.   A table column where the values stored are derived by computations involving data stored in other columns in the table.

DELETE.   A statement used to delete rows from a table.

Domain.   Describes the nature of the data that can be stored in a column; a *domain* of valid column values.

DROP. A statement used to drop a database object such as a table, for example, DROP TABLE <table_name>.

DROP INDEX. A statement used to drop or delete an index.

Foreign keys (FKs). Columns in one table that reference PK values in another table or in the same table.

INSERT. A statement used to insert values into a table.

Not NULL. A constraint meaning every data row must have a value for the column.

Precision. The total number of digits specified for a DECIMAL or other numeric data column specification.

Primary key (PK). A column or set of columns that uniquely identifies rows of data that are stored in the table.

Referential integrity. The enforcement of FOREIGN KEY constraints to ensure that values of a FK correspond to values of a PK in the table that is referenced.

ROLLBACK TRANSACTION. A statement used to reverse the effect of a data manipulation statement that is part of an explicit transaction.

Scale. The number of digits to be stored to the right of the decimal point for a DECIMAL specification.

Table. An object that stores organizational data.

Unique constraint. A constraint used to enforce uniqueness for a column value that is not a PK column.

UPDATE. A statement used to alter data values for rows that already exist within a table.

VARCHAR. A type of column data used to store variable-length, character data up to 8,000 characters per column entry.

CONCEPTS QUIZ

1. One of your colleagues is building a new information system that would normally access data from the organization's product table in the database. However, the system must store data about the quantity of each product that is on order and the current product table does not have a column that can be used to store this data. Your colleague insists that a new product table is needed to support the new application. What is your response and recommendation?

2. Briefly describe the use of each of the following data types:
   a. INT
   b. BIGINT
   c. DECIMAL (NUMERIC)
   d. MONEY
   e. CHAR (CHARACTER)
   f. NCHAR
   g. VARCHAR
   h. TEXT
   i. IMAGE
   j. DATETIME

3. With regard to the DECIMAL data type, describe how columns are specified in terms of precision and scale.

4. Would you specify a table column that can store telephone numbers as DECIMAL, CHAR, or VARCHAR? Justify your selection.

5. Exactly what type of information is stored in a column that is specified as the DATETIME data type?

6. Complete this statement: Table and column names should be _____ and reflect the _____ of the data to be stored.

7. What is the use and limitation with respect to NTEXT columns?

8. A column is specified as SMALLINT. An application program attempts to store the value 56728 to this column. How does SQL Server respond, and why?

9. If a date value is stored to a DATETIME column without specifying a time value, what value for time is stored?
10. Explain the rules that SQL Server uses for storing a century value to a date column when the system user or application program does not specify a century.
11. If you want to be able to store a NULL value for a column in a table, what must you do in specifying this capability with the CREATE TABLE statement?
12. What constraint type is built into the PRIMARY KEY constraint specification?
13. You are creating a table to store information about products. You want to require each product row to store a value for the *quantity_on_hand* column, and this value cannot be less than zero. What two constraints would you use?
14. You plan to use the ALTER TABLE statement to modify a column that already exists within a table. The table already has data rows stored to it. If the column has a size that is smaller than was originally specified, how does SQL Server respond to the ALTER TABLE statement?
15. In creating a *department* table for a university database, you wish to specify that each faculty member must be assigned to a department. What type of constraint is this?
16. You plan to insert some new data rows into a table, but do not have complete data row values to insert. Some of the fields are to remain blank. How do you accomplish this task?
17. When you specify a PRIMARY KEY constraint, what action does SQL Server take with regard to indexes?
18. You need to improve system response time performance for a program application that accesses employee row by a department code column. How can you accomplish this performance improvement?
19. You need to improve system response time for queries that access rows from tables based on several columns as part of the query. What type of index might improve system performance?

SQL CODING EXERCISES AND QUESTIONS: COMPANY DATABASE

In answering the SQL exercises and questions, submit a copy of each statement that you execute and any messages that SQL Server generates while executing your SQL statements. Also list the output for any result table that is generated by your SQL statements.

1. Create a table named *test_table*. This table should have two columns named *test_id* and *test_description*. These columns should be defined to store the following type of data, respectively: *test_id* stores whole number data that has a maximum value of 999; *test_description* stores variable character data that is a maximum of 25 characters in size.
2. Insert two rows into the *test_table*. You should create your own data.
3. Use the following SELECT statement to display the rows in the *test_table*.

```
SELECT * FROM test_table;
```

4. Use the DROP statement to drop the *test_table*.

5. Create the *department* table described in Appendix A. Do not define any foreign keys. Include all other constraint specifications required to ensure data integrity.
6. Add the data shown next to the *department* table. Leave the *dpt_mgrssn* and *dpt_mgr_start_date* values as NULL.

dpt_no	dpt_name	dpt_mgrssn	dpt_mgr_start_date
7	Production	NULL	NULL
3	Admin and Records	NULL	NULL
1	Headquarters	NULL	NULL

7. What statements would you use to mark the beginning and end of the three INSERT statements that you executed in Question 6 above if you wanted explicit transaction integrity specifications by using transaction delimiters? Show how the statements would be used by modifying your code for Question 7.
8. Use the following SELECT statement to display the rows in the *department* table.

```
SELECT *
FROM department;
```

9. Create the *employee* table described in Appendix A. Include all constraint specifications required to ensure data integrity. Create the referential integrity constraints needed to ensure that the department to which employees are assigned exists within the *department* table. Your integrity constraints should also allow employees to NOT be assigned to a department.
10. Add the data shown in Appendix A to the *employee* table. Add an additional row to the employee data consisting of data that describes you (your own employee row). Assign yourself a salary of 50,000, parking space 999, department 7, and supervisor SSN of '999444444'.
11. Use the following SELECT statement to display the rows in the *employee* table.

```
SELECT emp_ssn, emp_last_name
FROM employee;
```

12. Delete your row from the *employee* table. Use the SELECT statement given in Question 11 to display the employee rows. Verify that your row has been deleted.
13. Employee Zhu has reported that his address is incorrect. The correct street address is 6 Main St. Update the *emp_address* column of his data row accordingly. Verify that the row has been deleted.
14. Download the script needed to create the Company database shown in Appendix A from the textbook's website at www.prenhall.com/bordoloi to a disk. Save the file as a text file named *CreateCompanyDatabase.sql*. Prior to running the script, drop the *employee* and *department* tables. Run the script to create the entire database.
15. Alter the *employee* table to add a column that can be used to store the salary earned year-to-date. Name this column *salary_year_to_date* and use an appropriate data-type specification. You do not need to store any data to this column.
16. Create a nonunique index on the *employee* table for the employee zip code (*emp_zip*) column. Give the index an appropriate name.
17. Create a composite, nonunique index on the *employee* table for the employee zip code (*emp_zip*) and employee last name (*emp_last_name*) columns.

18. Create a script named **Item.sql** that creates a table named *item*, insert three rows of data as shown, and then display the data by using a SELECT statement. Use the SQL Query Analyzer to create and execute the script file.

Item Table

Column Name	Data Type	Constraint
item_id	SMALLINT	Primary Key
item_description	VARCHAR(25)	None
item_value	MONEY	None

Data to Insert		
item_id	**item_description**	**item_value**
2	Computer	979.95
4	Printer	152.59
7	Desk	385.98

SQL CODING EXERCISES AND QUESTIONS: RIVERBEND DATABASE

1. Create a table named *patient_archive*. This table can be used to store patient rows for inactive patients. Inactive patients are patients who have not visited the hospital facility for 5 years or more. The *patient_archive* table should have the same structure as the patient table except it should *not* have a column to store the *bed_number*—leave this column out of the table definition.
2. Store information about yourself to the *patient_archive* table as sample test data. Name each constraint, as is done for the *patient* table, except add the suffix *_archive* to each of the constraint names.
3. Use the following SELECT statement to display the rows in the *patient_archive* table.

```
SELECT * FROM patient_archive;
```

4. Use the DROP statement to drop the *patient_archive* table.
5. Create the *ward_dept* table described in Appendix B. Include all constraint specifications required to ensure data integrity. Do not define FKs for this question.
6. Add the data shown here to the *ward_dept* table.

Ward_id	Ward_dept_name	Office_location	Telephone_number
MEDS1	Medical Surgical Ward 1	SW1020	1005559201
MEDS2	Medical Surgical Ward 2	NW1018	1005559202
RADI1	Radiology Department	RA0070	1005559203

7. What two statements would you use to mark the beginning and end of the three INSERT statements that you executed for Question 6 above if you want explicit transaction integrity to be defined by using transaction delimiters? Show how you would modify the code to include these two new statements.
8. Use the following SELECT statement to display the rows in the *ward_dept* table:

```
SELECT * FROM ward_dept;
```

9. Create a table like the *staff* table described in Appendix B. Name your table *staff2*. Include all constraint specifications required to ensure data integrity. Create the referential integrity constraints needed to ensure that the *ward_dept* to which staff members are assigned for work exists within the *ward_dept* table. Your integrity constraints should also allow staff members to *not* be assigned to a ward or department. When naming the integrity constraints, replace the word *staff* with the word *staff2*.

10. Add data to the *staff2* table as shown below in the INSERT statements. Add an additional row to the *staff2* data consisting of data that describes yourself (your own staff2 row). Make up your own data.

```
INSERT INTO staff2 VALUES ('23232', '310223232', 'Eakin', 'Maxwell',
'E', 'MEDS1', 'SW4208', '6-JAN-98', 'M.D.', '1005559268', '0001',
'IL54386', 150000, NULL);

INSERT INTO staff2 VALUES ('23244', '316223244', 'Webber','Eugene',
NULL, 'RADI1', 'SW4392', '16-FEB-95', 'M.D.', '1005559270', '4410',
'IL383815', 175000, NULL);

INSERT INTO staff2 VALUES ('10044', '216223308', 'Sumner','Elizabeth',
NULL, 'MEDS2', 'SW4393', '16-FEB-01', 'M.D.','1005559271', '3201',
'IL419057', 165000, NULL);
```

11. Select specific columns from the *staff2* table by using the SELECT statement shown next.

```
SELECT staff_id, staff_ssn, staff_last_name
FROM staff2;
```

12. Delete your data row from the *staff2* table. Execute the SELECT statement given for Question 11 to demonstrate that the row has been deleted. Verify your record has been deleted.

13. Execute an UPDATE statement that changes the *office_location* column value for Eugene Webber to SW4000. Execute the SELECT statement shown to demonstrate that Webber's office has been updated:

```
SELECT staff_last_name, office_location
FROM staff2
WHERE staff_last_name = 'Webber';
```

14. Download the script needed to create the remaining tables of the Riverbend Hospital Database schema shown in Appendix B from the textbook's website at www.prenhall.com/bordoloi to a disk. Save the file as a text file named *CreateRiverbendDatabase.sql*. Prior to running the script, execute SQL statements to drop the *ward_dept* and *staff2* tables. Run the script to create the entire database.

15. Alter the *medicine* table to add a column that can be used to store the unit cost of each medicine. Name this column *med_unit_cost* and use an appropriate data-type specification. You do not need to store any data to this column.

16. Create a nonunique index on the *service_cat_id* column of the *service* table. Name the index *service_cat_id*.

SINGLE TABLE QUERY BASICS

This chapter focuses on learning to write SELECT statements to retrieve information from tables. This is termed querying a table, and this chapter covers single-table queries, meaning that the information retrieved comes from a single database table. As you have probably determined by this point in your studies, a database can be queried to produce both small and large quantities of information. Simple queries often tend to produce large quantities of information in terms of row output, whereas more complex queries are capable of extracting specific information from a database. If a query produces a large quantity of information, managers who need the information for decision making may be overwhelmed by the sheer volume of information. Usually managers need specific pieces of information to help them make decisions. In this chapter you initially learn to write simple queries, and progress to increasingly complex queries.

OBJECTIVES

You query a relational database through use of the SELECT statement. Chapter 1 introduces the SELECT statement. In this chapter you master the basics of the SELECT statement. You learn to write queries to select both specific rows and specific columns from a table. You also learn to sort the output in various ways. Additionally, you learn to avoid some of the common errors that can be made when writing a SELECT statement. The learning objectives for this chapter are:

- Write simple SELECT statements.
- Learn to use the COLUMN command to format output.
- Eliminate duplicate rows with the DISTINCT clause.
- Use the WHERE clause to specify selection criteria and conditions.
- Order rows with the ORDER BY clause.

SIMPLE SELECT STATEMENTS

The main element in a Structured Query Language (SQL) query is the SELECT statement. A properly written SELECT statement always produces a result in the form of one or more rows of output, providing there are rows in a table that satisfy the selection criteria. The SELECT statement chooses (selects) rows from one or more tables according to specific criteria. In this chapter we focus on selecting rows from a single table. SQL Example 3.1 shows the simplest form of a query.

```
/* SQL Example 3.1 */
SELECT *
FROM employee;


emp_ssn    emp_last_name  emp_first_name  emp_middle_name
---------  -------------  --------------  ---------------
999111111  Bock           Douglas         B
999222222  Amin           Hyder           NULL
999333333  Joshi          Dinesh          Null
more rows and columns will be displayed...
```

This query selects rows from the *employee* table. The asterisk (*) tells SQL Server to select (display) *all* columns contained in the table *employee*. The resulting output is termed a *result* table. The result table displayed in SQL Example 3.1 only lists the first three rows and first four columns of the result table. The full *employee* table is described in Appendix A and is part of the Company database. The full result table output wraps around your computer screen because the rows of data are too large to display to a single line. Additionally, you notice that the *emp_last_name, emp_first_name*, and *emp_middle_name* columns are quite wide when they display to your computer monitor because when the *employee* table was created, these columns were defined to be large enough to store the largest last, first, or middle name data values that might ever occur for an employee. Later in this chapter you learn to format the width of result table columns.

This particular type of query uses an asterisk (*) symbol to tell SQL Server: "Give me everything you have on employees. Do not hold anything back." All rows and all columns are selected. The SELECT statement in SQL Example 3.2 produces an identical result table by listing all column names in the *employee* table.

```
/* SQL Example 3.2 */
SELECT emp_ssn, emp_last_name, emp_first_name, emp_middle_name,
    emp_address, emp_city, emp_state, emp_zip, emp_date_of_birth,
    emp_salary, emp_parking_space, emp_gender,
    emp_dpt_number, emp_superssn
FROM employee;
```

Clearly, it is simpler to type the query in SQL Example 3.1 as opposed to the one given in SQL Example 3.2 that lists each column name individually, but you would only use the asterisk (*) in a SELECT statement if you wished to display all columns in the result table. Normally this is not the case.

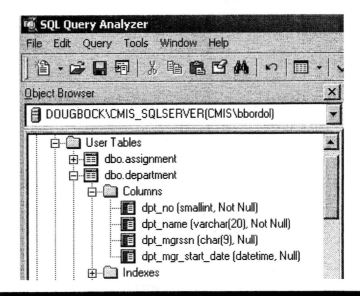

FIGURE 3.1

Note that a comma separates each column name. This syntax is required. The SELECT statement also specifies a table name in the FROM clause. Finally, the semi-colon at the end of the query, which is *optional* in Transact SQL (T-SQL), indicates that this is the end of the query. You may wonder about the ordering of the column names. It happens that the ordering of column names is immaterial except that the result table displays the columns in the order specified in the SELECT statement. Let us examine the data stored in the *department* table. We begin by first describing the *department* table using the Object Browser in SQL Query Analyzer, as shown in Figure 3.1.

There are only four columns in the *department* table. These columns store the department number, department name, department manager's social security number (SSN), and the date that each department manager was assigned to the job of department manager. The two queries in SQL Examples 3.3 and 3.4 produce exactly the same result table.

```
/* SQL Example 3.3 */
SELECT *
FROM department;
```

```
/* SQL Example 3.4 */
SELECT dpt_no, dpt_name, dpt_mgrssn, dpt_mgr_start_date
FROM department;

dpt_no dpt_name             dpt_mgrssn dpt_mgr_start_date
------ -------------------- ---------- -----------------------
   1   Headquarters         999666666  1981-06-19 00:00:00.000
   3   Admin and Records    999555555  2001-01-01 00:00:00.000
   7   Production           999444444  1998-05-22 00:00:00.000
```

SQL Example 3.5 is a revision of SQL Example 3.4 that simply reorders the order by which columns are listed in the result table. The output in terms of rows is identical, but the ordering of the columns changes to match the ordering in the SELECT statement.

```
/* SQL Example 3.5 */
SELECT dpt_name, dpt_no, dpt_mgr_start_date, dpt_mgrssn
FROM department;

dpt_name            dpt_no dpt_mgr_start_date      dpt_mgrssn
------------------- ------ ----------------------- ----------
Headquarters        1      1981-06-19 00:00:00.000 999666666
Admin and Records   3      2001-01-01 00:00:00.000 999555555
Production          7      1998-05-22 00:00:00.000 999444444
```

INDENTING SQL CODE

Have you noticed that we always start a new line for the FROM clause in a SELECT statement? We have also indented four characters in listing the columns to be displayed where the list of columns is too large to fit within a single line. It is fairly common to follow this type of indentation convention when writing a query because it makes a query easier to read. However, SQL Server can process a query regardless of whether you type an entire query on one line or several lines with or without indention. This is because SQL is a free-form language. This means that there are no rules about how many words you can put on a line or where you break a line. Also note that although we use a semicolon to mark the end of a query in almost all the examples in this book, the semicolon at end of the query is *optional* in T-SQL (versus required when using SQL for other databases such as Oracle). For example, the SQL statements in SQL Examples 3.6 and 3.7 are considered exactly the same in T-SQL.

```
/* SQL Example 3.6 */
SELECT * FROM employee;
```

```
/* SQL Example 3.7 */
SELECT
*
FROM
Employee;
```

Although not required, it is a good coding practice to start a new line for each clause in an SQL statement. This decreases application maintenance and increases readability. The following keywords are your signal to start a new line.

- SELECT
- FROM
- WHERE
- GROUP BY
- HAVING
- ORDER BY

SELECTING SPECIFIC COLUMNS

As you can see, using an asterisk (*) is a quick and easy way to list all column names in a table. However, in day-to-day queries you rarely need to specify all the available column names in a table. If you provided your boss with all the columns and rows from a table, the boss would likely tell you that you were providing too much detail. Let us suppose that your boss only wants a listing of employee SSNs, last names, and first names. The SELECT statement to produce this output is shown in SQL Example 3.8.

```
/* SQL Example 3.8 */
SELECT emp_ssn, emp_last_name, emp_first_name
FROM employee;

emp_ssn    emp_last_name          emp_first_name
---------  --------------------   --------------------
999111111  Bock                   Douglas
999222222  Amin                   Hyder
999333333  Joshi                  Dinesh
999444444  Zhu                    Waiman
more rows will be displayed...
```

NOTE: Throughout this manual, the rows of a result table produced by a query are limited to only the number of rows needed for you to understand the query. As you execute each query, you may sometimes see that we have omitted rows of data output for the purpose of brevity or clarity.

To review, the rules for writing a simple SELECT query in T-SQL are:

- Specify the column names you want displayed in the result set by typing the exact, complete column names.
- Separate each column name with a comma (,).
- The column names selected must belong to the table or tables named in the FROM clause.

FORMATTING DEFAULT OUTPUT

At times you may write a query where the columnar output does not fit onto a single display line in the Results pane of the SQL Query Analyzer; or if you save the output to a Results File, output may display lines that "wrap" around to the next line and the information may be difficult to read. SQL Example 3.9 produces this type of output (the output shown is from a Results File).

```
/* SQL Example 3.9 */
SELECT emp_ssn, emp_last_name, emp_first_name,
    emp_date_of_birth, emp_superssn
FROM employee;

emp_ssn    emp_last_name                   emp_first_name    emp_date_of_birth
                                                            emp_superssn

---------  -----------------------------   ----------------------------   -----------
-----------------------------------------------------   -------------
999111111  Bock                            Douglas                          1950-12-05
00:00:00.000                                           999444444
999222222  Amin                            Hyder                            1969-03-29
00:00:00.000                                           999555555
999333333  Joshi                           Dinesh                           1972-09-15
00:00:00.000                                           999444444
more rows will be displayed...
```

You can clean up the result table for such a query by modifying the output display size of specific columns. In SQL Server you can reformat the column output with automatic data type conversion by using the CAST and CONVERT functions in the SELECT statement.

USING THE CAST FUNCTION

SQL Example 3.10 illustrates the CAST function. The example reformats the *emp_last_name, emp_first_name*, and *emp_date_of_birth* columns to restrict their output to 12 characters each. This is significantly smaller than the column width specified for each of these columns in the *employee* table. The advantage is that each single row of output is displayed on a single line, thereby improving the readability of the information. Notice that CAST automatically converts the data type of *emp_date_of_birth* from the specified DATETIME to CHAR for purposes of display.

```
/* SQL Example 3.10 */
SELECT emp_ssn, CAST(emp_last_name As CHAR(12)),
    CAST(emp_first_name As CHAR(12)),
    CAST(emp_date_of_birth As CHAR(12)),
    emp_superssn
FROM employee;

emp_ssn                                                emp_superssn
---------  ---------   -----------   ------------   -------------
999111111  Bock        Douglas       Dec  5 1950    999444444
999222222  Amin        Hyder         Mar 29 1969    999555555
999333333  Joshi       Dinesh        Sep 15 1972    999444444
more rows will be displayed...
```

Did you notice that the reformatted columns, *emp_last_name, emp_first_name*, and *emp_date_of_birth* do not have column names (labels)? Because these columns have been manipulated, the default column names no longer apply. It is up to you to rename a column to reflect the manipulation. You learn how to do this in the next section.

RENAMING COLUMN NAMES

SQL Server does not label the results of built-in functions (such as CAST) or expressions in a SELECT clause. When you write SQL statements that produce output for use by managers, you need to keep in mind that a manager may not have access to the SQL statement—even if the manager did have access to the statement, the manager may not understand the statement. Therefore, unlabeled columns and their data are meaningless. You should always label the columns produced by a function or an expression. You can also assign a new name to an existing column name to make it more readable or more meaningful.

SQL Example 3.11 demonstrates how to label or rename display columns from the default column names. These are referred to as column *labels*. Sometimes they are also called *alias names*. The alias names here are denoted by the use of double quote marks. Note that there is no punctuation between the column to be displayed and the alias name.

```
/*SQL Example 3.11 */
SELECT emp_ssn, CAST(emp_last_name As CHAR(12)) "Last Name",
    CAST(emp_first_name As CHAR(12)) "First Name",
    CAST(emp_date_of_birth As CHAR(12))"Date of Birth" ,
    emp_superssn "Supervisor_SSN"
FROM employee;

emp_ssn   Last Name First Name Date of Birth Supervisor_SSN
--------- --------- ---------- ------------- --------------
999111111 Bock      Douglas    Dec  5 1950   999444444
999222222 Amin      Hyder      Mar 29 1969   999555555
999333333 Joshi     Dinesh     Sep 15 1972   999444444
more rows will be displayed...
```

When labeling or renaming display columns from the default column names, be sure to follow these rules.

- Enclose the label in quotes, either single or double.
- Do *not* separate the label from the expression with a comma.
- The label must follow the function or column name.

Here are some examples of errors that you may make when using labels. These examples use a function named COUNT(*). The function counts the number of rows in a table. In the first SELECT statement, to use Total Count as a column label, you must enclose the name with either single or double quotes. The second example is wrong because a comma separates the label from the function. You cannot use a comma as a syntax separator here.

```
WRONG:     SELECT COUNT(*) total count
WRONG:     SELECT COUNT(*), "total count"
```

Let us execute the second example shown above. It is displayed in SQL Example 3.12. When it executes, you note that SQL Server does not generate an error message. This is a legal SELECT statement, but the result table is not what you expect.

```
/*SQL Example 3.12 */
SELECT COUNT(*), 'total count'
FROM employee

----------- -----------
8           total count
```

In the last query the result table contains one row. It does count the number of employees in the *employee* table; however, the column has no heading (label). Additionally, a second column displays with the words "total count" as output. This is because of the erroneously placed comma in the query. You can see that it is important to learn all the details of the syntax of the SELECT statement.

USING THE CONVERT FUNCTION

SQL Example 3.11 formatted character data for output to a result table. You can also format the output of numeric columns. Consider SQL Example 3.13 which displays employee salary data.

```
/* SQL Example 3.13 */
SELECT emp_ssn, CAST(emp_last_name As CHAR(12)) "First Name",
    CAST(emp_first_name As CHAR(12)) "Last Name",
    CAST(emp_date_of_birth As CHAR(12)) "Date of Birth",
    emp_salary
FROM employee;

emp_ssn   First Name Last Name Date of Birth emp_salary
--------- ---------- --------- ------------- ----------
999111111 Bock       Douglas   Dec  5 1950   30000.0000
999222222 Amin       Hyder     Mar 29 1969   25000.0000
999333333 Joshi      Dinesh    Sep 15 1972   38000.0000
```

The *emp_salary* column is defined to be of data type MONEY; thus, the default output format displays four digits to the right of the decimal point. Additionally, the salaries are difficult to read because they are large numbers and do not have commas as would normally be the case when displaying a large number. Although the CAST function can be used to reformat both character and numeric data, the CONVERT function works better for certain data types such as MONEY and DATETIME. The CONVERT function includes a special parameter called the *style* parameter that enables you to use a variety of display formats when converting these special data types to character data.

SQL Example 3.14 shows the use of CONVERT function for the *emp_salary* column. As shown in the result table, the reformatted *emp_salary* data now has only two digits to the right of the decimal point and includes a comma for every three digits to the left of the decimal point. This was achieved by setting the *style* parameter value of the CONVERT function to "1" (boldfaced in the example). Also, the column heading label was changed to read *Salary* instead of the default column name (*emp_salary*).

```
/* SQL Example 3.14 */
SELECT emp_ssn, CAST (emp_last_name As CHAR(12)) "First Name",
    CAST (emp_first_name As CHAR(12)) "Last Name",
    CAST (emp_date_of_birth As CHAR(12))"Date of Birth",
    CONVERT (CHAR (10), emp_salary, 1) "Salary"
FROM employee;


emp_ssn    First Name  Last Name Date of Birth Salary
---------  ----------- --------- ------------- -------
999111111  Bock        Douglas   Dec  5 1950     30,000.00
999222222  Amin        Hyder     Mar 29 1969     25,000.00
999333333  Joshi       Dinesh    Sep 15 1972     38,000.00
more rows will be displayed...
```

We can improve the output for the *salary* column even further if we place a dollar sign ($) in front of the values for the employee salary figures. This result is achieved with SQL Example 3.15 by including a constant character "$" as a column name in the SELECT statement and *concatenating* this column with the *salary* column. The "+" sign, boldfaced in the example, is the concatenation symbol.

```
/* SQL Example 3.15 */
SELECT emp_ssn, CAST (emp_last_name As CHAR(12)) "First Name",
    CAST (emp_first_name As CHAR(12)) "Last Name",
    CAST (emp_date_of_birth As CHAR(12))"Date of Birth",
    '$' + CONVERT (CHAR (10), emp_salary, 1) "Salary"
FROM employee;


emp_ssn    First Name Last Name  Date of Birth Salary
---------  ---------- ---------- ------------- -----------
999111111  Bock       Douglas    Dec  5 1950   $ 30,000.00
999222222  Amin       Hyder      Mar 29 1969   $ 25,000.00
999333333  Joshi      Dinesh     Sep 15 1972   $ 38,000.00
more rows will be displayed...
```

Concatenation of two output columns is covered later in more detail. Concatenation simply means to add two strings of output together to form a single output column. We introduce the concept here simply to provide you some idea of the extent to which output in a result table can be tailored to meet the needs of business managers who may use the information in decision making.

COMMON ERRORS

Although SQL is a free-form language, there are still syntactical rules that you must follow or you may receive an error message instead of the desired result table. For example, if you violate any of the previously mentioned rules, SQL Server displays an error message indicating the possible cause of the error and the line number (in your query) where the error has occurred. Let us examine some example errors.

INVALID COLUMN NAME

The SELECT statement in SQL Example 3.16 has the employee SSN column name spelled incorrectly.

```
/* SQL Example 3.16 */
SELECT emp_socsecno
FROM employee;

Server: Msg 207, Level 16, State 3, Line 1
Invalid column name 'emp_socsecno'.
```

SQL Server responds by specifying which line has the error. Here the error is in line 1 where the employee SSN column should be *emp_ssn*, not *emp_socsecno*. If you receive this error message, check the spelling of the column name for typographical errors.

FROM KEYWORD MISSING

SQL Example 3.17 shows a SELECT statement that is missing the FROM clause so that no table name is specified. Without a table name, the database management system does not know which table to query. Note that SQL Query Analyzer thinks that the error is in line 1. This makes sense because there is only one line in the SELECT statement. It is your responsibility to analyze the error message and discover the root cause of the problem.

```
/* SQL Example 3.17 */
SELECT emp_ssn;

Server: Msg 207, Level 16, State 3, Line 1
Invalid column name 'emp_ssn'.
```

UNKNOWN COMMAND: INVALID COMMAND STRUCTURE

In SQL Example 3.18, the order of the SELECT and FROM clauses is reversed. SQL Server is very confused by this command and simply returns an 'incorrect syntax' error message.

```
/* SQL Example 3.18 */
FROM employee SELECT emp_ssn;

Server: Msg 156, Level 15, State 1, Line 1
Incorrect syntax near the keyword 'FROM'.
```

ERRORS IN PLACING COMMAS

Some syntax errors cause SQL Server to return an erroneous result table without any error messages. In SQL Example 3.19, a comma is missing after the *emp_last_name* column specification. Instead of reporting back that there is a syntax error or that a comma is missing, SQL Server produces a result set that is missing one column of data.

```
/* SQL Example 3.19 */
SELECT emp_ssn, emp_last_name emp_first_name
FROM employee;

emp_ssn    emp_first_name
---------  --------------------
999111111  Bock
999222222  Amin
999333333  Joshi
more rows will be displayed...
```

At first glance, it appears that the query executed satisfactorily, but wait—we wanted three columns of output and the SELECT statement only produced two columns of output—a listing with only the SSN and first name for each employee. However, a closer inspection of the output rows reveals that the last name of each employee is listed, but the column heading is wrong. SQL Server did not treat this as an error. Instead, SQL Server thought that you only wanted two columns of output, and that you wanted the second column to have a special column heading other than the default *emp_last_name*.

There is another possible type of comma placement error—placing a comma after the last column name specified in a SELECT statement, as is done in SQL Example 3.20. In this situation again, SQL Server gets very confused by the command and simply returns an incorrect syntax error message.

```
/* SQL Example 3.20 */
SELECT emp_ssn, emp_last_name, emp_first_name,
FROM employee;

Server: Msg 156, Level 15, State 1, Line 2
Incorrect syntax near the keyword 'FROM'.
```

DISTINCT CLAUSE: ELIMINATING DUPLICATE ROWS

As we learned in Chapter 2, tables are generally designed with a primary key that guarantees each row in a table is unique. Thus, if you select all columns from a table, no two rows in a result table are duplicates. However, if a SELECT statement does not select all columns, it is possible for a result table to contain duplicate rows. This can occur when the SELECT statement does not select the primary key column or columns as part of the output.

SQL Server provides a means for eliminating duplicate rows in a result table through use of the DISTINCT keyword. The SELECT statement in SQL Example 3.21 produces a simple listing of salaries paid to employees. The result table contains rows with duplicate values.

```
/* SQL Example 3.21 */
SELECT emp_salary
FROM employee;

emp_salary
-----------
30000.0000
25000.0000
38000.0000
43000.0000
43000.0000
55000.0000
25000.0000
25000.0000
(8 row(s) affected)
```

When row output is duplicated, it is possible for the duplicate values to obscure the relevant data that managers seek to use in making decisions. The query is rewritten in SQL Example 3.22 and uses the DISTINCT keyword to eliminate duplicate rows. When the DISTINCT keyword is used, the output ordering of rows may change unless the rows are explicitly sorted with the ORDER BY clause. Do not worry about row order for now as you can learn to control row output ordering later in this chapter.

```
/* SQL Example 3.22 */
SELECT DISTINCT emp_salary
FROM employee;

emp_salary
-----------
25000.0000
30000.0000
38000.0000
43000.0000
55000.0000
(5 row(s) affected)
```

The DISTINCT keyword must immediately follow the SELECT keyword and is not separated from the first column name with a comma. If you mistakenly place the DISTINCT keyword other than immediately following the SELECT statement, the query generates an error message, as shown in SQL Example 3.23.

```
/* SQL Example 3.23 */
SELECT emp_salary DISTINCT
FROM employee;

Server: Msg 156, Level 15, State 1, Line 2
Incorrect syntax near the keyword 'distinct'.
```

The DISTINCT keyword also eliminates duplicate rows where more than one column is displayed in the result table. SQL Example 3.24 shows a query of the *bed* table for the Riverbend Hospital database described in Appendix B. Note the duplicate rows highlighted in bold text.

```
/* SQL Example 3.24 */
SELECT room_id, bed_type_id
FROM bed;

room_id bed_type_id
------- -----------
SW1001  R1
SW1002  R1
SW1003  R2
SW1004  R1
SW1005  R2
SW1006  R1
SW1010  R1
SW1010  R2
SW1011  R2
SW1011  R2
SW1012  R1

(98 row(s) affected)
```

The DISTINCT clause eliminates duplicate row output as shown in SQL Example 3.25. The result table does not display all the rows—the key point is that the duplicate row for room SW1011, bed type R2 is no longer listed twice, nor are other duplicate rows listed.

```
/* SQL Example 3.25 */
SELECT DISTINCT room_id, bed_type_id
FROM bed;

room_id bed_type_id
------- -----------
. . .
SW1001  R1
SW1002  R1
SW1003  R1
. . .
SW1004  R2
SW1005  R2
SW1006  R1
SW1006  R2
SW1010  RE
SW1011  R2
SW1012  R1

(65 row(s) affected)
```

SELECTING ROWS: WHERE CLAUSE

You have learned how to display specific columns from a table, as well as how to reduce the number of rows displayed through use of the DISTINCT keyword. As you may recall from Chapter 1, displaying specific columns from a table is known as a *project* operation. We now focus on displaying specific rows of output. This is known as a *select* operation.

Specific rows can be selected by adding a WHERE clause to a SELECT query. Suppose that your boss is working on the quarterly budget for your organization. As part of this activity, it is necessary to produce a listing of each employee's SSN, last name, first name, and salary, but only for employees that are paid at least $35,000 annually. SQL Example 3.26 accomplishes this task. Note the use of the WHERE clause shown in bold text.

```
/* SQL Example 3.26 */
SELECT emp_ssn, emp_last_name, emp_first_name, emp_salary
FROM employee
WHERE emp_salary >= 35000;

emp_ssn    emp_last_name  emp_first_name emp_salary
---------  -------------- -------------- ----------
999333333  Joshi          Dinesh         38000.0000
999444444  Zhu            Waiman         43000.0000
999555555  Joyner         Suzanne        43000.0000
999666666  Bordoloi       Bijoy          55000.0000

(4 row(s) affected)
```

As you can see, the result table contains only rows where the *condition* (salary >= 35000) is met. Further, the dollar sign ($) and comma (,) are *not* used in specifying the numeric value for the employee salary in the WHERE clause. In this example we used the greater-than-or-equal-to operator (>=). You could just as easily request a list of employees that are paid less than $35,000 or any other value for employee salary, as is done in SQL Example 3.27.

```
/* SQL Example 3.27 */
SELECT emp_ssn, emp_last_name, emp_first_name, emp_salary
FROM employee
WHERE emp_salary < 35000;

emp_ssn    emp_last_name  emp_first_name emp_salary
---------  -------------- -------------- ----------
999111111  Bock           Douglas        30000.0000
999222222  Amin           Hyder          25000.0000
999887777  Markis         Marcia         25000.0000
999888888  Prescott       Sherri         25000.0000

(4 row(s) affected)
```

	TABLE 3.1	
	Operator	*Meaning*
	=	Equal to
	<	Less than
	>	Greater than
	>=	Greater than or equal to
	<=	Less than or equal to
	!=	Not equal to
	<>	Not equal to
	!>	Not greater than
	!<	Not less than

COMPARISON OPERATORS

SQL Server supports nine different *comparison operators*. These are listed in Table 3.1. These operators are used to express simple conditions where you are comparing two values. Their meaning when used in a condition is specified in the table. Note that they are written in exactly the same way that you speak them. You may also note that there are two operators that can be used to express "not equal to" – use the one of your choosing.

COMPARING CHARACTER DATA

The use of comparison operators is not limited to numeric data. They can also be used with columns containing character data. When comparing CHAR and VARCHAR data, the "less than" operator (<) means earlier in the alphabet (A comes before B), whereas the "greater than" operator (>) means later in the alphabet (Z comes after Y).

When you use comparison operators in a WHERE clause, the arguments (objects or values you are comparing) on both sides of the operator must be either *a column name,* or *a specific value.* If a specific value is specified, then the value must be either a numeric value or a literal, character string, for example, 'Bob', 'Main Street', 'Abc', 'Xyz', and the like. If the value is a character string—you must surround the value (string of characters) with which a column is compared with *single quotation* (') *marks* as is done in the examples.

Suppose your manager wants a listing of the SSN, last name, and first name for all male employees. The SELECT query requires a WHERE clause that selects rows based on employee gender. The *emp_gender* column stores coded data where M = male and F = female employees. SQL Example 3.28 shows a SELECT statement with the correct WHERE clause. Note that the values stored in the *emp_gender* column are compared to the literal character value 'M'.

```
/* SQL Example 3.28 */
SELECT emp_ssn, emp_last_name, emp_first_name
FROM employee
WHERE emp_gender = 'M';
```

```
emp_ssn     emp_last_name    emp_first_name
---------   --------------   --------------------
999111111 Bock               Douglas
999222222 Amin               Hyder
999333333 Joshi              Dinesh
999444444 Zhu                Waiman
999666666 Bordoloi           Bijoy

(5 row(s) affected)
```

Note that the *emp_gender* column name does not have to be specified in the listing of columns selected for display in the result table to use the column name in the WHERE clause. Now let us see what happens if you make a mistake and fail to enclose the employee gender code within single quote marks.

```
/* SQL Example 3.29 */
SELECT emp_ssn, emp_last_name, emp_first_name
FROM employee
WHERE emp_gender = M;

Server: Msg 207, Level 16, State 3, Line 3
Invalid column name 'M'.
```

SQL Server returns an error message indicating invalid column name. Although this error message does not tell you exactly what you did wrong, it does identify the line that has the error (line 3 above). Recall our earlier rule about the arguments in a WHERE clause. Because the literal string value was not enclosed by single quote marks, SQL Server assumed the letter M to be a column name. Of course, there is no column named M in the *employee* table so an error was returned. So, when you see this error with a reference to a line associated with a WHERE clause, you need to determine whether the column name referenced by the WHERE clause stores character data.

You can also write SELECT statements that use operators other than the equal sign. For example, suppose your manager needs a listing of employees that have a first name that begins with the letter 'J', or that begins with a letter that occurs later in the alphabet than the letter 'J'. SQL Example 3.30 shows the appropriate WHERE clause.

```
/* SQL Example 3.30 */
SELECT emp_last_name, emp_first_name
FROM employee
WHERE emp_last_name >= 'J';

emp_last_name        emp_first_name
-----------------    ----------------------
Joshi                Dinesh
Zhu                  Waiman
```

```
Joyner                Suzanne
Markis                Marcia
Prescott              Sherri


(5 row(s) affected)
```

ORDERING ROWS: ORDER BY CLAUSE

Normally, when rows are added to a table they are appended to the end of the table. This produces a table containing unordered rows. This is clear when examining the result table for SQL Example 3.30; the rows are not in alphabetic order.

When you display only a few rows of data, it may be unnecessary to sort the output; however, when you display numerous rows, managers may be aided in decision making by having the information sorted. Output from a SELECT statement can be sorted by using the optional ORDER BY clause. When you use the ORDER BY clause, the column name on which you are ordering must also be a column name that is specified in the SELECT clause.

The query from SQL Example 3.30 is expanded in SQL Example 3.31 to add an ORDER BY clause that sorts the result table by the *emp_last_name* column in ascending order. Ascending order is the default sort order.

```
/* SQL Example 3.31 */
SELECT emp_last_name, emp_first_name
FROM employee
WHERE emp_last_name >= 'J'
ORDER BY emp_last_name;

emp_last_name         emp_first_name
--------------------- ---------------------------
Joshi                 Dinesh
Joyner                Suzanne
Markis                Marcia
Prescott              Sherri
Zhu                   Waiman

(5 row(s) affected)
```

You can also sort data based on numeric column values. SQL Example 3.32 sorts employees based on their salary.

```
/* SQL Example 3.32 */
SELECT emp_last_name, emp_first_name, emp_salary
FROM employee
WHERE emp_salary > 35000
ORDER BY emp_salary;
```

```
emp_last_name        emp_first_name        emp_salary
-----------------    -----------------     ----------------
Joshi                Dinesh                38000.0000
Zhu                  Waiman                43000.0000
Joyner               Suzanne               43000.0000
Bordoloi             Bijoy                 55000.0000

(4 row(s) affected)
```

SORT ORDER

It is fairly intuitive that *numeric* columns sort by default from smallest to largest values. What about *character* data? The sorting of character data is language dependent. Table 3.2 displays the sort order that SQL Server uses when sorting the English language and special characters. The sort order is based on the American Standard Code for Information Interchange (ASCII) character coding scheme. Lowercase letters come *after* uppercase letters in the sort order.

ORDER BY WITH ASC AND DESC OPTIONS

By default, the ORDER BY clause sorts output rows in a result table in ascending order. However, there are situations when you may need to display results in descending order. Let us rewrite SQL Example 3.32 to display the rows in reverse-salary order, that is, highest salaries first. We use the keyword DESC (short for descending) to force this descending sort. The alternative default is ASC, which sorts in ascending order, but the ASC keyword is rarely used because it is the default.

When either the ASC or DESC optional keyword is used, it must follow the column name on which you are sorting in the WHERE clause. SQL Example 3.33 demonstrates the DESC keyword.

```
/* SQL Example 3.33 */
SELECT emp_last_name, emp_first_name, emp_salary
FROM employee
WHERE emp_salary > 35000
ORDER BY emp_salary DESC;

emp_last_name        emp_first_name        emp_salary
-----------------    -----------------     ----------------
Bordoloi             Bijoy                 55000.0000
Zhu                  Waiman                43000.0000
Joyner               Suzanne               43000.0000
Joshi                Dinesh                38000.0000

(4 row(s) affected)
```

TABLE 3.2   Characters, in ASCII Order
! " # $ % & ' ( ) * + , - . / 0 1 2 3 4 5 6 7 8 9 : ; < = > ? @
A B C D E F G H I J K L M N O P Q R S T U V W X Y Z [\ ] ^ _ `
a b c d e f g h i j k l m n o p q r s t u v w x y z {	} ~ ☐

SQL Example 3.34 shows what happens when you misplace the DESC keyword. Here the DESC is placed before *emp_salary* and the resulting error message is 'Incorrect syntax'.

```
/* SQL Example 3.34 */
SELECT emp_last_name, emp_first_name, emp_salary
FROM employee
WHERE emp_salary > 35000
ORDER BY DESC emp_salary;

Server: Msg 156, Level 15, State 1, Line 4
Incorrect syntax near the keyword 'DESC'.
```

ORDER BY WITH MORE THAN ONE COLUMN

Thus far you have learned how to sort output to a result table based on a single column; however, there are occasions where it is necessary to sort data based on more than one column. Sorting by multiple columns can improve the look and usability of information. As your boss learns more about the information you can extract from the Company database, the demands on your skills will undoubtedly increase.

The latest request is for a listing of employees sorted alphabetically within department. To meet this request for information, you may wish to study the *employee* table description provided in Appendix A or use the Object Browser in SQL Query Analyzer to examine the structure of the *employee* table. In addition to storing employee names and SSNs, you note that each row has a column named *emp_dpt_number*. This column stores values representing the department number to which employees are assigned.

The type of output desired by your manager involves a sort within a sort. We define the *emp_dpt_number* column as the major sort column. The *emp_last_name* column serves as the minor sort column. We shall sort employees by name within department by listing the major sort column first in the ORDER BY clause, followed by the minor sort column.

Note that the result shown in SQL Example 3.35 lists employees sorted by department number first. Within each department, employees are sorted by last name.

```
/* SQL Example 3.35 */
SELECT emp_dpt_number, emp_last_name, emp_first_name
FROM employee
ORDER BY emp_dpt_number, emp_last_name;

emp_dpt_number emp_last_name      emp_first_name
-------------- ------------------ --------------------
1              Bordoloi           Bijoy
3              Amin               Hyder
```

```
3                Joyner          Suzanne
3                Markis          Marcia
7                Bock            Douglas
7                Joshi           Dinesh
7                Prescott        Sherri
7                Zhu             Waiman

(8 row(s) affected)
```

You can combine both ascending and descending sort specifications within a single ORDER BY clause. Suppose that you wish to display the data shown above, but you need to sort the departments in descending order while maintaining the employee names within each department in ascending order by last name. SQL Example 3.36 shows the correct query.

```
/* SQL Example 3.36 */
SELECT emp_dpt_number, emp_last_name, emp_first_name
FROM employee
ORDER BY emp_dpt_number DESC, emp_last_name;

emp_dpt_number emp_last_name    emp_first_name
-------------- --------------   --------------
7                Bock            Douglas
7                Joshi           Dinesh
7                Prescott        Sherri
7                Zhu             Waiman
3                Amin            Hyder
3                Joyner          Suzanne
3                Markis          Marcia
1                Bordoloi        Bijoy

(8 row(s) affected)
```

Note that the department numbers are now in descending order, but within each department, the employee names are still displayed in alphabetic order by last name. In summary, the ORDER BY clause is a powerful tool for improving the usability of any result table listing, and it is easy to use with very few rules.

- You can include a maximum of 16 column names in the ORDER BY clause.
- You must separate column names within the ORDER BY clause with a comma (,) to avoid syntax error messages.

TOP KEYWORD

A SELECT statement that specifies the TOP keyword is particularly useful in business for producing listings of the top salespeople, top products sold, and the like. SQL Example 3.37 combines the use of the TOP keyword with the ORDER BY clause to list the employees with the two largest salaries. This lists the two largest salaries because of the parameter '2' included with the TOP keyword and because the rows are sorted in descending order due to the DESC keyword.

```
/* SQL Example 3.37 */
SELECT TOP 2 emp_ssn, emp_last_name, emp_salary
FROM employee
ORDER BY emp_salary DESC;

emp_ssn    emp_last_name      emp_salary
---------  -----------------  -----------------
999666666  Bordoloi           55000.0000
999444444  Zhu                43000.0000

(2 row(s) affected)
```

What if there are salary ties? SQL Example 3.37 actually displays the top two rows, and therefore does not include any employee who might also have a salary that is the same as that of Zhu. SQL Example 3.38 includes the WITH TIES keywords. As you can see, the two largest salaries were requested, but three employee fall into this category because of ties.

```
/* SQL Example 3.38 */
SELECT TOP 2 WITH TIES emp_ssn, emp_last_name, emp_salary
FROM employee
ORDER BY emp_salary DESC;

emp_ssn    emp_last_name      emp_salary
---------  -----------------  -----------------
999666666  Bordoloi           55000.0000
999444444  Zhu                43000.0000
999555555  Joyner             43000.0000

(3 row(s) affected)
```

If the PERCENT keyword is specified, only the specified percentage of rows is included in the result table. SQL Example 3.39 shows the PERCENT and WITH TIES keywords used to return the top 40% of employee salaries.

```
/* SQL Example 3.39 */
SELECT TOP 40 PERCENT WITH TIES emp_ssn, emp_last_name, emp_salary
FROM employee
ORDER BY emp_salary DESC;

emp_ssn    emp_last_name      emp_salary
---------  -----------------  -----------------
999666666  Bordoloi           55000.0000
999444444  Zhu                43000.0000
999555555  Joyner             43000.0000
999333333  Joshi              38000.0000

(4 row(s) affected)
```

INTO CLAUSE

The optional INTO clause of the SELECT statement is used to create temporary tables. This can be used to store the output of a result table for future manipulation. These temporary tables are not part of an organization's permanent, base tables; instead, they are simply an additional option to support managerial decision making.

SQL Example 3.40 shows the use of the INTO clause by modifying SQL Example 3.39 to create a temporary table named *top_salary_employees*. Now it is easy to select from the *top_salary_employees* if a middle-level manager needs to manipulate the data in some fashion. As you can see, the first query does not display a result table; instead, the output is stored to the temporary *top_salary_employees* table. The second query demonstrates that the rows are stored to the temporary table.

```
/* SQL Example 3.40 */
SELECT TOP 40 PERCENT WITH TIES emp_ssn, emp_last_name, emp_salary
INTO top_salary_employees
FROM employee
ORDER BY emp_salary DESC;

(4 row(s) affected)


SELECT *
FROM top_salary_employees;

emp_ssn     emp_last_name        emp_salary
---------   ------------------   --------------
999666666   Bordoloi             55000.0000
999444444   Zhu                  43000.0000
999555555   Joyner               43000.0000
999333333   Joshi                38000.0000

(4 row(s) affected)
```

SUMMARY

In this chapter we explored the power of simple SELECT statements. You learned to select specific rows and columns from individual tables by specifying column names to be displayed, and by using the WHERE clause to specify conditions for displaying rows. Additionally, you learned to sort the information displayed by using the ORDER BY clause. After completing the exercises at the end of this chapter you should be comfortable executing simple queries.

REVIEW EXERCISES

LEARN THESE TERMS

ASC. A keyword used to specify that the ORDER BY is ascending order. This is the default.

CAST and CONVERT. Data conversion functions to convert expressions of one data type to another data type. These conversion functions are also used to obtain a variety of special data display formats.

Comparison Operator. Operators used in WHERE clauses that are used to specify conditions for selecting rows. There are nine operators with means such as "equal to," "less than," "greater than," as well as others.

DESC. A keyword used to specify that the ORDER BY is in descending order.

DISTINCT. A keyword used to eliminate duplicate rows in a result table.

FROM. The SELECT statement clause used to specify the table or tables from which data are to be retrieved.

ORDER BY. A clause used to sort the display of rows in a result table. The column name or names on which you are sorting must be specified in the SELECT clause.

SELECT. The SQL statement used to query a database.

TOP. A keyword used to SELECT rows from the top of a result table; when combined with ORDER BY, this lists the largest values such as largest employee salaries.

WHERE. The clause in a query used to specify conditions for selecting rows to be displayed in the result table.

CONCEPTS QUIZ

1. Explain what the asterisk (*) means when used in a SELECT statement.
2. Which clause is used to specify the name of a table from which data are to be retrieved?
3. What can you do to create a result table such that columns are ordered in a specific sequence or ordering?
4. Why is a new line started for each clause in an SQL statement?
5. What does the following statement do?

```
SELECT CAST(emp_last_name As CHAR(12))
FROM employee;
```

6. What does the following statement do?

```
SELECT CAST(emp_last_name As CHAR(12)) "Last Name"
FROM employee;
```

7. What error message is returned by SQL Server when a SELECT statement specifies a column name that does not exist within the table that is queried?
8. How does SQL Server respond if the order of the SELECT and FROM clauses in a query is reversed?
9. How does SQL Server respond if your query is missing a comma between two column names?
10. What is the purpose of the DISTINCT keyword in a query?
11. Where is the DISTINCT keyword placed in a query?
12. What is the purpose of the WHERE clause in a query?
13. List the nine comparison operators and their meaning.
14. When comparing column values that are character data, what does the less than operator ($<$) mean?
15. If you are comparing a column value that is character to a literal string, what syntax is used to specify the literal string of characters?
16. What is the purpose of the ORDER BY clause?
17. How is the sort order for an ORDER BY clause determined when sorting by a character column?
18. What is the optional keyword used to specify descending order for an ORDER BY clause?

19. A manager wants a result table sorted by two columns, department number (*emp_dpt_number*), and employee last name (*emp_last_name*) within the department number. Which column is the major sort column and which one is the minor sort column, and how is this denoted in the ORDER BY clause?

20. What do the TOP, WITH TIES, and PERCENT keywords do when used in the SELECT clause of a SELECT statement?

SQL CODING EXERCISES AND QUESTIONS: COMPANY DATABASE

1. The senior project manager wants a listing that displays all the data from the *assignment* table. Write the query.

2. Write a query that selects all columns from the *assignment* table without using the (*) in your query. You may wish to use the Object Browser in SQL Query Analyzer to examine the structure of the *assignment* table.

3. The senior project manager wants the listing that you created for Question 2 above modified. The query should only list the employee SSN (*work_emp_ssn*) and number of hours an employee has worked on a project (*work_hours*) in the result table.

4. Rewrite the query from Question 3, but reverse the order in which the two columns are displayed. Display the *work_hours* column first and the *work_emp_ssn* column second.

5. The human resources manager requires a listing of employees from the organization's *employee* table to meet the reporting requirements for a government agency. The listing must include each employee's last name (*emp_last_name*), first name (*emp_first_name*), date of birth (*emp_date_of_birth*), and gender code (*emp_gender*). Write the query to display the output sorted by *emp_last_name*. Save your output to a Results File.

6. The last query caused the results table to display with rows wrapped because each line was too long to fit onto a single line of output. Use the appropriate statement or function to limit the output column width for the employee last and first names to 12 characters. Limit the output of the *emp_date_of_birth* column to 12 characters. Provide appropriate heading labels and sort the output as in Question 5. Execute the query to display the new result table.

7. The human resources manager has determined that the listing has the appropriate information; however, the data needs to be sorted first by employee gender (major sort column is *emp_gender*) and then by employee last name within gender (minor sort column is *emp_last_name*). As such, the *emp_gender* column should be displayed first, followed by the remainder of the columns used in Question 6 above. Rewrite the query keeping the column width settings specified in Question 6 above.

8. The Company's CEO is concerned about employee dependents. Your manager directs you to prepare a listing of dependent names (*dep_name*), dates of birth (*dep_date_of_birth*), and the relationship to employees (*dep_relationship*) from the *employee* table. The first column displayed should be the employee's SSN (*dep_emp_ssn*). All the data for this query is stored in the *dependent* table. Sort the output by *dep_emp_ssn* (major sort column) and by *dep_name* (minor sort column). Both the *dep_name* and the *dep_date_of_birth* columns should display no more than 12 characters of output.

9. Produce a second listing that displays only those employee dependents who are children (i.e., *dep_relationship* is either SON or DAUGHTER, but not SPOUSE). The result table should display the *dep_emp_ssn*, *dep_name*, and *dep_relationship* columns, and be sorted by *dep_emp_ssn* in descending order.

10. A new manager in the human resources department wants to know what dependent relationships are tracked within the *dependent* table. Produce a simple listing of the *dep_relationship* column that does not contain duplicate output rows.

11. The new manager in the human resources department needs a listing of departments and the cities where they are located. Examine the *dept_locations* table. Write a query to display the department number and department location. Sort the output in descending order by department number.

12. The chief executive officer (CEO) of the Company wants to know what the names and salaries are for the three most highly paid employees. Your query should include ties. Include only the *emp_last_name* and *emp_salary* columns.

13. The manager of projects for the Company needs a listing of the employee SSN values (*work_emp_ssn*) and the associated work hours (*work_hours*) from the *assignment* table for the employees who are part of the top 10% in terms of work hours.

14. Modify the query for Question 13 to store the rows returned to a temporary table named *top_workers*. Write a SELECT statement to display the rows in the temporary table.

SQL Coding Exercises and Questions: Riverbend Database

1. The Riverbend hospital administrator is new to the organization. This officer requests a listing of the rooms available at the hospital. Write a query to display all information about the rooms from the *room* table.

2. Write a query to display all information about rooms, as was done in Question 1, without using the asterisk (*) in your query. You can find information about the structure of the table in Appendix B.

3. The new chief of surgery needs a listing of services provided by the hospital. Write a query to display the identifier, description, and charge for each service in the *service* table. Use the appropriate statement or function to format the output of the *service_id* column to 10 characters and the *service_description* column to 30 characters. Provide appropriate column headings.

4. Rewrite the query from Question 3, but list the identifier, charge, and description in that order. Also, format the charge as decimal with two digits to the right of the decimal.

5. The hospital's human resources manager requires a listing of staff members from the organization's *staff* table to meet the reporting requirements for a government agency. The listing must include each employee's last name (*staff_last_name*), first name (*staff_first_name*), date hired (*date_hired*), and license number (*license_number*). Write the query to display the output sorted by *staff_last_name*. Limit the output for the last and first name to 15 characters each and the date hired to 12 characters.

6. Rewrite the last query to add the staff middle name in the result table. Display the output with the staff first name followed by the staff middle name and staff last

name. Use the appropriate command to limit the output column width for the staff last and first names to 12 characters. Limit the output column width for the staff middle name to 1 character.

7. Rewrite the query from Question 6 to sort the output by staff last name (major sort) within staff last name (minor sort). Keep all column width settings from Question 6.

8. The new hospital facilities coordinator needs a listing of beds of type 'RE' including the *bed_number*, *room_id*, and *bed_type_id* columns from the *bed* table. Sort the result table by *room_id* in ascending order.

9. The hospital pharmacist and chief of surgery are concerned about prescription medicines and the dosage prescribed for patients. Write a query to list each medicine code and dosage prescribed from the *prescription* table. Sort the rows of the result table by the medicine code.

10. Rewrite the query from Question 9 to eliminate duplicate rows in the result table.

11. The chief of nursing for the hospital needs a listing of *staff_id*, *specialty_code*, and date the specialty was awarded (*date_awarded*) for nurses with *specialty_code* of 'RN1' from the *staff_medspec* table. Sort the output by *staff_id*. Limit the output for the date the specialty was awarded to 12 characters.

12. Rewrite the query for Question 11 to display information for licensed practicing nurses with *specialty_code* of 'LPN' from the *staff_medspec* table.

13. The head of the prescription department is concerned about the stockage of medicines. Write a query to display the medicine code (*medicine_code*), common name (*med_common_name*), and quantity stocked (*quantity_stock*) from the *medicine* table for the four most medicines with the highest stockage levels, including ties if there are any. Restrict the display of the common name to 20 characters.

14. Rewrite the query for Question 13 to display the medicines that fall within the 10% of medicines with the smallest stockage levels.

15. Rewrite the query for Question 14 to store the rows returned to a temporary table named *low_stock_medicine*.

CHAPTER 4

ADDING POWER TO QUERIES

Chapter 3 teaches the basic SELECT statement including the FROM, WHERE, and ORDER BY clauses. As you are beginning to see, the SELECT statement is a very powerful tool for retrieving information from databases. This chapter focuses on teaching you how to add power to your queries by building on the capabilities of the WHERE clause.

OBJECTIVES

The SELECT statement's WHERE clause is one of the most important clauses because it has the ability to retrieve data through the use of many different operators. These special operators make it easy to retrieve data nonprocedurally. You will examine the power of logical operators named AND, OR, and NOT that can be used to link multiple WHERE conditions together. You will also examine the LIST operators that are used to retrieve rows where the data falls within a specified list of data values. Additionally, you will discover how the BETWEEN and LIKE operators can greatly simplify the task of writing WHERE clauses. As you see, these and more operators can add power to the WHERE clause. Your learning objectives for this chapter are:

- Use logical operators (AND, OR, NOT) to write complex query conditions.
- Use the IN and BETWEEN operators to write query conditions for lists of values and value ranges.
- Use the LIKE operator for character matching.
- Use the IS NULL operator when querying for unknown values.
- Use expressions in WHERE clauses.

LOGICAL OPERATORS (AND, OR, AND NOT)

In Chapter 3, you learned to write SELECT statements with a WHERE clause that has a single condition that specifies which data rows to retrieve from a table. You will now learn to use the logical operators, AND and OR, to add power to our queries.

This additional power comes from combining more than one condition in the WHERE clause. The NOT operator permits the creation of simple queries that otherwise would be unnecessarily bulky or complex.

> AND: joins two or more conditions, and returns results only when *all* the conditions are true.
>
> OR: joins two or more conditions, and it returns results when *any* of the conditions are true.
>
> NOT: negates the expression that follows it.

USING THE **AND** OPERATOR

The AND operator links two or more conditions in a WHERE clause. Suppose that one of our organizational managers needs a list of female employees. Further, the list should only contain employees with last names that begin with the letter "E" or last names that come later in the alphabet. Additionally, the result table should be sorted by employee last name. There are two conditions to be met. The WHERE clause may be written as: **WHERE emp_gender = 'F' AND emp_last_name >= 'E'.**

Note that both conditions must be met for the entire WHERE clause to evaluate as true. Structured Query Language (SQL) Example 4.1 shows the complete SELECT statement and result table.

```
/* SQL Example 4.1 */
SELECT emp_last_name, emp_first_name, emp_gender "Gender"
FROM employee
WHERE emp_gender = 'F' AND emp_last_name >= 'E'
ORDER BY emp_last_name;

emp_last_name          emp_first_name          Gender
---------------------  ----------------------- ------
Joyner                 Suzanne                 F
Markis                 Marcia                  F
Prescott               Sherri                  F
```

SQL Example 4.1 can be expanded to test additional conditions. We have also formatted the result table columns and added custom column heading labels. SQL Example 4.2 retrieves *employee* table data based on four different conditions. You may wish to review the *employee* table description provided in Appendix A to aid your understanding of the WHERE clause.

```
/* SQL Example 4.2 */
SELECT CAST(emp_last_name AS Char (12)) "Last Name",
    CAST(emp_first_name AS CHAR(2)) "First Name",
    CAST(emp_date_of_birth AS CHAR(12))"Birth Day",
    emp_gender "Gender", '$' +
    CONVERT (CHAR (10), emp_salary, 1) "Salary"
FROM employee
```

```
WHERE emp_last_name > 'E' AND
    emp_date_of_birth > '20-Jun-71' AND
    emp_gender = 'M' AND
    emp_salary > 20000
ORDER BY emp_last_name;

Last Name        First Name      Birth Day       Gender  Salary
---------------  --------------  --------------  ------  -----------
Joshi            Di              Sep 15 1972     M       $ 38,000.00
Zhu              Wa              Dec  8 1975     M       $ 43,000.00
```

The query in SQL Example 4.2 is a bit contrived simply because it is unlikely that a business manager needs a listing of employees with characteristics that exactly match the four conditions: (1) last name is greater than 'E', (2) birthday is after June 20, 1972, (3) gender is male, and (4) salary is greater than $20,000. However, the query is legal and can execute. We have provided this query simply to illustrate the power of the AND logical operator. Each employee listed in the result table satisfies all the query conditions. Imagine how long it would take for you to scan an *employee* table to create such a listing manually based on these four quite different conditions.

It is possible to write a WHERE clause using the AND operator that yields a result table that is empty. This is exactly what the query in SQL Example 4.3 does for the employees in the Company database.

```
/* SQL Example 4.3 */
SELECT emp_last_name, emp_first_name
FROM employee
WHERE emp_ssn = '999666666' AND emp_gender = 'F';

emp_last_name    emp_first_name
---------------  ---------------

(0 row(s) affected)
```

SQL Server returned an empty result table because none of the rows in the *employee* table meet both of the conditions specified in the WHERE clause. Employee 999-66-6666 is Bijoy Bordoloi, a male employee.

USING THE OR OPERATOR

Suppose that your organizational manager's requirements change a bit. Another employee listing is needed, but in this listing the employees may satisfy either (or both) of two conditions: (1) be female *or,* (2) have a last name that begins with the letter 'M' or a letter that comes later in the alphabet. Additionally, the result table should be sorted by employee last name. In this situation either of the two conditions can be met to satisfy the query. Female employees should be listed along with employees having a name that satisfies the second condition. The query is written with the OR logical operator, as is shown in SQL Example 4.4.

```
/* SQL Example 4.4 */
SELECT emp_last_name, emp_first_name, emp_gender
FROM employee
WHERE emp_gender = 'F' OR emp_last_name >= 'M'
ORDER BY emp_last_name;

emp_last_name        emp_first_name      emp_gender
-------------------  ------------------- ----------
Joyner               Suzanne             F
Markis               Marcia              F
Prescott             Sherri              F
Zhu                  Waiman              M

(4 row(s) affected)
```

The query produces a result table with four rows. Three of the rows are listed because the employee gender is female. The other row is listed because the employee's last name begins with the letter 'M' or later in the alphabet (Zhu). Additionally, two of the rows satisfy both conditions in the query (Markis and Prescott).

USING THE **NOT** OPERATOR

Suppose that one of your organization's managers requests a listing of employees that work in a specific department, such as department 7. Further, the listing should again be sorted alphabetically by last name. The query's WHERE clause is straightforward:

```
WHERE emp_dpt_number = 7
```

What if the request is for a listing of employees that do *not* work in department 7? The OR logical operator can be used to identify employees not in department 7 by simply specifying all department numbers except for department 7:

```
WHERE emp_dpt_number = 1 OR emp_dpt_number = 2 OR
      emp_dpt_number = 3 OR ... (more clauses)!
```

Clearly the WHERE clause given above is rather complex. Further, in an organization with dozens of departments, the use of the OR logical operator is too unwieldy or even infeasible to use. This is a classic situation that calls for use of the NOT operator to negate a simple condition. SQL Example 4.5 uses the NOT operator to simplify the WHERE clause.

```
/* SQL Example 4.5 */
SELECT emp_last_name, emp_first_name, emp_dpt_number
FROM employee
WHERE NOT emp_dpt_number = 7
ORDER BY emp_last_name;
```

```
emp_last_name          emp_first_name          emp_dpt_number
-------------------    -------------------     --------------
Amin                   Hyder                   3
Bordoloi               Bijoy                   1
Joyner                 Suzanne                 3
Markis                 Marcia                  3

(4 row(s) affected)
```

Notice that the NOT operator causes the condition to restrict the result table to rows where the department number is NOT 7. The query can also be written by using a "not equal to" comparison operator, as shown in SQL Example 4.6.

```
/* SQL Example 4.6 */
SELECT emp_last_name, emp_first_name, emp_dpt_number
FROM employee
WHERE emp_dpt_number <> 7
ORDER BY emp_last_name;

emp_last_name          emp_first_name          emp_dpt_number
-------------------    -------------------     --------------
Amin                   Hyder                   3
Bordoloi               Bijoy                   1
Joyner                 Suzanne                 3
Markis                 Marcia                  3

(4 row(s) affected)
```

You may wonder, if the "not equal to" comparison operator works just as well, why not simply rely on it? The answer is because there are occasions when the "not equal to" comparison operator can become unwieldy in a WHERE clause with several complex conditions. Suppose that a department manager requires a listing of all employees except those assigned to department 7 or those that are female. The NOT operator can simplify this WHERE clause so that it reads in an almost English-like fashion. SQL Example 4.7 demonstrates this use of the NOT operator.

```
/* SQL Example 4.7 */
SELECT emp_last_name, emp_first_name, emp_gender
FROM employee
WHERE NOT emp_dpt_number = 7 AND NOT emp_gender = 'F'
ORDER BY emp_last_name;

emp_last_name          emp_first_name          emp_gender
-------------------    -------------------     ----------
Amin                   Hyder                   M
Bordoloi               Bijoy                   M

(2 row(s) affected)
```

COMBINING **OR** AND **AND** OPERATORS

In the last section, you study examples with the OR logical operator used repeatedly to connect conditional statements. You can also use the AND logical operator repeatedly, and you can combine the AND and OR logical operators to create complex queries. However, you must exercise caution. There are pitfalls when combining the AND and OR operators. The next query gives an example of just such a pitfall. Examine the question, the query, and the result table carefully.

Using the *employee* table, provide a list of employees with a last name that begins with or is greater than the letter 'E', and who are either female or work in department number 1. SQL Example 4.8 provides the proposed WHERE clause.

```
/* SQL Example 4.8 */
SELECT CAST(emp_last_name AS CHAR(12)) "Last Name",
    CAST(emp_first_name AS CHAR(12)) "First Name",
    emp_gender, emp_dpt_number
FROM employee
WHERE emp_last_name >= 'E' AND emp_gender = 'F' OR emp_dpt_number = 1
ORDER BY emp_last_name;

Last Name     First Name     emp_gender emp_dpt_number
------------  -------------  ---------- --------------
Bordoloi      Bijoy          M          1
Joyner        Suzanne        F          3
Markis        Marcia         F          3
Prescott      Sherri         F          7

(4 row(s) affected)
```

The SELECT statement executes, but is it correct? The answer is no. The result table should not contain "Bijoy Bordoloi because his last name does not begin with a letter that is greater than or equal to the letter 'E'. This also underscores the importance of not simply accepting a result table as correct if an error message is not generated by the SELECT statement.

Where does this query go wrong? The answer is that there is a hierarchy of evaluation for the AND, OR, and NOT operators. When the AND operator is combined with the OR operator, SQL Server evaluates the conditions connected by the AND operator first. Following this SQL Server next evaluates the conditions connected by the OR operator. Let us break the WHERE clause into pieces to see how the conditions are evaluated.

There are three conditions to be evaluated. SQL Server begins by examining the two conditions connected by the AND operator. With this WHERE clause, a table row is a candidate for inclusion in the result table if both conditions connected by the AND operator are true. Essentially, SQL Server returns a value of either true or false from the AND operation.

```
Condition 1 AND Condition 2
emp_last_name >= 'E' AND emp_gender = 'F'
```

Next, SQL Server combines the result of the AND operation with the remaining condition in an OR operation. Let's suppose that the result of the AND operation was TRUE for a given row. The resulting OR operation looks like the following to SQL Server.

```
TRUE OR Condition 3
TRUE OR emp_dpt_number = 1
```

Regardless of the value for the *emp_dpt_number* column, the row can be included in the result table because the logical result of a TRUE value OR some other condition is always TRUE.

Now, suppose that the result of the AND operation for a given row yielded a FALSE value for that row. The row may still be a candidate for inclusion in the result table. The resulting OR operation looks like the following to SQL Server:

```
FALSE OR Condition 3
FALSE OR emp_dpt_number = 1
```

If the *emp_dpt_number* value equals 1 for the employee, then the row is included in the final result table. This is how Bijoy Bordoloi managed to sneak into the result table shown earlier. However, you can force a change in the hierarchy of evaluation for a complex condition by using parentheses to force the order of operation. This works exactly the same way as it does in mathematics. SQL Example 4.9 gives the correct rewritten query.

```
/* SQL Example 4.9 */
SELECT CAST(emp_last_name AS CHAR(12)) "Last Name",
    CAST(emp_first_name AS CHAR(12)) "First Name",
    emp_gender, emp_dpt_number
FROM employee
WHERE emp_last_name >= 'E' AND
    (emp_gender = 'F' OR emp_dpt_number = 1)
ORDER BY emp_last_name;

Last Name     First Name     emp_gender emp_dpt_number
------------  ------------   ---------- --------------
Joyner        Suzanne        F          3
Markis        Marcia         F          3
Prescott      Sherri         F          7

(3 row(s) affected)
```

SQL Server evaluates the complex condition beginning with the innermost set of parentheses. Here, SQL Server first tests a row to see whether the employee is female OR is in department 1. If a row passes that test, the query then tests to see whether the employee's name begins with a letter that is greater than or equal to 'E'.

The order in which the conditions are listed has no effect on the result table that is produced; however, the order of the conditions may affect the efficiency with which the computer processes an SQL statement. Our focus for now is on writing SQL statements that produce correct output. The last query could have been written, as shown in SQL Example 4.10 to produce the same result table.

```
/* SQL Example 4.10 */
SELECT CAST(emp_last_name AS CHAR(12)) "Last Name",
    CAST(emp_first_name AS CHAR(12)) "First Name",
    emp_gender, emp_dpt_number
FROM employee
WHERE (emp_gender = 'F' OR emp_dpt_number = 1) AND
        emp_last_name > 'E'
ORDER BY emp_last_name;

Last Name     First Name      emp_gender emp_dpt_number
------------  --------------  ---------- --------------
Joyner        Suzanne         F          3
Markis        Marcia          F          3
Prescott      Sherri          F          7

(3 row(s) affected)
```

As you gain experience with SQL, you find that writing queries becomes second nature. In contrast, it is never easy to understand exactly what a manager needs in terms of information. When you have doubt about what a manager has requested, ask questions.

LISTS (IN AND NOT IN)

There are two operators that are designed for testing whether data stored in a table column is either in or not in a list or set of values. These are the IN and NOT IN operators. These operators greatly simplify the task of writing queries that might otherwise require a large number of either OR logical operators or an unwieldy use of the NOT logical operator.

USING THE IN OPERATOR

Until this point, all queries have required you to compare the value stored in a single column of a table with another single value. To compare a column against several values, it is necessary to use the OR operator to combine multiple conditions. One of our organizational managers needs a listing of employees who earn specific annual salary figures of $43,000, $30,000, or $25,000 per year. Further, the listing is to be sorted by employee salary. The query can be written as shown in SQL Example 4.11.

```
/* SQL Example 4.11 */
SELECT CAST(emp_last_name AS Char (15)) "Last Name",
    CAST(emp_first_name AS CHAR(15)) "First Name",
    CAST(emp_salary AS DECIMAL(10,2)) "Salary"
```

```
FROM employee
WHERE emp_salary = 43000 OR emp_salary = 30000 OR emp_salary = 25000
ORDER BY emp_salary;

Last Name      First Name     Salary
-------------  -------------  ------------
Amin           Hyder          25000.00
Markis         Marcia         25000.00
Prescott       Sherri         25000.00
Bock           Douglas        30000.00
Zhu            Waiman         43000.00
Joyner         Suzanne        43000.00

(6 row(s) affected)
```

The use of the OR operator is unnecessarily complex. The IN operator can simplify the query. The revised query in SQL Example 4.12 tests to see the *emp_salary* column value matches any of the values in the list that is enclosed within parentheses.

```
/* SQL Example 4.12 */
SELECT CAST(emp_last_name AS Char (15)) "Last Name",
    CAST(emp_first_name AS CHAR(15)) "First Name",
    CAST(emp_salary AS DECIMAL(10,2)) "Salary"
FROM employee
WHERE emp_salary IN (43000, 30000, 25000)
ORDER BY emp_salary;

Last Name      First Name     Salary
-------------  -------------  ------------
Amin           Hyder          25000.00
Markis         Marcia         25000.00
Prescott       Sherri         25000.00
Bock           Douglas        30000.00
Zhu            Waiman         43000.00
Joyner         Suzanne        43000.00

(6 row(s) affected)
```

Because the WHERE clause has less code, the query is easier to read. Notice that each value in the list is separated by a comma (,).

What if the values in the list are character strings as would be the case if we were producing a listing of employees that reside in Marina, Edwardsville, or St. Louis? Character string values must be enclosed in single quotation marks. The resulting query sorted by employee city is shown in SQL Example 4.13.

```
/* SQL Example 4.13 */
SELECT CAST(emp_last_name AS Char (15)) "Last Name",
    CAST(emp_first_name AS CHAR(15)) "First Name",
```

```
    emp_city "City"
FROM employee
WHERE emp_city IN ('Marina', 'Edwardsville', 'St. Louis')
ORDER BY emp_city;

Last Name      First Name     City
-------------- -------------- --------------
Bordoloi       Bijoy          Edwardsville
Prescott       Sherri         Edwardsville
Amin           Hyder          Marina
Joyner         Suzanne        Marina
Bock           Douglas        St. Louis
Zhu            Waiman         St. Louis

(6 row(s) affected)
```

USING THE **NOT IN** OPERATOR

Okay, you have provided your department manager with the requested list of employees that earn $43,000, $30,000, or $25,000 per year. However, the manager now requests a listing of employees who *did not* earn one of those three salary figures listed in the previous SQL Example 4.12. With the possibility of a large number of employees having a salary value different from one of the three specified, writing the condition for the query appears to be a difficult if not an impossible task. However, the NOT IN operator was designed exactly to support this type of reporting requirement. The query in SQL Example 4.12 requires very little modification. Simply replace the IN operator with the NOT IN operator, as shown in SQL Example 4.14. The result table lists the two employees whose annual salary figures are NOT IN the prescribed list.

```
/* SQL Example 4.14 */
SELECT CAST(emp_last_name AS Char (15)) "Last Name",
    CAST(emp_first_name AS CHAR(15)) "First Name",
    CAST(emp_salary AS DECIMAL(10,2)) "Salary"
FROM employee
WHERE emp_salary NOT IN (43000, 30000, 25000)
ORDER BY emp_salary;

Last Name      First Name     Salary
-------------- -------------- --------------
Joshi          Dinesh         38000.00
Bordoloi       Bijoy          55000.00

(2 row(s) affected)
```

COMMON ERRORS WHEN USING **IN** AND **NOT IN** OPERATORS

There are some common errors that you need to avoid when using the IN and NOT IN operators. The query in SQL Example 4.15 is missing the required commas between the list items. The query in SQL Example 4.16 fails to include parentheses when coding the list of values. In both cases, SQL Server returns a rather cryptic error message.

```
/* SQL Example 4.15 */
SELECT CAST(emp_last_name AS Char (15)) "Last Name",
    CAST(emp_first_name AS CHAR(15)) "First Name",
    CAST(emp_salary AS DECIMAL(10,2)) "Salary"
FROM employee
WHERE emp_salary NOT IN (43000 30000 25000);

Server: Msg 170, Level 15, State 1, Line 5
Line 5: Incorrect syntax near '30000'.
```

```
/* SQL Example 4.16 */
SELECT CAST(emp_last_name AS Char (15)) "Last Name",
    CAST(emp_first_name AS CHAR(15)) "First Name",
    CAST(emp_salary AS DECIMAL(10,2)) "Salary"
FROM employee
WHERE emp_salary IN 43000, 30000, 25000;

Server: Msg 170, Level 15, State 1, Line 5
Line 5: Incorrect syntax near '43000'.
```

RANGES (BETWEEN AND NOT BETWEEN)

Writing a query with a condition that satisfies a range of values is similar to writing one that selects rows based on a list of values. Both query types allow you to compare values from a single table column against more than one value. However, with a list of values, your query can specify two or more exact values in the listing. When the number of values is quite large, it is often unwieldy or infeasible to use a simple listing. In this situation, your query needs to specify a range of values that a single table column may satisfy. SQL has two operators, BETWEEN and NOT BETWEEN that can simplify the expression of a range of values. Additionally, these two operators eliminate the need to use a more complex WHERE clause involving the use of the AND logical operator.

USING THE BETWEEN OPERATOR

You can use the BETWEEN operator to specify an *inclusive* range of values. When BETWEEN is used, the value from the table column used in the WHERE clause condition must fall within or between the lower and upper values specified by the BETWEEN operator. The range includes the end points specified by the range of values.

Suppose that one of our managers requires a listing of employees with annual salary figures that are between $25,000 and $40,000 per year. The query in SQL Example 4.17 produces the required result table with the output sorted by employee salary. Notice that the query uses the AND logical operator.

```
/* SQL Example 4.17 */
SELECT CAST(emp_last_name AS Char (15)) "Last Name",
    CAST(emp_first_name AS CHAR(15)) "First Name",
    '$' + Convert(char(10),emp_salary, 1) "Salary"
FROM employee
WHERE emp_salary >= 25000 AND emp_salary <= 40000
ORDER BY emp_salary;

Last Name          First Name        Salary
---------------    --------------    ----------
Amin               Hyder             $ 25,000.00
Markis             Marcia            $ 25,000.00
Prescott           Sherri            $ 25,000.00
Bock               Douglas           $ 30,000.00
Joshi              Dinesh            $ 38,000.00

(5 row(s) affected)
```

This query can be rewritten using the BETWEEN operator, as shown in SQL Example 4.18. This may make the WHERE clause easier to understand and less likely to be incorrectly coded by an SQL programmer.

```
/* SQL Example 4.18 */
SELECT CAST(emp_last_name AS Char (15)) "Last Name",
    CAST(emp_first_name AS CHAR(15)) "First Name",
    '$' + Convert(char(10),emp_salary, 1) "Salary"
FROM employee
WHERE emp_salary BETWEEN 25000 AND 40000
ORDER BY emp_salary;

Last Name          First Name        Salary
---------------    --------------    ----------
Amin               Hyder             $ 25,000.00
Markis             Marcia            $ 25,000.00
Prescott           Sherri            $ 25,000.00
Bock               Douglas           $ 30,000.00
Joshi              Dinesh            $ 38,000.00

(5 row(s) affected)
```

Specifying More than One Salary Range

If you need to specify two different salary ranges for employees, that is, $25,000 to $30,000 and $40,000 to $43,000, the query can include two BETWEEN clauses, as is done in SQL Example 4.19. This query displays rows for employees that have an annual salary that falls within one of the two specified salary ranges. Note that the specified range includes the end points for the two salary ranges.

```
/* SQL Example 4.19 */
SELECT CAST(emp_last_name AS Char (15)) "Last Name",
```

```
     '$' + Convert(char(10),emp_salary, 1) "Salary"
FROM employee
WHERE emp_salary BETWEEN 25000 AND 30000
    OR emp_salary BETWEEN 40000 AND 43000
ORDER BY emp_salary;

Last Name      Salary
-------------- -----------
Amin           $ 25,000.00
Markis         $ 25,000.00
Prescott       $ 25,000.00
Bock           $ 30,000.00
Zhu            $ 43,000.00
Joyner         $ 43,000.00

(6 row(s) affected)
```

USING THE **NOT BETWEEN** OPERATOR

The NOT BETWEEN operator is the mirror image of the BETWEEN operator. It is used to exclude a range of column values from a result table. For example, if one of your firm's managers needs a listing of employees with salaries that are either extremely high or extremely low, you can exclude salaries in a middle range of values with the NOT BETWEEN operator. The query in SQL Example 4.20 lists employees with salaries below $28,000 or above $50,000. You might also observe that using the NOT BETWEEN operator in this query is equivalent to using two BETWEEN operators combined with the OR logical operator that is used earlier in SQL Example 4.19.

```
/* SQL Example 4.20 */
SELECT CAST(emp_last_name AS Char (15)) "Last Name",
    '$' + Convert(char(10),emp_salary, 1) "Salary"
FROM employee
WHERE emp_salary NOT BETWEEN 28000 AND 50000
ORDER BY emp_salary;

Last Name      Salary
-------------- -----------
Amin           $ 25,000.00
Markis         $ 25,000.00
Prescott       $ 25,000.00
Bordoloi       $ 55,000.00

(4 row(s) affected)
```

COMMON ERRORS WHEN USING BETWEEN AND **NOT BETWEEN** OPERATORS

Like the IN and NOT IN operators, there are some common errors associated with the BETWEEN and NOT BETWEEN operators that need to be avoided. One typical error that even experienced programmers occasionally make is inserting a comma within a numeric value that is used to express the inclusive range of the BETWEEN search. The query in SQL Example 4.21 has this error. SQL Server returns the 'Incorrect syntax' error message and points you toward the problem.

```
/* SQL Example 4.21 */
SELECT CAST(emp_last_name AS Char (15)) "Last Name",
    '$' + Convert(char(10),emp_salary, 1) "Salary"
FROM employee
WHERE emp_salary BETWEEN 25,000 and 40,000;

Server: Msg 170, Level 15, State 1, Line 4
Line 4: Incorrect syntax near ','.
```

Another error that can occur is the misspecification of a SELECT statement by erroneously including too many AND logical operators in the WHERE clause. The query in SQL Example 4.22 has this particular error. SQL Server again returns the 'Incorrect syntax' error message and points you toward the problem.

```
/* SQL Example 4.22 */
SELECT CAST(emp_last_name AS Char (15)) "Last Name",
    '$' + Convert(char(10),emp_salary, 1) "Salary"
FROM employee
WHERE emp_salary BETWEEN 25000 AND 40000 AND 43000;

Server: Msg 170, Level 15, State 1, Line 4
Line 4: Incorrect syntax near ';'.
```

CHARACTER MATCHING (LIKE AND NOT LIKE)

Many of the SELECT statement examples shown thus far in the chapter have tested for specific instances of character data such as employee last names that have a beginning letter that is greater than **'E',** for example, **WHERE emp_last_name > 'E'.**

The LIKE and NOT LIKE operators can be used to search for data rows containing incomplete or partial character strings within a data column. For example, the query in SQL Example 4.23 searches the *employee* table for employee names that begin with the characters 'Bo'. The search is case sensitive meaning that 'Bo' is not equivalent to 'BO'.

```
/* SQL Example 4.23 */
SELECT CAST(emp_last_name AS Char (15)) "Last Name",
    CAST(emp_first_name AS CHAR(15)) "First Name"
FROM employee
WHERE emp_last_name LIKE 'Bo%';
```

```
Last Name      First Name
-------------  ---------------
Bock           Douglas
Bordoloi       Bijoy

(2 row(s) affected)
```

The percent (%) symbol is a wild card symbol used to represent one or more characters. There are four allowable wild card characters. The wild card operators and their uses are defined in Table 4.1.

Study the examples shown in Table 4.2. They can help you understand how to use the wild card characters with the LIKE operator. Typical results of a search are shown in parentheses ( ).

The SELECT statement shown in SQL Example 4.24 generates a result table that includes all DISTINCT rows where the employee SSN in the *assignment* table ends with the numbers 555.

```
/* SQL Example 4.24 */
SELECT DISTINCT work_emp_ssn "Emp SSN"
FROM assignment
WHERE work_emp_ssn LIKE '%555';

Emp SSN
---------
999555555
```

TABLE 4.1

Wild Card	Meaning
% (Percent)	Any string of zero or more characters
_(Underscore)	Any single character
[ ] (Brackets)	Any single character within a specified range such as **'a'** to **'d'**, inclusive **[a-d]** or a set of characters such as [aeiouy]
[^] (Not brackets)	Any single character **not** in the specified range or set. (e.g., [^a-f])

TABLE 4.2

LIKE '%inger' searches for every name that ends with 'inger' (**Ringer**, Str**inger**)

LIKE '%en%' searches for every name that has the letters 'en' in the name (Be**nn**et, Gre**en**, McBadd**en**)

LIKE '_heryl' searches for every six-letter name ending with 'heryl' (**Cheryl**); notice how this is different than '%heryl' which would return names that are six characters or more

LIKE '[CK]ars[eo]n' searches for every six-letter name that begins with a 'C' or 'K' and has the letter 'e' or 'o' between 'ars' and 'n' (e.g., '**Carsen**,' '**Karsen**,' '**Carson**,' and '**Karson**')

LIKE '[M-Z]inger' searches for all the names ending with 'inger' that begin with any single letter 'M' thru 'Z' (**Ringer**)

LIKE 'M[^c]%' searches for all the names that begin with 'M' not having 'c' as the second letter

Conversely, the NOT logical operator can be used in conjunction with the LIKE operator to find all DISTINCT employee rows that do not end with 555, as is done in SQL Example 4.25.

```
/* SQL Example 4.25 */
SELECT DISTINCT work_emp_ssn "Emp SSN"
FROM assignment
WHERE work_emp_ssn NOT LIKE '%555';

Emp SSN
----------
999111111
999222222
999333333
999444444
999666666
999887777
999888888

(7 row(s) affected)
```

There is a notable limitation when using wild card characters—you *cannot* use the comparison operators (=, >, <, etc.) with wild card characters. Wild cards used without the LIKE operator are interpreted as characters for which you wish to search. The query in SQL Example 4.26 attempts to find any employee SSN that consists of the four characters '%555' only. It cannot find employee SSNs ending with 555. In fact, it returns no rows from the *assignment* table because none of the SSNs have a percentage sign as part of the data. For this query to execute correctly, you must substitute the LIKE operator for the equal sign (=) comparison operator.

```
/* SQL Example 4.26 */
SELECT DISTINCT work_emp_ssn
FROM assignment
WHERE work_emp_ssn = '%555';

work_emp_ssn
-------------
(0 row(s) affected)
```

When a character search pattern contains single or double quotes within the string of characters, your query must be written by using the opposite type of quote marks to enclose the pattern. For example, the string shown below includes double quote marks around the word **Hello**. To search for this word, enclose the entire string with single quote marks as shown.

```
When this: "Hello," said Mark.
Do this: ' "Hello," said Mark. '
```

TABLE 4.3

Expression	Result
LIKE 5%	Returns any row where the column data value is '5' followed by any string of zero or more characters
LIKE 5[%]	Returns any row where the data value is 5%
LIKE _n	Returns any row where the column data value is a two-character value ending in the letter 'n', e.g., an, in, on, etc.
LIKE [_]n	Returns any row where the column data value is _n
LIKE [ ]]	Returns any row where the column data value is]

TABLE 4.4

Expression	Result
LIKE [a-ef]	Returns any row where the data value is a, b, c, d, e, or f
LIKE [-aef]	Returns any row where the data value is -, a, e, or f

What if the string of characters has one of the wild card characters as part of the string? To use a wild card such as the percentage sign, underscore, or left or right bracket—(%), (_) ([ ), or ( ])—as characters in a LIKE match string, enclose each wild card in brackets ([ ]). Table 4.3 summarizes this usage.

Earlier you learned that you can use the dash (–) symbol inside square brackets with a LIKE operator to express a range of characters in a search. If you want the dash (–) symbol to be one of the characters for which you are searching, you must place the dash symbol as the first character inside the set of brackets.

To search for a dash in a character string, place the dash as the first character inside a set of brackets. This usage is shown in Table 4.4.

UNKNOWN VALUES (IS NULL AND IS NOT NULL)

The term NULL is a keyword meaning the absence of any stored value. If a column in a data row is NULL, then there is no value stored in that column. Some of the rows in the *assignment* table shown in Appendix A may have a NULL value for the *work_hours* column if an employee has been assigned to a project, but has yet to report any hours worked. The SELECT statement shown in SQL Example 4.27 uses the IS NULL operator to query the *assignment* table to display all rows with a NULL value for *work_hours*.

```
/* SQL Example 4.27 */
SELECT *
FROM assignment
```

```
WHERE work_hours IS NULL;

work_emp_ssn work_pro_number work_hours work_hours_planned
------------ --------------- ---------- ------------------
999444444    1               NULL       NULL
999666666    20              NULL       15.5

(2 row(s) affected)
```

This query uses the IS NULL operator to test for a NULL value. You can also use the IS NOT NULL operator to retrieve rows where any value has been stored. You need to understand that a NULL value is *not synonymous* with "zero" (numerical values) or "blank" (character values). Instead, NULL values allow users to distinguish between a deliberate entry of zero or blank and a nonentry of data. You should think of NULL as meaning "unknown." Because of the nature of the NULL, when you compare a NULL with another value the results are **never TRUE;** a NULL value does not match anything, not even another NULL value. Stated another way, one unknown value cannot equal or be compared to another unknown value. However, NULL values are considered the same as each other when using the DISTINCT keyword to limit the number of rows displayed in a result table.

As you can see above, knowing the meaning of NULL allows you to write queries that can test for a NULL value. Rows can be included or excluded from a result table when a column contains a NULL value; however, the column must have been defined as capable of storing a NULL value when it was created. For example, it should be obvious that a column that is specified as a PRIMARY KEY cannot store a NULL value because every row in a table is required to have a PRIMARY KEY value.

The earlier query in SQL Example 4.27 is not the same as the one shown in SQL Example 4.28 that tests to see whether the *work_hours* column is equal to zero.

```
/* SQL Example 4.28 */
SELECT *
FROM assignment
WHERE work_hours = 0;

work_emp_ssn work_pro_number work_hours work_hours_planned
------------ --------------- ---------- ------------------

(0 row(s) affected)
```

SQL Example 4.28 returns no rows for the result table because none of the rows in the *assignment* table have a zero value for *work_hours*. Thus, you can see that zero (0) is a value, not an "unknown value."

On the other hand, although the actual output is not shown here, the next two queries can produce the same result table. The query in SQL Example 4.29 includes all rows where the *work_hours* column contains a value. The query in SQL Example 4.30 includes all rows where the *work_hours* is greater than or equal to zero.

```
/* SQL Example 4.29 */
SELECT *
FROM assignment
WHERE work_hours IS NOT NULL;

(15 row(s) affected)
```

```
/* SQL Example 4.30 */
SELECT *
FROM assignment
WHERE work_hours >= 0;

(15 row(s) affected)
```

USING EXPRESSIONS IN SELECT CLAUSES

Thus far we have used the SELECT clause of a SELECT statement to retrieve data and display result tables for data columns from a specified table. However, a SELECT clause can also contain expressions, or computed columns. Expressions, or computed columns, can also be used in a WHERE clause to manipulate column data. An expression is formed by combining a column name or constant with an arithmetic operator. The arithmetic operators used in SQL are given in Table 4.5.

Like logical operators, arithmetic operators have a hierarchy or order of evaluation. Multiplication, division, and modulo operations are performed before addition and subtraction. When an expression contains operators of the same order, the expression is evaluated from left to right. You can use parentheses to force a specific order of operation. The most deeply nested expression inside parentheses is performed first.

The Company database *employee* table stores annual salary figures for employees. However, suppose one of the organization's managers needs a result table that lists employee names and monthly salaries for purposes of preparing a monthly budget of some type. The SELECT statement shown in SQL Example 4.31 produces the required listing.

TABLE 4.5

Symbol	Operation	Order
*	Multiplication	1
/	Division	1
%	Modulo	1
+	Addition	2
−	Subtraction	2

```
/* SQL Example 4.31 */
SELECT CAST(emp_last_name AS Char (15)) "Last Name",
    CAST(emp_first_name AS CHAR(15)) "First Name",
    emp_salary/12 "Monthly Salary"
FROM employee
WHERE emp_salary/12 > 3500
ORDER BY emp_last_name;

Last Name       First Name       Monthly Salary
--------------  ---------------  -------------------
Bordoloi        Bijoy            4583.3333
Joyner          Suzanne          3583.3333
Zhu             Waiman           3583.3333

(3 row(s) affected)
```

Note that we have supplied an *alias* column name of "Monthly Salary" for this computed column (expression). Monthly salary is computed as the value from the *emp_salary* column divided by 12 (annual salary divided among 12 months). The expression is also used in the WHERE clause to restrict the rows that are displayed in the result table.

As you learned in Chapter 3, when a data column is manipulated, SQL Server does not provide a column name for the computed column in the result table, as demonstrated in SQL Example 4.32. For this reason, we supplied an alias column name to be used for the computed column (when the *alias* column name to be used consists of a single word such as "Salary," the double quote marks around the *alias* column name are not required). The *alias* column name provides meaning to the data displayed in the result table. As demonstrated in many previous examples thus far, you can make the output of SQL Example 4.31 even more readable by using the CAST and CONVERT commands combined the concatenation operator (+). The SELECT statement shown in SQL Example 4.33 produces the more readable result table.

```
/* SQL Example 4.32 */
SELECT emp_last_name "Last Name", emp_first_name "First Name",
    emp_salary/12
FROM employee
WHERE emp_salary/12 > 3500
ORDER BY emp_last_name;

Last Name                First Name
-----------------------  ------------------------------  -----------------------
Bordoloi                 Bijoy                           4583.3333
Joyner                   Suzanne                         3583.3333
Zhu                      Waiman                          3583.3333

(3 row(s) affected)
```

```
/* SQL Example 4.33 */
SELECT CAST(emp_last_name + ', ' + emp_first_name As CHAR(20)) "Full
Name", '$'+ CONVERT(CHAR(10), emp_salary/12, 1) "Monthly Salary"
From employee
WHERE emp_salary/12 > 3500
ORDER BY emp_last_name;

Full Name              Monthly Salary
------------------     --------------
Bordoloi, Bijoy        $   4,583.33
Joyner, Suzanne        $   3,583.33
Zhu, Waiman            $   3,583.33

(3 row(s) affected)
```

In the three previous SQL queries, *emp_salary* is divided by a numeric constant, 12. You can also form expressions that use column names on both sides of an arithmetic operator.

NULL values that are in columns that are used in computations can produce unexpected and sometimes confusing results. This occurs because the result of an arithmetic operation on a NULL is NULL or "unknown." For example, if you use a column as part of an expression, and some of the rows in the table contain NULL values for the column, then the result displayed will be NULL. SQL Example 4.34 displays data from the *assignment* table that is used to store the number of hours employees work on assigned projects. The query computes the average work hours per employee assigned to Project 1 based on a 40-hour work week. Notice that the employee with SSN 999-44-4444 has not reported any work hours for Project 1, thus the *work_hours* column is NULL. The computed "Average Per Week" column is also NULL, and is displayed as a NULL value.

```
/* SQL Example 4.34 */
SELECT work_emp_ssn "SSN", work_pro_number "Project",
    work_hours/40 "Avg Hours/Week"
FROM assignment
WHERE work_pro_number = 1
ORDER BY work_emp_ssn;

SSN         Project Avg Hours/Week
----------  ------- --------------
999111111   1       .785000
999444444   1       NULL
999888888   1       .525000

(3 row(s) affected)
```

If a business manager does not want rows with NULL values displayed in a result table, those rows can be eliminated through use of a WHERE clause that filters out rows with NULL values. The query shown in SQL Example 4.35 produces a result table for average work hours that filters out rows where the *work_hours* column value is NOT NULL. This also demonstrates the use of the AND logical operator.

```
/* SQL Example 4.35 */
SELECT work_emp_ssn "SSN", work_pro_number "Project",
    work_hours/40 "Avg Hours/Week"
FROM assignment
WHERE work_pro_number = 1 AND work_hours IS NOT NULL
ORDER BY work_emp_ssn;

SSN          Project Avg Hours/Week
-----------  ------- --------------
999111111    1       .785000
999888888    1       .525000

(2 row(s) affected)
```

It may seem redundant, but the output that results from expressions where NULL values are involved is very important and, sometimes, misunderstood. Consider the *contract_employee* table displayed in Table 4.6. The *contract_employee* table has four columns, *emp_id*, *emp_job*, *emp_salary*, and *emp_bonus*. The *emp_bonus* column is allowed to be NULL.

Management wants to determine the total compensation for each contract employee. Compensation is the employee salary added to the employee bonus. The query shown in SQL Example 4.36 produces two rows with NULL values for total compensation. This does not mean that the big boss and little boss are not paid. It simply means that because *emp_bonus* is NULL (unknown) for those two data rows, the total compensation cannot be computed.

TABLE 4.6 : contract_employee

emp_id, CHAR(2) NOT NULL	emp_job, VARCHAR2(12) NOT NULL	emp_salary, NUMBER NOT NULL	emp_bonus integer null
10	BIG BOSS	100000	NULL
20	LITTLE BOSS	50000	NULL
30	WARRIOR	10000	2000
40	WARRIOR	11000	3000

```
/* SQL Example 4.36 */
SELECT emp_id, emp_job, emp_salary+emp_bonus "Total Comp"
FROM contract_employee;

emp_id   emp_job        Total Comp
-------  -------------  ----------
10       BIG BOSS       NULL
20       LITTLE BOSS    NULL
```

```
 30      WORKER      12000.0000
 40      WORKER      14000.0000

(4 row(s) affected)
```

You may wish to create the *contract_employee* table and execute the query to satisfy yourself that the result table is accurate. This is left as SQL Coding Exercise 15 in the chapter review exercises for the Company database.

ORDER OF PRECEDENCE

At times you may write complex expressions that include more than one operator, such as the AND, OR, NOT, and arithmetic operators, among others. SQL has a prescribed order of precedence that determines which operator executes first—this affects the sequence of operations that are performed. Of course, the sequence of operations affects the result table that is produced. Table 4.7 summarizes the order of precedence for operators.

When an expression has more than one operator that is at the same precedence level, the operators are evaluated from left to right. Additionally, parentheses can be used to alter the precedence level among operators with the operators located within the innermost set of parentheses evaluated first.

TABLE 4.7

Operator Type	Operator
Unary operators	$+$ (Positive), $-$ (Negative), $\sim$ (Bitwise NOT)
Arithmetic operators	$*$ (Multiplication), $/$ (Division), $\%$ (Modulo)
Arithmetic operators	$+$ (Add), $(+$ Concatenate), $-$ (Subtract), $\&$ (Bitwise AND)
Comparison operators	$=, >, <, >=, <=, <>, !=, !>, !<$
Logical operators	NOT
Logical operators	AND
Logical operators	ALL, ANY, BETWEEN, IN, LIKE, OR, SOME
Assignment operator	$=$ (Assignment)

SUMMARY

This chapter focuses on adding power to your queries. The logical operators (AND, OR, NOT) can be used in WHERE clauses to develop complex criteria for row selection. The IN, NOT IN, BETWEEN, and NOT BETWEEN operators help you simplify WHERE clause criteria. The IS NULL and IS NOT NULL operators enable you to write queries that both identify and ignore rows with missing values. You also learned to write queries that use expressions in the SELECT and WHERE clauses. After completing the end-of-chapter exercises, you should be comfortable using the concepts covered here to add power to your queries.

REVIEW EXERCISES

LEARN THESE TERMS

AND operator. Joins two or more conditions, and returns results only when *all* the conditions are true.

BETWEEN operator. The value from the table column used in the WHERE clause condition must fall within or between the lower and upper values specified by the BETWEEN operator.

Computed column. A column of output in a result table that is produced by using an expression that contains an arithmetic operator or operators used to manipulate column data.

IN operator. Used to simplify a query by reducing the number of OR operators. This operator searches for column values that match values in a specified list.

LIKE operator. Used to search for data rows containing incomplete or partial character strings within a data column.

OR operator. Joins two or more conditions, and it returns results when *any* of the conditions are true.

NOT operator. Negates the expression that follows it.

NOT BETWEEN operator. Used to exclude a range of column values from a result table.

NOT IN operator. Negates the IN operator.

NOT LIKE operator. Negates the LIKE operator.

NULL. A keyword meaning the absence of any stored value. NOT NULL is the negation of NULL, meaning that there is a stored value. NULL is synonymous with unknown value.

Wild card. Different symbols used to represent one or more characters when specifying a WHERE clause using the LIKE or NOT LIKE operator, or a similar string search operator.

CONCEPTS QUIZ

1. You are examining the following WHERE clause in a SELECT statement. Explain when the clause evaluates to true and why?

```
WHERE emp_salary > 25000 AND emp_salary <= 45000
```

2. You are examining the following WHERE clause in a SELECT statement. Explain when the clause evaluates to true and why. Are there any potential problems with this WHERE clause?

```
WHERE emp_salary > 25000 OR emp_salary <= 45000
```

Situation. Use the following information to answer the next four questions. For a given data row, the column values are as follows: *emp_salary* = 45000, *emp_gender* = 'F', and *emp_superssn* = '123456789'.

3. Is the following WHERE clause True or False? Why?

```
WHERE emp_salary > 30000 AND emp_gender = 'F' OR
    emp_superssn = '44566778899';
```

4. Is the following WHERE clause True or False? Why?

```
WHERE emp_salary > 30000 OR emp_gender = 'F' AND
    emp_superssn = '44566778899';
```

5. Is the following WHERE clause True or False? Why?

```
WHERE (emp_salary > 30000 OR emp_gender = 'F') AND
    emp_superssn = '44566778899';
```

6. Is the following WHERE clause True or False? Why?

```
WHERE NOT (emp_salary > 30000 OR emp_gender = 'F' AND
    emp_superssn = '44566778899');
```

7. What is the purpose of the IN and NOT IN operators?
8. What is the purpose of the BETWEEN and NOT BETWEEN operators?
9. What is the purpose of the LIKE and NOT LIKE operators?
10. What data rows can be returned in a result table for a SELECT statement with the following WHERE clause?

```
WHERE emp_zip LIKE '62%';
```

11. Explain the concept of a NULL value.
12. What operators are used in expressions to create computed columns?

SQL CODING EXERCISES AND QUESTIONS: COMPANY DATABASE

In answering the SQL exercises and questions, submit a copy of each command that you execute and any messages that SQL Server generates while executing your SQL commands. Also list the output for any result table that is generated by your SQL statements.

1. Execute a query that displays all male employees in department number 7. The result table should list each employee's first name, last name, gender, and department number. To display each row on a single output line, format the employees first and last names such that their displays are limited to 12 characters in width for each column. Use meaningful column heading labels, such as "First Name."

2. Execute a query that displays all employees who earn more than $40,000, *and* are either in department 3 or are male. List each employee first name, last name, salary, gender, and department number formatted, as was done for Exercise 1.

3. Execute a query that displays all employees who earn exactly $43,000 or $55,000. List each employee's first name, last name, and salary. Use the IN operator.

4. Execute a query that displays all employees who DO NOT earn exactly $43,000 or $55,000. List each employee's first name, last name, and salary.

5. Execute a query that displays all employees who earn between $35,000 and $45,000, inclusive. List each employee's first name, last name, and salary. Use the BETWEEN operator. Sort the output by employee salary.

6. Execute a query that displays all employees who DO NOT earn between $29,000 and $45,000, inclusive. List each employee's first name, last name, and salary. Sort the output by employee salary.

7. Execute a query that displays all employees whose first name begins with the letter 'D'. List each employee's first and last name.

8. Execute a query that displays all employees whose last name contains the lower-case letter 'o'. List each employee's first and last name.

9. Execute a query that displays each employee's last name, annual salary, monthly salary, and weekly salary. Label the column names for annual salary, monthly salary, and weekly salary as Annual, Monthly, and Weekly, respectively. Sort the

output by employee last name. Format the columns named Annual, Monthly, and Weekly to include commas for every three digits to the left of the decimal point and have the dollar sign ($) as the prefix (e.g., $99,999.99).

10. Execute a query that lists all *employee* table rows that contain a null value in the *emp_superssn* column. List each employee's last name and supervisor SSN.

11. Execute a query that lists all female employees living in California ('CA'). List each employee's last name, first name, state of residence, and gender. Label the state of residence column as 'State.' Format the 'State' column as CHAR(5).

12. Execute a query for the *assignment* table to list each employee who has worked on either project 1 or 2, and who has worked more than 15 hours on the selected project. List each employee's SSN (*work_emp_ssn*), project number (*work_pro_number*), and hours worked (*work_hours*).

13. Execute a query for the *assignment* table to list each employee who has worked on project number 1, 15, 20, 22, 25, 28, or 30 (some of these projects may not exist in the database). List each employee's SSN (*work_emp_ssn*) and project number (*work_pro_number*).

14. Execute a query for the *assignment* table to list each employee who has worked 5 to 15 hours (inclusive) on any project, or where the hours worked is unknown. List each employee's SSN (*work_emp_ssn*), project number (*work_pro_number*), and hours worked (*work_hours*). Use the BETWEEN and OR operators.

15. Review the section on using expressions in SELECT clauses. Write the CREATE TABLE statement required to create the *contract_employee* table discussed in this chapter. Write INSERT commands to load the *contract_employee* table with the data shown earlier in this chapter. Execute a SELECT statement to compute contract employee total compensation to verify the accuracy of the result table shown in the text.

SQL Coding Exercises and Questions: Riverbend Database

1. A hospital administrator needs a listing of all patients with a zip code of '62025'. The result table should list each patient's last name, first name, city, state, and zip code. To display each row on a single output line, format the patient first and last name and patient city columns as CHAR(15). Use meaningful column names such as "First Name."

2. A hospital administrator needs a listing of staff members who are doctors (hospital_title = 'M.D.') in the oncology department (ward_dept_assigned = 'ONCOL'). The result table should include the staff member's last name, first name, hospital title, and ward and department to which they are assigned. Use meaningful column names such as "First Name."

3. Rewrite the query for Question 2. The hospital administrator has determined that the listing must *also* include physicians assigned to medical surgical department 1 (MEDS1).

4. Rewrite the query for Question 2. The hospital administrator needs the listing to include physicians assigned to any of four different wards/departments (ONCOL, MEDS1, CARD1, or RADI1). Use the IN operator. Sort the rows of the result table by the ward and department of assignment.

5. Rewrite the query for Question 4, but list physicians *not* assigned to one of the four specified wards and departments.

6. A hospital administrator needs a listing of all patients assigned to specific beds numbered 11 through 30, inclusive. The result table should list each patient's last name, first name, and bed number of assignment. To display each row on a single output line, format the patient first and last name as A15. Use meaningful column names such as "First Name." Use the BETWEEN operator. Sort the result table by bed number.

7. The hospital inventory manager needs a listing of medicines that are both overstocked and potentially understocked. List each medicine's code, common name, and quantity in stock (*medicine_code*, *med_name_common*, and *quantity_stock*) from the *medicine* table. List only medicines that have a *quantity_stock* value that is *not* between 500 and 25,000. Use the NOT BETWEEN operator. Use meaningful column names such as "Med Code."

8. An administrative worker needs a listing of all staff members who have a last name that begins with the letter 'B' and that have a hospital title of 'M.D.' List each staff member's last and first names as well as hospital title. Sort the output by last name then by first name. Use meaningful column names.

9. Rewrite the query for Question 8, but list staff members who have a last name that contains the lowercase letter 'o' with all other requirements remaining the same.

10. The administrator in charge of payroll budgeting needs a listing that displays each salaried staff member's last name, first name, annual salary, monthly salary, and weekly salary. Label the column names for annual salary, monthly salary, and weekly salary as Annual, Monthly, and Weekly, respectively. Sort the output by employee last name, then first name. Format the columns named Annual, Monthly, and Weekly to include commas for every three digits to the left of the decimal point and have the dollar sign ($) as the prefix (e.g., $99,999.99). Do not display output for hourly workers (the value of *wage_rate* is NULL for salaried workers).

11. The hospital administrator in charge of patient census needs a listing of current patients that have not been assigned a bed number to complete bed assignments for the day. The result table should list the patient's last name and bed number (which is to be NULL). Use the IS NULL operator. Use meaningful column names.

12. Dr. Quattromani, a cardiologist at the Riverbend Hospital, has requested a listing of patient identifications to whom she prescribed (*prescription* table) either Lanoxin or Alupent (medicine_code is 9999012 or 9999013). Dr. Quattromani's staff identification is 66425. List the prescription number, patient ID, medicine code, and staff ID.

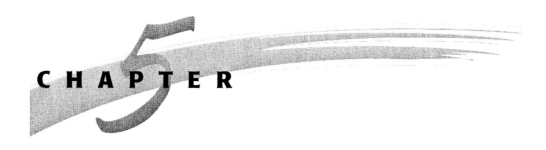

AGGREGATE FUNCTIONS AND GROUPING OF DATA

Business managers often need aggregate information to support various decision-making tasks. These types of managerial questions tend to focus on information that represents exceptional situations. Exception information is information that falls outside of the normal expectations for business operations. Sometimes exception information represents undesirable situations, such as low product sales. At other times, exception information represents very good situations, such as sales that exceed corporate goals. At still other times, managers may need information about averages or counting values to compare performance across time periods, across departments, or across employee groups.

Typical managerial questions include: What product experienced the largest sales volume last quarter? What is the average salary for employees within a specific job type? How many employees in a specific department are female or male? What is the average number of hours employees devoted to completing a specific project or group of projects? Who are the employees with a salary that is higher than the average salary of the entire company? These questions require your Structured Query Language (SQL) queries to display data that is exceptional in some fashion, and this information must be aggregated in some fashion. SQL has numerous predefined *aggregate functions* that can be used to write queries to produce exactly this kind of information.

OBJECTIVES

In this chapter you learn to use many of the SQL aggregate functions to write queries. You also learn the GROUP BY and HAVING clauses. The GROUP BY clause specifies how to group rows from a data table when you are aggregating information, whereas the HAVING clause filters out rows that do not belong in specified groups. Your learning objectives for the chapter are:

- Write queries with aggregate functions: SUM, AVG, COUNT, MAX, and MIN.
- Use the GROUP BY clause to answer complex managerial questions.
- Use the GROUP BY clause with NULL values.
- Use the GROUP BY clause with the WHERE and ORDER BY clauses.
- Use the HAVING clause to filter out rows from a result table.

IMPLEMENTING AGGREGATE FUNCTIONS

Aggregate functions perform a variety of actions such as counting all the rows in a table, averaging a column's data, and summing numeric data. Aggregates can also search a table to find the highest "MAX" or lowest "MIN" values in a column. As with other types of queries, you can restrict or filter out the rows these functions act on using the WHERE clause.

For example, if a manager needs to know how many employees work in an organization, the aggregate function named COUNT(*) can produce this information. The COUNT(*) function shown in SQL Example 5.1 counts all rows in a table. The wild card asterisk (*) is used as the parameter or argument in the function—it means to count all the rows.

```
/* SQL Example 5.1 */
SELECT COUNT(*)
FROM employee;
------------
    8
```

The result table for the COUNT(*) function is a single column from a single row known as a *scalar* result or value. Notice that the result table has no column heading. As you learned in Chapter 3, the output column can be assigned a meaningful column name termed a *label* or *alias,* as shown in SQL Example 5.2. Remember that if the *label* is more than one word, then it must be enclosed in double quotes.

```
/* SQL Example 5.2 */
SELECT COUNT(*) "Number of Employees"
FROM employee;

Number of Employees
-------------------
    8
```

Table 5.1 lists some of the commonly used aggregate functions including their syntax and use.

The ALL and DISTINCT keywords are optional, and perform as they do with the SELECT clauses that you have learned to write. The ALL keyword is the default where the option is allowed. The *expression* listed in the syntax can be a constant, a function, or any combination of column names, constants, and functions connected by arithmetic operators; however, aggregate functions are most often used with a column name.

TABLE. 5.1	
Function Syntax	*Function Use*
SUM([ALL I DISTINCT] expression)	The total of the (distinct) values in a numeric column or expression
AVG([ALL I DISTINCT] expression)	The average of the (distinct) values in a numeric column or expression
COUNT([ALL I DISTINCT] expression)	The number of (distinct) non-NULL values in a column or expression
COUNT(*)	The number of selected rows
MAX(expression)	The highest value in a column or expression
MIN(expression)	The lowest value in a column or expression

There are two rules that you must understand and follow when using aggregates:

- Aggregate functions can be used in both the SELECT and HAVING clauses—the HAVING clause is covered later in this chapter.
- Aggregate functions cannot be used in a WHERE clause.

Consider the query in SQL Example 5.3. This query is wrong because it violates one of the two rules to follow when using aggregates—it attempts to use the AVG aggregate function in the WHERE clause. SQL Server 2000 responds with the error message shown. We have not studied the topic of subqueries yet (see Chapter 7), but the error message makes it clear that this is an attempted misuse of the aggregate function.

```
/* SQL Example 5.3 */
SELECT *
FROM employee
WHERE AVG(emp_salary) > 40000;

Server: Msg 147, Level 15, State 1, Line 4
An aggregate may not appear in the WHERE clause unless it is in a subquery
contained in a HAVING clause or a select list, and the column being
aggregated is an outer reference.
```

If you think about what an aggregate function does and what the purpose of a WHERE clause is, then this error makes perfect sense. Remember, a WHERE clause includes or excludes rows from a result table based on user-defined criteria. The aggregate function then acts on all rows or a subset of rows that satisfy the criteria specified by the WHERE clause. Because the WHERE clause must execute *before* the aggregate function takes effect, you cannot include an aggregate function in a WHERE clause. Later in this chapter you learn how to use the HAVING clause to filter out rows with grouped data—*after* aggregate functions have been calculated.

USING THE AVERAGE (AVG) FUNCTION

Suppose that managers need to determine the average salary of employees for the firm for budgeting or some similar purpose. You can use the AVG function to compute the average value for the *emp_salary* column in the *employee* table. The query in SQL Example 5.4 does this task easily. Additionally, so that managers can understand the result table without any problem we have formatted the data and labeled the output. As with the COUNT(*) function, the result table for AVG here is a *scalar* value.

```
/* SQL Example 5.4 */
SELECT '$'+ CONVERT(Char(10), AVG(emp_salary), 1) "Average Employee
Salary"
FROM employee;

Average Employee Salary
-------------------------
$ 35,500.00
```

Now suppose that a similar, yet different management question is posed. What is the average salary *offered* to employees? This question asks you to incorporate the concept of computing the average of the distinct salaries paid by the organization. The same query with the DISTINCT keyword in the aggregate function returns a different average as shown in SQL Example 5.5. Notice the syntax used for placing the DISTINCT keyword in the query.

```
/* SQL Example 5.5 */
SELECT '$'+ CONVERT(Char(10), AVG(DISTINCT emp_salary), 1) "Average
Employee Salary"
FROM employee;

Average Employee Salary
-------------------------
$ 38,200
```

The difference between the two queries occurs because the DISTINCT keyword causes T-SQL to omit duplicate values from the processing. Although you could not determine this from the result table, SQL Example 5.4 used eight employee rows including three that each had a salary of $25,000 in computing the average displayed in the result table. In SQL Example 5.5 the salary of $25,000, or any other salary figure that is paid to more than one employee is only used once in computing the average DISTINCT salary. Thus, the two computed averages are different.

USING THE SUM (SUM) FUNCTION

Suppose that a senior manager needs to know the total salary paid currently to the entire organization—such a figure would be useful in analyzing aggregate budget questions for a firm. This question can be answered by using the SUM function. The SUM function computes the total of a column of numeric data in a table—do not attempt to produce a SUM of a column that stores character data. The SELECT statement shown in SQL Example 5.6 returns the requested total of the *emp_salary* column from the *employee* table.

```
/* SQL Example 5.6 */
SELECT '$'+ CONVERT(Char(10), SUM(emp_salary), 1) "Total Salary"
FROM employee;

Total Salary
------------
$ 284,000
```

If management is preparing a budget for various departments, you may be asked to write a query to compute the total salary for different departments. The query shown in SQL Example 5.7 computes the total *emp_salary* for employees assigned to department 7.

```
/* SQL Example 5.7 */
SELECT '$'+ CONVERT(Char(10), SUM(emp_salary), 1) "Total Salary Dept 7"
FROM employee
WHERE emp_dpt_number = 7;

Total Salary Dept 7
-------------------
$ 136,000
```

Keep in mind that SQL is not case sensitive with respect to keywords. Query 5.7 could also have been typed in lowercase, as is shown in SQL Example 5.8.

```
/* SQL Example 5.8 */
select '$'+ convert(char(10), sum(emp_salary), 1) "Total Salary Dept 7"
from employee
where emp_dpt_number = 7;
```

Regardless, the result table is identical. This is just to remind you that keywords may be entered in either lowercase or uppercase, and this rule also applies to aggregate function names. By convention, we type keywords in uppercase to differentiate between keywords and column or table names.

USING THE MINIMUM (MIN) AND MAXIMUM (MAX) FUNCTIONS

At times managers need to know which value in a column is the largest or smallest of all values. Questions such as what product was sold the most or least, which employee is paid the largest or smallest salary, and similar questions arise continually in business.

SQL provides two aggregate functions to assist you in writing queries to answer these types of questions. The MIN function returns the lowest value stored in a data column. Similarly, the MAX function returns the largest value stored in a data column. However, unlike SUM and AVG, the MIN and MAX functions work with both numeric and character data columns.

SQL Example 5.9 gives a query that uses the MIN function to find the lowest value stored in the *emp_last_name* column of the *employee* table. This is analogous to determine which employee's last name comes first in the alphabet. The example also demonstrates using the MAX function to list the employee row for the *emp_last_name* column where last name comes last (highest) in the alphabet.

```
/* SQL Example 5.9 */
SELECT MIN(emp_last_name), MAX(emp_last_name)
FROM employee;


-------------------------    -------------------------
Amin                         Zhu
```

More often you can use the MIN and MAX functions to manipulate numeric data columns. Let us return to the management question of what are the highest and lowest salaries paid to employees of the firm. The query shown in SQL Example 5.10 uses the MIN and MAX function to answer this question. Notice that the query does not provide the actual names of the employees with these salary values. We learn later in this chapter how to combine aggregate functions with column names to answer such a question.

```
/* SQL Example 5.10 */
SELECT '$'+ CONVERT(Char(10), MAX(emp_salary), 1) "Highest Salary",
       '$'+ CONVERT(Char(10), MIN(emp_salary), 1) "Lowest Salary"
FROM employee;

Highest Salary Lowest Salary
-------------- -------------
$ 55,000       $ 25,000
```

USING THE COUNT (COUNT) FUNCTION

At the beginning of this chapter we use the COUNT(*) function to count the number of rows in a table. The COUNT function does essentially the same thing. The difference is that you can define a specific column to be counted. When the COUNT function processes a specified column, rows containing a NULL value in the named column are omitted from the count. Recall that a NULL value stands for unknown, and that this should not be confused with a blank or a zero value.

The query shown in SQL Example 5.11 counts the number of employees that are assigned a supervisor. Employees not assigned a supervisor may have a NULL value for the supervisor's Social Security number (SSN) column (*emp_superssn*). SQL Server issues a warning to let you know that rows were not included that had NULL values.

```
/* SQL Example 5.11 */
SELECT COUNT(emp_superssn) "Number of Supervised Employees"
FROM employee;

Number of Supervised Employees
------------------------------
7
```

```
(1 row(s) affected)

Warning: Null value is eliminated by an aggregate or other SET
operation.
```

In contrast, the COUNT(*) function in SQL Example 5.12 counts each employee row regardless of NULL values.

```
/* SQL Example 5.12 */
SELECT COUNT(*) "Number of Employees"
FROM employee;

Number of Employees
-------------------
8
```

GROUPING DATA: GROUP BY CLAUSE

Now that you have gained familiarity with aggregate functions, you are ready to add power to your queries. The power of aggregate functions is greater when combined with the GROUP BY clause. In fact, the GROUP BY clause is rarely used without an aggregate function. Although it is possible to use the GROUP BY clause without aggregates, such a construction has very limited functionality, and could lead to a result table that is confusing or misleading. We focus on using the GROUP BY clause with aggregate clauses.

When properly used, the GROUP BY clause enables you to use aggregate functions to answer more complex managerial questions such as:

- What is the average salary of employees in each department?
- How many employees work in each department?
- How many employees are working on a particular project?

Return to the query posed earlier in SQL Example 5.7. This particular query uses aggregate functions to answer questions concerning a single department in the Company database. However, if a manager needs information about the average salary for *each* department, then you would need to write a separate query for each department using the approach demonstrated thus far. This would be quite a bit of work for a large organization with dozens of departments. Clearly, there has to be a better way. SQL comes to the rescue with the GROUP BY clause and enables you to answer questions about each department by writing only a single query.

The query in SQL Example 5.13 answers the managerial question, how many employees work for each department? The count produced by the COUNT(*) aggregate function is grouped by department based on the *emp_dpt_number* column value. The result table is termed a *vector* aggregate, as opposed to *scalar*, because it produces an aggregate value for each group identified by the GROUP BY clause.

```
/* SQL Example 5.13 */
SELECT emp_dpt_number "Department", COUNT(*) "Employee Count"
FROM employee
GROUP BY emp_dpt_number;


Department Employee Count
---------- --------------
1           1
3           3
7           4
```

SQL Server provides considerable flexibility in specifying the GROUP BY clause. The column name used in a GROUP BY clause does not have to be listed in the SELECT clause; however, it must be a column name from one of the tables listed in the FROM clause. We can rewrite the query in SQL Example 5.14 without specifying the *emp_dpt_number* column as part of the result table; however, as you can see from the result table for SQL Example 5.14, the results are rather cryptic without the *emp_dpt_number* column to identify the meaning of the aggregate count.

```
/* SQL Example 5.14 */
SELECT COUNT(*) "Employee Count"
FROM employee
GROUP BY emp_dpt_number;


Employee Count
--------------
1
3
4
```

Note, however, that if your SELECT clause includes *both* column names and aggregate functions, as was the case with the query in SQL Example 5.12, then you must also have a GROUP BY clause in your query. Additionally, the column name or names in the GROUP BY clause *must* match the column name or names listed in the SELECT clause. Otherwise, SQL Server return errors messages, as shown below in SQL Examples 5.15 and 5.16.

```
/* SQL Example 5.15 */
SELECT emp_dpt_number "Department", COUNT(*) "Employee Count"
FROM employee;


Server: Msg 8118, Level 16, State 1, Line 2
Column 'employee.emp_dpt_number' is invalid in the select list because it
is not contained in an aggregate function and there is no GROUP BY clause.
```

In SQL Example 5.15, SQL Server does not accept the mixing of column names and aggregate functions in the SELECT clause because the GROUP BY clause is missing. SQL Server considers the use of the *emp_dpt_number* column name (denoted as *employee.emp_dpt_number*) invalid.

In SQL Example 5.16, a similar error message is generated because the GROUP BY clause does not specify a column name that matches a column name in the SELECT clause.

```
/* SQL Example 5.16 */
SELECT emp_dpt_number "Department", COUNT(*) "Employee Count"
FROM employee
GROUP BY emp_city;

Server: Msg 8120, Level 16, State 1, Line 2
Column 'employee.emp_dpt_number' is invalid in the select list because it
is not contained in an aggregate function and there is no GROUP BY clause.
```

The GROUP BY clause does have some limitations. For example, you cannot use an aggregate function in a GROUP BY clause. SQL Server returns an error message, as demonstrated by SQL Example 5.17.

```
/* SQL Example 5.17 */
SELECT AVG(emp_salary), emp_salary * 1.25
FROM employee
GROUP BY AVG(salary);

Server: Msg 144, Level 15, State 1, Line 4
Cannot use an aggregate or a subquery in an expression used for the
group by list of a GROUP BY clause.
```

USING GROUP BY WITH EXPRESSIONS

In addition to column names, any expression listed in a SELECT clause can also be used with a GROUP BY clause. Suppose one of our managers needs to know the average salary of employees for our organization. Further, the manager needs to know what the new average salary figures will be if all employees receive a 25% raise—a great business year for the firm. SQL Example 5.18 produces the needed information by grouping on the expression, *emp_salary * 1.25*, as opposed to a column name. The expression is highlighted for easy identification.

```
/* SQL Example 5.18 */
SELECT CAST(AVG(emp_salary) AS Decimal(10,2)) "Current Average Salary",
       CAST(AVG(emp_salary * 1.25) AS Decimal(10,2)) "New Average Salary"
FROM employee
GROUP BY emp_salary * 1.25;

Current Average Salary New Average Salary
---------------------- ------------------
25000.00               31250.00
30000.00               37500.00
```

```
38000.00              47500.00
43000.00              53750.00
55000.00              68750.00
```

Perhaps a more typical management question might be: What is the average salary for each department, and what would be the new average salary after an across-the-board 25% pay raise? The revised query in SQL Example 5.19 changes the condition in the GROUP BY clause to group on department number.

```
/* SQL Example 5.19 */
SELECT emp_dpt_number "Department",
    CAST(AVG(emp_salary) AS Decimal(10,2)) "Current Average Salary",
    CAST(AVG(emp_salary * 1.25)AS Decimal(10,2)) "New Average Salary"
FROM employee
GROUP BY emp_dpt_number;

Department Current Average Salary New Average Salary
---------- --------------------- ------------------
1              55000.00              68750.00
3              31000.00              38750.00
7              34000.00              42500.00
```

USING **GROUP BY** WITH A **WHERE** CLAUSE

You can combine the WHERE and GROUP BY clauses in a SELECT statement. The WHERE clause works to eliminates data table rows from consideration before any grouping takes place. SQL Example 5.20 is a query that produces an average hours worked result table for employees with an SSN that is larger than the specified SSN, 999-66-0000. Notice that the row for the employee with SSN 999-66-6666 contains a NULL value for the total work hours because the *work_hours* column value is NULL for that employee.

```
/* SQL Example 5.20 */
SELECT work_emp_ssn SSN, AVG(work_hours) "Average Hours Worked"
FROM assignment
WHERE work_emp_ssn > 999660000
GROUP BY work_emp_ssn;

SSN        Average Hours Worked
---------- ----------------------------------------------
999666666 NULL
999887777 20.500000
999888888 21.500000

(3 row(s) affected)

Warning: Null value is eliminated by an aggregate or other SET operation.
```

USING **GROUP BY** WITH AN **ORDER BY** CLAUSE

As you learned in studying Chapter 3, the ORDER BY clause allows you to specify how to sort rows in a result table. The default ordering is from smallest to largest value. Similarly, a GROUP BY clause in a SELECT statement determines the sort order of rows in a result table with aggregate results. The sort order can be changed by specifying an ORDER BY clause after the GROUP BY clause. This allows you to specify a sort order based on a data column that is different from that specified in the GROUP BY clause.

SQL Example 5.21 has a query that provides managers with information about the average salary of employees in each department. The result table is sorted from smallest to largest by the average salary figure. Without the ORDER BY clause, the output would be sorted by the *emp_dpt_number* column specified in the GROUP BY clause.

```
/* SQL Example 5.21 */
SELECT emp_dpt_number "Department",
'$' + CONVERT(Char(10), AVG(emp_salary), 1) "Average Salary"
FROM employee
GROUP BY emp_dpt_number
ORDER BY AVG(emp_salary);


Department Average Salary
---------- --------------
3              $ 31,000.00
7              $ 34,000.00
1              $ 55,000.00
```

If management wants the result table to display average salaries from highest to lowest, you can specify the DESC keyword (the abbreviation for descending) in the ORDER BY clause. SQL Example 5.22 shows the revised query. Note the syntax placement of the DESC keyword.

```
/* SQL Example 5.22 */
SELECT emp_dpt_number "Department",
'$' + CONVERT(Char(10), AVG(emp_salary), 1) "Average Salary"
FROM employee
GROUP BY emp_dpt_number
ORDER BY AVG(emp_salary)DESC;

Department Average Salary
---------- --------------
1              $ 55,000.00
7              $ 34,000.00
3              $ 31,000.00
```

FILTERING GROUPED DATA: THE HAVING CLAUSE

Earlier you learn that you cannot use an aggregate function in a WHERE clause. SQL Server returns an error message and fails to process the query. The HAVING clause is used for aggregate functions in the same way that a WHERE clause is used for column names and expressions. Essentially, the HAVING and WHERE clauses do the same thing, that is, filter rows from inclusion in a result table based on some conditions. Although it may appear that a HAVING clause filters out groups, it does not. Instead, a HAVING clause filters rows. When all rows for a group are eliminated so is the group.

To summarize, the important differences between the WHERE and HAVING clauses are:

- A WHERE clause is used to filter rows *BEFORE* the GROUPING action (i.e., before the calculation of the aggregate functions).
- A HAVING clause filters rows *AFTER* the GROUPING action (i.e., after the calculation of the aggregate functions).

Suppose that a manager in the accounting department requires a listing of departments where the average salary is greater than $33,000. We know that we cannot use the condition "AVG(*emp_salary*) > 33000" in the WHERE clause because SQL Server returns an error message due to the AVG aggregate function in the WHERE clause. We can remedy this problem by using a HAVING clause to filter rows after the grouping action. SQL Example 5.23 gives a query with the appropriate SELECT statement. The usage of a condition in a HAVING clause is like that for a WHERE clause.

```
/* SQL Example 5.23 */
SELECT emp_dpt_number "Department",
'$' + CONVERT(Char(10), AVG(emp_salary), 1) "Average Salary"
FROM employee
GROUP BY emp_dpt_number
HAVING AVG(emp_salary) > 33000;


Department Average Salary
---------- --------------
1          $ 55,000.00
7          $ 34,000.00
```

Now, suppose this same manager is not interested in the budget for department 1, but has the same question concerning average salaries for the other departments in our organization. This gives rise to a situation where we can combine the use of the WHERE and HAVING clauses. SQL Example 5.24 gives the SELECT statement needed to produce a result table for this query.

```
/* SQL Example 5.24 */
SELECT emp_dpt_number "Department",
'$' + CONVERT(Char(10), AVG(emp_salary), 1) "Average Salary"
FROM employee
WHERE emp_dpt_number <> 1
GROUP BY emp_dpt_number
HAVING AVG(emp_salary) > 33000;


Department Average Salary
---------- --------------
7          $ 34,000.00
```

Of course, having completed this series of SELECT statements in sequence, we knew in advance that only one department would satisfy all the conditions of the query, and this helps us to prove the accuracy of the query. Conceptually, SQL performs the following steps in the query given in SQL Example 5.24.

1. The WHERE clause filters rows that do not meet the condition *emp_dpt_number* <> 1.
2. The GROUP BY clause collects the surviving rows into one or more groups for each unique *emp_dpt_number*.
3. The aggregate function calculates the average salary for each *emp_dpt_number* grouping.
4. The HAVING clause filters out the rows from the result table that do not meet the condition: average salary greater than $33,000.

All this represents quite a bit of work on the part of your SQL query and your SQL Server software. The good news is that you do not have to do the processing by hand, or do you really have to worry about how it all happens. How SQL Server handles the query does not matter because it interprets your query and creates its own plan of action.

STANDARD SQL RULES

The most common use of a HAVING clause is to create result tables containing one row per group, with one or more summary values in a row. To do this your query must meet the following conditions:

1. Columns listed in a SELECT clause must also be listed in the GROUP BY expression or they must be arguments of aggregate functions.
2. A GROUP BY expression can only contain column names that are in the SELECT clause listing.
3. Columns in a HAVING expression must be either:
   - Single-valued arguments of an aggregate function, for instance, or
   - Listed in the SELECT clause listing or GROUP BY clause.

The SELECT statement in SQL Example 5.25 is an example of a query that complies with these rules. First, the *emp_dpt_number* column listed in the SELECT clause listing is also listed in the GROUP BY clause. The second expression in the SELECT clause listing is the aggregate function, COUNT(*). Second, the GROUP BY expression only contains column names listed in the SELECT clause column listing (*emp_dpt_number*). Third, the HAVING expression is an argument of an aggregate function. The query returns a single row per group in the result table, and groups the rows from the *employee* table by the *emp_dpt_number* column. The query eliminates departments that have less than two employees.

```
/* SQL Example 5.25 */
SELECT emp_dpt_number "Department", COUNT(*) "Employee Count"
FROM employee
GROUP BY emp_dpt_number
HAVING COUNT(*) >= 2;
```

```
Department Employee Count
---------- --------------
   3           3
   7           4
```

Let us see what happens when we add a column name, *emp_gender*, to the SELECT clause listing of the above query, but do not include this column in the GROUP BY clause. As shown in SQL Example 5.26, SQL Server returns an error message that is very explicit and clear. Of course departments do not have a gender. Gender is a characteristic of the department employees.

```
/* SQL Example 5.26 */
SELECT emp_dpt_number "Department", emp_gender, COUNT(*) "Employee
Count"
FROM employee
GROUP BY emp_dpt_number
HAVING COUNT(*) >= 2;

Server: Msg 8120, Level 16, State 1, Line 2
Column 'employee.emp_gender' is invalid in the select list because
it is not contained in either an aggregate function or the GROUP BY
clause.
```

We can remedy this problem by including the *emp_gender* column name in the GROUP BY clause, as demonstrated in SQL Example 5.27. Notice, however, that the meaning (and output) of this query is quite different from that of SQL Example 5.25. SQL Example 5.25 displayed the department number and the number of employees for those departments that have more than two employees, irrespective of gender. The basis for computing the aggregate function, COUNT(*), was only one group, *emp_dpt_number*. In contrast, SQL Example 5.27 has two grouping factors, *emp_dpt_number* and *emp_gender*. Hence, the COUNT function counts the number of rows for each gender group within each department. The employee department is considered the major grouping factor whereas employee gender is a subgrouping within each department. The query displays the number of employees of a specific gender for those departments that have more than two employees of the same gender as a result of the HAVING clause. It happens that department 3 does not have more than two male employees and department 7 does not have more than two female employees, thus, there are no groupings for those genders within the two departments.

```
/* SQL Example 5.27 */
SELECT emp_dpt_number "Department", emp_gender,
   COUNT(*) "Employee Count"
FROM employee
GROUP BY emp_dpt_number, emp_gender
HAVING COUNT(*) >= 2;
```

```
Department emp_gender Employee Count
----------- ----------- --------------
3           F           2
7           M           3
```

Further, let us see what happens when two additional aggregate functions are added to the SELECT clause listing of SQL Example 5.25. The modified query in SQL Example 5.28 counts the number of employees in a department and simultaneously computes both the largest and smallest employee salary for each department.

```
/* SQL Example 5.28 */
SELECT emp_dpt_number "Department", COUNT(*) "Employee Count",
    '$' + CONVERT(Char(10), MAX(emp_salary), 1) "Top Salary",
    '$' + CONVERT(Char(10), MIN(emp_salary), 1) "Low Salary"
FROM employee
GROUP BY emp_dpt_number
HAVING COUNT(*) >= 2;

Department Employee Count Top Salary  Low Salary
---------- -------------- ----------- -----------
3          3              $ 43,000.00 $ 25,000.00
7          4              $ 43,000.00 $ 25,000.00
```

By adding the MAX(*emp_salary*) and MIN(*emp_salary*) columns to the query, you gain additional columns in the result table, but the exact same groups are displayed. This query conforms to Standard SQL because the *emp_salary* column name is included as an argument in the MAX and MIN aggregate functions. It is simply chance that the largest and smallest employee salary figures for department 3 and 7 are identical in the *employee* table.

SQL EXTENSIONS TO GROUP BY AND HAVING CLAUSES

Various relational database management systems, such as SQL Server, provide extensions to the standard SQL. These extensions provide flexibility in displaying data in result tables by allowing references to columns and expressions that are not used to create groups or summary calculations. You need to understand that these extensions are NOT part of the American National Standards Institute (ANSI) standard for SQL. Before using these, ensure that the database management system software that you are using supports these language extensions.

- A SELECT clause listing that includes aggregate functions can also include columns that are not arguments of aggregate functions, or that are not included in the GROUP BY clause.
- The GROUP BY clause can include column names or expressions that are not included in the SELECT clause listing (SQL Example 5.29 demonstrates this).
- The GROUP BY ALL clause displays all groups, even those excluded from calculations by a WHERE clause.

- The HAVING clause can include columns or expressions that are not listed in the SELECT clause or in a GROUP BY clause.

```
/* SQL Example 5.29 */
SELECT emp_dpt_number "Department", COUNT(*) "Employee Count"
FROM employee
GROUP BY emp_dpt_number, emp_gender
HAVING COUNT(*) >= 2;

Department Employee Count
---------- --------------
3              2
7              3
```

As exemplified in SQL Example 5.29, if not properly formulated, SQL extensions can result in query output that is difficult to interpret. Compare the result of this query with that of SQL Example 5.25. The employee counts are different because the grouping includes employee gender as a subgroup, and eliminates subgroupings with fewer than two employees.

Table 5.2 summarizes what you need to do if you are writing a query that involves grouping and summarizing column data.

Using HAVING Without a GROUP BY Clause

The HAVING clause is a conditional option that is directly related to the GROUP BY clause option because a HAVING clause eliminates rows from a result table based on the result of a GROUP BY clause. Many relational database management systems including SQL Server cannot process a query with a HAVING clause that is not accompanied by a GROUP BY clause. The following query in SQL Example 5.30 attempts to use a HAVING clause without a GROUP BY clause. SQL Server generates error messages.

TABLE 5.2   Grouping and Summarizing

To Get This Effect:	*Do This:*
Exclude rows before grouping	Use a WHERE clause
Divide a result table into groups	Use a GROUP BY clause
Calculate summary values for each group	Include one or more aggregates in the SELECT clause listing
Exclude groups from the result table	Use a HAVING clause

If This Happens:	*Look For This:*
All qualified rows in all qualified groups display	The SELECT clause listing contains a column name that is not in the GROUP BY clause
All excluded groups display	Query includes GROUP BY ALL

```
/* SQL Example 5.30 */
SELECT emp_dpt_number, AVG(emp_salary)
FROM employee
HAVING AVG(emp_salary) > 33000;

Server: Msg 8118, Level 16, State 1, Line 2
Column 'employee.emp_dpt_number' is invalid in the select list because it
is not contained in an aggregate function and there is no GROUP BY clause.
```

SUMMARY

In this chapter you develop an understanding of the use of aggregate functions. The GROUP BY clause enables you to produce complex data manipulations with ease through the use of clearly understandable queries. The HAVING clause restricts rows in a result table to those rows that meet conditions that involve the use of an aggregate function.

The WHERE and ORDER BY clauses are also covered in conjunction with the GROUP BY clause and aggregate functions. Numerous examples demonstrate how to use these clauses to order the display of rows in a result table according to management specifications, and to eliminate information that is not desired in a final result table.

The chapter also summarizes SQL extensions for the GROUP BY and HAVING clauses. You are now ready to reinforce your learning by completing the review exercises.

REVIEW EXERCISES

LEARN THESE TERMS

Aggregate functions.   Used to write queries to produce *summary* data.

AVG.   The average of values in a numeric column or expression.

COUNT.   The number of non-NULL values in a column or an expression.

COUNT(*).   The number of selected rows.

DISTINCT.   A keyword that causes SQL to omit duplicate values from processing.

GROUP BY clause.   Used to specify which rows from a data table can be included when aggregating information by groups.

HAVING clause.   Used to filter rows after the execution of aggregate functions.

MAX.   The highest value in a column or an expression.

MIN.   The lowest value in a column or an expression.

Scalar aggregate.   A scalar aggregate function produces a *single value* in a result table from a SELECT statement that does not include a GROUP BY clause.

SUM.   The total of values in a numeric column or expression.

Vector aggregate.   A vector aggregate yields a result table that has many values due to the use of a GROUP BY clause.

CONCEPTS QUIZ

1. Explain the use of each of the aggregate functions: SUM, AVG, COUNT, COUNT(*), MAX, and MIN.
2. What is the purpose of the DISTINCT keyword when used with an aggregate function?
3. What is the rule concerning the use of aggregate functions in SELECT, HAVING, and WHERE clauses?

4. What aggregate functions work with both numeric and character data columns?
5. If you write a query using the COUNT (Column Name) aggregate function, what happens to rows that contain a NULL value for the column to be queried?
6. If you write a query using the COUNT(*) aggregate function, what happens to rows that contain NULL values?
7. What is the purpose of the GROUP BY clause?
8. Name one limitation of the GROUP BY clause with respect to aggregate functions.
9. How many values are in a result table that is produced by using a scalar aggregate function without a GROUP BY clause?
10. How many values are in a result table that is produced by using a vector aggregate function with a GROUP BY clause?
11. What happens to a result table when a GROUP BY clause processes data columns that contain NULL values?
12. How does a WHERE clause affect the production of a result table from a SELECT statement that has a GROUP BY clause?
13. Why would you use an ORDER BY clause to order output when a GROUP BY clause normally determines the sort order of rows in a result table?
14. What is the keyword used to display result table rows from highest to lowest value based on a data column where the ORDER BY clause is used for sorting?
15. What is the purpose of a HAVING clause and what advantage does it offer to you in developing queries?
16. If you need to create a result table containing more than one summary value in each row, what conditions must be met in using a HAVING clause along with aggregate functions?

SQL Coding Exercises and Questions: Company Database

1. A manager from the human resources department needs you to write a query to count the total number of dependents for all employees in the Company. Write a query to display this number. Label the output column **Number of Dependents**.
2. The *dep_date_of_birth* column in the *dependent* table stores date of birth information for dependents of employees of the Company. Write a query to display the date of birth of the youngest dependent listed in the table. Label the output column with a reasonable label.
3. The department table stores information about departments within the Company. The *dpt_mgr_start_date* column stores the date on which an employee started working as a department manager. Write a query to display the date for the manager that has worked as a department manager the longest. Label the output column **Longest Working Manager**.
4. Accountants working on the Company's annual budgeting process need to know the average salary (*emp_salary*) for employees and the sum of all employee salaries. The information is stored in the *employee* table. The result table should have two columns based on a single query. Label the columns **Average Salary** and **Total Salary**. Format the output as $999,999.99.
5. A new government reporting regulation requires you to develop a query that can count the number of male dependents of employees of the Company. The

information is stored in the *dep_gender* column of the *dependent* table. The result table should have a single output column labeled **Number Male Dependents**.

6. A revision to the government reporting regulation cited in Question 5 requires the report to count the number of male and female dependents of the Company. Display the information as two columns, one for gender and one for the associated count. The result table should have two rows, one for each gender as shown here. Use a single query. Additionally, the gender output column should be formatted as CHAR(6) and have a heading label of **Gender**. The count column should have a heading label of **Number Counted**.

```
Gender Number Counted
------ --------------
F      10
M      3
```

7. The government reporting regulation cited in Questions 5 and 6 also require a report of the count of each type of dependent (spouse, daughter, and son). Write a query that can produce a result table with two columns labeled **Dependent Type** (use the *dep_relationship* column) and **Dependent Count** from the *dependent* table.

8. Modify the query written for Question 7 above to restrict output to the result table such that spouses are not listed. Only a count of daughters and sons should be listed in the output. Label the columns as specified in Question 7.

9. Modify the query written for Question 7 above to sort the output by the count of the number of dependents in each category with the largest counts listed first. Label the columns as specified in Question 7.

10. Modify the query written for Question 7 above to restrict the output to only count dependents who were born after December 31, 1970. Use the *dep_date_of_birth* column in your query to refer to each dependent's date of birth. Label the columns as specified in Question 7.

11. The Company's Executive Director for project manager needs to know the number of projects each department is working on based on the information stored in the *project* table. The result table should have two columns labeled **Department** and **Project Count**. You need to refer to the *pro_dept_number* column that stores the department number and the *pro_number* column that stores the project number information.

12. Rewrite the query from Question 11 above to exclude projects located in Edwardsville. You need to use the *pro_location* column that stores the project location in writing your query. Label the columns as specified in Question 11.

13. Rewrite the query from Question 11 above to exclude any group that does not have at least two projects. Label the columns as specified in Question 11.

14. Write a query to provide the Executive Director with the total hours worked per project. Use the *work_pro_number* and *work_hours* columns from the *assignment* table to obtain the project numbers and hours worked, respectively. Label the two columns **Project Number** and **Total Hours**, respectively.

15. Rewrite the query for Question 14 to exclude projects where the total *work_hours* column value is less than 15 hours. Sort the output by **Total Hours** from smallest to largest.

SQL CODING EXERCISES AND QUESTIONS: RIVERBEND DATABASE

1. A manager from the human resources department needs you to write a query to count the number of staff members of the Riverbend Hospital. Count the number of rows in the *staff* table. Label the output column **Number of Staff Members**.

2. The *date_hired* column in the *staff* table stores date hired information for staff members of the Riverbend Hospital. A hospital administrator wishes to present an award at an upcoming organizational award ceremony to the staff member who has worked the longest at the hospital. Write a query to display the date hired for the oldest staff member listed in the table. No special output column label is required.

3. Rewrite the query for Question 2 to display the date hired for the newest staff member at the hospital. No special output column is required.

4. Accountants working on the hospital's annual budgeting process need to know the average salary (*emp_salary*) for staff members and the sum of all staff member salaries. The information is stored in the *staff* table. The result table should have two columns based on a single query. Label the columns **Average Salary** and **Total Salary**. Format the output as $9,999,999.99. HINT: Use CHAR(12). Keep in mind that not all staff members are salaried.

5. Write a query that is comparable to that for Question 4, but this query should list the average wage and total wage for staff members who are paid a wage. Format the output as $999,999.99. Label the columns **Average Wage** and **Total Wage**.

6. A new government reporting regulation requires the hospital to report the number of regular beds in use by the hospital. The *bed_type* codes for these beds are "R1" and "R2". The information is stored in the *bed_type_id* column of the *bed* table. The result table should have a single output column labeled **Number Regular Beds**.

7. A change in the government reporting regulation concerning available hospital beds requires a count by type of all types of beds that are available. Display the information as two columns, one for *bed_type_id* and one for the associated count. The result table should have several rows, one for each bed type. Use a single query. Additionally, the *bed_type_id* output column should be formatted as A15 and have a heading of **Bed Type**. The count column should have a heading of **Number Counted**. Use a GROUP BY clause.

8. Another government regulation requires a report of the number of services provided by the hospital counted by the standard service categories. Display the result table as two columns, one for *service_cat_id* and one for the associated count. The result table should have several rows, one for each service category. Use a single query. The column headings should be "Service Category" and "Number of Services" and the data comes from the *service* table. You need to use a GROUP BY clause.

9. Rewrite the query for Question 8 to exclude the counting of services in categories injections and laboratories (codes = INJ, LAB).

10. Modify the query written for Question 9 to sort the output by the count of the number of services in each category with the largest counts listed first. Label the columns as specified in Question 8.

11. The hospital's chief of surgery needs to know the number of treatments provided by each staff member (use *treatment* table). The result table should have two columns labeled **Staff Member ID** and **Treatment Count**. You need to refer to the

staff_id column that stores the staff member identification and the *service_id* column that stores the service identification provided as a treatment to a patient.

12. Rewrite the query for Question 11 to exclude from the listing staff members providing fewer than 10 treatments. Hint: Use a HAVING clause.

13. Rewrite the query for Question 12 to exclude from the listing staff members providing fewer than 10 treatments and staff members with *staff_id* values of 66432 and 66444.

14. Write a query to provide the hospital budgeting officer with information about the average charge of each treatment for patients by *service_id*. Base the average value on the *service_id* and *actual_charge* columns of the *treatment* table. Order the output by *service_id*. Format the average charge as $999,999.99.

15. Rewrite the query for Question 14 to exclude average charges that are less than $1,000. Order the output by average charge.

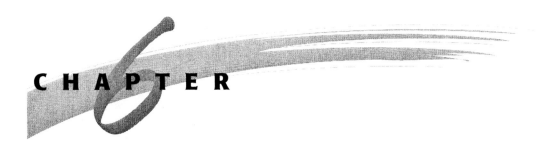

CHAPTER 6

JOINS

This chapter focuses on JOIN operations. Thus far your study of the Structured Query Language (SQL) has focused on writing queries that retrieve data stored in a single table. However, large databases have many related tables. Managers often need information that requires the retrieval of data rows from one or more related tables. For example, a human resources manager may want a listing of employees by name as well as the names of their dependents. This requires retrieving related data rows from both the *employee* and *dependent* tables of the Company database. Queries of this type are termed JOIN operations, and may include data rows from two, three, or even more related tables. Having mastered single table queries, you are not ready to learn to write queries that join multiple tables.

OBJECTIVES

The related tables of a large database are linked through the use of *foreign keys* (FKs) or what are often referred to as *common columns*. In Chapter 2, you learned to create tables that are linked by foreign keys to enforce REFERENTIAL INTEGRITY constraints. In this chapter, you learn to use primary key (PK) and FK columns to join tables together—this enables you to produce a single result table with the data from the joined tables to provide the information that managers need to address increasingly complex problem-solving tasks. Writing table join queries is a task SQL programmers routinely accomplish. Your learning objectives for this chapter include:

- Learn the basic join operation rules.
- Write legacy equijoin and inequality join queries by using the WHERE clause.
- Write equijoin and inequality join queries by using the JOIN keyword.
- Write complex join queries with more than two tables, and more than two columns.
- Write outer join queries.
- Write self-join (recursive) queries.

TYPICAL JOIN OPERATION

Figure 6.1 diagrams two relationships for the *employee* and *department* tables. The figure illustrates the concept of a JOIN operation by connecting related data columns within each table with a line. In fact, Figure 6.1 depicts two different JOIN operations. We first focus on the line that connects the *employee* table's *emp_dpt_number* column with the *department* table's *dpt_no* column. Even though these two columns have different names, the data stored in the columns share a common *domain* of values; that is, the values stored in the *employee* table's *emp_dpt_number* column consists of valid department numbers found in the *department* table's *dpt_no* column. This JOIN operation enables the selection of employees assigned to specific departments.

The second line connects the *employee* table's *emp_ssn* column to the *department* table's *dpt_mgrssn* column. This line represents a second, different JOIN operation that enables the display of detailed information about a department's manager. A typical managerial request might be to prepare a listing of department information that includes the name of each department manager. Because the only information stored in the *department* table about each department's manager is the manager's social security number (SSN) (*dpt_mgrssn*), a JOIN operation of the two tables is necessary.

We begin our study of JOIN operations by focusing on the relationship between the *employee* and *department* tables represented by the common department number values. The query in SQL Example 6.1 lists employee names and department numbers. This is a single-table query—it only retrieves data from the *employee* table.

```
/* SQL Example 6.1 */
SELECT CAST(emp_last_name As CHAR(12)) "Last Name",
       CAST(emp_first_name As CHAR(12)) "First Name",
       CAST(emp_dpt_number As CHAR(4)) "Dept"
FROM employee;

Last Name      First Name   Dept
------------   ------------ ----
Bock           Douglas      7
Amin           Hyder        3
Joshi          Dinesh       7
Zhu            Waiman       7
more rows will be displayed . . .
```

A large organization can have dozens or even hundreds of departments. Thus, the numbers displayed in the department column shown above may not be very meaningful. In fact, they may be meaningless. In this situation, a manager may want the result table to display the department name instead of the department number. This requires you to retrieve information from two tables because department names are stored in the *department* table. Hence, your query needs to join the *employee* and the *department* tables to produce the desired result table.

Joins can be specified in either the FROM or WHERE clauses. The join conditions combine with the WHERE and HAVING search conditions to control the rows that are selected from the tables referenced in the FROM clause. Early standards for SQL specified the use of a WHERE clause to join tables. The newer American National

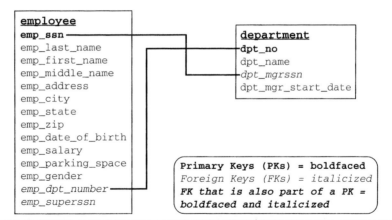

FIGURE 6.1

Standards Institute (ANSI) and International Standards Organization (ISO) ANSI/ISO SQL-92 standard uses the FROM clause to carry out a JOIN operation. The older syntax is, however, still valid, and is expected to remain valid in the future (except for OUTER JOIN operations discussed later in this chapter). We first examine a JOIN operation using the WHERE clause because you are already familiar with WHERE clauses.

Study the query in SQL Example 6.2. In this query the join condition, *e.emp_dpt_number = d.dpt_no*, in the WHERE clause *links* the rows of the two tables, *employee* and *department*, by matching the values in *employee* table's *emp_dpt_number* column to the values in *department* table's *dpt_no* column. Because the query retrieves row data from two tables, each table is listed in the FROM clause. Further, each table is provided with a table *alias name*. The use of an alias name is optional. The *employee* table's alias name is simply the letter "e" whereas the *department* table's alias is the letter "d"—you select an alias name that you prefer to use. A common practice is to use a single letter. Table alias names are used to enable an abbreviated method for referencing a table name within the query. This shorthand method for referring to a table simplifies writing a query. The query is also shown without the use of alias names in SQL Example 6.3.

```
/* SQL Example 6.2 - Query with alias names */
SELECT CAST(emp_last_name As CHAR(12)) "Last Name",
       CAST(emp_first_name As CHAR(12)) "First Name",
       dpt_name "Department Name"
FROM employee e, department d
WHERE e.emp_dpt_number = d.dpt_no;
```

```
/* SQL Example 6.3 - Same query using full table names */
SELECT CAST(emp_last_name As CHAR(12)) "Last Name",
       CAST(emp_first_name As CHAR(12)) "First Name",
       dpt_name "Department Name"
FROM employee, department
WHERE emp_dpt_number = dpt_no;
```

```
Last Name      First Name    Department Name
------------   -----------   -----------------
Bock           Douglas       Production
Amin           Hyder         Admin and Records
Joshi          Dinesh        Production
Zhu            Waiman        Production
more rows will be displayed . . .
```

The newer syntax based on the ANSI/ISO SQL-92 standard writes the join condition explicitly by using a combination of JOIN and ON keywords within the FROM clause. This allows the WHERE clause to be focused on specifying the criteria for selecting the data rows to be included in the result table. This syntax is shown in SQL Example 6.4. Note that the WHERE clause does not handle the join condition. The FROM clause explicitly specifies the JOIN in addition to listing the tables and assigning the aliases. Notice that there is no comma between the table names. The parentheses around the join condition are optional. Finally, notice that the output is identical for both queries. For the rest of the examples in this chapter, we interchangeably use both techniques so that you can learn to specify the join conditions in both the FROM and WHERE clauses.

```
/* SQL Example 6.4 - Query with alias names */
SELECT CAST(emp_last_name As CHAR(12)) "Last Name",
       CAST(emp_first_name As CHAR(12)) "First Name",
       dpt_name "Department Name"
FROM employee e JOIN department d ON (e.emp_dpt_number = d.dpt_no);

Last Name      First Name    Department Name
------------   -----------   -----------------
Bock           Douglas       Production
Amin           Hyder         Admin and Records
Joshi          Dinesh        Production
Zhu            Waiman        Production
more rows will be displayed . . .
```

HOW JOINS ARE PROCESSED

Now that you have seen a basic JOIN query, it is time to learn what SQL is doing for you behind the scenes. Conceptually, when two tables are joined, SQL creates a *Cartesian* product of the tables. A Cartesian product consists of all possible combinations of the rows from each of the tables regardless of whether the rows are related to one another. Therefore, when a table with 10 rows is joined with a table with 20 rows, the Cartesian product is 200 rows ($10 \times 20 = 200$). For example, joining the *employee* table with eight rows and the *department* table with three rows produces a Cartesian product table of 24 rows ($8 \times 3 = 24$).

It is important to understand how JOIN queries are processed to develop your knowledge of this important concept. Therefore, we examine a series of examples to aid you in understanding the JOIN operation process. Table 6.1 shows two tables simply named *table_1* and *table_2*. Each table has a single column named *col_1*. Each table also has three rows with simple alphabetic values stored in the *col_1* column.

A Cartesian product of these tables yields a result table with nine rows ($3 \times 3 = 9$). The query in SQL Example 6.5 that produces the Cartesian product is elementary.

```
/* SQL Example 6.5 */
SELECT *
FROM table_1, table_2;

COL_1 COL_1
_____ _____
a     a
b     a
c     a
a     b
b     b
c     b
a     c
b     c
c     c
```

An examination of the result table reveals that the first row of *table_1* was joined with every row of *table_2*. Likewise, the second row of *table_1* was joined with every row of *table_2*, and so forth.

A Cartesian product result table is normally not very useful. In fact, such a result table can be terribly misleading. As exemplified in SQL Example 6.5, if you execute this type of query for the *employee* and *department* tables, the result table implies that every employee has a relationship with every department, and we know that this is simply not the case.

The query in SQL Example 6.5 requires a join condition in the FROM or the WHERE clause to specify the nature of the relationship between the two tables. This prevents the error of joining rows that are *not* related. SQL Example 6.6 gives the revised query. The join condition (boldfaced) in the WHERE clause specifies that only

TABLE 6.1	
Table_1 *Col_1*	*Table_2* *Col_1*
========	========
a	a
b	b
c	c

related rows are to be displayed in the result table; in other words, where values in *table_1* match the values in *table_2*.

```
/* SQL Example 6.6 */
SELECT *
FROM table_1 t1, table_2 t2
WHERE t1.col_1 = t2.col_1;

COL_1 COL_1
----- -----
a     a
b     b
c     c
```

The join condition in the WHERE clause filters out rows that are not related. Conceptually, it is important to understand that the join condition, whether it is in the WHERE clause or in the FROM clause, is the key to joining tables. A *join condition* defines the criteria to be evaluated for each pair of joined rows.

We next return to SQL Example 6.3 where we join the *employee* and *department* tables; however, we restrict the result table to a listing of employees that work in a specific department. The revised query shown in SQL Example 6.7 specifies the listing of employees in the Production Department (department 7). This is accomplished by using the AND logical operator and adding a condition to the WHERE clause.

```
/* SQL Example 6.7 */
SELECT CAST(emp_last_name As CHAR(12)) "Last Name",
       CAST(emp_first_name As CHAR(12)) "First Name",
       dpt_name "Department Name"
FROM employee e, department d
WHERE e.emp_dpt_number = d.dpt_no
      AND e.emp_dpt_number = 7;

Last Name    First Name      Department Name
-----------  ------------    -------------------
Bock         Douglas         Production
Joshi        Dinesh          Production
Zhu          Waiman          Production
Prescott     Sherri          Production
```

As you can see from SQL Example 6.7, a WHERE clause can both JOIN tables as well as restrict the rows displayed in the result table based on specified criteria. However, if you use the ANSI/ISO SQL-92 syntax for joining tables using the FROM clause, then you can include the join condition and specific data row selection criteria within the FROM clause as shown in SQL Example 6.8. Note that this syntax does not use a WHERE clause.

```
/* SQL Example 6.8 */
SELECT CAST(emp_last_name As CHAR(12)) "Last Name",
```

```
        CAST(emp_first_name As CHAR(12)) "First Name",
        dpt_name "Department Name"
FROM employee e JOIN department d ON (e.emp_dpt_number = d.dpt_no)
     AND e.emp_dpt_number = 7;


Last Name       First Name      Department Name
------------    ------------    ------------------
Bock            Douglas         Production
Joshi           Dinesh          Production
Zhu             Waiman          Production
Prescott        Sherri          Production
```

Alternatively, you can specify the join condition in the FROM clause and specify the specific data row selection criteria in the WHERE clause, as shown in SQL Example 6.9. All three examples produce exactly the same result. The method shown in SQL Example 6.9, however, is the *recommended* method because it separates the listing of join conditions from the specific data row selection criteria. This should add to query understandability and maintainability as the number of joins and specific criteria in a query increase.

```
/* SQL Example 6.9 */
SELECT CAST(emp_last_name As CHAR(12)) "Last Name",
       CAST(emp_first_name As CHAR(12)) "First Name",
       dpt_name "Department Name"
FROM employee e JOIN department d ON (e.emp_dpt_number = d.dpt_no)
WHERE e.emp_dpt_number = 7;


Last Name       First Name      Department Name
------------    ------------    ------------------
Bock            Douglas         Production
Joshi           Dinesh          Production
Zhu             Waiman          Production
Prescott        Sherri          Production
```

JOIN OPERATION RULES

JOINS AND THE SELECT CLAUSE

Now that you have studied several JOIN examples, we review the detailed rules that you need to understand to produce successful JOIN operations. As with any query, a JOIN query always begins with a SELECT clause. List the columns to be displayed in the result table after the SELECT keyword.

Further, the result table column order reflects the order in which column names are listed in the SELECT clause. If you want to modify the order of the columns, you simply rearrange the order of the column listing in the SELECT clause. SQL Example 6.10 moves the Department Name column to the first column position in the result table.

```
/* SQL Example 6.10 */
SELECT dpt_name "Department Name",
    CAST(emp_last_name As CHAR(12)) "Last Name",
    CAST(emp_first_name As CHAR(12)) "First Name"
FROM employee e JOIN department d ON (e.emp_dpt_number = d.dpt_no)
WHERE e.emp_dpt_number = 7;

Department Name       Last Name      First Name
------------------    ------------   ------------
Production            Bock           Douglas
Production            Joshi          Dinesh
Production            Zhu            Waiman
Production            Prescott       Sherri
```

JOIN operations also support the specification of all columns by the use of a simple asterisk (*) in a SELECT clause. The result table for a query like the one shown in SQL Example 6.11 contains all columns from both the *employee* and *department* tables. When the asterisk (*) is used, the column order of the result table is based on the order in which tables are listed in the FROM clause; thus, the order in which the columns are listed is to be all *employee* columns followed by all *department* columns. For purposes of brevity, we have omitted the result table for this query, but you may wish to execute the query yourself to examine the output.

```
/* SQL Example 6.11 */
SELECT *
FROM employee e JOIN department d ON (e.emp_dpt_number = d.dpt_no)
WHERE e.emp_dpt_number = 7;
```

JOINS AND THE FROM CLAUSE

Any SELECT statement that has two or more table names (or view names—see Chapter 8) listed in a FROM clause is a JOIN query. By definition, a JOIN operation retrieves rows from two or more tables.

You can always use the FROM clause to list the tables from which columns are to be retrieved by a JOIN query. The FROM clause listing has a limit of 256 table names—not much of a limit at all because it is unusual to join more than three or four tables in a single SQL statement. The order of table name listings is irrelevant to the production of the result table with the one exception noted above; that is, if you use an asterisk (*) in the SELECT clause, then the column order in the result table reflects the order in which tables are listed in the FROM clause.

As explained earlier, you can specify the join conditions in a FROM clause by explicitly using the JOIN clause within the FROM clause. You can also specify the *type* of JOIN such as INNER, LEFT OUTER, RIGHT OUTER, or FULL OUTER. If you do not specify the *type* of join then, by default, the join operation is always an INNER join. We did not indicate the type of join in any of the example queries thus far. So, they are all examples of INNER join operations. The various OUTER join operations are covered later in this chapter.

JOINS AND THE WHERE CLAUSE

As you learned earlier, the WHERE clause can be used to specify the relationship between tables listed in the FROM clause along with specifying row selection criteria for display in the result table. For all practical purposes, you may specify as many selection criteria as are necessary to produce the desired result table. Additionally, although the queries shown thus far have always specified the JOIN operation before specifying selection criteria, the order of selection criteria or JOIN operations is not important. For example, SQL Example 6.7 can be rewritten, as is shown in SQL Example 6.12. Here the criteria for row selection and table joins in the WHERE clause are reversed, yet the result table output is the same.

```
/* SQL Example 6.12 */
SELECT CAST(emp_last_name As CHAR(12)) "Last Name",
       CAST(emp_first_name As CHAR(12)) "First Name",
       dpt_name "Department Name"
FROM employee e, department d
WHERE e.emp_dpt_number = 7
AND e.emp_dpt_number = d.dpt_no;

Last Name     First Name    Department Name
------------  ------------  ------------------
Bock          Douglas       Production
Joshi         Dinesh        Production
Zhu           Waiman        Production
Prescott      Sherri        Production
```

A note of caution though! The scenario exemplified in SQL Example 6.12 applies only if you are joining tables using the WHERE clause. If you elect to both join tables and specify row selection criteria in a FROM clause as is allowed in the newer ANSI/ISO-92 standard, then you MUST specify the JOIN operation *before* specifying the row selection criteria. Otherwise, SQL Server generates an error message, as illustrated in SQL Example 6.13. This is another good reason to use the JOIN keyword with the FROM clause for joining tables while using the WHERE clause to specify row selection criteria.

```
/* SQL Example 6.13 */
SELECT CAST(emp_last_name As CHAR(12)) "Last Name",
       CAST(emp_first_name As CHAR(12)) "First Name",
       dpt_name "Department Name"
FROM emp_dpt_number = 7 and
     employee e JOIN department d ON (e.emp_dpt_number = d.dpt_no);

Server: Msg 170, Level 15, State 1, Line 5
Line 5: Incorrect syntax near '='.
```

QUALIFYING COLUMN NAMES AND ALIASES

Normally you do not need to create alias names for tables. This is optional. However, when column names are *ambiguous* you must qualify the column names. A column name is ambiguous when the same column name is used in different tables. The Company database described in Appendix A avoids ambiguity by naming each column with a prefix to denote the table to which the column belongs. However, this naming convention is not required. Recall our earlier example with the tables named *Table_1* and *Table_2*. The query used to JOIN these tables is shown in SQL Example 6.14.

```
/* SQL Example 6.14 */
SELECT *
FROM table_1, table_2
WHERE table_1.col_1 = table_2.col_1;

Col_1 Col_1
----- -----
a     a
b     b
c     c
```

Because each table has a column named *col_1*, the column names used in the WHERE clause to accomplish the JOIN operation are *qualified* by referencing the table name, "dot," and the column name. If the column names were not qualified, the query would look like the one shown below, and SQL Server returns an error message. The query shown in SQL Example 6.15 fails to process because of ambiguity in the column names (*col_1*).

```
/* SQL Example 6.15 */
SELECT *
FROM table_1, table_2
WHERE col_1 = col_1;

Server: Msg 209, Level 16, State 1, Line 2
Ambiguous column name 'Col_1'.
```

This error message tells you that you have included a column name somewhere in the query that exists in more than one of the tables listed in the FROM clause. The error is in the WHERE clause; however, it is also possible to make a similar error in the SELECT clause. The SELECT statement shown below fails to qualify the *col_1* name in the SELECT clause, and SQL Server again produces an error message.

```
/* SQL Example 6.16 */
SELECT col_1
FROM table_1, table_2
WHERE table_1.col_1 = table_2.col_1;

Server: Msg 209, Level 16, State 1, Line 2
Ambiguous column name 'Col_1'.
```

As you have seen, an ambiguous column name is qualified by using the DOT (. connector to connect the table name and column name. Sometimes it is easier to qualify column names by using table alias names. As was demonstrated earlier, a table can be assigned an alias name for a query by simply listing a unique identifier for the table name in the FROM clause. Often, a single letter is used as an alias name to reduce keystroke requirements as was done earlier in the JOIN query for the *employee* and *department* tables shown here as SQL Example 6.17.

```
/* SQL Example 6.17 */
SELECT CAST(e.emp_last_name As CHAR(12)) "Last Name",
       CAST(e.emp_first_name As CHAR(12)) "First Name",
       dpt_name "Department Name"
FROM employee e JOIN department d ON (e.emp_dpt_number = d.dpt_no)
WHERE e.emp_dpt_number = 7;

Last Name      First Name      Department Name
-----------    -----------     ---------------
Bock           Douglas         Production
Joshi          Dinesh          Production
Zhu            Waiman          Production
Prescott       Sherri          Production
```

The use of the letters "e" and "d" is completely arbitrary; "t1" and "t2" or any other unique aliases could be used. The important points to learn are:

- The alias name must follow a table name.
- Use a space to separate a table name and its alias name.
- The alias name must be unique within the SELECT statement.

When column names are not identical you are *not* required to qualify them. Sometimes they are qualified anyway because it can be helpful in terms of documenting the query. In this fashion, it becomes clear, for example, that the *dpt_name* column is retrieved from the *department* table. Likewise, the *emp_last_name* and *emp_first_name* columns are retrieved from the *employee* table. Although not required by the database management system processing the SQL statement, the additional qualification may help you and future programmers decipher the query should it ever need to be modified.

JOIN: RELATIONAL OPERATORS

The JOIN operators shown in Table 6.2 determine the basis by which columns are matched, and are called *relational operators*. You may recognize them as the comparison operators that you learned earlier. The most commonly used JOIN operator is the "equal" (=) sign.

JOIN OPERATIONS USING INEQUALITY OPERATORS (<, >, < >)

The JOIN queries covered thus far are termed *equijoins* because the relational operator used in the JOIN operation is the equal sign (=). However, you may use any relational operator in a JOIN query. This query in SQL Example 6.18 uses an inequality operator, the *not equal to* (< >) relational operator.

TABLE 6.2

Operator	Meaning
=	Equal to
<	Less than
>	Greater than
>=	Greater than or equal to
<=	Less than or equal to
!=	Not equal to
<>	Not equal to
!>	Not greater than
!<	Not less than

```
/* SQL Example 6.18 */
SELECT CAST(emp_last_name As CHAR(12)) "Emp Last Name",
       CAST(dep_name AS CHAR(12)) "Dependent Name"
FROM employee e JOIN dependent d ON (e.emp_ssn <> d.dep_emp_ssn)
WHERE e.emp_last_name IN ('Bordoloi', 'Bock')
ORDER BY emp_last_name;

Emp Last Name Dependent Name
------------- --------------
Bock          Jo Ellen
    .             .
    .             .
    .             .
Bock          Rita
Bordoloi      Deanna
    .             .
    .             .
Bordoloi      Allen
```

Query 6.18 produces a result table where the dependent names listed are *not* dependents of the respective employees who are listed. The query may not make a lot of sense to you as an SQL programmer, but its usefulness depends on management's need for the information.

As it happens, JOIN operations using inequality operators are not used very often. Most queries are equijoins because a JOIN operation based on equality often makes the most sense. Conceptually, a JOIN operation involving an inequality operator works the same way as an equijoin. A Cartesian product is formed from the *employee* and *dependent* tables. The result table is then populated based on the inequality JOIN condition and selection criteria.

COMPLEX JOIN OPERATIONS

Although the examples given thus far have joined rows from two tables, you can specify up to 256 tables in a JOIN operation—a very large number. Although it is somewhat common to join three or four tables in a JOIN operation, it would be very

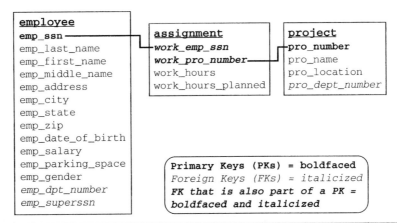

FIGURE 6.2

unusual to exceed this number; thus, it turns out that, for all intensive purposes, you are unlimited when joining tables. You do need to understand that the greater the number of tables included in a JOIN operation, the longer the query takes to process, especially when the tables are large with millions of rows per table.

JOINING THREE TABLES

The example shown in Figure 6.2 joins three tables to produce a result table based on two, different relationships. The bold lines show that the *assignment* table is related to the *employee* table through the employee social security number (SSN) domain of values. Similarly, the *assignment* table is related to the *project* table through the project number domain of values. The *assignment* table is classified as an *association* table because the rows in it relate to or associate both the *employee* and *project* tables simultaneously.

An association table relates or associates two or more base tables where the base tables are related in a many-to-many fashion. Here, the *assignment* table depicts the fact that many employees can be assigned to work on a project, and a project can simultaneously have many employees assigned to it. Association tables are also termed *intersection* or *conjunction* tables.

SQL Example 6.19 uses the FROM clause to the join the three tables depicted in Figure 6.2. This is the most acceptable format for a multiple table join operation.

```
/* SQL Example 6.19 */
SELECT CAST(emp_last_name As CHAR(12)) "Last Name",
       CAST(emp_first_name As CHAR(12)) "First Name",
       '$' + CONVERT (CHAR (12), 1.10*emp_salary, 1) "Raised Salary",
       p.pro_name "Project"
FROM employee e JOIN assignment a ON (e.emp_ssn = a.work_emp_ssn)
                JOIN project p ON (a.work_pro_number = p.pro_number)
WHERE p.pro_name = 'Inventory';
```

```
Last Name      First Name     Raised Salary Project
------------   ------------   ------------- ------------
Amin           Hyder          $27500.000000 Inventory
Zhu            Waiman         $47300.000000 Inventory
Markis         Marcia         $27500.000000 Inventory
```

SQL Example 6.20 uses a WHERE clause to join the three tables. Both queries produce the same result table.

```
/* SQL Example 6.20 */
SELECT CAST(emp_last_name As CHAR(12)) "Last Name",
    CAST(emp_first_name As CHAR(12)) "First Name",
    '$' + CONVERT(CHAR (12), emp_salary * CONVERT(MONEY,1.10), 1)
       "Raised Salary",
    p.pro_name "Project"
FROM employee e, assignment a, project p
WHERE e.emp_ssn = a.work_emp_ssn AND
    a.work_pro_number = p.pro_number AND
    p.pro_name = 'Inventory';

Last Name      First Name     Raised Salary Project
------------   ------------   ------------- ------------
Amin           Hyder          $    27,500.00 Inventory
Zhu            Waiman         $    47,300.00 Inventory
Markis         Marcia         $    27,500.00 Inventory
```

This is a good example of a situation where joining more than two tables produces information that managers may find extremely helpful. The result table shown provides information about what employee salaries would be if each worker on the Inventory project is given a 10% raise. The Raised Salary value is a computed column. The *emp_salary* column value is defined as data type MONEY and is multiplied by 110% (converted to MONEY with the CONVERT statement) to arrive at the Raised Salary value.

Let us take a closer look at these two queries. It may help you to refer to the description of the Company database that is provided in Appendix A. This may seem strange, but did you notice that the *assignment* table does not contribute any columns to the result table? Also none of the columns used to specify the JOIN operation are included in the result table. Even when columns are not represented in a result table, you may still use them to formulate a query.

How many tables you need to include in your JOIN operation depends on the conditional requirements of the management questions that you are trying to answer. You may need to display data only from, say, two tables, as illustrated in SQL Examples 6.19 and 6.20. However, as depicted in Figure 6.2, the two tables, *employee* and *project,* are not directly joinable as they do not have any *direct* relationship represented by 'primary–foreign key' relationships. A typical join condition specifies a foreign key from one table and its associated primary key in the other table. To display data from tables linked through an association table, you may need to join three or four or even more tables. Note, however, that you can join only two tables at a time. That is, you can have only two table names in each join condition. Thus, if you are joining *two* tables then you must have at least *one* join condition; if you are joining *three* tables then you must have at least *two* join conditions; and if you are joining *n* tables, then you must have at least *n* – 1 join conditions.

Examine Figure 6.2 again. The bold lines connecting the tables depict the fact that the JOIN operation involves two different conditions that are stated in SQL Examples 6.19 and 6.20. The first condition joins the *employee* and *assignment* tables based on each employee's SSN. Thus, only employees who are assigned to a project are included in the result table. The second condition joins the *assignment* and *project* tables based on the project number columns in each table. This means that only projects that have associated rows in the *assignment* table can be included in the result table.

```
/* Join conditions in SQL Example 6.19 */
FROM employee e JOIN assignment a
    ON (e.emp_ssn = a.work_emp_ssn)                    /* Condition #1 */
JOIN project p ON (a.work_pro_number = p.pro_number)  /* Condition #2 */
WHERE p.pro_name = 'Inventory';                        /* Condition #3 */

/* Join conditions in SQL Example 6.20 */
WHERE e.emp_ssn = w.work_emp_ssn AND                   /* Condition #1 */
    w.work_pro_number = p.pro_number AND               /* Condition #2 */
    p.pro_name = 'Inventory';                          /* Condition #3 */
```

Finally, there is a third condition that does not join any tables; instead, it specifies the criteria for row selection to restrict the result table rows to only those employees who are working on the project named "Inventory." Conceptually, a Cartesian product of the three tables is formed, and then only those rows satisfying the conditions stated in the FROM or WHERE clause are retained for the result table.

JOINING FOUR TABLES

Figure 6.3 depicts what is termed a *ternary* relationship. Some textbooks on database modeling may also term this type of relationship a gerund. This example comes from the Riverbend Hospital database case described in Appendix B. A ternary relationship is a relationship among three base tables (*staff*, *patient*, and *service*) at the same time, and it is implemented by creating three one-to-many relationships where the three base tables are related to a single association table (*treatment*) by creating foreign key columns in the association table.

Study Figure 6.3. This relationship represents the storage of information about which service (identified by *service_id*) was provided by which staff member (identified by *staff_id*) to which patient (identified by *pat_id*). Many different services can be provided by many different staff members to many different patients. For example, an appendectomy or tonsillectomy can be provided by Dr. Bordoloi or Dr. Bock to patient Smith or patient Jones.

The *treatment* association table has a composite primary key identifier of *treatment_number* and *treatment_date* along with three foreign key columns, *service_id*, *staff_id*, and *patient_id* as links to reference data rows in the three base

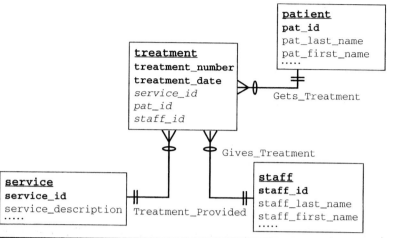

FIGURE 6.3

tables. The *treatment_date* column is included as part of the composite PK because the same service may be provided by the same staff member to the same patient on many different days and times. The chief of physicians may require a report listing the names of patients receiving treatment where the result table displays the patient name, service description, and staff member names as well as the date on which the service was provided by Dr. Quattromani. This requires a join operation that joins the four tables.

SQL Example 6.21 gives a SELECT statement that joins the tables through use of the FROM clause with the JOIN key word. SQL Example 6.22 joins the tables by using a WHERE clause. Both examples produce the same result table.

```
/* SQL Example 6.21 */
SELECT CAST(pat_last_name + ', ' + pat_first_name AS CHAR(20))
    "Patient",
    CAST(s.service_description AS CHAR(20)) "Treatment Svc",
    CAST(staff_last_name + ', ' + staff_first_name AS CHAR(20))
    "Staff Member"
FROM patient p JOIN treatment t ON (p.pat_id = t.pat_id)
    JOIN staff st ON (st.staff_id = t.staff_id)
    JOIN service s ON (s.service_id = t.service_id)
WHERE st.staff_last_name = 'QUATTROMANI'
ORDER BY pat_last_name, pat_first_name;


Patient               Treatment Svc     Staff Member
-------------------   ---------------   -------------------
Ridgeway, Ricardo     EKG/Interp        Quattromani, Toni
Ridgeway, Ricardo     Therapeutic Inj   Quattromani, Toni
```

Note the join conditions in SQL Example 6.21. Each base table (*service*, *staff*, and *patient*) is joined to the *treatment* association table by setting the primary key column from each base table equal to the associated FK column in treatment, for example:

```
FROM patient p JOIN treatment t
    ON (p.pat_id = t.pat_id)              /* condition 1 */
```

SQL Example 6.22 joins the tables and specifies the search criteria in the WHERE clause through liberal use of the AND operator. You may find the syntax in SQL Example 6.22 to be easier to understand than that shown in SQL Example 6.21. Still, the syntax of SQL Example 6.21 is the current ANSI/ISO-92 standard for SQL.

```
/* SQL Example 6.22 */
SELECT CAST(pat_last_name + ', ' + pat_first_name AS CHAR(20))
    "Patient",
    CAST(s.service_description AS CHAR(20)) "Treatment Svc",
    CAST(staff_last_name + ', ' + staff_first_name AS CHAR(20))
    "Staff Member"
FROM patient p, treatment t, staff st, service s
WHERE p.pat_id = t.pat_id AND
    st.staff_id = t.staff_id AND
    s.service_id = t.service_id AND
    st.staff_last_name = 'QUATTROMANI'
ORDER BY pat_last_name, pat_first_name;


Patient                 Treatment Svc           Staff Member
----------------------  ----------------------  ----------------------
Ridgeway, Ricardo       EKG/Interp              Quattromani, Toni
Ridgeway, Ricardo       Therapeutic Inj         Quattromani, Toni
```

JOINING TABLES BY USING TWO COLUMNS

Study the diagram in Figure 6.4. This diagram depicts the relationship at a university where students enroll in course sections. The *enrollment* table stores rows describing enrollments in various course sections and is identified by a composite key that includes the student SSN, course number, and section number columns. The *section* table stores information about sections of courses that are offered in a given term, and has rows identified by a composite key that includes the course number and section number. To join the *enrollment* and *section* tables, the JOIN operation needs to specify a complex JOIN condition that includes both the *course_number* and *section_number* columns from both tables. This is because neither *course_number* nor *section_number* columns are sufficient by themselves to identify the associated rows

FIGURE 6.4

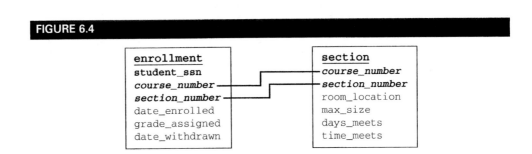

for a given student and section. This example can be extended to three or more columns and to three or more tables.

The SELECT statement that accomplishes the JOIN based on two columns is shown in SQL Example 6.23. Again, this situation arises when the related tables have *composite primary key* columns. You may recall that a composite primary key is required when a single column is not sufficient to guarantee the unique identification of table rows.

```
/* SQL Example 6.23 */
/* Join conditions in the WHERE clause */
SELECT s.course_title "Course Title", e.student_ssn "Student SSN"
FROM enrollment e, section s
WHERE e.course_number = s.course_number AND
      e.section_number = s.section_number;

/* Join conditions in the FROM clause */
SELECT s.course_title "Course Title", e.student_ssn "Student SSN"
FROM enrollment e JOIN section s
    ON (e.course_number = s.course_number) AND
       (e.section_number = s.section_number);
```

OUTER JOIN OPERATIONS

The type of JOIN you have been exposed to thus far is an INNER JOIN, more specifically an *equijoin* where tables are joined based on equality of values in *common* columns. This is what most people refer to when they use the term JOIN. There is, however, another class of join operations called OUTER JOINs. This type of join has a limited, but very important and specific purpose. It is used to identify situations where rows in one table do *not* match rows in a second table, even though the two tables are related. Inner joins drop rows of the first table if they do not have matching rows in the second table. If you want to keep these unmatched rows instead of dropping them, you need to use an OUTER JOIN.

Such would be the situation if management wants to know what products are available but have never been sold to a customer. Clearly management would want to eliminate the stockage of poorly selling products. Whereas a *product* table stores information about all products that are for sale, a *sales* table only stores rows about products that have actually sold. If a product is not listed in the *sales* table, then it has not sold and would have no corresponding rows in the *sales* table. An OUTER JOIN would allow rows from the *product* table to appear in a result table even when there are no matching rows in the *sales* table to which it is joined.

TYPES OF OUTER JOIN

There are three types of outer joins: the LEFT, RIGHT, and FULL OUTER JOIN. They all begin with an INNER JOIN, and then they add back some of the rows that have been dropped. A LEFT OUTER JOIN adds back all the rows that are dropped from the first (left) table in the join condition, and output columns from the second (right) table are set to NULL. A RIGHT OUTER JOIN adds back all the rows that

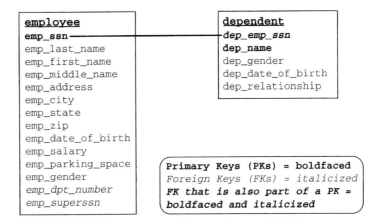

FIGURE 6.5

are dropped from the second (right) table in the join condition, and output columns from the first (left) table are set to NULL. The FULL OUTER JOIN adds back all the rows that are dropped from both the tables. We do not address the FULL OUTER JOIN in this text.

Let us examine an OUTER JOIN situation for the Company database. Suppose management needs a listing of *all* employees of the firm as well as their dependents, if they have any dependents. Figure 6.5 shows the relationship between the *employee* and *dependent* tables. The *dep_emp_ssn* column is a foreign key in the *dependent* table and has a shared domain with the *emp_ssn* column of the *employee* table. Individual dependents have a single employee to whom they belong, but some employees do not have any dependents. This is analogous to the product sales situation described earlier because some products have no sales history. We can use an OUTER JOIN to join the *employee* and *dependent* tables even when employees have no dependents.

The query in SQL Example 6.24 produces the desired result table. Note that, unlike the situation with INNER JOIN, which could be specified either in the WHERE or in the FROM clause, Microsoft recommends that an OUTER JOIN be specified only in the FROM clause because planned future releases of SQL Server may *not* support OUTER JOINs in the WHERE clause. Hence, we provide the syntax for only the FROM clause in our example. In our example, we carry out a LEFT OUTER JOIN because we want the query to return *all* the rows from the *employee* table that is listed on the *left* side of the join condition in the FROM clause. The *dep_name* and *dep_relationship* column values from the *dependent* table (on the *right* side of the join condition) can be set to NULL for the unmatched rows.

```
/* SQL Example 6.24 */
SELECT CAST(emp_last_name As CHAR(12)) "Last Name",
       CAST(emp_first_name As CHAR(12)) "First Name",
       CAST(dep_name As CHAR(12)) "Dependent",
       CAST(dep_relationship As CHAR(8)) "Relationship"
FROM employee LEFT OUTER JOIN dependent ON (emp_ssn = dep_emp_ssn);
```

```
Last Name    First Name   Dependent    Relationship
------------ ------------ ------------ ------------
Bock         Douglas      Deanna       DAUGHTER
Bock         Douglas      Jeffery      SON
Bock         Douglas      Mary Ellen   SPOUSE
Bock         Douglas      Michelle     DAUGHTER
Bock         Douglas      Rachael      DAUGHTER
Amin         Hyder        NULL         NULL
Joshi        Dinesh       NULL         NULL
Zhu          Waiman       Andrew       SON
Zhu          Waiman       Jo Ellen     DAUGHTER
Zhu          Waiman       Susan        SPOUSE
Joyner       Suzanne      Allen        SPOUSE
Bordoloi     Bijoy        Anita        DAUGHTER
Bordoloi     Bijoy        Mita         SPOUSE
Bordoloi     Bijoy        Monica       DAUGHTER
Bordoloi     Bijoy        Rita         DAUGHTER
Markis       Marcia       NULL         NULL
Prescott     Sherri       NULL         NULL

(17 row(s) affected)
```

The result table lists some employees more than once. This happens when an employee has more than one dependent. Also, some employees do not have any dependents listed. The *dep_name* and *dep_relationship* columns of these employees are NULL.

OUTER JOINS AND NULL VALUES

The result table produced by SQL Example 6.24 is useful, but what if your manager wants the listing of employees to be restricted to only those employees who do *not* have any dependents. Again, this is analogous to the sales order situation described earlier where it might be advantageous to produce a listing of only those products that have never sold. This would enable our firm to advertise those products and to get them off our store's shelves. Similarly, management might desire a listing of employees with no dependents to satisfy some governmental reporting requirement.

Now, you may argue that for the small number of rows given in our result table, a manager could manually "line through" any employees listed in the result table that have dependents and obtain the required information. However, if the result table is large with hundreds of rows, most managers will find this approach to be unacceptable. They will want the computer to generate the employee listing.

We can take advantage of the fact that the *dep_name* column is NULL for employees with no dependents, and simply add a criterion to the WHERE clause to exclude employees where the *dep_name* column is NULL. The revised query is shown in SQL Example 6.25.

```
/* SQL Example 6.25 */
SELECT CAST(emp_last_name As CHAR(12)) "Last Name",
       CAST(emp_first_name As CHAR(12)) "First Name",
       CAST(dep_name As CHAR(12)) "Dependent",
       CAST(dep_relationship As CHAR(8)) "Relationship"
```

```
FROM employee LEFT OUTER JOIN dependent ON (emp_ssn = dep_emp_ssn)
WHERE dep_name IS NULL;


Last Name     First Name    Dependent     Relationship
------------  ------------  ------------  ---------------
Amin          Hyder         NULL          NULL
Joshi         Dinesh        NULL          NULL
Markis        Marcia        NULL          NULL
Prescott      Sherri        NULL          NULL
```

Finally, we can tidy up the result table by eliminating the dependent and relationship columns as output because they are NULL. We simply remove these column names from the SELECT clause listing. SQL Example 6.26 produces a clean result table that provides only the essential information needed by management.

```
/* SQL Example 6.26 */
SELECT CAST(emp_last_name As CHAR(12)) "Last Name",
       CAST(emp_first_name As CHAR(12)) "First Name"
FROM employee LEFT OUTER JOIN dependent ON (emp_ssn = dep_emp_ssn)
WHERE dep_name IS NULL;


Last Name     First Name
------------  ------------
Amin          Hyder
Joshi         Dinesh
Markis        Marcia
Prescott      Sherri
```

LEFT AND RIGHT OUTER JOIN OPERATIONS

Eventually, as your career as an SQL programmer blossoms, you may hear arguments about RIGHT OUTER JOIN and LEFT OUTER JOIN. These terms refer to ordering of the tables in a join operation as well as the order by which tables are depicted in an entity–relationship diagram. Earlier we noted that the OUTER JOIN between the *employee* and *dependent* tables is a LEFT OUTER JOIN. However, if the *employee* table were to be depicted on the right side of the relationship in Figure 6.5, and if it is outer joined with the *dependent* table depicted on the left side of the relationship, then we need to specify this join operation as a RIGHT OUTER JOIN.

Now if you think about it, the entity–relationship diagram could just as easily have been drawn with the *dependent* table on the left and the *employee* table on the right. Does the fact that this is now a RIGHT OUTER JOIN make any difference to SQL? The answer is no. The query in SQL Example 6.24 can be rewritten, as is done in SQL Example 6.27. Can you find the slight difference? We have highlighted it for you. The join condition in the FROM clause is now specified as a RIGHT OUTER JOIN, but the query is still returning *all* the rows from the *employee* table. The query has the order of tables names in the JOIN operation in the FROM clause reversed from its earlier specification. Regardless, SQL dutifully produces exactly the same result table!

```
/* SQL Example 6.27 */
SELECT CAST(emp_last_name As CHAR(12)) "Last Name",
       CAST(emp_first_name As CHAR(12)) "First Name",
       CAST(dep_name As CHAR(12)) "Dependent",
       CAST(dep_relationship As CHAR(8)) "Relationship"
FROM dependent RIGHT OUTER JOIN employee
ON (emp_ssn = dep_emp_ssn);

Last Name    First Name    Dependent    Relationship
-----------  -----------   -----------  ---------------

Bock         Douglas       Deanna       DAUGHTER
Bock         Douglas       Jeffery      SON
Bock         Douglas       Mary Ellen   SPOUSE
Bock         Douglas       Michelle     DAUGHTER
Bock         Douglas       Rachael      DAUGHTER
Amin         Hyder         NULL         NULL
Joshi        Dinesh        NULL         NULL
Zhu          Waiman        Andrew       SON
Zhu          Waiman        Jo Ellen     DAUGHTER
Zhu          Waiman        Susan        SPOUSE
Joyner       Suzanne       Allen        SPOUSE
Bordoloi     Bijoy         Anita        DAUGHTER
Bordoloi     Bijoy         Mita         SPOUSE
Bordoloi     Bijoy         Monica       DAUGHTER
Bordoloi     Bijoy         Rita         DAUGHTER
Markis       Marcia        NULL         NULL
Prescott     Sherri        NULL         NULL

(17 row(s) affected)
```

So remember, if a colleague wants to "quibble" about whether a JOIN operation is a LEFT versus RIGHT OUTER JOIN, the difference is basically semantic.

SELF-JOIN OPERATIONS

A self-join operation produces a result table when the relationship of interest exists among rows that are stored within a single table. This means that rows within a table are associated with other rows in the same table. This is the case for the Company's *employee* table for the **supervise** relationship depicted in Figure 6.6. Individual employees are identified by their SSN (*emp_ssn*). Likewise, each employee row has a column to store the supervisor's SSN (*emp_superssn*). A supervisor is simply an employee who performs supervisory functions, and so we did not create a separate table to store supervisor rows. If you study the data for the *employee* table given in Appendix A, you will discover that the employee that is in charge of the Company has a NULL value for the *emp_superssn* column.

The queries in SQL Examples 6.28 and 6.29 produce a listing of employees and their supervisors. SQL Example 6.28 uses the FROM clause whereas SQL Example 6.29 uses the WHERE clause to carry out the self-join. Both queries produce the same output.

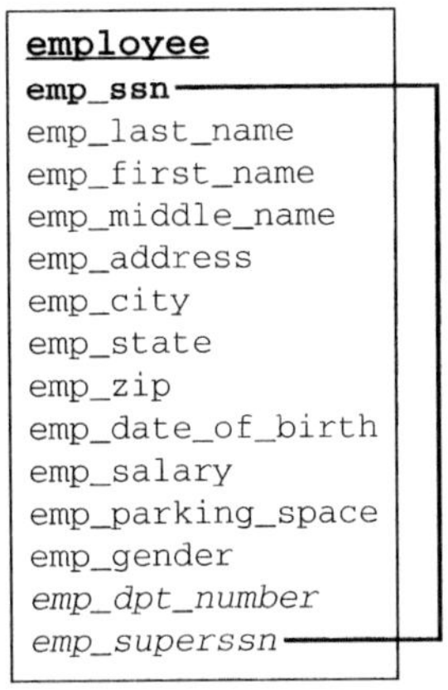

```
employee
emp_ssn
emp_last_name
emp_first_name
emp_middle_name
emp_address
emp_city
emp_state
emp_zip
emp_date_of_birth
emp_salary
emp_parking_space
emp_gender
emp_dpt_number
emp_superssn
```

FIGURE 6.6

```
/* SQL Example 6.28 */
SELECT CAST(e1.emp_last_name + ', ' + e1.emp_first_name As CHAR(20))
        "Supervisor",
     CAST(e2.emp_last_name + ', ' + e2.emp_first_name As CHAR(20))
        "Employee"
FROM employee e1 JOIN employee e2 ON (e1.emp_ssn = e2.emp_superssn)
ORDER BY e2.emp_superssn;
```

```
/* SQL Example 6.29 */
SELECT CAST(e1.emp_last_name + ', ' + e1.emp_first_name As CHAR(20))
        "Supervisor",
     CAST(e2.emp_last_name + ', ' + e2.emp_first_name As CHAR(20))
        "Employee"
FROM employee e1, employee e2
WHERE e1.emp_ssn = e2.emp_superssn
ORDER BY e2.emp_superssn;
```

```
Supervisor             Employee
-------------------    --------------------
Zhu, Waiman            Bock, Douglas
Zhu, Waiman            Joshi, Dinesh
Zhu, Waiman            Prescott, Sherri
Joyner, Suzanne        Markis, Marcia
Joyner, Suzanne        Amin, Hyder
Bordoloi, Bijoy        Zhu, Waiman
Bordoloi, Bijoy        Joyner, Suzanne
```

We use the concatenation operator + (plus sign) in the SELECT clause to concatenate each supervisor's last and first names along with a comma separator between names into a single output column. This is also done for employees that are supervised.

The FROM clause specifies the *employee* table twice, each time with a different table alias name (*e1* and *e2*). This is necessary to create a conceptual Cartesian product between what appear to be two different and separate *employee* tables named *e1* and *e2* when, in fact, we have only a single *employee* table. The alias table names are used to specify the self-join operation in the FROM or the WHERE clause. Rows are joined where an employee's supervisor SSN equals the employee SSN of another row.

Did you notice that one row is missing from the result table? This is the row for employee Bordoloi because he has no supervisor. He is in charge of the Company and, as was noted earlier, the *emp_superssn* column value for Bordoloi's row is NULL. If we wish to produce a complete listing of employees including Bordoloi, we can execute a self-RIGHT OUTER JOIN, as is done in SQL Example 6.30.

```
/* SQL Example 6.30 */
SELECT CAST(e1.emp_last_name + ', ' + e1.emp_first_name As CHAR(20))
       "Supervisor",
    CAST(e2.emp_last_name + ', ' + e2.emp_first_name As CHAR(20))
       "Employee"
FROM employee e1 RIGHT OUTER JOIN employee e2 ON (e1.emp_ssn =
e2.emp_superssn)
ORDER BY e2.emp_superssn;

Supervisor                 Employee
-------------------        -------------------
NULL                       Bordoloi, Bijoy
Zhu, Waiman                Prescott, Sherri
Zhu, Waiman                Bock, Douglas
Zhu, Waiman                Joshi, Dinesh
Joyner, Suzanne            Amin, Hyder
Joyner, Suzanne            Markis, Marcia
Bordoloi, Bijoy            Zhu, Waiman
Bordoloi, Bijoy            Joyner, Suzanne
```

SUMMARY

In this chapter you learn to write queries to display information that is retrieved from related tables. You can use either the FROM or the WHERE clause to produce join operations for up to 256 tables at a time, although two, three, or four tables are more common. The recommended method for joining tables is through use of the JOIN keyword within a FROM clause.

A join of more than two tables requires that you specify a relatively more complex join condition that uses the AND logical operator. You also learn how to join two or more tables that have composite primary keys.

You learn to use outer join operations to produce queries where tables have rows that may or may not have related rows in other tables. Finally, you learn how to use a self-join operation to join rows from a table that are related to rows in the same table. Completing the review exercises will enable you to master the basic concepts associated with joining tables. You should now have a basic understanding of the process that the SQL Server uses to execute a join query.

REVIEW EXERCISES

LEARN THESE TERMS

Alias name.   A shorthand method for referring to a table to simplify query writing.

Ambiguous column names.   When two tables have columns named with identical names. The column names must be qualified.

Association table.   A table that relates or associates two other tables where the relationship between those two other tables would be many to many.

Cartesian product.   A result table consists of all possible combinations of the rows from each of the tables.

Common column.   Another term for a foreign key in a table.

Composite primary key.   When a table is identified uniquely by more than one column because a single column is not sufficient to guarantee uniqueness.

Concatenate operator.   A + sign used to concatenate two or more column values or literals for display as a single column.

Domain.   A specified set of values that are valid for store in a column of a database table.

Equijoin.   A join operation that uses an equal sign as the relational operator.

Foreign key.   A column used to link a table to another related table. It may also be an internal link within the table used to link rows with other related rows.

JOIN.   An operation used to connect (link) two or more tables based on a common domain of values stored to common columns or foreign key columns.

OUTER JOIN operation.   Allows rows from one table to appear in a result table even if there is no matching value in the table to which it is joined.

SELF-JOIN operation.   A join operation that produces a result table when the relationship of interest exists among rows that are stored within a single table.

Ternary relationship.   A relationship among three base tables at the same time.

CONCEPTS QUIZ

1. Explain the concept of a *domain* of values, and relate this concept to join operations.
2. Which clauses in a SELECT statement can be used to join tables and how is this typically accomplished?
3. What is an alias table name? Is it optional or mandatory?
4. What is a Cartesian product? Why is it important?
5. What specifies the order by which columns are displayed in a result table produced by a JOIN operation where only specific columns are selected?
6. What specifies the order by which columns are displayed in a result table produced by a JOIN operation where all columns are selected through use of an asterisk (*) in the SELECT clause?
7. You have written a query that fails to execute. The SQL Server returns the following error message. What do you need to do to correct the error condition?

   ```
   ORA-00918: column ambiguously defined
   ```

8. You need to qualify a column named *emp_ssn* that is stored in both the *employee* and *benefits* tables. How do you refer to this column in a FROM or WHERE clause that has no alias names?
9. Assume that the alias names for the *employee* and *benefits* tables referenced in Question 8 above are "e" and "b," respectively. Now how would you reference the ambiguous *emp_ssn* columns?
10. Why would you qualify column names that are NOT ambiguous?

11. What is the limit on using different selection criteria in the WHERE clause of a SELECT statement that is joining tables?
12. What is an equijoin as opposed to an inequality join?
13. What is the maximum number of tables that can be listed in a JOIN operation?
14. What is an association table?
15. When would your JOIN query have to join two or more tables by using more than one column from each table in the JOIN condition?
16. What is an OUTER JOIN?
17. Suppose that our firm tracks repair parts inventory in a table named *inventory* and the use of those parts in a second table named *parts_used*. What type of JOIN would be used to produce a listing of parts that have not been used and how would the JOIN operation conceptually produce the listing?
18. Continuing with the situation described in Question 17 above, suppose that some parts are manufactured by using other parts from inventory; thus, there is a relationship among the rows within the *inventory* table. What type of JOIN would be used to produce a listing of which parts are used to manufacture other parts?

SQL CODING EXERCISES AND QUESTIONS: COMPANY DATABASE

In answering the SQL exercises and questions, submit a copy of each command that you execute and any messages that SQL Server generates while executing your SQL commands. Also list the output for any result table that is generated by your SQL statements. Unless stated otherwise in the question, always use the ANSI/ISO-92 standard technique of specifying join conditions with a JOIN keyword in the FROM clause when answering these exercises and questions.

1. Write a query to produce a result table that is a Cartesian product of the *department* and *dept_locations* tables. The result table should include the *dpt_no* and *dpt_name* columns from *department* and the *dpt_location* column from *dept_locations*.
2. The Cartesian product produced in Question 1 above is not terribly useful. A new manager in the production area needs a report that shows where departments are located. Alter the query for Question 1 above to restrict row output by joining the two tables.
3. The manager in the human resources department needs a listing of department managers and their salaries and assigned parking spaces. The query must display the department number (*dpt_no*), department name (*dpt_name*), employee first and last name (concatenate the *emp_first_name* and *emp_last_name* columns into a single column), employee salary (*emp_salary*), and employee parking space (*emp_parking_space*). Use the *employee* and *department* tables. Name the columns in the result table as follows: Dept #., Department, Employee, Salary, and Parking, respectively. Use CAST and CONVERT statements to produce a listing that fits easily on one page.
4. The Company's vice-president for project management wants to know which projects are controlled by which departments. The result table needs to display the department name (*dpt_name*), project number (*pro_number*), project name (*pro_name*), and project location (*pro_location*). Give each output column an appropriate column name.

5. Revise the query written for Question 4 to restrict output to projects located in Edwardsville or supervised by the production department.

6. The Company's vice-president for project management needs a listing of all employees and the number of hours they have worked on various projects. The result table should list the employee's last and first names (*emp_last_name* and *emp_first_name*), project number (*work_pro_number*), and hours worked (*work_hours*). The result table should list all employees, whether they are assigned to work on a project. Use alias names for the table names. Give each column an appropriate column name. Use CAST and CONVERT commands to produce a listing that fits easily on one page. Sort the output by *emp_last_name* and *emp_first_name*. Which employee or employees are assigned to a project, but have not worked any hours on a project?

7. Revise the query for Question 6 above to only list employees who have *not* worked any hours for an assigned project. This provides the vice-president of project management with a "needs to be motivated" list of employees.

8. Revise the query for Question 6 above. Replace the project number as an output column with the project name (*pro_name*). The project name information must be retrieved from the *project* table. Rename the column Project. All other requirements remain the same.

9. The human resources manager needs a listing of employees by last name, their dependents first name, and dependent birth dates. The relevant output columns are *emp_last_name* from the *employee* table and *dep_name* and *dep_date_of_birth* from the *dependent* table. Use alias table names. Name each column appropriately. Sort the result table by *emp_last_name*. Use the CAST statement to produce a listing that fits easily on one page.

10. Produce a listing of employees that are supervised by the manager of department 7. The result table should have the following columns: Manager Last Name, Department Name, and Employee Last Name. Name each column "Supervisor," "Department," and "Employee Supervised," respectively. Be careful in determining the tables and the columns that are required to produce the result table.

11. Revise the query written for Question 10 above to specify the entire JOIN operation in the WHERE clause instead of the FROM clause.

12. Produce a query that lists all employee last names, employee gender, dependent names, and dependent gender for those employees who have dependents of the opposite gender. Also list the dependent relationship. The columns needed in the result table are *emp_last_name*, *emp_gender*, *dep_name*, *dep_gender*, and *dep_relationship*. Name each output column appropriately. Use the CAST command to reformat the output columns to produce a listing that fits easily on one page. Sort the result table by *emp_last_name*.

13. Revise the query written for Question 12 above to specify the entire JOIN operation in the WHERE clause instead of the FROM clause.

SQL CODING EXERCISES AND QUESTIONS: RIVERBEND DATABASE

1. Several physicians have requested that you write a query that displays the patient history for hospital patients. Your result table displays the *pat_id* and *pat_last_name* columns from the patient table and the *note_comment* column from

the *patient_note* table. Join the tables and use the default column headings. Submit just the output from the first three patient rows displayed. How many rows in the result table are produced by your query?

2. Modify the query for Question 1 to only list the patient history for the patient with identification 100303. All other requirements remain the same.

3. The hospital's human resources manager needs a listing of staff members and the name of the ward or department to which they are assigned. The result table should display each staff member's last and first name (*staff_last_name* and *staff_first_name*) concatenated as a single column with the heading "Staff Member" as well as a column listing the ward or department name (*ward_dept_name*). These columns come from the *staff* and *ward_dept* tables. Sort the output by the ward and department name first, and then by staff member name.

4. The chief of surgery requires a listing of services provided by service category. Your query uses the *service* and *service_cat* tables. Display four columns as follows: *service_cat_id*, *service_cat_desc*, *service_id*, and *service_description*. Use headings of "Category," "Category Description," "Service," and "Service Description," respectively. Sort the output by *service_cat_id,* then by *service_id*.

5. Revise the query for Question 4 to restrict the output to service categories with identifiers of 'CAR' and 'LAB'. All other requirements remain the same.

6. The chief of hospital resource utilization needs a listing of patients assigned to beds. The result table needs to include the patient name (last and first names concatenated as a single column), bed number, and bed type identifier. These columns are *pat_last_name*, *pat_first_name*, *bed_number*, and *bed_type_id* from the *patient* and *bed* tables. Use meaningful column names and sort the result table rows by the bed number.

7. The chief of hospital resource utilization is happy with the listing produced for Question 6, but now requests that you replace the *bed_type_id* column with the *bed_description* column from the *bed_type* table. Your new query joins three tables.

8. The chief of hospital resource utilization is visiting you again, this time to ask you to add a fourth column for the result table produced for Question 7. Add the *room_description* column from the *room* table. Display this column as 15 characters. Your new query joins four tables.

9. There is concern about patient care. Revise the query for Question 6 to list patients *not* yet assigned to a bed. The result table needs to include the patient name (last and first names concatenated as a single column) and bed number. This second column should be null. Sort the result table by patient last and then first names.

10. The chief of physicians requires a listing of patients receiving treatment. The result table must display the patient name (last and first concatenated from the *patient* table), *service_description* column (*service* table), and staff member name providing the treatment (last and first name concatenated from the *staff* table). Sort the result table by the patient last then first name. Your query joins four tables. Use CAST statements to restrict the result table to displaying each of the three columns as CHAR(20).

11. Rewrite the query for Question 10 above by specifying the entire JOIN operation in the WHERE clause instead of the FROM clause.

12. The chief of pharmacy requires a listing of patients receiving prescriptions. The result table must display the patient name (last and first concatenated from the *patient* table), medicine common name (*med_name_common* from the *medicine* table), and staff member who prescribed the medicine (last and first name concatenated from the *staff* table). Sort the result table by the patient last then first name. Your query joins four tables. Use CAST statements to restrict the result table to displaying each of the three columns as CHAR(20).

13. Rewrite the query for Question 12 above by specifying the entire JOIN operation in the WHERE clause instead of the FROM clause.

14. Modify the query for Question 12 to display rows only for patients prescribed Demerol.

15. Modify the query for Question 12 to only display rows for patients prescribed medicine by Dr. Toni Quattromani (*staff_id* = 66425).

16. Modify the query for Question 12 to display rows for patients either who were prescribed Lanoxin or where the doctor writing the prescription was Dr. Quattromani.

CHAPTER 7

SUBQUERIES

Thus far you have learned to write queries where all the information needed to specify row retrieval criteria is known at *design time*. The term *design time* simply means that you are in the process of writing or designing a query. This contrasts with *run time,* which refers to the actual execution and processing of a query. In this chapter you expand your understanding of the SELECT statement to include the topic of subqueries. Quite simply, a *subquery* is a query within a query. Subqueries enable you to write queries that select data rows for criteria that are actually developed while the query is executing at *run time*.

OBJECTIVES

To understand the subquery approach to information retrieval, you first review what you have learned to this point about the SELECT statement. Your learning objectives for this chapter include:

- Learn the formal subquery definition and write a subquery.
- Learn the subquery restrictions.
- Use the IN operator when writing a subquery.
- Nest subqueries at multiple levels.
- Use comparison operators when writing a subquery.
- Use the ALL and ANY keywords when writing a subquery.
- Write a *correlated subquery* including the use of the EXISTS operator.
- Use the ORDER BY clause when writing a subquery.

SUBQUERY EXAMPLE

Structured Query Language (SQL) Example 7.1 queries the *employee* table. In this example you, as the SQL programmer, know at design time that you want to retrieve employee information where employee salaries are at or above $25,000, and employees work in department 3 or 7. Additionally, the actual criteria values used in row selection are hard coded—$25,000 for the employee salary and departments 3 and 7 for the department number.

```
/* SQL Example 7.1 */
SELECT CAST(emp_last_name As CHAR(12)) "Last Name",
       CAST(emp_first_name As CHAR(12)) "First Name",
       emp_dpt_number "Dept",
       '$' + CONVERT(CHAR (10), emp_salary, 1) "Salary"
FROM employee
WHERE emp_salary >= 25000
      AND emp_dpt_number IN (3, 7);

Last Name       First Name     Dept     Salary
-----------     -----------    ------   -----------
Bock            Douglas         7       $ 30,000.00
Amin            Hyder           3       $ 25,000.00
Joshi           Dinesh          7       $ 38,000.00
more rows are displayed . . .
```

However, suppose you need to write a query where the criteria values for a WHERE clause are unknown at design time. As an example, consider a situation where the human resources manager needs a list of the names of all employees who earn a salary equal to the minimum salary amount paid within your organization. The problem is that at design time, you do not know what the minimum salary amount is. Further, over time, the minimum salary will surely change as employee's are hired or leave the firm, and as salaries change.

Let us begin by breaking the query into two subtasks. First, write a query to determine the Company's minimum salary amount. This is accomplished in SQL Example 7.2.

```
/* SQL Example 7.2 */
SELECT MIN(emp_salary) "Min Salary"
FROM employee;

Min Salary
--------------------
25000.0000
```

You could now proceed by substituting the value $25,000 for the minimum employee salary into the WHERE clause of a second query. Of course, every time the minimum employee salary changes, you need to make a minor revision to the WHERE clause to specify the new minimum salary value.

The subquery approach allows you to combine these two separate queries into one query as is illustrated in SQL Example 7.3. Notice that the subquery is essentially the first query from SQL Example 7.2 that you used in the two-part query approach. Also, the subquery is the object of the equal comparison operator (=).

```
/* SQL Example 7.3 */
SELECT CAST(emp_last_name As CHAR(12)) "Last Name",
       CAST(emp_first_name As CHAR(12)) "First Name",
       '$' + CONVERT(CHAR(10), emp_salary, 1) "Salary"
FROM employee
WHERE emp_salary =
    (SELECT MIN(emp_salary)
     FROM employee);


Last Name      First Name     Salary
------------   ------------   ------------
Amin           Hyder          $ 25,000.00
Markis         Marcia         $ 25,000.00
Prescott       Sherri         $ 25,000.00
```

Okay, so the subquery does not appear to be such a big deal. In fact, you can quickly scan the *employee* table listed in Appendix A and find the same result. What if the *employee* table has thousands or even millions of rows? The query in SQL Example 7.3 produces a quick listing whereas the manual approach could take hours or even days to complete the task.

This is a very important learning point—you should note that there are no hard-coded parameters in the WHERE clause except for the table and column names. The criteria for row selection used for the WHERE clause come from the result table produced by the subquery. We say that data for the subquery is derived at *run time*. As such, the value returned by this subquery can, and most probably changes depending on the contents of a table, yet the query always produces accurate and dependable results without any modification whatsoever.

DEFINITION OF SUBQUERY

Now that you have seen an example subquery, it may help you to learn the concept by formally defining subqueries.

FORMAL DEFINITION

As stated earlier, a subquery is a query inside another query. More formally, it is the use of a SELECT statement inside one of the clauses of another SELECT statement. In fact, a subquery can also be nested inside INSERT, UPDATE, and DELETE statements. In fact, a subquery can be contained inside another subquery, which is inside another subquery, and so forth. A subquery is allowed any place that an expression is allowed providing the subquery returns a single, *scalar* value.

The subquery in SQL Example 7.3 is an example of a subquery inside a WHERE clause. This is termed a *nested subquery,* an *inner query,* or an *inner select.* The term *outer query* is sometimes used to refer to a SELECT statement that contains a subquery.

Because it can be used any place where an expression is allowed, providing it returns a single value, a subquery can also be listed as an object in a FROM clause listing. This is termed an *inline view* because when a subquery is used as part of a FROM clause, it is treated like a virtual table or view (views are covered in Chapter 8). In this chapter, we focus on the use of subqueries with WHERE and HAVING clauses of SELECT statements. Subqueries with FROM clauses are not covered because the technique is not used very often.

SQL Server allows a maximum nesting of 32 subqueries; however, you are more likely to be limited by available memory. In practice, the limit of 32 levels is not really a limit at all because it is rare to encounter subqueries nested beyond three or four levels. In fact, the practice of nesting one SELECT statement inside another is the reason for the use of the word *structured* in the name Structured Query Language.

SUBQUERY TYPES

There are three basic types of subqueries. We study each of these in the remainder of this chapter.

1. Subqueries that operate on lists by use of the IN operator or with a comparison operator modified by the ANY or ALL optional keywords. These subqueries can return a group of values, but the values must be from a single column of a table. In other words, the SELECT clause of the subquery must contain only one parameter (i.e., only one column name, only one expression, *or* only one aggregate function).

2. Subqueries that use an unmodified comparison operator ($=, <, >, <>$). These subqueries must return only a single, *scalar* value.

3. Correlated subqueries which (unlike regular subqueries) depend on data provided by the outer query. This type of subquery also includes subqueries that use the EXISTS operator to test the *existence* of data rows satisfying specified criteria.

SUBQUERY SYNTAX: GENERAL RULES

A subquery SELECT statement is very similar to the SELECT statement used to begin a regular or outer query. The complete syntax of a subquery is:

```
( SELECT [DISTINCT] subquery_select_parameter
  FROM {table_name | view_name}
               {table_name | view_name} ...
  [WHERE search_conditions]
  [GROUP BY column_name [,column_name ] ...]
  [HAVING search_conditions] )
```

You should notice a few minor differences between a subquery and regular query syntax. For example, the ORDER BY clause cannot be used in writing the subquery part of a query unless the TOP keyword is specified; thus, we do not show the use of the ORDER BY clause in the standard syntax. There are additional clauses that are restricted including the COMPUTE and FOR BROWSE clauses—these clauses are beyond the scope of this text. Subqueries can be nested inside both the WHERE and HAVING clauses of an outer SELECT, or inside another subquery. Additionally, a subquery is always enclosed in parentheses.

SUBQUERY RESTRICTONS

CLAUSE RESTRICTIONS

Generally speaking, a SELECT clause of a subquery contains only one expression, only one aggregate function, or only one column name. Additionally, the value or values returned by a subquery must be *join compatible* with the WHERE or HAVING clause of the outer query. This last point is made clearer through the example SELECT statement shown in SQL Example 7.4. This query lists the names of employees who have dependents, a typical type of listing requested by human resources managers. The domain of values in the *dependent* table's *dep_emp_ssn* column is all valid employee Social Security numbers (SSNs). Thus, the values returned from this column in the *dependent* table in the subquery are join compatible with values stored in the *employee* table's *emp_ssn* column of the outer query because they are the same type of data and the data values come from the same domain of possible values.

```
/* SQL Example 7.4 */
SELECT CAST(emp_last_name As CHAR(12)) "Last Name",
       CAST(emp_first_name As CHAR(12)) "First Name"
FROM employee
WHERE emp_ssn IN
   (SELECT dep_emp_ssn
    FROM dependent);

Last Name First Name
--------- ----------

Bock      Douglas
Zhu       Waiman
Joyner    Suzanne
Bordoloi  Bijoy
```

Notice that the *emp_last_name* and *emp_first_name* columns are not stored in the *dependent* table. These columns only occur in the *employee* table. The strategy used in developing this query first focuses on producing an intermediate result table that contains the employee SSNs for those employees who have dependents. This is accomplished by the subquery.

Next the outer SELECT statement qualifies the employee names to be displayed (employee rows) through use of the IN operator. Any employees with an SSN that is IN the list produced by the subquery have their data row displayed in the final result table.

DATA-TYPE JOIN COMPATIBILITY

In addition to concerns about the domain of values returned from a subquery, the data type of the returned column value or values must be *join compatible*. Join compatible data types are data types that SQL Server automatically converts when matching data in criteria conditions. For example, it would not make any sense to compare the values stored in the *emp_ssn* column of the *employee* table to values stored in *dep_date_of_birth* column of the *dependent* table because the *emp_ssn* column is the data type CHAR and the *dep_date_of_birth* column is the data type DATETIME. Attempts to compare values from these two columns would be like comparing apples to oranges.

As we learn in Chapter 2, there are a fairly small number of Transact Structured Query Language (T-SQL) data types, but these data types enable you to store all types of data. Although T-SQL data types vary somewhat from those specified by the American National Standards Institute (ANSI) standard for SQL, SQL Server maps the ANSI standard data types to the T-SQL data types. For example, SQL Server automatically converts among any of the following ANSI numeric data types when making comparisons of numeric values because they all map into the T-SQL NUMERIC data type.

- int (integer)
- smallint (small integer)
- decimal
- float

Remember that SQL Server does not make comparisons based on column names. Columns from two tables that are compared may have different names as long as they have a shared domain and the same data type or convertible data types.

JOIN-COMPATIBLE DATA COLUMNS

Table 7.1 shows columns from two different tables with different column names. Both of these columns store student identification values. They are join compatible because they store the same data type.

NOT JOIN COMPATIBLE

Table 7.2 shows two columns with different types that have the same column name. Even though the column names are identical, and even though both columns store student identification values, one column is CHAR and the other is SMALLINT. Because these data types are different, SQL server fails to process the join request—they are not join compatible.

TABLE 7.1

Column Name	Data Type
stu_id	CHAR
student_id	CHAR

TABLE 7.2

Column Name	Data Type
stu_id	CHAR
stu_id	SMALLINT

OTHER RESTRICTIONS

There are additional restrictions for subqueries.

- The DISTINCT keyword *cannot* be used in subqueries that include a GROUP BY clause.
- Subqueries cannot manipulate their results internally. This means that a subquery cannot include the ORDER BY clause (unless a TOP keyword appears in the SELECT clause), the COMPUTE clause, or the INTO keyword. As you may recall, the INTO keyword is used to create temporary tables and is not applicable to subqueries.
- Output in a result table can only include columns from a table that is named in the FROM clause of the outer query—if a table name appears only in a subquery, then the result table cannot contain columns from that table.

SUBQUERIES AND IN OPERATOR

IN OPERATOR

The IN operator should be familiar to you. In earlier chapters you use it to write queries that defined row selection criteria based on the use of lists of data enclosed in parenthesis. The only difference in the use of the IN operator with subqueries is that the list does not consist of hard-coded values. The query shown in SQL Example 7.5 illustrates the use of hard-coded department numbers of 1 and 7 as values of the IN keyword.

```
/* SQL Example 7.5 */
SELECT CAST(emp_last_name As CHAR(12)) "Last Name",
       CAST(emp_first_name As CHAR(12)) "First Name",
       emp_dpt_number "Dept"
FROM employee
WHERE emp_dpt_number IN (1, 7);


Last Name      First Name    Dept
------------   ------------  -------
Bock           Douglas       7
Joshi          Dinesh        7
Zhu            Waiman        7
Bordoloi       Bijoy         1
Prescott       Sherri        7
```

The WHERE clause of a query that includes the IN operator used with a subquery takes the general form shown as follows:

```
WHERE <expression> [NOT] IN (subquery)
```

Now let us turn to an example with a subquery where the IN keyword operates on a list of values returned by an inner subquery. In this situation, the values returned are not hard coded—they can vary over time. Suppose that a manager i the human resources department requires a listing of employees that have male dependents, but not a listing of the actual dependents themselves. We can write a subquery that retrieves the employee SSN (*dep_emp_ssn*) from the *dependent* table where the dependent's gender is male. The outer query then lists employees that have an employee SSN (*emp_ssn*) that is found in the listing produced by the subquery, as illustrated in SQL Example 7.6.

```
/* SQL Example 7.6 */
SELECT CAST(emp_last_name As CHAR(12)) "Last Name",
       CAST(emp_first_name As CHAR(12)) "First Name"
FROM employee
WHERE emp_ssn IN
    (SELECT dep_emp_ssn
     FROM dependent
     WHERE dep_gender = 'M');

Last Name      First Name
-----------    ------------
Bock           Douglas
Zhu            Waiman
Joyner         Suzanne
```

Let us review the conceptual steps involved in evaluating the query. First, the subquery returns the SSNs of those employees that have male dependents from the *dependent* table.

```
/* SQL Example 7.7 */
SELECT dep_emp_ssn
FROM dependent
WHERE dep_gender = 'M';

dep_emp_ssn
-----------
999111111
999444444
999555555
```

There are three male dependents and the intermediate result table produced by the subquery lists the SSNs of the employees to which these dependents belong. Next, these SSN values are substituted into the outer query as the listing that is the object of the IN operator. So, from a conceptual perspective, the outer query now looks like the following:

```
/* SQL Example 7.8 */
SELECT CAST(emp_last_name As CHAR(12)) "Last Name",
       CAST(emp_first_name As CHAR(12)) "First Name"
FROM employee
WHERE emp_ssn IN (999444444, 999555555, 999111111);
```

```
Last Name      First Name
-----------    -----------
Bock           Douglas
Zhu            Waiman
Joyner         Suzanne
```

The preceding queries, like many subqueries, can also be formulated as *join queries*. As you may recall from your study of Chapter 6, a join query connects the *employee* and *dependent* tables based on the common domain of values stored in the *employee* table's *emp_ssn column* and the *dependent* table's *dep_emp_ssn* column. The SQL Example 7.9 illustrates this join query approach.

```
/* SQL Example 7.9 */
SELECT CAST(emp_last_name As CHAR(12)) "Last Name",
       CAST(emp_first_name As CHAR(12)) "First Name"
FROM employee e JOIN dependent d ON (e.emp_ssn = d.dep_emp_ssn)
WHERE d.dep_gender = 'M';

Last Name      First Name
-----------    -----------
Bock           Douglas
Zhu            Waiman
Joyner         Suzanne
```

Both the join and the subquery version produce identical result tables, although the order of the rows in the result table may differ. Each query is equally correct. This begs the question, "Which approach is most appropriate?" The general, basic rules of thumb are:

- Use a subquery when the result table displays columns from a single table.
- Use a join query when the result displays columns from two or more tables.
- Use a join query when the existence of values must be checked with the EXISTS operator—a join query may perform better than a subquery. The EXISTS operator is discussed later in this chapter.

NOT IN OPERATOR

Like the IN operator, the NOT IN operator can take the result of a subquery as the operator object. Earlier we produced listing of employees with dependents. Suppose that a human resources manager, to meet a government-reporting requirement, requires a listing of employees who do *not* have any dependents. The NOT IN operator is especially good for producing this type of result table, as shown in SQL Example 7.10.

```
/* SQL Example 7.10 */
SELECT CAST(emp_last_name As CHAR(12)) "Last Name",
       CAST(emp_first_name As CHAR(12)) "First Name"
FROM employee
```

```
WHERE emp_ssn NOT IN
    (SELECT dep_emp_ssn
    FROM dependent);

Last Name        First Name
-----------      -----------
Amin             Hyder
Joshi            Dinesh
Markis           Marcia
Prescott         Sherri
```

The subquery produces an intermediate result table containing the SSNs of employees who have dependents in the *dependent* table. Conceptually, the outer query compares each row of the *employee* table against the result table. If the employee SSN is *not* found in the result table produced by the inner query, then it is included in the final result table.

MULTIPLE LEVELS OF NESTING

Thus far we have studied subqueries nested one level in depth. However, subqueries may themselves contain subqueries. When the WHERE clause of a subquery has as its object another subquery, these are termed *nested subqueries*. The manager of the project named Order Entry requires a listing of employees that worked more than 10 hours on the project. A subquery is appropriate because the result table only lists columns from a single table—the *employee* table. The result table produced by SQL Example 7.11 only displays employee last and first names.

```
/* SQL Example 7.11 */
SELECT CAST(emp_last_name As CHAR(12)) "Last Name",
       CAST(emp_first_name As CHAR(12)) "First Name"
FROM employee
WHERE emp_ssn IN
    (SELECT work_emp_ssn
    FROM assignment
    WHERE work_hours > 10 AND work_pro_number IN
        (SELECT pro_number
        FROM project
        WHERE pro_name = 'Order Entry') );

Last Name        First Name
-----------      -----------
Bock             Douglas
Prescott         Sherri
```

To understand how this query executes, we begin our examination with the lowest subquery. We execute it independently of the outer queries. It is important to note that this subquery is useful where the project name is known, but the associated project number is not known. SQL Example 7.12 gives the query and result table. The result is a single column from a single row known as a scalar result, meaning a single value is returned by the query (you study the meaning of this term in detail later in this chapter).

```
/* SQL Example 7.12 */
SELECT pro_number
FROM project
WHERE pro_name = 'Order Entry';

pro_number
----------
1
```

Now, let us substitute the project number into the IN operator list for the intermediate subquery and execute it, as shown in SQL Example 7.13. The intermediate result table lists two employee SSNs for employees that worked more than 10 hours on project 1.

```
/* SQL Example 7.13 */
SELECT work_emp_ssn
FROM assignment
WHERE work_hours > 10 AND work_pro_number IN (1);

work_emp_ssn
------------
999111111
999888888
```

Finally, we substitute these two SSNs into the IN operator listing for the outer query in place of the subquery.

```
/* SQL Example 7.14 */
SELECT CAST(emp_last_name As CHAR(12)) "Last Name",
       CAST(emp_first_name As CHAR(12)) "First Name"
FROM employee
WHERE emp_ssn IN (999111111, 999888888);


Last Name     First Name
----------    ----------
Bock          Douglas
Prescott      Sherri
```

As you can see, the final result table matches the results produced when the entire query with two nested subqueries is executed. This *decomposition approach* to studying queries can also help you in writing nested subqueries.

SUBQUERIES AND COMPARISON OPERATORS

COMPARISON OPERATORS AND ERRORS

This section discusses subqueries that use a comparison operator in the WHERE clause. Table 7.3 provides a listing of the SQL comparison operators and their meaning for your convenience.

TABLE 7.3	
Comparison Operator	*Meaning*
=	Equal to
<	Less than
>	Greater than
>=	Greater than or equal to
<=	Less than or equal to
!=	Not equal to
<>	Not equal to
!>	Not greater than
!<	Not less than

The general form of the WHERE clause with a comparison operator is similar to that used thus far in the text. Note that the subquery is again enclosed by parentheses.

```
WHERE <expression> <comparison_operator> (subquery)
```

Let us consider an earlier example of the equal sign (=) comparison operator, as follows:

```
WHERE emp_salary =
(SELECT MIN(emp_salary)
FROM employee);
```

The most important point to remember when using a subquery with a comparison operator is that the subquery can only return a single or *scalar* value. This is also termed a *scalar subquery* because a single column of a single row is returned by the subquery. If a subquery returns more than one value, SQL Server generates an error message, and the query fails to execute. Let us examine a subquery that cannot execute because it violates the "single value" rule. The query in SQL Example 7.15 returns multiple values for the *emp_salary* column.

```
/* SQL Example 7.15 */
SELECT emp_salary
FROM employee
WHERE emp_salary > 40000;
```

```
emp_salary
--------------------
43000.0000
43000.0000
55000.0000
```

Now, if we substitute this query as a subquery in another SELECT statement, then that SELECT statement fails. This is demonstrated in SQL Example 7.16. The SQL code fails with Server Error Message 512 because the subquery uses the greater than (>) comparison operator and the subquery returns multiple values.

```
/* SQL Example 7.16 */
SELECT emp_ssn
FROM employee
WHERE emp_salary >
    (SELECT emp_salary
     FROM employee
     WHERE emp_salary > 40000);

Server: Msg 512, Level 16, State 1, Line 2
Subquery returned more than 1 value. This is not permitted when the
subquery follows =, !=, <, <= , >, >= or when the subquery is used as
an expression.
```

To use a subquery as the object of a comparison operator, you must be familiar enough with the data stored in the relevant tables and with the nature of the programming problem to know with certainty that the subquery can return a scalar value. You can also test the subquery to determine whether it returns a scalar value, although this approach does not always guarantee a scalar value is returned when the data values change over time.

AGGREGATE FUNCTIONS AND COMPARISON OPERATORS

As you may recall, the aggregate functions (AVG, SUM, MAX, MIN, and COUNT) always return a *scalar* result table. Thus, a subquery with an aggregate function as the object of a comparison operator always executes provided you have formulated the query properly.

Suppose a payroll manager needs a listing of employees who have a salary level greater than the average salary for all employees. SQL Example 7.17 uses the AVG aggregate function in the subquery to produce the desired result.

```
/* SQL Example 7.17 */
SELECT CAST(emp_last_name As CHAR(12)) "Last Name",
       CAST(emp_first_name As CHAR(12)) "First Name",
        '$' + CONVERT (CHAR (10), emp_salary, 1) "Salary"
FROM employee
WHERE emp_salary >
```

```
    (SELECT AVG(emp_salary)
     FROM employee);


Last Name       First Name      Salary
-----------     -----------     -----------
Joshi           Dinesh          $ 38,000.00
Zhu             Waiman          $ 43,000.00
Joyner          Suzanne         $ 43,000.00
Bordoloi        Bijoy           $ 55,000.00
```

The subquery produces a scalar result table with a single value—the average salary of all employees. In fact, the average salary is $35,500. The outer query then lists employees who have a salary that exceeds the average salary.

COMPARISON OPERATORS MODIFIED WITH ALL OR ANY KEYWORDS

The ALL and ANY keywords can modify a comparison operator to allow an outer query to accept multiple values from a subquery. The general form of the WHERE clause for this type of query is:

```
WHERE <expression> <comparison_operator> [ALL | ANY] (subquery)
```

The ALL and ANY keywords can produce a result table that has zero, one, or more than one value. Subqueries that use these keywords may also include GROUP BY and HAVING clauses.

ALL KEYWORD

To understand the ALL keyword, let us examine its effect on the "greater than" (>) comparison operator in a SELECT statement. Suppose our payroll manager needs an employee list of those employees with a salary that is greater than the salary of all the employees in department 7. In SQL Example 7.18, the ALL keyword modifies the greater than comparison operator to mean greater than *all* values. Only a single row is returned in the result table.

```
/* SQL Example 7.18 */
SELECT CAST(emp_last_name As CHAR(12)) "Last Name",
       CAST(emp_first_name As CHAR(12)) "First Name" ,
       '$' + CONVERT (CHAR (10), emp_salary, 1) "Salary"
FROM employee
WHERE emp_salary > ALL
    (SELECT emp_salary
     FROM employee
     WHERE emp_dpt_number = 7);


Last Name       First Name      Salary
-----------     -----------     -----------
Bordoloi        Bijoy           $ 55,000.00
```

Conceptually, for each row in the *employee* table, the inner query creates a final listing of salaries of employees who work in department 7. We can determine these salaries by executing the inner query alone.

```
/* SQL Example 7.19 */
SELECT emp_salary
FROM employee
WHERE emp_dpt_number = 7;


emp_salary
--------------------
30000.0000
38000.0000
43000.0000
25000.0000
```

The outer query finds the largest salary value in the list for department 7. This is $43,000. Next the outer query compares the salary of each employee to this largest value one row at a time. The result table includes only employees who have a salary larger than that of anyone else who works in department 7. In this case, only Bordoloi has such a salary.

ANY KEYWORD

The ANY keyword is not as restrictive as the ALL keyword. When used with the greater than comparison operator, "> ANY" means greater than *some* value. Let us examine the ANY keyword when used within the SELECT statement in SQL Example 7.20. The firm's payroll manager needs the employee name and salary of any employee who has a salary greater than that of *any* employee with a salary that exceeds $30,000. This query is not the same as asking for a listing of employees with salaries that exceed $30,000. We can see how it differs by examining the execution of the SELECT statement in detail.

```
/* SQL Example 7.20 */
SELECT CAST(emp_last_name As CHAR(12)) "Last Name",
       CAST(emp_first_name As CHAR(12)) "First Name" ,
       '$' + CONVERT (CHAR (10), emp_salary, 1) "Salary"
FROM employee
WHERE emp_salary > ANY
    (SELECT emp_salary
     FROM employee
     WHERE emp_salary > 30000);


Last Name       First Name      Salary
-------------   -------------   -------------
Zhu             Waiman          $ 43,000.00
Joyner          Suzanne         $ 43,000.00
Bordoloi        Bijoy           $ 55,000.00
```

For each employee, the inner query finds a list of salaries greater than $30,000. Let us execute the inner query alone to see the listing that is produced.

```
/* SQL Example 7.21 */
SELECT emp_salary
FROM employee
WHERE emp_salary > 30000;


emp_salary
----------------------
38000.0000
43000.0000
43000.0000
55000.0000
```

Four employee salaries are listed in the intermediate result table produced by the inner query, and the smallest of these is $38,000. The outer query looks at all the values in the list and determines whether the employee currently under consideration earns more than *any* of the salaries in the intermediate result table—this means more than $38,000. The employees listed in the final result table all earn more than the $38,000 listed in the intermediate result table.

"= ANY" (EQUAL ANY) EXAMPLE

The "= ANY" operator is exactly equivalent to the IN operator. For example, to find the names of employees who have male dependents, you can use either IN or "= ANY"—both the queries in SQL Example 7.22 and SQL Example 7.23 produce identical result tables.

```
/* SQL Example 7.22 */
SELECT CAST(emp_last_name As CHAR(12)) "Last Name",
       CAST(emp_first_name As CHAR(12)) "First Name"
FROM employee
WHERE emp_ssn IN
    (SELECT dep_emp_ssn
     FROM dependent
     WHERE dep_gender = 'M');
```

```
/* SQL Example 7.23 */
SELECT CAST(emp_last_name As CHAR(12)) "Last Name",
       CAST(emp_first_name As CHAR(12)) "First Name"
FROM employee
WHERE emp_ssn = ANY
    (SELECT dep_emp_ssn
     FROM dependent
     WHERE dep_gender = 'M');


Last Name       First Name
-----------     -------------
Bock            Douglas
Zhu             Waiman
Joyner          Suzanne
```

"!= ANY" (Not Equal Any) Example

As we saw on page 183, the "= ANY" is identical to the IN operator. However, the "!= ANY" (not equal any) is *not* equivalent to the NOT IN operator. If a subquery of employee salaries produces an intermediate result table with the salaries $38,000, $43,000, and $55,000, then the WHERE clause with the NOT IN operator shown below means "NOT $38,000" AND "NOT $43,000" AND "NOT $55,000."

```
WHERE NOT IN (38000, 43000, 55000);
```

However, the "!= ANY" comparison operator and keyword combination shown in this next WHERE clause with the != ANY operator means "NOT $38,000" OR "NOT $43,000" OR "NOT $55,000."

```
WHERE != ANY (38000, 43000, 55000);
```

Let us consider another situation. Suppose a human resource manager needs a listing of employees who do not have dependents. You might write the following erroneous query:

```
/* SQL Example 7.24 */
SELECT CAST(emp_last_name As CHAR(12)) "Last Name",
       CAST(emp_first_name As CHAR(12)) "First Name"
FROM employee
WHERE emp_ssn != ANY
    (SELECT DISTINCT dep_emp_ssn
     FROM dependent);

Last Name     First Name
------------  ------------
Bock          Douglas
Amin          Hyder
Joshi         Dinesh
Zhu           Waiman
Joyner        Suzanne
Bordoloi      Bijoy
Markis        Marcia
Prescott      Sherri
```

The query produces output, but the query actually fails because the result table lists *every employee* in the *employee* table. This occurs because the inner query returns all SSNs for employees with dependents from the *dependent* table. Then, for each *dep_emp_ssn* value, the outer query finds all employee SSNs that do not match one of the *dep_emp_ssn* values. However, because there are four values in the intermediate result table, the "!= ANY" operator is like an "OR" operator during the comparison and, of course, each employee SSN fails to match at least one of the *dep_emp_ssn* values. In this example, the **"!= ANY"** operator *always* returns a TRUE value. Remember, when OR is used, a value is returned when any one of the conditions tested is TRUE.

So, how can we answer the management query? The solution approach was actually covered earlier in this chapter—use the NOT IN operator, as is done in SQL Example 7.25.

```
/* SQL Example 7.25 */
SELECT CAST(emp_last_name As CHAR(12)) "Last Name",
       CAST(emp_first_name As CHAR(12)) "First Name"
FROM employee
WHERE emp_ssn NOT IN
    (SELECT DISTINCT dep_emp_ssn
     FROM dependent);


Last Name       First Name
-------------   --------------
Amin            Hyder
Joshi           Dinesh
Markis          Marcia
Prescott        Sherri
```

CORRELATED SUBQUERIES

The type of subquery we have discussed so far is the type where the outer query depends on values provided by the inner query and the inner query is resolved independently of the outer query. As opposed to this (regular) type of subquery, a *correlated subquery* is one where the inner query *also* depends on values provided by the outer query. A *correlated* subquery contains a column name which refers to a table name specified in the FROM clause of the outer query. This means that in a *correlated subquery,* the inner query is executed repeatedly, once for each row that might be selected by the outer query. SQL Example 7.26 demonstrates this concept.

Correlated subqueries can produce result tables that answer complex management questions. *Suppose our payroll manager needs a listing of the most highly paid employee from each department.* Clearly, the MAX aggregate function should be used somewhere in the SELECT statement; and, sure enough, it is used in the inner query of the SELECT statement, shown in SQL Example 7.26.

```
/* SQL Example 7.26 */
SELECT CAST(emp_last_name As CHAR(12)) "Last Name",
       CAST(emp_first_name As CHAR(12)) "First Name" ,
       emp_dpt_number "Dept",
       '$' + CONVERT(CHAR(10), emp_salary, 1) "Salary"
FROM employee e1
WHERE emp_salary =
    (SELECT MAX(emp_salary)
     FROM employee
     WHERE emp_dpt_number = e1.emp_dpt_number);
```

Last Name	First Name	Dept	Salary
Zhu	Waiman	7	$ 43,000.00
Joyner	Suzanne	3	$ 43,000.00
Bordoloi	Bijoy	1	$ 55,000.00

Unlike the subqueries previously considered, the subquery in this SELECT statement cannot be resolved independently of the outer query. Notice that the outer query specifies that rows are selected from the *employee* table with an alias name of *e1*. The inner query compares the employee department number column (*emp_dpt_number*) of the *employee* table to the same column for the alias table name *e1* specified in the FROM clause of the outer query. The value of *e1.emp_dpt_number* is treated like a variable—it changes as SQL Server examines each row of the employee table as per the SELECT statement of the outer query. The subquery's results are correlated with each individual row of the main query—thus, the term *correlated subquery*.

In this query, SQL Server considers each row of the *employee* table for inclusion in the result table by substituting the value of the employee's department number for each row into the inner query. Unlike the previous subqueries, the above query generates a new set of values for *each row* in the *employee* table.

This may be easier to understand by actually working through the data stored in the *employee* table found in Appendix A. The first row stores data for employee Bijoy Bordoloi of department 1. SQL Server retrieves Bordoloi's department number and inserts it as the value for *e1.emp_dpt_number* in the inner query. The inner query uses the MAX function to compute the maximum salary for all the employees in department 1. Because this value is $55,000, and Bijoy is paid $55,000, his name is included in the final result table.

The second row stores data for employee Suzanne Joyner with a salary of $43,000 in department 3. Again, SQL Server retrieves Joyner's department number and inserts it as the *new* value for *e1.emp_dpt_number* in the inner query. The maximum salary for department 3 is $43,000. Because Joyner is paid $43,000, her name is also included in the final result table.

Let us skip to the fourth row. This row belongs to Marcia Markis with a salary of $25,000 in department 3. Again, SQL Server retrieves Markis' department number and inserts it into the inner query. Again, the maximum salary for department 3 is computed as $43,000. Because Markis' salary is $25,000 and this is less than the maximum for department 3, her row is *not* included in the final result table. You should be able to work through the remaining rows and determine whether a row can be included in the final result table.

SUBQUERIES AND EXISTS OPERATOR

A special type of *correlated* subquery uses the EXISTS operator. This type of subquery functions as an *existence test*. In other words, the WHERE clause of the outer query tests for the existence of rows returned by the inner query. The subquery does not actually produce any data; instead, it returns a value of TRUE or FALSE.

The general format of a subquery WHERE clause with an EXISTS operator is shown next. Note that the NOT operator can optionally be used to negate the result of the EXISTS operator.

```
WHERE [NOT] EXISTS (subquery)
```

Again, we return to the question of listing all employees that have dependents. This query can be written using the EXISTS operator shown in SQL Example 7.27.

```
/* SQL Example 7.27 */
SELECT CAST(emp_last_name As CHAR(12)) "Last Name",
       CAST(emp_first_name As CHAR(12)) "First Name"
FROM employee
WHERE EXISTS
    (SELECT *
     FROM dependent
     WHERE emp_ssn = dep_emp_ssn);

Last Name      First Name
------------   ------------
Bock           Douglas
Zhu            Waiman
Joyner         Suzanne
Bordoloi       Bijoy
```

Do you notice that this SELECT statement is a *correlated* subquery? The inner query depends on values (the *emp_ssn* column) provided by a table (*employee*) specified in the FROM clause of the outer query. Therefore, the subquery executes for each row contained in the *employee* table. When the subquery executes, it searches the *dependent* table for a row or rows that meet the criteria stated in the subquery WHERE clause. If at least one row is found, the subquery returns a TRUE value to the outer query. If the subquery cannot find a row that meets the criteria, it returns a FALSE value. When the outer query receives a TRUE value, the employee row under evaluation is included in the result table.

Notice that subqueries using the EXISTS operator are a bit different from other subqueries in the following ways:

- The keyword EXISTS is not preceded by a column name, constant, or other expression.
- The parameter in the SELECT clause of a subquery that uses an EXISTS operator almost always consists of an asterisk (*). This is because there is no real point in listing any column name because you are simply testing for the existence of rows that meet the conditions specified in the subquery.
- The subquery evaluates to TRUE or FALSE instead of returning any data.
- A subquery that uses an EXISTS operator always is a correlated subquery.

The EXISTS operator is very important, because there is often no alternative to its use. All queries that use the IN operator or a modified comparison operator ($=, <, >$, etc.

modified by ANY or ALL) can be expressed with the EXISTS operator. However, some queries formulated with EXISTS cannot be expressed in any other way. Why then should we not simply write all the earlier queries by using the EXISTS operator? The answer concerns query-processing efficiency. Consider the two queries shown in SQL Examples 7.28 and 7.29. Each query produces identical result tables of employees who have dependents.

```
/* SQL Example 7.28 */                /* SQL Example 7.29 */
SELECT emp_last_name                  SELECT emp_last_name
FROM employee                         FROM employee
WHERE emp_ssn = ANY                   WHERE EXISTS
    (SELECT dep_emp_ssn                   (SELECT *
    FROM dependent);                      FROM dependent
                                          WHERE emp_ssn = dep_emp_ssn);


emp_last_name                         emp_last_name
-------------                         -------------
Bock                                  Bock
Zhu                                   Zhu
Joyner                                Joyner
Bordoloi                              Bordoloi
```

Suppose the *employee* table has 5 million rows, as might be the case for a very large government agency. In SQL Example 7.28, the subquery executes only once. The outer query then processes the *employee* table against values returned by the subquery. The *employee* table will have 5 million rows processed. SQL Example 7.29 has a correlated subquery; therefore, the subquery processes once for every row processed by the outer query. If the outer query processes 5 million rows, then the subquery also processes 5 million times. Obviously the first query is more efficient.

The NOT EXISTS operator is the mirror image of the EXISTS operator. A query that uses NOT EXISTS in the WHERE clause is satisfied if the subquery returns *no* rows.

SUBQUERIES AND ORDER BY CLAUSE

Let us return to the SQL Example 7.29. If the result table is large, management may request that the output be sorted by employee name. The SELECT statement shown in SQL Example 7.30 adds the ORDER BY clause to specify sorting by first name within last name. Note that the ORDER BY clause is placed after the WHERE clause, and that this includes the subquery as part of the WHERE clause.

```
/* SQL Example 7.30 */
SELECT CAST(emp_last_name As CHAR(12)) "Last Name",
       CAST(emp_first_name As CHAR(12)) "First Name"
FROM employee
WHERE EXISTS
    (SELECT *
    FROM dependent
    WHERE emp_ssn = dep_emp_ssn)
ORDER BY emp_last_name, emp_first_name;
```

```
Last Name      First Name
------------   ------------
Bock           Douglas
Bordoloi       Bijoy
Joyner         Suzanne
Zhu            Waiman
```

SUMMARY

This chapter introduces the topic of subqueries. A subquery is simply a query inside another query. You learned that a subquery can also have a subquery as an object of its WHERE clause. Subqueries can enable the production of result tables without hard coding the criteria used for row selection. To use a subquery, the data type of the value or values produced by a subquery must be *join compatible* with the expression in the WHERE clause of the outer query.

You also studied the use of various operators with subqueries. These include the IN and NOT IN operators that are useful for processing subqueries that return a list of values. You examined the use of multiple levels of nesting and learn to decompose queries when writing them and when studying how they process tables. Additionally, you saw how the ALL and ANY keywords can modify the effect of a comparison operator. Aggregate functions are commonly used in subqueries to return a *scalar* result table.

The *correlated subquery* is one where the inner query also depends on values provided by the outer query. This type of subquery can produce result tables that enable you to answer complex management questions. You also learned to use the EXISTS operator for subqueries testing the existence of rows that satisfy a specified criterion. These subqueries return a TRUE or FALSE value. Finally, you studied the relationship between correlated subqueries that use the EXISTS operator and subqueries that use the IN operator. You also learned where to place the ORDER BY clause for an outer query.

After completing the review exercises given in the next section, you should have good expertise in using subqueries to query a database. In addition, you should understand the method of processing correlated subqueries.

REVIEW EXERCISES

LEARN THESE TERMS

ALL keyword.   A keyword that can modify a comparison operator (e.g., the ALL keyword modifies the greater than comparison operator to mean greater than *all* values).

ANY keyword.   A keyword that can modify a comparison operator (e.g., the ANY keyword modifies the greater than operator to mean greater than *some* value).

Correlated subquery.   A subquery where the inner query depends on values that are provided by the outer query.

Design time.   Refers to your mode of operation when you are writing or designing a query.

EXISTS operator.   An operator used in a subquery to function as an "existence test" where the subquery returns a value of TRUE or FALSE.

Inner query. Another name for a nested subquery; also termed an *inner select*.

Join-compatible. The values returned by a subquery are compatible in terms of data type and domain of values with the WHERE clause specified in an outer query.

Nested subqueries. A query that is the object of a WHERE clause; also when the WHERE clause of a subquery has as its object another subquery.

Outer query. A term sometimes used to refer to a SELECT statement that contains a subquery.

Run time. Refers to the actual execution and processing of a query.

Scalar result. When a result table is a single column from a single row. This is also termed a *scalar subquery*.

Subquery. A query within a query.

CONCEPTS QUIZ

1. What term is used to refer to the SELECT statement that contains a subquery?
2. How many levels of subqueries can be used within a WHERE clause?
3. The IN operator is used for what type of subquery?
4. Name a clause that *cannot* be used in writing the subquery portion of a query.
5. Complete this sentence: A subquery is always enclosed in _____.
6. Complete this sentence. Generally speaking, the SELECT clause of a subquery contains _____, _____, or _____.
7. What does the term *join compatible* mean with respect to data types?
8. Explain conceptually how the following query is processed by the SQL server.

```
SELECT emp_last_name "Last Name", emp_first_name "First Name"
FROM employee
WHERE emp_ssn IN
   (SELECT dep_emp_ssn
    FROM dependent
    WHERE dep_gender = 'M');
```

9. What are the general, basic rules of thumb concerning when to use a join versus a subquery approach in writing queries?
10. Suppose that you want to produce a listing of employees who are not assigned to work on a specific project listing. What operator is most appropriate for this type of query?
11. Complete this sentence. This _____ _____ to studying queries can also help you in writing nested subqueries.
12. Study the WHERE clause shown next. What can happen when a query executes with this WHERE clause?

```
WHERE emp_salary >
   (SELECT emp_salary
    FROM employee
    WHERE emp_salary > 30000);
```

13. What type of result table do aggregate functions produce?
14. Suppose that a payroll manager desires a list of employees who have a salary that is greater than the salary of all the employees in department 5. Which keyword would you use to modify the comparison operator?
15. Suppose that a payroll manager wants to know the employee name and salary of any employee who has a salary greater than that of any employee with a salary exceeding $30,000. Which keyword would you use to modify the comparison operator?

16. The "= ANY" comparison operator and keyword are identical to the _____ operator.
17. What is a correlated subquery?
18. When writing a correlated subquery involving a single table, what method is used for specifying the table name listed in the outer query's FROM clause referenced in the WHERE clause of the subquery?
19. Complete this sentence. When a subquery uses the EXISTS operator, the subquery functions as an _____ _____.
20. Complete this sentence. A subquery that is the object of an EXISTS operator evaluates to either _____ or _____.

SQL Coding Exercises and Questions: Company Database

NOTE: Create meaningful column names for the result tables produced by the queries that you write in working the following exercises.

1. The *assignment* table stores data about the hours that employees are working on specific projects. A senior project manager desires a listing of employees (last and first name) who are currently working on project 10, 20, or 30. Use a subquery approach.

2. Modify the query you wrote for Question 1 above by sorting the rows of the result table by employee last name.

3. Management needs a listing of employee names (last and first) who have worked on a project, but have not worked on project 10, 20, or 30. You must use the NOT IN operator. Use a subquery approach and sort the rows of the result table by employee last name.

4. The manager of the 'Payroll' project needs a listing of employee names (last and first) who worked more than 8 hours on the Project. Your query should have a subquery within a subquery.

5. Management is concerned with employees who are nearing retirement. The human resources manager needs a listing of employees (last and first names) and their date of birth, but only if the employee was born before *all* employees in department 3. Hint: Use the MIN aggregate function to determine the age of the oldest employee in department 3 based on the *emp_date_of_birth* column. Format the output for each of the three columns as CHAR(12).

6. Management is concerned that some employees are not putting in sufficient work hours on assigned projects 1, 2, and 3. List the names of employees (last and first) for employees who worked on one of these three projects fewer hours than the average number of hours worked on each of these three projects combined. Hint: Compute the average hours worked on projects 1, 2, and 3 in a subquery. Some employees have no work hours recorded for some of the projects.

7. Management is still concerned about work productivity. Write a query that produces a listing of each employee who worked the *least* on each project (each project has only a single employee listed unless two employees tied for putting forth the least effort). Include the employee SSNs (*work_emp_ssn,*) hours worked (*work_hours,*), and project number (*work_pro_number*) columns in the result table. Hint: Use a correlated subquery. Sort the output by *work_pro_number.*

8. Management is again concerned with productivity. It is believed that employees may not be paid sufficiently well to motivate their work. Produce a listing of names (last and first) of each employee who receives the lowest salary in each department (some departments may have more than one poorly paid employee). The result table should list the *emp_ssn, emp_last_name, emp_first_name, emp_dpt_number,* and *emp_salary* columns with meaningful column names, sorted by *emp_dpt_number*. Based on the results of this question and Question 7 on page 191, is there any evidence that poorly paid employees also performed poorly in terms of their hours worked on assigned projects?

9. Management also has concerns about the salaries of younger employees. Write a query to display the last and first names, department number, salary, and birth date of the youngest employee in each department. Hint: Use the MAX function. Based on the results of this question and Question 8 above, is there any evidence that younger employees are paid poorly?

10. Review the requirements for Question 4 on page 191. Rewrite the query to add the number of hours worked (*work_hours*) column with a modified column name *Payroll Hours Worked* to the result table. Try answering this question using a combination of the join query and the subquery approaches.

11. Using a subquery approach, list the names of employees (last and first name) who are managers of departments. Use the EXISTS operator.

12. The Company's chief executive officer (CEO) needs to know the department with the *highest* average salary. The result table should have two columns labeled **Department** and **Highest Average Salary.**

SQL CODING EXERCISES AND QUESTIONS: RIVERBEND DATABASE

1. The *treatment* table stores data about the treatment services that patients have received. The chief of physicians needs a listing of patients (last and first name) who have received either a blood glucose or an antibiotic injection (*service_id* = '82947' or '90788'). Use a subquery approach.

2. Modify your query for Question 1 to sort the output by patient last name, and then by patient first name.

3. Modify the query for Question 1 to produce a listing of patients who have *not* received either a blood glucose or an antibiotic injection (*service_id* = '82947' or '90788'). Use a subquery approach. Use the NOT IN operator. Sort the output by patient last name, and then by patient first name.

4. The *prescription* table stores data about the medicines that have been prescribed for patients. The chief of pharmacology needs a listing of patients (last and first name) who have received either Valium or Demerol (*medicine_code* = '9999003' or '9999002'). Use a subquery approach.

5. Modify the query for Question 4 to display the output sorted by patient last name, and then by patient first name.

6. The chief of general surgical procedures needs a listing of patient names (last and first) who have received a service treatment **'General Panel'**; however, you do not know the *service_id* for this service. Your query should have a subquery within a subquery using the *patient, treatment,* and *service* tables. Sort the output by patient last name, and then by patient first name.

7. The director of human resources for the hospital is concerned about employee retention. One of the hospital directors has suggested that the hospital has difficulty retaining employees except for registered nurses (*hospital_title* = 'R.N.'). Produce a listing of staff members (last and first names) and the date they were hired to work at the hospital, but only list staff members who were hired before any nurse with a hospital title of 'R.N.' Hint: Use the MIN aggregate function to determine the date hired for the oldest registered nurse based on the *date_hired* column. The result table must also list the employee's hospital title and date hired. Format the output such that each column has a meaningful name and is an appropriate width such that each row fits on a single line of output.

8. The head of the hospital's accounting department is concerned about the prescribed charge for services versus the actual charge for services in the surgery category of services (*service_cat_id* = 'SUR'). Produce a listing of surgery services listed in the *treatment* table by *service_id* where the prescribed *service_charge* differs from the *actual_charge* recorded in the *treatment* table. The result table should also include the *service_charge* and *actual_charge*. Use a subquery approach to produce a listing of *service_id* values from the *service* table that belong to the 'SUR' category of services. Display the result table with the service and actual charges formatted to include the dollar sign ($).

9. Alter the above query to only list services where the difference between the *service_charge* and *actual_charge* is greater than the *average* difference between these two charges for services in the 'SUR' category of services. The result table should only list the *service_id* and *service_description* columns from the *service* table. Hint: Compute the average difference between these two charges for 'SUR' services in a subquery.

10. The head of hospital auditing wants to know which patients were charged the most for a treatment. The result able should list three columns from the *treatment* table appropriately labeled: *pat_id, actual_charge,* and *service_id*. Only list rows where the patient was charged the most for a treatment. This may result in some rows where patients were charged identical amounts to other patients. Sort the rows by *service_id*. Use a correlated subquery. Format the output appropriately.

11. The chief of administration for the hospital is concerned with productivity. It is believed that physicians may not be paid sufficiently well to motivate their work. Produce a listing of names (last and first) of each physician (*hospital_title* = 'M.D.') who receives the lowest salary in each ward or department. Some wards or departments may have more than one poorly paid physician. The result table should list the *staff_last_name* and *staff_first_name* (concatenated as a single column), *ward_dept_assigned,* and *salary* columns with meaningful column names, sorted by *ward_dept_assigned*. Use the COLUMN commands shown here to format the output.

12. Modify the query for Question 11 to list physicians from each ward or department who are paid the highest salaries.

13. Management has decided to extend the study of salary payments to employees in all salaried categories (do not include hourly wage employees). Write a query to display the last and first names (as a single column), ward or department assigned identification (ID) code, salary, and date hired of the employee in each ward or

department who has worked the least amount of time at the hospital. Hint: Use the MAX function and a correlated subquery.

14. Review the requirement for Question 13. Rewrite the query to add the ward or department name to the result table. Delete the employee first name and the ward or department assigned ID code. This requires a combination of join and subquery approaches.

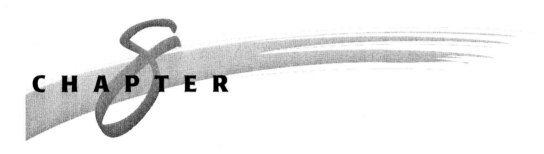

CHAPTER

VIEWS AND TABLES WITH THE IDENTITY PROPERTY

This chapter covers two important types of database topics. The first is *views*. A *view* is a *logical* or *virtual table*. Views have several uses. A major advantage of a view is that it can simplify query writing such that system users without an extensive background in Structured Query Language (SQL) can write some of their own queries to access database information. Views can also provide an element of data security by limiting the data that a system user can access.

This chapter also examines use of the *identity* property when defining table columns through use of the CREATE TABLE statement. The identity property is an optional clause used when defining columns. Columns defined in this fashion must be of data-type integer. Identity columns have the column values assigned by the system—some Microsoft products such as Microsoft Access define these as "AutoNumber" columns. This supports the automatic generation of integer values that are often used as surrogate primary key values for tables in situations where primary key values do not exist in reality. For example, order numbers for customer sales orders can be automatically generated by the database system, thereby ensuring that no two sales orders have the same assigned sales order number.

OBJECTIVES

Your learning objectives include the creation and maintenance of each of these database constructs. In the review section of the chapter, you are presented with a number of exercises designed to reinforce key learning points for views and the use of identity property columns. Your learning should focus on the following objectives:

- Create a single table view.
- Create a join table view—include functions.
- Insert, update, and delete table rows using a view.
- Create a view with errors.

- Drop a view.
- Create a table with column specifications that include the *identity* property.
- Insert data rows into tables with a column specified with the *identity* property.
- Use SCOPE_IDENTITY function to insert data rows into tables that are related to a table that has a column specified with the *identity* property.

VIEWS

A database view is a *logical* or *virtual table* based on a query. Figure 8.1 illustrates this concept. Managers often need to access information from more than one table; however, they rarely need to access data from all the columns in a table. Figure 8.1 shows the *employee* and *department* tables that, as you know, are related to one another. Managers working with employee salaries may want to access employee Social Security numbers (SSNs), salary levels, and associated department number to which an employee is assigned, as well as department name. This is made easier for a manager through the creation of the *emp_dept* view.

In fact, it is useful to think of a view as a stored query because views are created with a CREATE VIEW statement that incorporates use of a SELECT statement. Further, views are queried just like tables. This means that from your perspective as a developer or from a database system user's perspective, a view looks like a table. However, the actual data retrieved by a SELECT query of a view is not stored as part of a database. Instead, the data is "gathered together" each time a view is queried from the database tables for which a view is defined. In fact, SQL Server stores information about the definition of a view as an object. SQL Server also stores the *execution plan* for creating the view.

To understand views better, let us begin with a very simple example. Examine the *employee* table definition provided in Appendix A. The *employee* table has a fairly large number of columns. It is unlikely that all managers may be interested in all the columns in this table. Instead, you may find that the manager of employee parking is only concerned with which employees are assigned to which parking spaces, whereas a human resources department manager is only concerned with facts such as employee name and gender.

FIGURE 8.1

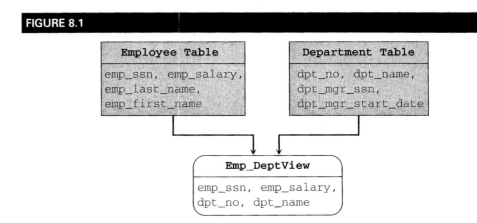

The view definition provided in SQL Example 8.1 creates a view named *employee_parking*. One of the nice features of the *employee_parking* view is that it is simple. If you manage employee parking, you can select information about employees without having to deal with columns of data that are irrelevant to your job.

```
/* SQL Example 8.1 */
CREATE VIEW employee_parking (parking_space, last_name,
    first_name, ssn) AS
SELECT emp_parking_space, emp_last_name, emp_first_name, emp_ssn
FROM employee
```

NOTE: SQL Server does not allow the termination of a CREATE VIEW statement with a semicolon. If you create views with other relational DBMS products such as Oracle, a semicolon at the end of the statement is required.

Views also provide a form of security. For example, the *employee_parking* view limits the information that parking managers and personnel can access; thus, columns containing information such as employee salaries are hidden from members of the parking department. After all, parking managers do not have a "need to know" with regard to everyone's salary in an organization. Let us examine the information provided by the view with a SELECT query, as shown in SQL Example 8.2.

```
/* SQL Example 8.2 */
SELECT *
FROM employee_parking
ORDER BY last_name, first_name;

parking_space    last_name    first_name    ssn
-------------    ---------    ----------    ---------
422              Amin         Hyder         999222222
542              Bock         Douglas       999111111
1                Bordoloi     Bijoy         999666666
more rows will be displayed . . .
```

Notice that the only columns in the query are those defined as part of the view. Additionally, we have renamed the columns in the view so that they are slightly different from the column names in the underlying *employee* table. Further, the rows can be sorted based on any column or set of columns defined for the view by using the same ORDER BY clause for the view selection that you would use when selecting from a table.

CREATING VIEWS

Now that you have studied an example view, we examine the full syntax of the CREATE VIEW statement.

CREATE VIEW SYNTAX

The general syntax is given below. The CREATE VIEW statement has a number of options and you learn about each of these in this section.

```
CREATE VIEW [ < database_name > . ] [ < owner > . ] view_name [ (
column_name1 [,column_name2, ... column_name_n ] ) ]
[ WITH < view_attribute1 > [, view_attribute2, ... view_attribute_n ] ]
AS
    SELECT
    [ WITH CHECK OPTION ]
```

The specification of a database name and owner name for view objects is optional. View names must themselves comply with the rules for naming identifiers in SQL Server. Columns to be included in views may be optionally named. Renaming columns in this fashion enables the system designer to select column names that are particularly meaningful to the intended system users for the view. There are, however, times when you may be required to name a column. Columns must be named when:

- A column is derived through use of an arithmetic expression, function, or constant.
- A join causes the selection of two columns from different tables, but with the same name because of a JOIN operation—one of the columns must be named.

If you do not name view columns, then the columns have the same column names as the columns specified in the SELECT clause listing.

The AS keyword is required. The actual columns that comprise a view are defined with a SELECT statement. You can select columns from a single table, multiple tables through a JOIN operation, or columns from other views. You must have SELECT privileges on the table and view columns selected for the view definition. Restrictions on the SELECT clause of the CREATE VIEW statement include:

- The COMPUTE and COMPUTE BY clauses cannot be used.
- The ORDER BY clause cannot be used unless the TOP clause is used in the SELECT statement.
- The INTO keyword cannot be used.
- A temporary table or table variable cannot be listed in the SELECT listing.
- A maximum of 1,024 columns can be defined for an individual view.

EXAMPLE CREATE VIEW COMMANDS

The CREATE VIEW command shown in SQL Example 8.3 creates a view named *empview7*. This view enables the selection of each employee's SSN, first name, and last name, but only for employees assigned to department 7. The view has a different structure than the *employee* table in terms of the columns in the view. The view stores a subset of the *employee* table rows because the rows accessible through the view are restricted to employees assigned to department 7. Also, the WITH CHECK OPTION clause ensures that any data manipulation language (DML) statements executed against the view restrict the UPDATE, INSERT, or DELETE operations to employees in department 7.

```
/* SQL Example 8.3 */
CREATE VIEW empview7 (SSN, FirstName, LastName, Dept) AS
SELECT emp_ssn, emp_first_name, emp_last_name, emp_dpt_number
FROM employee
WHERE emp_dpt_number=7
WITH CHECK OPTION
```

SQL Example 8.4 shows a simple query of the *empview7* view. Note that the column names assigned in the view differ from those used in the *employee* table.

```
/* SQL Example 8.4 */
SELECT *
FROM empview7;

SSN         FirstName          LastName         Dept
_____   _____   _____   _____
999111111   Douglas            Bock             7
999333333   Dinesh             Joshi            7
999444444   Waiman             Zhu              7
999888888   Sherri             Prescott         7
```

It is also possible to create a view that has exactly the same structure as an existing database table. The view named *dept_view* in SQL Example 8.5 has exactly the same structure as *department* table. Further, the view provides access to all the rows of the *department* table.

```
/* SQL Example 8.5 */
CREATE VIEW dept_view (DepartmentNo, Name, ManagerSSN,
    StartDate) AS
SELECT dpt_no, dpt_name,
    LEFT(dpt_mgrssn,3)+'-'+SUBSTRING(dpt_mgrssn,4,2)+'-'+
    RIGHT(dpt_mgrssn,4), CAST(dpt_mgr_start_date As CHAR(11))
FROM department
```

Now it appears that a view that duplicates a table exactly in terms of data row accessibility may not be terribly useful. However, the *dept_view* view has column names that may be more meaningful to the system user than those assigned to the table according to the firm's naming convention. Additionally, the department manager's SSN has been formatted through the use of SQL functions (you learn about the LEFT, SUBSTRING, and RIGHT functions when you study Chapter 9). Also, the date on which individual managers were assigned to their position (*dpt_mgr_start_date*) has been cast as a character column in the view. SQL Example 8.6 shows the selection of data from the view.

```
/* SQL Example 8.6 */
SELECT *
FROM dept_view;
```

```
DepartmentNo Name              ManagerSSN  StartDate
------------ ---------------   ----------  ----------
1            Headquarters      999-66-6666 Jun 19 1981
3            Admin and Records 999-55-5555 Jan  1 2001
7            Production        999-44-4444 May 22 1998
```

Compare the result table for the view with the result table produced by SQL Example 8.7 where data rows are selected from the *department* table. The result table for SQL Example 8.6 probably is easier for a system user to quickly interpret.

```
/* SQL Example 8.7 */
SELECT *
FROM department;

dpt_no dpt_name          dpt_mgrssn dpt_mgr_start_date
------ ---------------   --------- ----  ----------------------
1      Headquarters      999666666  1981-06-19 00:00:00.000
3      Admin and Records 999555555  2001-01-01 00:00:00.000
7      Production        999444444  1998-05-22 00:00:00.000
```

FUNCTIONS AND VIEWS: JOIN VIEWS

In addition to specifying columns from existing tables, you can use single row functions consisting of number, character, date, and group functions as well as expressions to create additional columns in views. This can be extremely useful because the system user has access to data without having to understand how to use the underlying functions.

Consider the query in SQL Example 8.8, which illustrates the usage of the MAX and MIN functions within a *join view*. The columns to be displayed are selected from two different tables: *employee* and *department*.

```
/* SQL Example 8.8 */
CREATE VIEW dept_salary
    (Name, MinSalary, MaxSalary, AvgSalary) AS
SELECT d.dpt_name, MIN(e.emp_salary),
    MAX(e.emp_salary), AVG(e.emp_salary)
FROM employee e JOIN department d ON (e.emp_dpt_number=d.dpt_no)
GROUP BY d.dpt_name
```

The *dept_salary* view can be queried to produce a result table with the department name (from the *department* table), as well as three computed columns. These three columns store the minimum, maximum, and average salaries for members of the department, but the data used to produce a result table with these three columns actually come from the *employee* table. Thus, this view is also known as a *join view* because it joins the *department* and *employee* tables. Further, the data can be grouped by department name.

Now we execute the SELECT statement shown in SQL Example 8.9 to display data from the *dept_salary* view. Notice how simple the query is to write as compared to the query used to create the view. This query can be executed by a system user with limited SQL training and provide the system user with easy access to information that may be used repeatedly over time.

```
/* SQL Example 8.9 */
SELECT *
FROM dept_salary;

Name                MinSalary      MaxSalary      AvgSalary
-----------------   ------------   ------------   ----------
Admin and Records   25000.0000     43000.0000     31000.0000
Headquarters        55000.0000     55000.0000     55000.0000
Production          25000.0000     43000.0000     34000.0000
```

DROPPING VIEWS

A database administrator (DBA) or view owner can drop a view with the DROP VIEW statement. SQL Example 8.10 drops the *dept_view* object.

```
/* SQL Example 8.10 */
DROP VIEW dept_view;
```

VIEW STABILITY

Remember that a view does not actually store any data. The data needed to support view queries are retrieved from the underlying database tables and displayed to a result table at the time that a view is queried. The result table is stored only temporarily.

If a table that underlies a view is dropped, then the view is no longer valid. We examine this by creating a *test* table with a single column. SQL Examples 8.11, 8.12, and 8.13 create a table named *test*, store two data rows to the table, and display all the data from the table.

```
/* SQL Example 8.11 */
CREATE TABLE test (
    test_row VARCHAR(10)
);
```

```
/* SQL Example 8.12 */
INSERT INTO test VALUES ('Test row 1');
INSERT INTO test VALUES ('Test row 2');
```

```
/* SQL Example 8.13 */
SELECT *
FROM test;

test_row
-----------
Test row 1
Test row 2
```

As you can see, the *test* table was created and we were able to access data from the table. SQL Example 8.14 creates a view named *test_view* with the same structure and data as our *test* table. The query in SQL Example 8.15 displays all the data from the view *test_view*.

```
/* SQL Example 8.14 */
CREATE VIEW test_view AS
SELECT *
FROM test
```

```
/* SQL Example 8.15 */
SELECT *
FROM test_view;

test_row
-----------
Test row 1
Test row 2
```

Not surprisingly, the result table for the *test_view* is identical to the result table for the *test* table. Now let us drop the *test* table and query the *test_view* again. SQL Server returns two error messages. The first message specifies that the table named *test* that is referenced by the view is an invalid object name. The second message informs you that *test_view* could not be used due to binding errors—of course, it is impossible for the view to bind to a nonexistent table.

```
/* SQL Example 8.16 */
DROP TABLE test;
```

```
/* SQL Example 8.17 */
SELECT *
FROM test_view;

Server: Msg 208, Level 16, State 1, Procedure test_view, Line 3
Invalid object name 'test'.
```

```
Server: Msg 4413, Level 16, State 1, Line 1
Could not use view or function 'test_view' because of binding errors.
```

What do you think will happen if we simply recreate the test table and again insert the two data rows into the table—will a SELECT statement accessing the view work? This is tested by SQL Examples 8.18 to 8.20. The test table is again created and rows are inserted.

```
/* SQL Example 8.18 */
CREATE TABLE test (
    test_row VARCHAR(10)
);
```

```
/* SQL Example 8.19 */
INSERT INTO test VALUES ('Test row 1');
INSERT INTO test VALUES ('Test row 2');
```

The query of *test_view* in SQL Example 8.20 again produces the expected result table. This demonstrates that view definitions are stable, but this only holds if the table that is recreated exactly matches the original table definition.

```
/* SQL Example 8.20 */
SELECT *
FROM test_view;

test_row
----------
Test row 1
Test row 2
```

INSERTING, UPDATING, AND DELETING ROWS THROUGH VIEWS

In this section, you learn basic concepts concerning how to insert, update, and delete table rows through the use of views. The concept of inserting rows into tables through views is a complex one. Likewise, updating existing table rows through views is equally or more complex. Deleting rows is considerably simpler.

When you execute an UPDATE, DELETE, or INSERT DML statement on a view, you are actually manipulating the data rows for the base table or tables on which the view is defined. There are restrictions on the use of UPDATE, DELETE, and INSERT statements with views.

First, to use the UPDATE, DELETE, or INSERT statement with a view, the view must be *updateable*. A view is updateable if the SELECT clause does not specify any aggregate function in the SELECT listing. Additionally, the view could not have been created through use of a TOP, GROUP BY, DISTINCT, or UNION clause or clauses. It is permissible for aggregate functions to be used in a SELECT subquery in a FROM clause. Also, the view cannot have any derived columns in the SELECT list. When you study Chapter 10, you learn a method that can be used to work around part of this first restriction.

Next, if a view is created as the result of a JOIN operation (a join view), the UPDATE and INSERT statements can only modify or insert rows into one of the base tables at a time. You cannot modify rows from two or more tables with a single DML statement.

Finally, the DELETE statement can only execute against a view if a table is referenced in a FROM clause. This simply means that you cannot delete rows from a table that has not been specified.

INSERTING ROWS

Basically, you can insert a row in a table by inserting a row in a view only if the view is updateable. Additionally, the INSERT statement cannot violate any constraints on the underlying tables. The rule concerning constraint violations also applies to UPDATE and DELETE commands. We focus on a single-table update, although it is possible to update base tables accessed through views that are defined for two or more joined tables through the use of multiple DML statements.

The *dept_view2* view created in SQL Example 8.21 allows managers to easily display department number and name information. Note that *dept_view2* has only two columns whereas the *department* table has four columns. The two *department* table columns not included in *dept_view* are both allowed to store NULL values, and there are no constraints on the columns.

```
/* SQL Example 8.21 */
CREATE VIEW dept_view2 AS
SELECT dpt_no, dpt_name
FROM department
```

The INSERT statements in SQL Example 8.22 insert two new rows into the *department* table by using *dept_view2*. Notice that we have erroneously entered the department name of the new department 19 as "Department 20." We address this a bit later in this section.

```
/* SQL Example 8.22 */
INSERT INTO dept_view2 VALUES (18, 'Department 18');
INSERT INTO dept_view2 VALUES (19, 'Department 20');
```

SQL Example 8.23 confirms the row insertions by selecting from the view. The result table displays the original three rows from the *department* table as well as the newly inserted rows for departments 18 and 19.

```
/* SQL Example 8.23 */
SELECT *
FROM dept_view2;

dpt_no dpt_name
------ ------------------
1      Headquarters
3      Admin and Records
7      Production
18     Department 18
19     Department 20
```

UPDATING ROWS

The UPDATE statement in SQL Example 8.24 corrects the error in the department name for department 19 by changing the name to "Department 19." SQL Example 8.25 queries the *department* table to determine whether the rows in the base table were updated through the view.

```
/* SQL Example 8.24 */
UPDATE dept_view2 SET dpt_name = 'Department 19' WHERE dpt_no = 19;
(1 row(s) affected)
```

```
/* SQL Example 8.25 */
SELECT *
FROM department;

dpt_no dpt_name                dpt_mgrssn dpt_mgr_start_date
------ ------------------      ---------- -----------------------
1      Headquarters            999666666  1981-06-19 00:00:00.000
3      Admin and Records       999555555  2001-01-01 00:00:00.000
7      Production              999444444  1998-05-22 00:00:00.000
18     Department 18           NULL       NULL
19     Department 19           NULL       NULL
```

Success! The *department* table has two new rows. The INSERT statements updated the *department* table through the *dept_view2* view. Likewise, the UPDATE statement updated the department name for department 19. Note that the department manager's SSN and start date columns are NULL for the two new rows because data for these columns are not entered with the INSERT statements in SQL Example 8.22.

There are some limitations on use of the UPDATE statement that you need to understand. If you attempt to update a row in a table through a view by referencing a column that is defined for the table, but not for the view, SQL Server returns an error message.

DELETING ROWS

Now let us try the DELETE statement. SQL Example 8.26 deletes the rows for departments 18 and 19 through the *dept_view2* object. SQL Example 8.27 verifies that these two rows no longer exist in the department table. That was pretty straightforward.

```
/* SQL Example 8.26 */
DELETE dept_view2
WHERE dpt_no = 18 OR dpt_no = 19;
(2 row(s) affected)
```

```
/* SQL Example 8.27 */
SELECT *
FROM department;

dpt_no dpt_name          dpt_mgrssn dpt_mgr_start_date
------ ------------------ ---------- ----------------------
1      Headquarters       999666666  1981-06-19 00:00:00.000
3      Admin and Records  999555555  2001-01-01 00:00:00.000
7      Production         999444444  1998-05-22 00:00:00.000
```

SUMMARY OF VIEW FACTS

Now let us examine a summary of the facts that we have learned about views that is presented in Table 8.1. Some of these facts underscore advantages of views whereas others underscore limitations of views.

IDENTITY PROPERTY

Have you ever wondered how certain numeric identifiers are created? For example, suppose a furniture store needs to produce unique numbers that can be used to identify sales orders. What are the possible origins of these identification numbers? If management directs sales clerks to create sales order numbers, sooner or later two different sales clerks can use the same number to identify two different sales orders. The solution to this type of data processing problem is to let the computer system generate a series of unique sales order numbers. SQL Server provides the capability to generate sequence of unique numbers for this type of use at the time that tables are created through use of the *identity* property clause.

CREATE TABLE SYNTAX WITH IDENTITY COLUMN

Prior to defining the sales order table, you need to learn the syntax of a CREATE TABLE statement that includes an *identity* column. Given your familiarity with the CREATE TABLE command, we can demonstrate the use of the identity column with an actual table. Let us continue the use our furniture store example to examine the concept in detail.

TABLE 8.1   A Summary of View Facts

A view does not store data; instead, a view displays data through a SELECT query as if the data were stored in the view

A view definition as provided by the CREATE VIEW statement is stored in the database; further, SQL Server develops what is termed an *execution plan* that is used to "gather up" the data that need to be displayed by a view; this execution plan is also stored in the database

A view can simplify data presentation as well as provide a kind of data security by limiting access to data based on a "need to know"

A view can display data from more than one table; we say that views hide *data complexity;* for example, a single view can be defined by joining two or more tables

A view can display data from more than one table; we say that views hide the resulting view, however, treated as a single table, thereby hiding the fact that the view rows actually originate from several tables; this also simplifies data access

Views can be used to update the underlying tables

Views can change the appearance of data; for example, a view can be used to rename and recast columns from tables without affecting the base table

A view that has columns from more than one table cannot be modified by an INSERT, DELETE, or UPDATE command if a grouping function GROUP BY clause is part of the view definition

A row cannot be inserted in a view in which the base table has a column with a NOT NULL or other constraint that cannot be satisfied by the new row data

Columns in a join view (a view defined with two or more base tables) are subject to DML operations only if one of the underlying tables is affected by the DML statement

Management at the furniture store wishes to identify each sales order by a unique order number. Further, the order number needs to be generated by the application program that is used by sales personnel to record sales information. As the application developer, you coordinate with your organizational DBA in defining the sales order table. The CREATE TABLE statement is shown in SQL Example 8.28.

```
/* SQL Example 8.28 */
CREATE TABLE sales_order (
    so_number              INTEGER IDENTITY(100,1)
        CONSTRAINT pk_sales_order PRIMARY KEY,
    so_value               DECIMAL(9,2),
    so_emp_ssn             CHAR(9),
CONSTRAINT fk_so_emp_ssn
    FOREIGN KEY (so_emp_ssn) REFERENCES employee  );
```

The *sales_order* table shown in SQL Example 8.28 is quite simple, but it is sufficient to illustrate the use of the identity column. Three columns can store data: the *so_number* (sales order number), *so_value* (sales order value), and *so_emp_ssn* (employee SSN of the employee who enters the sales order information).

The IDENTITY clause is highlighted in SQL Example 8.28. This clause causes the database system to automatically generate values for the *so_number* column. By default, an identity column has an initial value of 1 and an increment of 1. This means that the numbers generated are a simple sequence 1, 2, 3, 4, and so forth.

However, you can specify the initial value and increment in parentheses, as is done in SQL Example 8.28. The column must also be defined to store the INTEGER data type.

Management has apparently determined that they want sales order numbers to initially start with number 100 and be incremented by 1. The general syntax of the IDENTITY clause is:

```
IDENTITY [ ( initial_value , increment ) ]
```

The INSERT statements in SQL Example 8.29 insert three rows into the *sales_order* table. Remember that the table has three columns; however, the INSERT statements only insert values for two columns for each row. This is because the *so_number* column has its value automatically generated.

```
/* SQL Example 8.29 */
INSERT INTO sales_order VALUES (155.59, '999111111');
INSERT INTO sales_order VALUES (450.00, '999444444');
INSERT INTO sales_order VALUES (16.95,  '999444444');
```

Now, let us examine the *sales_order* table by querying the table (SQL Example 8.30) to display the rows that were inserted. Note that the sales order numbers stored in the *so_number* column were properly generated as the sequence 100, 101 and 102. Do you know what number is to be assigned to the next sales order? Yes the answer is 103.

```
/* SQL Example 8.30 */
SELECT *
FROM sales_order;

so_number   so_value   so_emp_ssn
----------  ---------  ----------
100         155.59     999111111
101         450.00     999444444
102         16.95      999444444
```

Often, a table like *sales_order* can be related to another table that stores sale order details. Let us create a simple *order_details* table, as shown in SQL Example 8.31 to illustrate how you can enforce referential integrity between the two tables.

```
/* SQL Example 8.31 */
CREATE TABLE order_details (
    od_number               INTEGER,
    od_row                  INTEGER,
    od_product_desc         VARCHAR(15),
    od_quantity_ordered     INTEGER,
    od_product_price        DECIMAL(9,2),
```

```
CONSTRAINT pk_order_details
    PRIMARY KEY (od_number, od_row),
CONSTRAINT fk_order_number FOREIGN KEY (od_number)
    REFERENCES sales_order  );
```

Note that the *order_details* table has a composite primary key that includes both the *od_number* and *od_row* columns. The *od_row* is simply a way of numbering each item ordered on a specific order. Use of the *od_row* value is necessary to arrive at a unique identifier for each row in the *order_details* table because the *od_number* column value that is system generated is not sufficient to guarantee primary key uniqueness. For each order row, the system stores the product description, quantity ordered, and product price. The *order_details* table has a FOREIGN KEY reference to the *sales_order* table through the *od_number* column.

Now, let us use the INSERT statement to store information about sales orders and order details. As each row is inserted into the *sales_order* table, related rows about the products sold on the order are inserted into the *order_details* table. SQL Example 8.32 gives INSERT statements that store a *sales_order* row with a total value of $200 along with two *order_detail* rows. Additionally, we first delete the rows that were previously inserted into the *sales_order* table.

```
/* SQL Example 8.32 */
/* First delete the existing sales_order rows */
DELETE FROM sales_order;
GO
/* Now insert a new sales_order row and two order_detail rows */
INSERT INTO sales_order VALUES(200.00, '999111111' );
GO
BEGIN
    DECLARE @so_number INTEGER
    SELECT @so_number = (SELECT SCOPE_IDENTITY())
    INSERT INTO order_details
        VALUES (@so_number, 1, 'End Table', 1, 100.00);
    INSERT INTO order_details
        VALUES (@so_number, 2, 'Table Lamp', 2, 50.00);
END
```

SQL Example 8.32 introduces the concept of defining of a variable with the DECLARE statement. Here the variable is named *@so_number* and is an INTEGER variable. Further, the function SCOPE_IDENTITY is used to return from the database system tables the value of the last identity number (or sequence number if you prefer that terminology) that was generated by the system within the same procedure. The SCOPE_IDENTITY function is predefined in SQL Server for your use. The last identity number generated in this procedure was 103 (for the *so_number* column in the *sales_order* table). This identity number, 103, is stored to the *@so_number* variable, and then the variable's value is inserted into the *order_details* rows. You learn more about writing short procedures using declared variables and functions when you study Chapter 10.

The SELECT statements in SQL Examples 8.33 and 8.34 display the rows in these two tables, respectively.

```
/* SQL Example 8.33 */
SELECT *
FROM sales_order;

so_number    so_value    so_emp_ssn
-----------  ----------  ----------
103          200.00      999111111
```

```
/* SQL Example 8.34 */
SELECT od_number "So Number", od_row "Row",
    od_product_desc "Description",
    CAST(od_quantity_ordered As CHAR(3)) "Qty",
    od_product_price "Price"
FROM order_details;

So Number   Row    Description   Qty   Price
----------  -----  ------------  ----  ------
103         1      End Table     1     100.00
103         2      Table Lamp    2     50.00

(2 row(s) affected)
```

The use of the identity property for the *so_number* column of the *sales_order* table enables the generation of the next identity number in the sequence for use as the primary key. This identity number value is then retrieved from the database's system tables by the SCOPE_IDENTITY function and this value is used when inserting the two rows in the *order_details* table. Without this approach, the *so_number* in the *sales_order* table would *not* match the *od_number* column value in the *order_detail* table, and we would have a referential integrity problem. As you can see the sales order number matches the order details number and so the two tables are linked through these two columns with common values.

SUMMARY

In this chapter, you learn that *views* are an important mechanism to facilitate the display of selected columns from tables. Views can also provide a type of database security by restricting access to database information by limiting the columns displayed by a view.

You also learn about the use of *identity* columns in tables for automatically generating sequences of integers that can be used as primary key values. This approach to autonumbering is important when primary key values do not exist in reality and must be system generated. The SCOPE_IDENTITY function can be used to retrieve the last identity number generated by the computer system from a database's system tables, and then the identity number can be used to ensure that referential integrity exists between two or more tables.

REVIEW EXERCISES

LEARN THESE TERMS

CREATE VIEW.   Command that uses a SELECT statement to create a view.

DROP VIEW.   A command used to delete an existing view.

Execution plan.   The plan SQL Server stores that is used to "gather together" the data required to be presented by a view.

Identity column.   A column that stores a number generated automatically as part of a sequence of numbers; used to identify rows uniquely in a table.

Join view.   A view definition that can be queried to display data that results from a join of two or more database tables.

SCOPE_IDENTITY.   A function that is used to return from the database system tables the value of the last identity number (or sequence number if you prefer that terminology) that was generated by the system within a procedure.

Updateable view.   A view that enables the use of DML statements to update the rows in the base table or tables that underlie a view definition.

View.   A logical table; also termed a virtual table.

Virtual table.   Another term for a database view.

CONCEPTS QUIZ

1. Where is the data for a view stored?
2. What statement is used to query a view?
3. How do views provide a form of security?
4. Which information is optional when the CREATE VIEW statement is executed?
5. What are the rules for naming a view and the columns in a view?
6. When are columns in a view required to be named?
7. What are the restrictions on the SELECT clause of the CREATE VIEW statement?
8. What is the purpose of the WITH CHECK OPTION clause of the CREATE VIEW statement?
9. Why might you create a view with the exact same column structure as a table?
10. What is the purpose of a join view?
11. What happens if a table that underlies a view is dropped, the view is queried, and then the table is created again with the same structure that it had before it was dropped?
12. If you execute an UPDATE, DELETE, or INSERT DML statement on a view, are you manipulating the data rows stored in the view?
13. Discuss the restrictions on the use of DML statements with views.
14. What makes a view updateable?
15. If a table that underlies a view has a constraint, does this constraint apply to INSERT, UPDATE, and DELETE statements that are used to manipulate rows accessible through the view?
16. Discuss a limitation of using the UPDATE statement with a view.
17. What is the purpose of the identity property clause?
18. What is the default initial value and increment of an identity column?
19. What data type must be used for an identity column?
20. What function is used to return from the database system tables the value of the last identity number generated by the system within a procedure?

SQL Coding Exercises and Questions: Company Database

1. The payroll department needs to regularly access information about employee salary information. The DBA of the company has directed you to create a view based on the *employee* table named *salary_view*. This view should include employee SSN (*emp_ssn*), employee last and first names (*emp_last_name* and *emp_first_name*), and salary for each employee (*emp_salary*). Name the columns of the view as follows: *ssn, last_name, first_name,* and *salary*. Write the Transact Structured Query Language (T-SQL) code needed to create this view. Write a SELECT statement to display rows from the view for employees with salaries at or above $30,000.

2. Drop the view named *salary_view* created in Question 1 and replace it with a new view (same name) that also includes the *emp_dpt_number* column. Name this column *department* in the new view. Write a SELECT statement to display rows from the view where employees are in department 7 and their salary is at or above $30,000.

3. Clerical employees in the human resources department only need access to information about employee dependents. Create a view named *dependent_view* that has the same structure as the *dependent* table; however, use more meaningful column names for the columns than are used in the current *dependent* table.

4. Create a view named *project_hours* that can be used by the senior project manager to access information about work hours that have been reported for different projects. The view should join the *project* and *assignment* tables. The view should show each project's name (*pro_name*) as well as the average hours worked on each project. Name the columns *project_name* and *average_hours* in the view. The rows in the view should be grouped by the project name. Write a SELECT statement to display projects where the average hours is at or greater than 15.

5. The Company's senior project manager needs to access information about departments that manage projects for a specific set of projects, namely, those located in either Edwardsville or Marina. Create a view named *department_projects* that includes the *dpt_no* and *dpt_name* columns from the *department* table and the *pro_name* and *pro_location* from the *project* table. The view should only reference rows for projects that are located in either Edwardsville or Marina. The columns in the view should be named *dept_no, department, project,* and *location,* respectively. Write a SELECT statement to display all the rows that are accessible through the view. The *project* and *location* view columns should be defined with a CAST function to be CHAR(15). The *department* view column should be defined to be CHAR(17).

6. The senior project manager has requested that the *department_projects* view also include the project number. Replace the *department_projects* view described in Question 5 with a new view that includes the *pro_number* column from the *project* table. Name this column *pro_no* in the view. All other requirements remain unchanged. Write a SELECT statement to display all the rows that are accessible through the view.

7. Demonstrate the use of the view named *department_projects* for the senior project manager by writing a SELECT command to query the *department_projects* view created in Question 6 to display all row information for projects belonging to department 3.

8. The senior project manager no longer needs the views named *department_projects* and *project_hours*. Write commands to drop these views.

9. Create the table named *sales_order* described earlier in the chapter. The table should have an identity column named *so_number*. Store information for three sales orders as shown in SQL Example 8.29. Add an INSERT statement to insert a fourth sales order in the amount of $15.95 sold by the employee whose SSN is 999-11-1111. Write a SELECT statement to display all the information in the *sales_order* table.

10. Create the *order_details* table described earlier in the chapter as SQL Example 8.31. Delete the rows inserted earlier into the *sales_order* table. Execute the code shown in SQL Example 8.32 to insert a new row into the *sales_order* table and the two associated rows in the *order_details* table. Execute SELECT statements to display the rows in the two tables.

11. Create a view named *sales* that displays all the columns from the *sales_order* and *order_details* tables that you created for Exercise 10 above; however, do not repeat the sales order number column more than once and do not list the *od_row* column. Execute a SELECT statement to display the rows.

12. The senior vice president for resource management desires to number new departments within the company sequentially beginning with number 40. Create a table named *new_department* that has the same structure as the existing *department* table except that the *dpt_no* column should be an identity column. The department numbering is to be in increments of 1. Write the code needed to create the new table, and then insert the following rows into the new table.

TABLE DATA: new_department

dpt_no	dpt_name	dpt_mgrssn	dpt_mgr_start_date
40	Production	NULL	NULL
41	Admin and records	NULL	NULL
42	Headquarters	NULL	NULL

Write a SELECT statement to display the rows.

SQL CODING EXERCISES AND QUESTIONS: RIVERBEND DATABASE

1. The pharmacy at the Riverbend Hospital regularly accesses information about medicines that are stocked. The hospital DBA has directed you to create a view based on the *medicine* table named *medicine_view*. This view should include the medicine code (*medicine_code*), common medicine name (*med_name_common*), scientific medicine name (*med_name_sci*), quantity in stock (*quantity_stock*), and unit of measure (*unit_measure*) for each medicine. Name the columns of the view as follows: *med_code*, *common_name*, *scientific_name*, *quantity*, and *units*. CAST the *common_name* view column as CHAR(18), the *scientific_name* view column as CHAR(16) and the *units* view column as CHAR(20). Write the SQL code needed to create this view. Write a SELECT statement to display rows from the view for medicines with a quantity in stock level that is at or below 1,000.

2. Replace the view named *medicine_view* created in Question 1 with a new view (same name) that also includes the *normal_dosage* column. Name this column

dosage in the new view. All other view requirements remain the same. Write a SELECT statement to display rows from the view where medicine code is greater than or equal to 9999010 and the quantity in stock is at or above 10,000. List the medicine code, common name, quantity, and dosage for the medicines.

3. Employees in the patient services department only need limited access to information about patients. Create a view named *patient_view* that has the same structure as the *patient* table, but includes only the *pat_id*, *pat_last_name*, *pat_first_name*, and *pat_date_of_birth* columns. The view should have more meaningful column names for the columns than are used in the current *patient* table. The last and first name columns should be CAST as CHAR(15) and the date of birth column should be CAST as CHAR(12). Write a SELECT statement to display information from patient_view where the patient identification (ID) value is greater than or equal to '60000'.

4. Create a view named *patient_record* that can be used by hospital physicians and nurses to access information about patients and the notes recorded for patients. The view should join the *patient* and *patient_note* tables. The view should show each patient's name (*pat_last_name* and *pat_first_name* concatenated as a single column that is limited to 20 characters), SSN (*pat_ssn*), bed assigned (*bed_number* —CAST as CHAR(3)), note comments (*note_comment*), and date the note was taken (*note_date*—CAST AS CHAR(12)) for each patient. Name the columns in the view appropriate names. Write a SELECT statement to display the patient record where the patient's SSN is 666-66-6666.

5. The hospital pharmacy directory needs a view created named *prescription_view* that has the following information: prescription number, prescription date (CAST as CHAR(12) column), dosage prescribed, dosage directions, medicine common name, patient name (last and first as a single column limited to 20 characters), and staff member identification (*staff_id*) and name (*staff_last_name*) who wrote the prescription. Name the columns in the view appropriate names. Write a SELECT statement to display prescription information for prescription 755444020.

6. The directory of patient treatment planning needs a view created named *treatment_view* that has the following information: treatment number, service identifier, service description, treatment date (column limited to 12 characters), patient name (last and first as a single column limited to 20 characters), staff member identification (*staff_id*), and name (*staff_last_name*) who provided the treatment actual charge for the treatment, and comments on the treatment. Name the columns in the view appropriate names. Write a SELECT statement to display treatment information for treatment 18.

7. The chief of physicians requests a view named *staff_location_view* that lists staff members and the ward or department to which they are currently assigned. The view should list the staff member's name (last and first as a single column limited to 20 characters), staff identifier, ward or department ID, ward or department name to which assigned, and work telephone number (not the office telephone number), and phone extension. Name the columns in the view appropriate names. Write a SELECT statement to display staff location information for staff members assigned to the ward with identifier MEDS1.

8. Revise the view named *staff_location_view* to only include rows for staff members assigned to wards or departments with the following identifiers: MEDS1, CARD1

ONCOL, and SURG1. Write a SELECT statement to display staff location information for staff members in ward CARD1. Your result table should just display the staff member name, ward or department identifier, and ward or department name.

9. The hospital's management no longer needs the views named *staff_location_view* or *treatment_view*. Write commands to drop these views.

10. The hospital chief of administration wants to assign patient identifiers for new patients arriving at the hospital numbers sequentially beginning with number 700,000. The patient numbering will be in increments of 1. Create a table named *patient2* where the *pat_id* column is an identity column. The *patient2* table should have referential integrity to the *bed* table, as is currently explained in Appendix B. You need to create new names for the constraints listed in Appendix B.

11. Write an INSERT command to insert two new rows into the *patient2* table created in Question 10. The patient SSNs as well as last and first names are shown below. Leave the other column values NULL. Write a SELECT statement to display the *pat_id*, *pat_ssn*, *pat_last_name*, and *pat_first_name* columns for all rows from the *patient2* table.

Patient SSN (pat_ssn)	Last Name (pat_last_name)	First Name (pat_first_name)
900-00-0000	Zucker	Zina
900-00-0001	Zucker	Zachary

12. Write a statement to drop the *patient2* table.

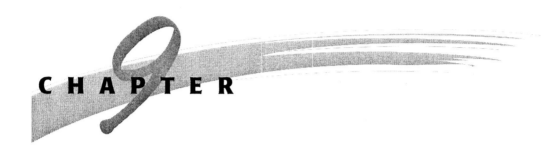

CHAPTER

ADDITIONAL FUNCTIONS

Chapter 5 covered the use of numeric, aggregate functions such as AVG, MAX and MIN. Structured Query Language (SQL) Server has many additional functions. Some of these functions are used in writing procedural Transact-SQL (T-SQL) program code for stored procedure and trigger scripts that you study in Chapter 10. However, there are numerous functions that are used with nonprocedural SELECT statements. These functions can provide additional capabilities that add power to your queries, and this makes life easier for you as an SQL programmer. This chapter focuses on a subset of SQL Server functions that are used quite often with SELECT statements. To help you learn the functions, we have classified them according to their use as: (1) string and text, (2) mathematical, (3) conversion, and (4) date functions.

OBJECTIVES

String and text functions allow you to manipulate a string of characters that can include letters, numbers, and special characters. These functions also allow you to examine data stored in columns defined as various CHARACTER data types. Mathematical functions, as the name implies, manipulate values stored in table columns that are defined as one of the various numeric data types. Conversion functions convert data explicitly from one data type to another. Date functions manipulate data stored in DATETIME columns. Remember that a DATETIME column stores both date and time information—this means that the date functions enable you to manipulate both the date and time values stored in these columns. Your learning objectives are:

- Use string and text functions to manipulate character and text data.
- Use mathematical functions to manipulate numeric data.
- Use conversion functions to convert data from one data type to another.
- Use date and time functions to manipulate date and time data.

GENERAL NOTATION

As discussed in Chapter 5, the general notation for functions is as follows:

```
FUNCTION (argument1 [,optional_argument2] [, optional_argument_n] )
```

The function name is given in capital letters. The parameter *argument1* is a place-holder that may be filled by a string of characters enclosed in single quote marks, a numeric value, an expression, or a column name. Some functions require more than one argument or expression. As was the case with aggregate functions, each function has a single set of parentheses, and all arguments are enclosed by these parentheses. The number of required or optional argument clauses may vary among the different functions.

STRING AND TEXT FUNCTIONS

String and text functions manipulate *character strings* as well as *text* and *image* data. Quite simply, a character string refers to a group of characters where the characters can be alphabetic letters, numbers, spaces, and special characters. Examples of character string values are shown in Table 9.1. Did you notice that strings of numbers are treated as character strings if they are not manipulated mathematically? For example, you would never add two telephone numbers together, nor would you subtract two product numbers; therefore, telephone numbers and product numbers are actually character strings—not numbers.

Table 9.2 summarizes the string and text functions that you examine in this section. The functions are listed alphabetically; however, we have grouped the functions according to the task they perform in our coverage to aid you in learning their use.

ASCII, UNICODE, CHAR, AND STR FUNCTIONS

The functions discussed in this section are most often used for specialized SQL programming needs. They do not have many direct business uses in terms of providing information that business managers use to solve problems; however, you need to be

TABLE 9.1	
Type of Data to Be Stored	***Example Values***
Customer street address	100 South Main Street
Customer telephone number	(618) 555-1212
Customer name	Bijoy Bordoloi or Douglas Bock
Social Security number (SSN)	999-99-9999
Product number	13496

TABLE 9.2

Function	Use/Definition
ASCII	Returns the ASCII code value of the leftmost character of a character string
CHAR	Converts an integer ASCII code value to the equivalent character
CHARINDEX	Returns the starting position of a specified substring found within a character string
LEFT	Returns the specified number of characters from the leftmost portion of a character string
LEN	Returns a numeric value equivalent to the number of characters in a string of characters, excluding trailing blanks
LOWER	Returns a character string that is all lowercase
LTRIM	Removes leading blanks from a character string
REPLACE	Replaces all occurrences of a character substring with another specified character substring within a character string
RIGHT	Returns the specified number of characters from the rightmost portion of a character string
RTRIM	Removes trailing blanks from a character string
STR	Returns character data that is converted from numeric data
SUBSTRING	Returns a string of specified *length* from a larger character string beginning at a specified character *position*
UNICODE	Returns an integer value for the first character of an expression as defined for the Unicode standard
UPPER	Returns a character string that is all uppercase

aware of these functions in the event that you should become involved in a programming project where they are used.

The American Standard Code of Information Interchange (ASCII) and CHAR functions are mirror images of one another. ASCII returns the ASCII code value as an INT numeric value for the leftmost character in a character string. The character string must be of data type CHAR or VARCHAR. The CHAR function, on the other hand, returns the ASCII character for a supplied argument of data type INT. The integer value supplied as an argument to the CHAR function must be an integer between the values 0 through 255, inclusive. If the INTEGER argument for the CHAR function is not within the specified range of 0 through 255, the function returns a NULL value. The general syntax for ASCII and CHAR follows:

```
ASCII(character_string)

CHAR(integer_value)
```

SQL Example 9.1 shows the result of a SELECT statement that uses these two functions. The ASCII equivalent for the first letter of the name 'Bijoy' is the integer value 66, whereas the character equivalent for ASCII value 98 is the letter 'b'.

```
/* SQL Example 9.1 */
SELECT ASCII('Bijoy') "ASCII", CHAR(98) "Character"

ASCII        Character
----------   ---------
66           b
```

SQL Example 9.2 shows a SELECT statement that uses the ASCII function with the *emp_last_name* column from the *employee* table. The result table shows the last names and the ASCII values for the first character of each name.

```
/* SQL Example 9.2 */
SELECT emp_last_name "Last Name", ASCII(emp_last_name) "ASCII Value"
FROM employee;

Last Name     ASCII Value
-----------   -----------
Bock          66
Amin          65
Joshi         74
```

The UNICODE function works like the ASCII function except that it returns an INT value according to the Unicode standard for the first character of the expression. The Unicode string of characters must be of data type NCHAR or NVARCHAR. The general syntax of UNICODE is:

```
UNICODE(unicode_string)
```

SQL Example 9.3 shows a SELECT statement that uses the UNICODE function. The result table displays the UNICODE equivalency for the dollar sign ($) and the Malta lira (£).

```
/* SQL Example 9.3 */
SELECT UNICODE('$10,000') "Value of $ Sign",
    UNICODE('£') "Value of £ Sign"

Value of $ Sign Value of £ Sign
--------------- ---------------
36              163
```

The STR function converts numeric data to a character string. This conversion function requires a FLOAT data type with a decimal point as a required argument. It also has two optional arguments that can be used to specify the length of the returned character string (including decimal point, sign, digits, and spaces), and the number of digits in the string to the right of the decimal point. The default value for the length of the returned character string is 10 characters. The general syntax for STR is:

```
STR(float_expression [, length [, decimal]])
```

SQL Example 9.4 uses the STR function to display several FLOAT values. The first two numbers demonstrate how STR rounds up or down when the number of digits to be displayed to the right of the decimal are fewer than the actual precision of the number. The third number is not displayed because a length of '4' was specified and the number 12345 cannot fit into four characters. If STR cannot store significant digits to the left of the decimal point into the specified strength length, then the function returns a string of asterisks to warn you that your specification is not sufficiently large. The last number shows the display with no digits specified to the right of the decimal. The value is rounded to the nearest whole number. Remember, all these values are now treated as strings.

```
/* SQL Example 9.4 */
SELECT STR(12345.6789,8,2) "Rounded Up",
    STR(12345.6744,8,2) "Rounded Down",
    STR(12345.6789,4,2) "Length Too Short",
    STR(12345.6789,6) "No Decimal Value";

Rounded Up  Rounded Down  Length Too Short  No Decimal Value
----------  ------------  ----------------  ----------------
12345.68    12345.67      ****                         12346
```

SQL Example 9.5 shows the display of values from the *emp_salary* column of the *employee* table. The first column is displayed by using the STR function whereas the second column displays the data as stored in the table.

```
/* SQL Example 9.5 */
SELECT STR(emp_salary,7,0) "Salary As String",
    emp_salary "Salary as Money"
FROM employee;

Salary As String  Salary as Money
----------------  ---------------
    30000         30000.0000
    25000         25000.0000
    38000         38000.0000
more rows will be displayed...
```

LEFT AND RIGHT FUNCTIONS

The LEFT and RIGHT functions are string extraction functions. That is, both of these extract substrings from strings. Generally, a substring is simply a smaller string of characters that are a subset of a larger string. For example, the substring of the first four characters of the character string 'Bordoloi' is 'Bord'. The LEFT function returns the left part of a character string for the specified number of characters, whereas the

RIGHT function returns the right part of a character string for the specified number of characters. Both functions have two required arguments. The general syntax for the LEFT and RIGHT function is:

```
LEFT(character_string, integer_value)

RIGHT(character_string, integer_value)
```

The character string argument may be any data type that can be implicitly converted to VARCHAR or NVARCHAR, but cannot be TEXT or NTEXT. The integer value must be a positive value that specifies the number of characters to extract (return) from the character string. SQL Example 9.6 shows the use of both of these functions for columns in the *employee* table.

```
/* SQL Example 9.6 */
SELECT emp_last_name "Full Name",
    LEFT(emp_last_name, 5) "First 5",
    RIGHT(emp_last_name, 5) "Last 5"
FROM employee;

Full Name       First 5 Last 5
------------    ------- ------

Bock            Bock    Bock
Amin            Amin    Amin
Joshi           Joshi   Joshi
Zhu             Zhu     Zhu
Joyner          Joyne   oyner
Bordoloi        Bordo   doloi
Markis          Marki   arkis
Prescott        Presc   scott
```

Here, the LEFT function extracts the first five characters from the *emp_last_name* column whereas the RIGHT function extracts the last five characters from the column. Notice the result for employees with five or fewer characters in their last name.

LEN, LTRIM, AND RTRIM FUNCTIONS

The LEN function returns a numeric value equivalent to the number of characters (not bytes) in a specified character string while ignoring trailing blank characters. LEN is usually used in conjunction with other functions for tasks such as determining how much space needs to be allocated for a column of output on a report. The general syntax of the LEN function is:

```
LEN(character_string)
```

We have seen that SQL Server usually stores character string data using the CHAR or VARCHAR data types. CHAR columns are fixed length and SQL Server blank pads, that is, add blanks to character strings that do not completely fill a CHAR column. VARCHAR columns are variable length. Since the LEN function ignores trailing blanks in character strings, the count of characters returned is the same for CHAR and VARCHAR columns.

The SELECT statement in SQL Example 9.7 produces a result table listing the cities where employees reside. It also displays the numeric length of each city name. Additionally, because the *emp_city* column is defined as VARCHAR, the field is not blank padded.

```
/* SQL Example 9.7 */
SELECT DISTINCT emp_city "City", LEN(emp_city) "Length"
FROM employee;

City             Length
---------------- -------------
Collinsville     12
Edwardsville     12
Marina           6
Monterey         8
St. Louis        9
```

The LTRIM and RTRIM functions trim blank characters from the left and right ends of strings, respectively. The syntax for each of these functions is:

```
RTRIM(character_string)
```

```
LTRIM(character_string)
```

Suppose that a data table has two fixed-length columns defined as CHAR(15), but these columns actually store values of variable length, such as the names of drugs and the unit of measurement. Further, suppose that we wish to concatenate these two columns for purposes of display in a result table. Because CHAR data fields are automatically blank padded when values are not sufficiently large to fill up all the column space, concatenating the columns would display values with too much blank space between the drug name and the unit of measurement. However, you can use the RTRIM function when concatenating to produce a more pleasing display.

Let us test this by creating a table named *drug_table*, and by inserting three rows of data into the table as shown by the sequence of commands in SQL Example 9.8.

```
/* SQL Example 9.8 */
CREATE TABLE drug_table (
drug_name       CHAR(15),
drug_unit       CHAR(15));

INSERT INTO drug_table VALUES ('Aspirin', '25 mg');
INSERT INTO drug_table VALUES ('Toprol', '0.05 mg');
INSERT INTO drug_table VALUES ('Ibuprofen', '800 mg');
```

Now, suppose that a business manager requests a report listing drugs and their unit of measure for prescriptions. The SELECT statement in SQL Example 9.9 displays the drug names and units of measure concatenated without and with the use of the RTRIM function. The display in the second column is easier for a business manager to read.

```
/* SQL Example 9.9 */
SELECT drug_name + drug_unit "Drug",
    RTRIM(drug_name) + ' ' + RTRIM(drug_unit) "Concatenated"
FROM drug_table;


Drug                           Concatenated
------------------------------ -----------------
Aspirin         25 mg          Aspirin 25 mg
Toprol          0.05 mg        Toprol 0.05 mg
Ibuprofen       800 mg         Ibuprofen 800 mg
```

UPPER and LOWER Functions

The UPPER and LOWER functions can alter the appearance of information displayed in a result table. Again, the appearance of information may be important for business managers. The UPPER function converts character string data to uppercase letters. The LOWER function, on the other hand, converts character string data to lowercase letters. The general syntax of these functions is:

```
LOWER(char_value)
```

```
UPPER(char_value)
```

The query in SQL Example 9.10 selects data from the *employee* table. The *emp_gender* column stores a single-character coded value of "M" for male or "F" for female, and these values are stored in capitalized format. The first expression in the SELECT clause uses the LOWER function to display these coded gender values in lowercase. The second expression in the SELECT clause uses the UPPER function to display employee last names as all capital letters.

```
/* SQL Example 9.10 */
SELECT LOWER(emp_gender) "Gender",
    UPPER(emp_last_name) "Last Name"
FROM employee;

Gender Last Name
------ -----------
  m      BOCK
  m      AMIN
  m      JOSHI
more rows will be displayed...
```

Each employee's state of residence is stored as a two-character abbreviation, such as "CA" for California and "NY" for New York. If it is desirable to display these values with only the first letter capitalized, the LOWER function can first return the lowercase equivalents of these two-character abbreviations. First, we know each state abbreviation is two characters. We can use LOWER to return the lowercase equivalent of the second character in a state abbreviation by extracting it with the RIGHT function. We then concatenate this single character to the first character of the state abbreviation by extracting the first character with the LEFT function. If we do not know for certain that the first letter is capitalized, we can embed the LEFT function within an UPPER function to ensure the desired result. The resulting state abbreviation can be displayed with just the first letter capitalized as demonstrated by SQL Example 9.11.

```
/* SQL Example 9.11 */
SELECT LTRIM(emp_last_name) "Last Name",
    UPPER(LEFT(emp_state,1)) + LOWER(RIGHT(emp_state,1)) "State"
FROM employee;

Last Name                          State
---------------------------------  -----
Bock                               Mo
Amin                               Ca
Joshi                              Il
more rows will be displayed...
```

CHARINDEX AND REPLACE FUNCTIONS

The CHARINDEX function returns the INT value of the starting position for a substring within a character string. This function is useful for identifying the starting position so that we can confirm that the substring can be found within the larger string. The general syntax is:

```
CHARINDEX( character_string1, character_string2 [, start_position])
```

The first character string argument is the substring to be found in the second character string argument. The second character string argument is usually expressed as a column from a table. The start position argument is optional and can be used to specify a character position starting point for the search. The default start position for the search is the first character of the second character string. If the search is unsuccessful, CHARINDEX returns a value of zero.

All this is quite abstract and a concrete example can help you understand the use of this function. Suppose one of the business managers needs a listing of all employees by name and address who live on High Street (abbreviated High St.). SQL Example 9.12 gives a SELECT statement that searches the *emp_address* column of the *employee* table along with the result table.

```
/* SQL Example 9.12 */
SELECT RTRIM(emp_last_name) + ', ' + RTRIM(emp_first_name) "Employee",
    emp_address "Address"
FROM employee
WHERE CHARINDEX('High St', emp_address) != 0;


Employee           Address
-----------------  --------------
Markis, Marcia     High St. #14
```

The CHARINDEX function is used within the WHERE clause. Recall that if the substring is found within the *emp_address*, then the INT value returned is NOT zero; however, if the substring is not found, then the INT value is zero. Thus, we tested for the return value NOT EQUAL TO 0. Only one employee was found to live on High Street.

This function is complex enough that it warrants another example. SQL Example 9.13 uses the Riverbend Hospital database (Appendix B) to list patients who were 'admitted from ER' to the hospital for treatment. This is a typical listing that a hospital administer might require. This particular SELECT statement requires joining the *patient* and *patient_note* tables on the common patient identification numbers (*pat_id* columns). The CHARINDEX function is used to filter the patient listing to those who have been admitted from ER.

```
/* SQL Example 9.13 */
SELECT RTRIM(pat_last_name)+', '+RTRIM(pat_first_name) "Patient",
    note_comment
FROM patient p INNER JOIN patient_note pn ON p.pat_id = pn.pat_id
WHERE CHARINDEX('admitted from ER', note_comment) != 0
ORDER BY note_date;


Patient                 note_comment
---------------------   ------------------------------------------
Howard, Ronald          Patient admitted from ER at 0022 hours
Lakeside, Lillian       Patient admitted from ER at 1235 hours
Algebra, Albert         Patient admitted from ER at 0725 hours
more rows will be displayed...
```

The REPLACE function scans a character string and replaces all occurrences of a character substring with another specified character substring. The general syntax is:

```
REPLACE(character_string, substring1, substring2)
```

Extending SQL Example 9.13, management at the Riverbend Hospital wants to replace the acronym "ER" with the words "Emergency room." Such might be the case for a report listing that is prepared for individuals who do not normally work in hospitals. SQL Example 9.14 uses the REPLACE function to modify SQL Example 9.13 to accomplish this.

```
/* SQL Example 9.14 */
SELECT RTRIM(pat_last_name)+', '+RTRIM(pat_first_name) "Patient",
    REPLACE(note_comment, 'ER', 'Emergency room') "Note Comment"
FROM patient p INNER JOIN patient_note pn ON p.pat_id = pn.pat_id
WHERE CHARINDEX('admitted from ER', note_comment) != 0
ORDER BY note_date;


Patient             Note Comment
----------------    -------------------------------------------------------
Howard, Ronald      Patient admitted from Emergency room at 0022 hours
Lakeside, Lillian   Patient admitted from Emergency room at 1235 hours
Algebra, Albert     Patient admitted from Emergency room at 0725 hours
more rows will be displayed...
```

SUBSTRING FUNCTION

The SUBSTRING function is a very powerful function that can extract a substring from a string of characters. This is useful for displaying portions of a larger stored text character string, and the function can operate on character, binary, text, or image data. The general format of the function is:

```
SUBSTRING(character_string, start_position, number_of_characters])
```

The function has three required arguments. The first is the character_string that is the object of the extraction process. The second argument is an INT value that specifies the start position of the substring to be extracted. The third argument is an INT value that specifies the number of characters to be extracted. The SELECT statement in SQL Example 9.15 extracts the last four digits of each employee's SSN for display in a result table for department 3.

```
/* SQL Example 9.15 */
SELECT RTRIM(emp_last_name) + ', ' + RTRIM(emp_first_name) "Employee",
    SUBSTRING(emp_ssn,6,4) "Last 4 SSN"
FROM employee
WHERE emp_dpt_number = 3;


Employee                Last 4 SSN
--------------------    ----------
Amin, Hyder             2222
Joyner, Suzanne         5555
Markis, Marcia          7777
```

The above example also demonstrates, as was done earlier, the use of the plus symbol as a *concatenation operator* (+). You can also use functions with the concatenation operator. Recall that employee SSNs are stored without the normal dashes used when displaying these values. However, business managers normally expect data reports and listings to provide formatted SSNs. SQL Example 9.16

demonstrates formatting employee SSNs for a result table. The concatenation operator is also used to format each employee name (last and first name) for display as a single column.

```
/* SQL Example 9.16 */
SELECT emp_last_name+', '+emp_first_name "Employee ",
    SUBSTRING(emp_ssn,1,3)+'-'+SUBSTRING(emp_ssn,4,2)+'-'+
    SUBSTRING(emp_ssn,6,4) "SSN"
FROM employee
WHERE emp_dpt_number = 3;

Employee                 SSN
-----------------------  ------------
Amin, Hyder              999-22-2222
Joyner, Suzanne          999-55-5555
Markis, Marcia           999-88-7777
```

The SELECT clause concatenates each employee last name with a comma and blank space. This string is then concatenated to the employee first name. The SSN is formatted by using the first SUBSTRING function to extract the first three numbers from the employee SSN character string beginning in character position 1. The concatenation operator appends these three numbers to a dash (-) symbol. Another concatenation operator appends a second SUBSTRING function that extracts the next two numbers of the SSN. Another set of concatenation operators append another dash, and then the third SUBSTRING extracts the last four digits of the SSN. You should also note that this particular expression is quite long. T-SQL allows you to break the expression to start a new line—a convenient break point is right before or after the use of a concatenation operator.

MATHEMATICAL FUNCTIONS

SQL Server has a large number of functions for manipulating columns that store the various types of numeric data. Aggregate row functions used to manipulate numeric data were covered in Chapter 5. In this chapter, you will learn about additional numeric functions that act on single values and that perform special mathematical manipulations.

SINGLE-VALUE FUNCTIONS

You may find that single-value functions are really quite simple. These functions can be combined with the arithmetic operator symbols for addition, subtraction, multiplication, division, and modulus division ($+ - * / \%$) to develop complex expressions for display in result tables. Numeric functions accept numeric arguments, such as expressions or column names defined as one of the numeric data types, and then they return numeric values. The type of data values returned vary from one function to the next. Table 9.3 lists some common single-value numeric functions and their use and definition. We examine several of these functions in detail.

TABLE 9.3	
Function	*Use/Definition*
ABS	The absolute value of a numeric expression; ABS(-5) returns 5
ACOS	The arccosine of a FLOAT; arguments must be between -1 and 1 and the returned value ranges from 0 to *pi* in radians; ACOS(0.5) = 1.047
ASIN	The arcsine of a FLOAT; arguments must be between -1 and 1 and the returned value ranges from *pi*/2 to *pi*/2 in radians; ASIN(0.5) = 0.524
ATAN	The arctangent of a FLOAT; arguments are unbounded and the returned value ranges from $-pi$/2 to *pi*/2 in radians; ATAN(0.5) = 0.464
ATAN2	The arctangent whose tangent is between two FLOAT values; arguments are unbounded and the returned value ranges from $-pi$ to *pi*; ATAN2(0.5, 5.0) = 0.0997
CEILING	The smallest integer value that is greater than or equal to a NUMERIC value; CEILING(6.6) = 7
COS	The cosine of a FLOAT expressed in radians; COS(0.5) = 0.8776
DEGREES	The angle in degrees of a numeric value given in radians; DEGREES(0.5) = 29
EXP	The value of the mathematical constant 'e' raised to the *n*th power; EXP(1) = 2.718
FLOOR	The largest integer value that is less than or equal to a number; FLOOR(6.7) = 6
LOG	The natural logarithm of a FLOAT number where the number is greater than zero; LOG(0.5) = -0.693
LOG10	The base-10 logarithm of a FLOAT number; LOG10(0.5) = -0.301
ISNULL	A replacement function; if value1 is NULL, ISNULL returns value2; otherwise, ISNULL returns value1; ISNULL(work_hours,0) substitutes a value of 0 for any NULL value in the *work_hours* column
PI	Returns the constant value of PI; requires no argument; PI( ) = 3.14
POWER	The number1 raised to the number2 power; if number1 is negative, number2 must be an integer; POWER(5.00, 0.5) = 2.24
ROUND	Rounds a number1 to number2 decimal places; ROUND(15.34563, 2) = 15.35000
SIGN	Evaluates number1; returns -1 if number1 is negative, 0 if number1 is 0, 1 if number1 is positive; SIGN(0.5) = 1.0
SIN	The sine of a FLOAT expressed in radians; SIN(0.5) = 0.479
SQRT	The square root of a FLOAT; the FLOAT must be positive; SQRT(5.0) = 2.236
SQUARE	The square of a given FLOAT expression; SQUARE(2.2) = 4.84
TAN	The tangent of a number expressed in radians; TAN(0.5) = 0.546

TRANSCENDENTAL FUNCTIONS

The transcendental functions include the single-value functions named ACOS, ASIN, ATAN, ATAN2, COS, EXP, LOG, LOG10, SIN, and TAN. Business programming rarely requires these functions, and we do not define each of them here. For the most part, they are used in scientific applications. There is also some applicability in the quantitative business areas such as finance and marketing research. The query in SQL Example 9.17 demonstrates how to generate values for selected transcendental functions.

```
/* SQL Example 9.17 */
SELECT COS(0.5) "COS", EXP(1) "EXP", LOG(0.5) "LOG",
    LOG10(0.5) "LOG10";


COS        EXP        LOG         LOG10
--------   ---------  ----------  ----------
0.877582 2.7182818 -0.6931472 -0.3010300
more precision is displayed with SQL Query Analyzer
```

ISNULL FUNCTION FOR NULL VALUE SUBSTITUTION

You have learned that NULL values actually represent an unknown value. Sometimes when values in tables are unknown, it is possible to substitute a reasonable guess or average value where a NULL value exists. At other times you may wish to highlight the absence of a value by substituting another value, such as zero for the NULL value. The query in SQL Example 9.18 reveals that some employees have NULL values for the *work_hours* column in the *assignment* table for projects 1 and 20.

```
/* SQL Example 9.18 */
SELECT work_emp_ssn "SSN", work_pro_number "Project",
    work_hours "Hours"
FROM assignment
WHERE work_pro_number IN (1,20);


SSN         Project Hours
----------  ------- -----
999111111 1         31.4
999444444 1         NULL
999444444 20        11.8
999555555 20        14.8
999666666 20        NULL
999888888 1         21.0
```

Suppose that the senior project manager has requested that you produce a result table and substitute the value 0.0 where NULL values exist in the *assignment* table. You can accomplish this task with the ISNULL function. ISNULL is a substitution function and it allows you to substitute a specified value where the stored value in a row is NULL. The general format of the ISNULL function is:

```
ISNULL(check_expression, replacement_value)
```

The ISNULL function works with numeric, character, date, and other data types. If *check_expression* is NULL, ISNULL returns the *replacement_value*; otherwise, ISNULL returns the *check_expression*. SQL Example 9.19 produces the result requested by the senior project manager by listing a value of .0 where *work_hours* is NULL.

```
/* SQL Example 9.19 */
SELECT work_emp_ssn "SSN", work_pro_number "Project",
    ISNULL(work_hours, 0) "Hours"
FROM assignment
WHERE work_pro_number IN (1,20);

SSN        Project Hours
---------- ------- -----
999111111 1        31.4
999444444 1        .0
999444444 20       11.8
999555555 20       14.8
999666666 20       .0
999888888 1        21.0
```

ABS FUNCTION

The absolute value is a mathematical measure of magnitude. The general format of the ABS function is:

```
ABS(numeric_value)
```

SQL Server provides the ABS function for use in computing the absolute value of a numeric value or expression. Business managers may be interested in the magnitude by which a particular value deviates from some standard or average value. For example, suppose that the senior project manager has established 20 hours as the desired standard for working on assigned projects. The manager may wish to know which employees have deviated significantly from this standard on a project, either by not working enough (less than 10 hours) or by exceeding expectations (more than 30 hours). The query in SQL Example 9.20 addresses the senior project manager's concerns.

```
/* SQL Example 9.20 */
SELECT work_emp_ssn "SSN", work_pro_number "Project #",
    work_hours "Hours Worked", ABS(work_hours - 20) "Difference"
FROM assignment
WHERE ABS(work_hours - 20) >= 10
ORDER BY ABS(work_hours - 20);

SSN        Project # Hours Worked Difference
---------- --------- ------------ ----------
999887777 30         30.8         10.8
999111111 1          31.4         11.4
999111111 2          8.5          11.5
999222222 10         34.5         14.5
999222222 30         5.1          14.9
999333333 3          42.1         22.1
```

The result table lists each employee SSN, project number, hours worked on the project, and number of hours by which the hours worked deviates from the standard of 20 hours. Note how the ABS function is used in the SELECT clause to compute the Difference column, in the WHERE clause to specify the criteria for row selection, and in the ORDER BY clause to order the result table by the degree of work deviation.

POWER, SQRT, SQUARE, AND ROUND FUNCTIONS

The POWER, SQRT (square root), and SQUARE are typically used in scientific computing, but they may also be used in writing expressions for queries in the financial or marketing research areas. The ROUND function has general applicability to many business applications where output data needs to be rounded. The general format for these functions is:

```
POWER(numeric_value1, numeric_value2)

SQRT(float_value)

SQUARE(float_value)

ROUND(numeric_value, integer_value)
```

The POWER function raises *numeric value1* to a specified positive exponent, *numeric value2*. The SQUARE function squares any FLOAT numeric value. The SQRT function computes the square root of a numeric value, expression, or numeric column value. You may have noted that SQRT(*float_value*) is equivalent to POWER(*numeric_value1*, 0.5), whereas SQUARE(*float_value*) is equivalent to POWER(*numeric_value1*, 2). The sample query in SQL Example 9.21 demonstrates the use of these three functions.

```
/* SQL Example 9.21 */
SELECT POWER(25.0, 3.0) "Cubed",
    POWER(25.0, 0.5) "0.5 Power",
    SQRT(25) "Square Root", SQUARE(25.0) "Squared";

Cubed          0.5 Power      Square Root      Squared
-------------- -------------- ---------------- --------
15625.0        5.0            5.0              625.0
```

The ROUND function displays numeric values to specific levels of mathematical precision. The general format is:

```
ROUND(numeric_value, integer_value)
```

The ROUND function rounds *numeric value* to the specified number of digits of precision, an integer value shown in the formal definition as *integer_value*. Usually, we round numbers to some number of digits after the decimal; however, rounding to whole numbers is also allowed. Suppose that a manager needs a listing of hours worked by employees assigned to projects, but wishes the listing to be rounded to the nearest whole hour. Another manager may require a similar listing, but desires the hours to be rounded to the nearest 10 hours. The query in SQL Example 9.22 produces a result table that supports both managerial needs. Note the use of the negative value (-1) for rounding to the nearest 10 hours.

```
/* SQL Example 9.22 */
SELECT work_emp_ssn "SSN", work_hours "Hours",
    ROUND(work_hours,0) "Rounded 0 Hours",
    ROUND(work_hours,-1) "Rounded 10 Hours"
FROM assignment
ORDER BY work_emp_ssn;

SSN        Hours   Rounded 0 Hours Rounded 10 Hours
---------- ------- --------------- ----------------
999111111 31.4    31.0            30.0
999111111 8.5     9.0             10.0
999222222 34.5    35.0            30.0
more rows will be displayed...
```

CONVERSION FUNCTIONS

The conversion functions were introduced in Chapter 3 and have been used throughout much of the textbook. They were used to aid you in formatting result table output in a rudimentary fashion. However, the real purpose of conversion functions is to convert one data type to another data type. This is termed *explicit casting* or simply *conversion*. For certain data types and operations, SQL Server supports *implicit casting*, which is the automatic conversion of one data type to another data type. For example, if you compare a CHAR expression with a DATETIME expression, SQL Server automatically converts the two expressions for purposes of the comparison.

SQL Server provides the CONVERT and CAST functions for explicit casting. The CONVERT function can do everything and even more than the CAST function However, the CAST is provided for compatibility to the SQL-92 standard for the SQL

CONVERT FUNCTION

The CONVERT function is quite versatile and supports any SQL Server valid data type. You can use the CONVERT function in both SELECT and WHERE clauses. In fact, you can use CONVERT anywhere you would normally use an expression. The function requires two arguments and has a third optional argument as shown by the following general syntax:

```
CONVERT(data_type, value_to_convert [,style])
```

If the data type requires a length argument that specifies the length of the returned value, you pass the length in the parentheses that enclose the data type. Style is optional and is used when the data type to which you are converting can take on different style changes. For example, style would be selected when converting DATETIME to CHAR for purposes of specifying how to display the date or time.

SQL Example 9.23 demonstrates formatting of an output column size of a result table for the *emp_last_name* column of the *employee* table. The *emp_last_name* and *emp_first_name* columns are both defined as VARCHAR(25) in the *employee* table. A company manager may request a listing of employees with the full name displayed as a single column and limited to a display of 12 characters in width. We can do this by converting the output display to the fixed character string CHAR(12). This can prevent output lines with several columns that would otherwise be quite wide from wrapping around in the result table. Output that does not fit within the width specification is truncated as was done for several of the names.

```
/* SQL Example 9.23 */
SELECT CONVERT(CHAR(12), emp_last_name+', '+emp_first_name) "Name"
FROM employee;

Name
------------
Bock, Dougla
Amin, Hyder
Joshi, Dines
Zhu, Waiman
Joyner, Suza
Bordoloi, Bi
Markis, Marc
Prescott, Sh
```

SQL Example 9.24 shows the use of the CONVERT function with employee names to display the last name, a comma, and then simply the first initial of the first name followed by a period. Notice that:

```
/* SQL Example 9.24 */
SELECT emp_last_name + ', '+CONVERT(CHAR(1), emp_first_name)+'.' "Name"
FROM employee;

Name
----------
Bock, D.
Amin, H.
Joshi, D.
more rows will be displayed...
```

SQL Example 9.25 shows the conversion of the *emp_date_of_birth* column, which is defined as a DATETIME column in the *employee* table to a CHAR display. Note the use of style 107 as a parameter. The various values for the style parameter are given in

Table 9.4. The designation (24) indicates use of the 24-hour clock commonly referred to as military time.

```
/* SQL Example 9.25 */
SELECT CONVERT(CHAR(15), RTRIM(emp_last_name) + ', ' +
    RTRIM(emp_first_name)) "Employee",
    CONVERT(CHAR(27), emp_date_of_birth, 107) "Birthday"
FROM employee;


Employee          Birthday
---------------   ------------
Bock, Douglas     Dec 05, 1950
Amin, Hyder       Mar 29, 1969
Joshi, Dinesh     Sep 15, 1972
more rows will be displayed...
```

TABLE 9.4

Style Code for 2-Digit Year	Style Code for 4-Digit Year	Standard for	Date Format
—	—	Default	mon dd yyyy hh:miAM
1	101	USA	mm/dd/yy
2	102	ANSI	yy.mm.dd
3	103	British and French	dd/mm/yy
4	104	German	dd.mm.yy
5	105	Italian	dd-mm-yy
6	106	—	dd mon yy
7	107	—	mon dd, yy
8	108	—	hh:mi:ss
—	9 and 109	Default + milliseconds	mon dd yyyy hh:mi:ss:mmmAM
10	110	USA	mm-dd-yy
11	111	Japan	yy/mm/dd
12	112	ISO	Yymmdd
—	13 and 113	European default + milliseconds	dd mm yyyy hh:mi:ss:mmm(24)
14	114	—	hh:mi:ss:mmm(24)
—	20 and 120	ODBC canonical	yyyy-mm-dd hh:mi:ss(24)
—	21 and 121	ODBC canonical (with milliseconds)	yyyy-mm-dd hh:mi:ss:mmm(24)
—	126	ISO8601	yyyy-mm-dd Thh:mm:ss.mmm (no spaces)
	130	Hijri calendar (Kuwait)	hh:mi:ss:mmmAM
	131	Hijri calendar (Kuwait)	dd/mm/yy hh:mi:ss:mmmAM

There are several characteristics of data conversions behaviors that you need to understand. These include:

- An error is generated if a conversion is not possible. For example, you cannot convert the character string '123xyz' to an integer because of the presence of letters in the character string.
- The default length for a conversion is 30 characters.
- When converting from character to DATETIME and SMALLDATETIME, an error is generated when you try to convert a character string not recognized by SQL Server as a valid date. This also applies when converting DATETIME to SMALLDATETIME. The dates converted must fall within the allowable range of values for a SMALLDATETIME (e.g., Jan. 1, 1990 to Jun. 6, 2079).
- When converting INT to MONEY or SMALLMONEY, integer values are assumed to be whole dollars for conversions to U.S. currency, or whole money equivalents for other currencies).
- When converting FLOAT to MONEY, the FLOAT value is rounded to four digits to the right of the decimal.
- When converting from CHAR or VARCHAR to MONEY, the character string can include a currency sign such as $ and a decimal point (optional), but cannot contain letter characters or a comma.
- When converting character strings to any data type where the character string is too long to fit within the data type, the character string value is truncated. SQL Server displays an asterisk.
- You can convert TEXT to CHAR or VARCHAR and IMAGE to BINARY or VARBINARY, subject to the size limit of the data type to which you are converting. This also applies to conversions of NTEXT to NCHAR and NVARCHAR.

CAST FUNCTION

The CAST function produces identical output to the CONVERT function except the CAST function does not support the style argument when converting to a target data type that can have more than one style for conversion, as noted for DATETIME above. The syntax for CAST is, however, different. It requires two arguments and the required keyword, AS.

```
CAST(value_to_convert AS data_type)
```

SQL Example 9.26 demonstrates the use of CAST to produce a result table identical to that produced earlier by SQL Example 9.23.

```
/* SQL Example 9.26 */
SELECT CAST(emp_last_name+', '+emp_first_name AS CHAR(12)) "Name"
FROM employee;
```

```
Name
-------------
Bock, Dougla
Amin, Hyder
Joshi, Dines
Zhu, Waiman
Joyner, Suza
Bordoloi, Bi
Markis, Marc
Prescott, Sh
```

DATE FUNCTIONS

From your study of Chapter 2 and subsequent chapters, you may recall that the DATETIME and SMALLDATETIME data types store both date and time information, including the hour, minute, and second. Further, the DATETIME data type also stores time information accurate to 3.33 milliseconds (msec). SQL Server provides numerous date functions to support date and time manipulations. We focus on the date functions that you may use most often as a T-SQL programmer. These are described in Table 9.5.

GETDATE AND GETUTCDATE FUNCTIONS

The GETDATE function returns the current date and time from the computer's operating system. You can use GETDATE in any SELECT statement to display the current system date. You can also use GETDATE in INSERT statements as well as in the DEFAULT clause of the CREATE TABLE command for setting the default value for a DATETIME column. In the example shown in SQL Example 9.27, the GETDATE function displays the current date and time. This also shows the default format date and time that is output for SQL Server.

TABLE 9.5	
Function	*Use/Definition*
DATEADD	Adds a specified interval to a specified date
DATEDIFF	Returns the difference in terms of date and time boundaries between two specified dates
DATENAME	Returns a character string for a specified part of a specified date
DAY	Returns an integer value for the day part of a specified date
GETDATE	Returns the current system date and time using the SQL Server standard internal format for DATETIME values
GETUTCDATE	Returns the current system date and time using the universal time coordinate (also termed greenwich mean time)
MONTH	Returns an integer value for the month part of a specified date
YEAR	Returns an integer value for the year part of a specified date

```
/* SQL Example 9.27 */
SELECT GETDATE() "Current Date and Time";

Current Date and Time
-------------------------
2003-02-06 19:22:08.153
```

DATEPART TABLE

Several date functions require an argument parameter commonly referred to in Microsoft documentation as *datepart*. Additionally, there is a DATEPART function, but we do not cover it in this textbook. The *datepart* argument is used to specify the part of a date to return by a function. Table 9.6 defines the possible values for *datepart* as well as accepted abbreviations to use for this argument. You will notice the use of *datepart* throughout the remainder of this section.

DATE ARITHMETIC, AND **DATEADD** AND **DATEDIFF** FUNCTIONS

SQL Server provides the capability to perform date arithmetic through use of the DATEADD and DATEDIFF functions. The general syntax for DATEADD is:

```
DATEADD(datepart, number, date)
```

The argument *datepart* is as specified in Table 9.6. If you wish to add days to a specified date, you could use the accepted abbreviation *dd*. The *number* argument is the increment and must be an integer value. Specifying a noninteger such as 1.65 simply causes the 0.65 portion of the number to be discarded. Finally, the *date* argument is a DATETIME or SMALLDATE expression, usually a table column name (that stores a date value). It can also be a character string that is in one of the acceptable date formats. For example, if you add seven (7) to a value stored in a DATETIME or SMALLDATETIME column, SQL Server produces a date that is 1 week later than the stored date. Adding 7 is equivalent to adding 7 days to the date. Likewise, subtracting 7 from a stored date by adding a −7, produces a date that is a week earlier than the stored date.

TABLE 9.6			
Datepart	*Abbreviation*	*Datepart*	*Abbreviation*
Year	yy, yyyy	Day	dd, d
Quarter	qq, q	Hour	hh
Month	mm, m	Minute	mi, n
Dayofyear	dy, y	Second	ss, s
Week	wk, ww	Millisecond	Ms
Day of week *	dw		

* Not an accepted abbreviation for *datepart*—use the abbreviation *dw* instead.

Suppose one of our company managers wants a listing of employees along with the date on which each employee will turn 65 years of age, this the firm's mandatory retirement age. SQL Example 9.28 provides the required result table by adding 65 years to the employee's date of birth that is stored in the *employee* table. This also demonstrates why the date of birth is stored as opposed to the employee's age because the age value would require constant maintenance to update stored age values.

```
/* SQL Example 9.28 */
SELECT CONVERT(CHAR(15), RTRIM(emp_last_name) + ', ' +
    RTRIM(emp_first_name)) "Employee",
    DATEADD(year, 65, emp_date_of_birth) "Date Turns 65"
FROM employee;

Employee         Date Turns 65
---------------- ------------------------
Bock, Douglas    2015-12-05 00:00:00.000
Amin, Hyder      2034-03-29 00:00:00.000
Joshi, Dinesh    2037-09-15 00:00:00.000
more rows will be displayed...
```

The DATEDIFF function performs date subtraction. Subtracting two DATETIME or SMALLDATE columns can be used to produce the number of years, quarters, months, weeks, days, and so forth, between two dates. The general syntax is:

```
DATEDIFF(datepart, start_date, end_date)
```

Again, the argument *datepart* is as specified in Table 9.6. The start_date and end_date arguments are valid date expressions or character strings in valid date formats. Suppose that a human resources manager needs to know how many months the department manager of department 3 has worked in this assigned position. The query in SQL Example 9.29 produces the desired result table by combining use of the DATEDIFF and GETDATE functions.

```
/* SQL Example 9.29 */
SELECT dpt_mgrssn "SSN", emp_last_name "Last Name",
    DATEDIFF(mm, dpt_mgr_start_date, GETDATE()) "Number of Months"
FROM department d INNER JOIN employee e ON d.dpt_mgrssn = e.emp_ssn
WHERE dpt_no = 3;

SSN        Last Name  Number of Months
---------- ---------- -----------------
999555555  Joyner     25
Your answer will vary depending on when you execute the query.
```

DATENAME, DAY, MONTH, AND YEAR FUNCTIONS

The DATENAME function performs exactly as its name implies—it returns a character string specifying the desired *datepart* of a specified date. The general syntax is:

```
DATENAME(datepart, date)
```

Likewise, the DAY, MONTH, and YEAR functions perform exactly as their names imply—each returns an INT data type value representing the desired portion of a specified date. The general syntax for these functions is:

```
DAY(date)
```

```
MONTH(date)
```

```
YEAR(date)
```

SQL Example 9.30 shows the use for each of these four functions. At times business managers may wish to have result tables display portions of dates using one of these functions.

```
/* SQL Example 9.30 */
SELECT CAST(emp_last_name AS CHAR(12)) "Last Name",
    CAST(DATENAME(mm, emp_date_of_birth) AS CHAR(12)) "Month Born",
    DAY(emp_date_of_birth) "Day Born",
    MONTH(emp_date_of_birth) "Month As Number",
    YEAR(emp_date_of_birth) "Year Born"
FROM employee;

Last Name     Month Born   Day Born   Month As Number   Year Born
----------    ----------   --------   ---------------   ---------
Bock          December     5          12                1950
Amin          March        29         3                 1969
Joshi         September    15         9                 1972
more rows will display...
```

SUMMARY

In this chapter, you learned numerous additional functions that add power to SQL queries. Character functions are used to manipulate character string data. The ASCII, UNICODE, CHAR, and STR functions can convert values from one data type to another. The LEFT and RIGHT functions are used to extract substrings whereas LEN, LTRIM, and RTRIM can compute the number of characters in a character string and trim off leading and trailing blanks. The UPPER and LOWER functions alter the appearance of information displayed in a result table by displaying data as all upper- or lowercase letters. The CHARINDEX function searches for a substring within a larger string whereas REPLACE replaces occurrences of a substring in a character string. Finally, the SUBSTRING function can extract a substring from a character string.

Mathematical functions manipulate numeric data types. There are numerous transcendental functions such as ACOS and ASIN used for scientific applications. The ISNULL function is used to substitute values where data are otherwise NULL in value. The ABS function can be used to compute absolute differences between two values. The POWER, SQRT, SQUARE, and ROUND functions are used to raise numeric values to specified exponential values, to compute square roots, to square numeric values, and to round numeric values to specified precision levels, respectively.

The conversion functions CONVERT and CAST are used to convert data from one data type to another. CAST is provided for compatibility with the SQL-92 standard.

The Date functions GETDATE and GETUTCDATE generate the system date in both standard and UTC date formats. Date arithmetic is made possible through the DATEADD and DATEDIFF functions. Different parts of dates can be extracted and displayed in different formats through use of the DATENAME, DAY, MONTH, and YEAR functions.

REVIEW EXERCISES

LEARN THESE TERMS

ABS. Computes the absolute value of a number or numeric expression.

ASCII. Returns the ASCII code value of the leftmost character of a character string.

CAST. Converts one data type to another data type, but does not support the style argument that CONVERT supports.

CHAR. Converts an integer ASCII code value to the equivalent character.

CHARINDEX. Returns the starting position of a specified substring found within a character string.

CONVERT. Converts one data type to another data type—supports any SQL Server valid data type.

DATEADD. Adds a specified interval to a specified date.

DATEDIFF. Returns the difference between two specified dates.

DATENAME. Returns a character string from a specified date where the character string can be specified to be the year, month, day, hours, etc.

DAY. Returns an integer value for the day part of a specified date.

Explicit casting. The conversion of one data type to another data type.

GETDATE. Returns the current system date and time.

GETUTCDATE. Returns the current date and time using the universal time coordinate.

ISNULL. A function that allows a programmer to substitute a specified value wherein stored values are NULL.

LEFT. Returns the specified number of characters from the leftmost portion of a character string.

LEN. Returns a numeric value equivalent to the number of characters in a string of characters.

LOWER. Returns a character value that is all lowercase.

LTRIM. Trims specified characters from the left end of a string.

MONTH. Returns an integer value for the month part of a specified date.

POWER. Raises a numeric value to a specified positive exponent.

REPLACE. Replaces all occurrences of a character substring with another specified character substring within a character string.

RIGHT. Returns the specified number of characters from the rightmost portion of a character string.

ROUND. Displays numeric values to specific levels of mathematical precision.

RTRIM. Removes trailing blanks from a character string.

SQRT. Computes the square root of a numeric value, expression, or numeric column value.

SQUARE. Squares any FLOAT numeric value.

STR. Returns character data that is converted from numeric data.

SUBSTRING. Returns a string of specified length from a larger character string beginning at a specified character position.

UNICODE. Returns an integer value for the first character of an expression as defined for the Unicode standard.

UPPER. Returns a character value that is all uppercase.

YEAR. Returns an integer value for the year part of a specified date.

CONCEPTS QUIZ

1. Are numbers such as telephone numbers and product numbers treated as character or numeric data? Explain why?
2. What is the purpose of the UPPER and LOWER functions?
3. What does the LEN function do?
4. What is the purpose of the SUBSTRING function? What can the following SELECT statement do?

```
SELECT SUBSTRING(emp_ssn,6,4)
FROM employee;
```

5. What is the purpose of the LTRIM and RTRIM functions?
6. When using the CHARINDEX function to search a character string (substring), what does the function return if the character string is found, and is not found?
7. What is the purpose of the ISNULL function?
8. Which function would you use to measure the magnitude by which a particular value deviates from some standard or average value?
9. Explain the use of the CONVERT function. How is it different from CAST?
10. What values are turned by the GETDATE function?
11. How is the GETUTCDATE function different from GETDATE?
12. State what value is returned by the following expression: GETDATE() + 1.
13. You wish to know the date 6 months from now. Which function is best for displaying this value? Write the function specification to return a date 6 months from today's date.
14. What is the purpose of the DATENAME, DAY, MONTH, and YEAR functions?
15. How does the ROUND function round values?

SQL CODING EXERCISES AND QUESTIONS: COMPANY DATABASE

In answering the SQL exercises and questions, submit a copy of each command that you execute and any messages that Oracle generates while executing your SQL commands. Also list the output for any result table that is generated by your SQL statements.

1. Management requires a listing of employees by last name, first name, and middle initial. The last name should be displayed in all capital letters. The entire name should be concatenated together so as to display in a single column with a column heading of "Employee Name." The rows should be sorted by employee last name, then employee first name. The last and first names should be separated by a comma, for example, Bock, Douglas B. Do not worry about displaying a period after the middle initial.
2. Use the ASCII to display the ASCII equivalent of the first letter of each employee's last name. Assign an appropriate column heading to the output of the result table. The result table must also display each employee's last name to verify that the output of the ASCII function is correct.
3. To simplify output to a result table for a budgeting manager, you decide to write a query to display each employee's last name and salary as a single column. Convert the salary value to a character string and display the salary in whole dollars to the nearest dollar. Allocate eight characters for display of the salary. Order the output by employee last name and use the column heading "Name and Salary." Use the STR function.

4. Write a query that displays the department name and the length in number of characters of each department's name. Use the *department* table. Label the column headings appropriately.

5. Rewrite the query for Question 1 to only list employees who have the character string "oy" in the name. Use the CHARINDEX function.

6. Management wants a listing of department numbers and locations (use the *dept_locations* table)—display the output as a single column with the heading "Department Locations." Use the CONVERT function.

7. Write a query that displays the first four characters of each employee's last name and the last four digits of each employee's SSN. Label the column headings "Name" and "SSN." Order the result table rows by employee last name. Use the SUBSTRING function.

8. Produce a result table for management with a listing of employee last names and their street address, but only for employees who live on a street type address, for example, High St. Replace the abbreviation "St" with the word "Street."

9. Write a query to display a listing of employee last names and the SSN of the employee's supervisor. If the employee has no supervisor, display the message "Top Dog." Provide appropriate headings. Sort the result table by employee last name.

10. Develop for the company's senior project manager a listing of employees who reported working between 15 and 25 hours on assigned projects. List the employee last name, project number, and hours worked. Use the ABS function. Use meaningful column headings. Sort the rows of the result table by employee last name. Hint: 20 is the midpoint between 15 and 25 hours; the absolute value of the difference would be 5 hours.

11. The senior project manager needs a listing by employee last name, project number, and hours worked with the *work_hours* column rounded to the nearest integer value for projects 2 and 10. Sort the result table by employee last name within project number. Use meaningful column names.

12. Write a query to display dependent information for the human resources manager. Display each dependent's name, gender, and date of birth. The date of birth should be displayed as: Month Name (three-character abbreviation), two-digit day, and four-digit year (e.g., Dec 12, 1970).

13. Write a query to display each dependent's name, date of birth, and date on which the dependent turned or will turn 65 years of age. Use meaningful column names. Display each date using the DD MON YYYY format.

14. Write a short query to display the current day of the week from the operating system date.

15. The human resources manager needs a listing of dependents including their name and gender, but only for female dependents. Instead of displaying the coded value for gender, your result table must display the term "female." Use meaningful column headings. Sort the result table by dependent name.

SQL CODING EXERCISES AND QUESTIONS: RIVERBEND DATABASE

1. The chief of physicians requires a listing of staff members by last name, first name, and middle name. The last name should be displayed in all capital letters. The entire name should be concatenated together so as to display in a single field with

a column heading of "Staff Name." The rows should be sorted by staff member last name, then first name, and finally middle name. Separate the last and first names by a comma and sort the listing by last name.

2. Write a query that displays the scientific medicine name and the length in number of characters of each medicine name. Use the *medicine* table. Label the column headings appropriately.

3. Rewrite the query for Question 1 to only list staff members who have the character string "ou" in either the last or first name.

4. Rewrite the query for Question 3 to list staff members who have the character strings "ou" or "rd" in the name.

5. The hospital's chief of administration wants a listing of rooms and bed numbers. Display the *room_id* and *bed_number* columns from the *bed* table as a single column with the heading **Rooms/Beds**. Order the output by *room_id*.

6. Write a query that displays the first four characters of each staff member's last name and the last four digits of each staff member's SSN. Label the column headings "Name" and "SSN." Order the result table rows by staff member last name.

7. The chief of staff for the hospital needs a listing of staff members by last and first name along with their salary. If the staff member is paid a wage, the salary is NULL— do not list these staff members. Provide appropriate column headings and format the salary to include the dollar sign '$'. Sort the result table by staff member last name.

8. One of the hospital's financial analysts needs to compare actual treatment charges charged to patients to the established normal service charges for a treatment. Display the *service_id* and *service_charge* columns from the *service* table, and the *actual_charge* from the *treatment* table. The analyst is concerned with treatments where the actual difference between the service and actual charge is more than $50.00 above or below the normal serve charge (either high or low). Also display a computed column that is the difference between the service and actual charge (as a positive number). Use appropriate column sizes and headings and format the charges with a dollar sign ($) and appropriate comma and decimal point with two digits to the right of the decimal point.

9. The hospital's financial analyst has decided to focus on situations where there is a difference between the service and actual charge, but only where the actual charge was less than the established normal service charge. The analyst is concerned that there may be too many instances where the hospital is not charging a sufficient amount for services rendered. Modify the query for Question 8 above to meet these requirements. Sort the output by differences from largest to smallest. The columns to be displayed are the same as for Question 8.

10. Prepare a standard listing for the hospital's financial analyst that lists the *service_id* and *service_charge* for high-value services and round the *service_charge* to the nearest $10 dollars. Order the output by *service_id*. Display only services that have a *service_charge* value equal to or more than $1,000. A sample result table looks something like this:

```
Service Rounded Charge
------- --------------
12001   $  6,200.00
12002   $  6,500.00
12003   $  9,500.00
```

11. Write a query to display staff member information for the human resources manager. Display each staff member's last and first name (concatenated and restricted to 30 characters), hospital title (limited to 20 characters), and date hired. The date hired should be displayed as: Month Name (abbreviated to 3 characters, e.g., Jan, Feb, Mar), two-digit day, and four-digit year (e.g., Dec 05, 2002). Use the COLUMN commands shown to format the first two columns of output. Sort the output by date hired.

12. The hospital has a staff member recognition program that provides awards for staff members who have served the hospital 10 years or more. Write a query to display each staff member's last and first name (concatenated and restricted to 30 characters), date hired, and date on which the staff member celebrated or will celebrate 10 years of employment with the Riverbend Hospital. Use meaningful column names. Display each date using the DD-MON-YYYY format. Order the rows in the result table by the date hired.

13. Part of the hospital's patient recognition program (this program is for patients instead of staff members) recognizes patients who reach 60 years of age. Write a query to display each patient's last and first name (concatenated and limited to 30 characters of output), date of birth, and date on which the patient will be 60 years old. Use meaningful column names. Display each date using the DD-MON-YYYY format. Order the rows in the result table by the patient's date of birth.

14. The hospital's patient census manager needs a listing of beds by room and whether a bed is occupied. Instead of displaying the coded values for the *bed_availability* column, your result table must display the term "Occupied" if a patient is already assigned to the bed; otherwise, display the value for available from the *bed_availability* column that is the letter "N". Use meaningful column headings. Sort the result table by *bed_number* within *room_id*. The result table displays the *room_id*, *bed_number*, and *bed_availability* columns and look something like the listing shown here.

```
Room # Bed    Availability
------ -----  ------------
ER0001 50     Occupied
ER0001 51     N
ER0001 52     Occupied
ER0001 53     Occupied
ER0001 59     Occupied
ER0002 54     N
. . .
more rows will display
```

15. Modify your query in Question 14 to include the *bed_description* column (limited to 30 characters for output) from the *bed_type* table.

16. Modify your query in Question 15 to only list beds that have as part of the *bed_description* the word "fixed" (upper- or lowercase or any combination).

STORED PROCEDURES
AND TRIGGERS

In this chapter you learn some aspects of procedural programming with Microsoft's Transact Structured Query Language (T-SQL) procedural extensions of SQL. Our focus is on using procedural programming statements to develop *stored procedures* and *triggers*. A stored procedure is a small computer program that is maintained as a database object. Stored procedures are used to automate batch processing, that is, tasks that are performed repetitively. Typical uses of stored procedures are to control database access and to create audit trails of actions taken by system users and application programs that modify data stored in database tables. Additionally, stored procedures, as database objects, can be called (executed) by programs written in other programming languages.

A trigger is another type of small computer program. Triggers differ from stored procedures because a trigger executes whenever a specific data manipulation event for a database table or view occurs. Examples of events include the insertion or deletion of a row to or from a table. Triggers may also be programmed such that they execute in lieu of an actual data manipulation event.

OBJECTIVES

Thus far you have learned to use the nonprocedural capabilities of T-SQL to write queries and to manipulate data in tables. This chapter provides you an introduction to some of the procedural capabilities of T-SQL. Your learning objectives are:

- Learn the advantages of stored procedures.
- Learn about the permissions required to create stored procedures.
- Create and execute stored procedures.
- Write stored procedures with multiple parameters.
- Learn to avoid stored procedure parameter errors.
- Drop stored procedures.
- Learn how triggers work.

- Learn the different types of triggers.
- Write program code to create AFTER and INSTEAD OF triggers.
- Define the order of trigger execution for tables with multiple triggers.

STORED PROCEDURES

As you learned in the chapter introduction, a *stored procedure* is a kind of computer program that is used to process tasks that are repetitive in nature—meaning these computerized tasks are conducted over and over during the course of business.

Consider a situation where there is a need to control which employees can store new rows to a table. Storing data to database tables is a typical repetitive task. Suppose that your company operates retail stores that sell clothing. When clothing is sold, it is desirable for the sales data to be captured at the point of sale. Clearly, you would not expect even experienced salespersons to store sales data by using SQL INSERT statement because of the potential for errors to be made with this approach. Can you visualize a sales clerk typing an SQL INSERT statement at a computer workstation? Probably not. It just is not reasonable to expect employees in most job classifications to learn to use data manipulation language commands.

Now, try to visualize this same sales clerk using a computer application system that runs on a cash register (actually a special computer terminal) with a graphic user interface. The clerk would point-and-click with a computer mouse and type information into data entry text boxes that are part of a user-friendly computer application window, and very little training would be required. The clerk would not have to remember the syntax of an INSERT statement because a stored procedure could automate the row insertion task as part of the computer program.

ADVANTAGES OF STORED PROCEDURES

The scenario described above outlines one of the advantages of stored procedures—the ability to automate repetitive tasks. Stored procedures as database objects in SQL Server can be called from application programs by using many different programming languages, including Visual Basic.NET and Visual C++.

Another advantage of stored procedures is that SQL Server generates and maintains (stores) an execution plan for a stored procedure. The execution plan is the manner by which SQL Server plans to always execute the procedure. Further, the execution plan is stored as part of a database; and when a procedure is used, there is no need for the system to regenerate the execution plan. Thus, the stored procedure executes very efficiently.

Still another advantage of stored procedures is that you can grant permission to execute stored procedures that modify database objects such as tables without granting explicit permission to modify the database objects directly. These two different sets of permissions, that is, the permission to execute a stored procedure that accesses a database object (such as a table) versus the permission to access a database object directly, are independent of one another. This means you can grant a salesperson the permission to run a computer program that updates a *sales* table without granting explicit permission to directly modify the *sales* table. Chapter 12 provides detailed information about different database permissions to perform specific tasks and execute specific T-SQL statements.

PERMISSION TO CREATE PROCEDURES

Procedures are created by executing the CREATE PROCEDURE statement. Before we explain the use of this T-SQL command, you need to understand that to execute a CREATE PROCEDURE statement you must first be granted an explicit permission to do so. Normally the person granting you this permission is a database administrator (DBA). A DBA can execute a GRANT CREATE PROCEDURE command to grant you this specific permission.

When you study Chapter 12, you learn that DBAs are granted very broad permissions to manage SQL Server because they fulfill certain *roles* as a DBA. Roles are actual database objects and have names such as *sysadmin, db_owner,* and *db_ddladmin.* These are role names that are short for system administrator, database owner, and database data definition language administrator, respectively. Individuals authorized to work in these roles can grant you the permission to create stored procedures. For now you do not need to worry about these roles. Your instructor can grant you the permission you need to practice creating procedures. However, if you find that you cannot execute the CREATE PROCEDURE statement, then you probably have not been granted permission to do so.

CREATE PROCEDURE SYNTAX

A simplified version of the general syntax of the CREATE PROCEDURE statement is shown here. In fact, the statement can be abbreviated to CREATE PROC—you do not need to spell out the entire word.

```
CREATE PROCEDURE [owner.]procedure_name [(@parameter1 datatype1
   [=DEFAULT], [{@parameter2 datatype2 [=DEFAULT],...})]
   AS {INSERT | UPDATE | DELELTE} table_name
      {code to execute for the procedure}
```

The *owner* of a procedure is the system user account that is assigned ownership through this particular option. Often ownership is assigned to a system user who works as a DBA, or alternatively to an application programmer.

Procedures may have optional parameters (@parameter1, @parameter2, ...) enclosed within parentheses of specified data types (datatype1, datatype2, ...). When parameters are used, the parameter name and data type are paired and multiple parameter and data-type pairs are separated by commas. Parameters may or may not be assigned default values—the assignment of a default value depends on the programming application requirements and the rules of the business that the procedure is implementing. It is legal to assign a default value of NULL to a parameter. Parameters are used to pass values to the stored procedure—they can also pass values back to a calling procedure.

STORED PROCEDURE EXAMPLE 1: PAY RAISE

The CREATE PROCEDURE statement shown in SQL Example 10.1 creates a procedure named *pay_raise.* This procedure receives the percentage value of the raise to be assigned through the parameter named *@percent_raise.* The default value is 3%;

however, the parameter can be used to pass any percentage raise value to the stored procedure. If a value is passed to the stored procedure, then this value supercedes the default pay raise of 3%. Thus, the procedure allows the assignment of any size pay raise to an employee from 00.0% up to and including 99.9%.

```
/* SQL Example 10.1 */
CREATE PROCEDURE pay_raise (@percent_raise DECIMAL(3,1)=3.0)
    AS UPDATE employee
        SET emp_salary = emp_salary + (emp_salary * @percent_raise/100);
```

This is an UPDATE procedure that updates each employee record by increasing the salary through the SET clause. The T-SQL UPDATE statement is the object of the AS clause. It takes the current value of the *emp_salary* column and multiplies the value by the percentage raise. This value is then added back to the current *emp_salary* to arrive at a new value for the *emp_salary* column.

Figure 10.1 shows the SQL Query Analyzer as a tool for creating procedures. The procedure in SQL Example 10.1 has executed successfully. The object browser can be used to examine any existing procedure including a listing of the parameters with the associated data types. If you are unfamiliar with an existing stored procedure, the object browser is a good tool to use to gain familiarity when you are new on the job.

EXECUTING A STORED PROCEDURE

Stored procedures can be executed with the SQL Query Analyzer through use of the EXECUTE statement. This statement may be abbreviated as EXEC. The simplified, general syntax of the EXEC statement is:

```
EXEC procedure_name [(@parameter1=value1 {, @parameter2=value2, ...})]
```

You have the option of naming the parameters and assigning values, as shown in the syntax. Often, however, you may simply list the parameter values in the

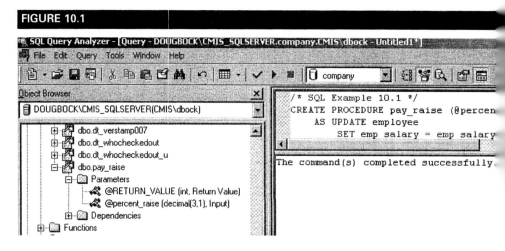

FIGURE 10.1

order in which they were defined for the stored procedure. SQL Example 10.2 gives a SELECT statement that lists employee Social Security numbers (SSNs) and their current salary levels for the first three employees prior to execution of the *pay_raise* procedure.

```
/* SQL Example 10.2 */
SELECT emp_ssn "SSN", emp_last_name "Last Name",
    CONVERT (CHAR (10), emp_salary, 1) "Salary"
FROM employee
ORDER BY emp_ssn;

SSN        Last Name           Salary
---------- ------------------- ----------
999111111  Bock                30,000.00
999222222  Amin                25,000.00
999333333  Joshi               38,000.00
more rows will display . . .
```

SQL Example 10.3 shows the execution of the *pay_raise* procedure and the system response that *8 row(s) were affected*. This example raises every employee's salary by 7.5% — a very healthy raise under most economic conditions. The parameter value of 7.5% is simply listed because the procedure only has a single input parameter.

```
/* SQL Example 10.3 */
EXEC pay_raise 7.5
```

Finally, SQL Example 10.4 executes the same SELECT statement as SQL Example 10.2 to show the new salary levels. The procedure raised all employee salaries by 7.5%.

```
/* SQL Example 10.4 */
SELECT emp_ssn "SSN", emp_last_name "Last Name",
    CONVERT (CHAR (10), emp_salary, 1) "Salary"
FROM employee
ORDER BY emp_ssn;

SSN        Last Name           Salary
---------- ------------------- ----------
999111111  Bock                32,250.00
999222222  Amin                26,875.00
999333333  Joshi               40,850.00
more rows will display . . .
```

STORED PROCEDURE EXAMPLE 2: INDIVIDUAL RAISE

One of the problems with the *pay_raise* procedure is that every employee receives a raise. This is fine if the company decides to grant every employee the same blanket raise; however, this is often not the case in the real world. It is more likely that employees may be granted different raises and even at different times of the year. You need to revise the *pay_raise* procedure to accommodate this more likely scenario.

SQL Example 10.5 shows a new procedure named *individual_raise*. This procedure takes two input parameter values. The first is the SSN *(@emp_ssn)* of the employee to receive a raise. The second is our familiar percentage value of the raise.

```
/* SQL Example 10.5 */
CREATE PROCEDURE individual_raise (@emp_ssn CHAR(9),
    @percent_raise DECIMAL(3,1))
    AS  SELECT emp_ssn "SSN", emp_last_name "Last Name",
            CONVERT (CHAR (10), emp_salary, 1) "Old Salary"
        FROM employee
        WHERE emp_ssn = @emp_ssn
    UPDATE employee
        SET emp_salary = emp_salary + (emp_salary * @percent_raise/100)
            WHERE emp_ssn = @emp_ssn
    SELECT emp_ssn "SSN", emp_last_name "Last Name",
            CONVERT (CHAR (10), emp_salary, 1) "New Salary"
        FROM employee
        WHERE emp_ssn = @emp_ssn;
```

This procedure not only processes individual employee raises but also displays information from the *employee* table about the individual's salary prior to, and after execution of, the UPDATE statement. This is accomplished by the two SELECT statements in the stored procedure. As you can see, stored procedures actually are like small computer programs.

SQL Example 10.6 executes the *individual_raise* procedure and displays the output for the employee with SSN = 999-55-5555. The *(1 row(s) affected)* message in the middle of the output simply means that the procedure executed only for employee Joyner because of the specification of the WHERE clause in the UPDATE statement. A 10% raise for Joyner amounts to an additional $4,300 on top of the earlier raise that all employees received.

```
/* SQL Example 10.6 */
EXEC individual_raise @emp_ssn=999555555, @percent_raise=10.0

SSN         Last Name       Old Salary
---------   -------------   ----------
999555555   Joyner          46,225.00

(1 row(s) affected)
(1 row(s) affected)

SSN         Last Name       New Salary
---------   -------------   ----------
999555555   Joyner          50,847.50

(1 row(s) affected)
```

DEFAULT PARAMETER OPTION

Let us return to the *pay_raise* procedure to learn about the use of the DEFAULT parameter value. Earlier in this chapter you study the *pay_raise* procedure and may recall that the procedure specified a default pay raise of 3% for all employees. Quite simply, this means that if you execute the procedure without specifying any pay raise, each employee gets a 3% raise. SQL Example 10.7 shows the execution of the *pay_raise* procedure with no percentage raise specified. Earlier employee Bock received the 7.5% pay raise that all employees received. Bock's new salary was $32,250. The additional 3% pay raise granted to all employees by the DEFAULT parameter raises Bock's salary to $33,217.50. This is true of the other employees. You should verify that each employee did receive the default pay raise of 3%.

```
/* SQL Example 10.7 */
EXEC pay_raise

SELECT emp_ssn "SSN", emp_last_name "Last Name",
    CONVERT (CHAR (10), emp_salary, 1) "Salary"
FROM employee
ORDER BY emp_ssn;

SSN         Last Name       Salary
---------   -------------   ---------
999111111   Bock            33,217.50
999222222   Amin            27,681.25
999333333   Joshi           42,075.50
more rows will display . . .
```

STORED PROCEDURE PARAMETER ERRORS

It is possible to make a number of errors when executing stored procedures. Usually these errors occur when values passed to a stored procedure are of the incorrect data type, or when you fail to pass parameter values that are required for a procedure to execute properly.

SQL Example 10.8 shows an attempt to execute the procedure named *individual_raise* without specifying the amount of the raise. You might not have noticed, but the *individual_raise* procedure does *not* have a DEFAULT value specified for the *@percent_raise* parameter. SQL Server returns an error message indicating that a required parameter was not supplied in the EXEC statement.

```
/* SQL Example 10.8 */
EXEC individual_raise @emp_ssn=999666666

Server: Msg 201, Level 16, State 3, Procedure individual_raise, Line 0
Procedure 'individual_raise' expects parameter '@percent_raise', which
was not supplied.
```

SQL Example 10.9 shows an attempt to execute the *individual_raise* procedure without specifying the SSN. The same error message was generated, but for a different expected parameter error.

```
/* SQL Example 10.9 */
EXEC individual_raise @percent_raise=5.0

Server: Msg 201, Level 16, State 3, Procedure individual_raise, Line 0
Procedure 'individual_raise' expects parameter '@emp_ssn', which was not
supplied.
```

Finally, SQL Example 10.10 shows an attempt to execute the *individual_raise* procedure by specifying the SSN and percentage of raise in reverse order without specifying the names of the parameters—specifying the parameters when they are not in the order that the procedure expects. SQL Server generates an error message indicating that the data type *int* could not be converted to *decimal* (those data types expected by the procedure).

```
/* SQL Example 10.10 */
EXEC individual_raise 7.5, 999666666

Server: Msg 8114, Level 16, State 1, Procedure individual_raise, Line 0
Error converting data type int to decimal.
```

DROPPING STORED PROCEDURES

Stored procedures are dropped with the DROP PROCEDURE statement. To drop a stored procedure, you must be the owner of the procedure, or a DBA with the *db_owner* or *sysadmin* role permissions. SQL Example 10.11 drops the procedure named *pay_raise*.

```
/* SQL Example 10.11 */
DROP PROCEDURE pay_raise;

The command(s) completed successfully.
```

TRIGGERS

As you learn in the chapter introduction, *triggers* are program code objects in a database that are invoked whenever a specific action occurs to a table. With early database management systems (DBMS), computer scientists referred to the *firing* of a trigger; hence the adoption and continued use of the term *trigger*. Triggers can be invoked by any action that inserts rows into a table, updates existing table rows, or deletes table rows.

In Chapter 2 you learned to create tables and to incorporate the use of integrity constraints into the table definitions. You also learned to create NOT NULL constraints, PRIMARY KEY constraints, REFERENTIAL INTEGRITY constraints, and others. When DBMS software was first created, triggers were used to enforce REFERENTIAL INTEGRITY and other types of constraints. At that time, DBMS software lacked much of the capabilities that now exist with various CREATE TABLE and ALTER TABLE statement clauses.

Modern DBMS products like SQL Server use triggers to enforce a new type of constraint termed a PROCEDURAL INTEGRITY constraint. This means that triggers enforce what business managers refer to as *business rules*. For example, the Company may have a policy (business rule) that employees cannot receive a raise that exceeds 10% of their current salary level. We can write a trigger to enforce this rule whenever someone attempts to modify (UPDATE) an employee's salary and the raise exceeds the 10% policy level. In fact, enforcing business rules is one of the primary purposes of triggers. You can still enforce other integrity constraints with triggers, but this is done less often.

Earlier you learned about the permission to execute the CREATE PROCEDURE statement. Triggers require no such permission. Instead, you have permission to create a trigger for a specific table if you are the owner of the table. A system user with an account that is designated as a data definition language administrator or a database owner can also create a trigger for a table.

TRIGGER SYNTAX

Triggers have four components: (1) the trigger name, (2) the table or view name to which the trigger is assigned, (3) the timing of the trigger action and associated DML action, and (4) the program code to be executed. The simplified, general syntax of the CREATE TRIGGER statement is as follows:

```
CREATE TRIGGER trigger_name ON {table_name | view_name }
    {FOR | AFTER | INSTEAD OF } {[INSERT,] [UPDATE,] [DELETE]}
AS {batch code | IF UPDATE(column_name)}
```

Trigger_name is the name of the trigger as an object stored in the database. The table or view on which the trigger acts is specified as part of the ON clause. SQL Server provides for specification of triggers on views. Prior to this, SQL Server did not support triggers on views.

The FOR, AFTER, and INSTEAD OF options are used to define when a trigger acts. The FOR and AFTER clauses both specify that a trigger fires after the event that triggers the firing. This is because the AFTER and FOR keyword options are synonymous—they do the same thing. The INSTEAD OF clause allows you to specify that the trigger should execute instead of the event that would normally activate (fire) the trigger. Additionally, you need to understand that AFTER triggers are only supported on tables, not views.

The INSERT, UPDATE, and DELETE statement options are used to specify which DML event causes a trigger to fire. You can combine these DML options in a trigger; however, you cannot specify a DELETE statement option whenever a trigger has an IF UPDATE clause. Finally, the AS clause is used to specify whether the trigger executes a series of procedural and nonprocedural T-SQL statements or an

TABLE 10.1 Table: audit_employee	
Column Name	*Column Data Type and Size*
emp_ssn	CHAR(9)
old_salary	MONEY
new_salary	MONEY
system_user_name	CHAR(20)
datetime_changed	DATETIME

IF UPDATE clause. All this becomes much clearer once you have seen the programming code for a typical CREATE TRIGGER statement.

TRIGGER EXAMPLE 1: UPDATING EMPLOYEE SALARY

Suppose that management is concerned about security of the database and directs you to develop an automated means of keeping track of which employees modify the *emp_salary* column of the *employee* table. In most companies, only certain employees are authorized to make modifications to employee salary data, and modifications by other employees would be highly suspect.

You determine that you need to develop a means for keeping an audit trail of who makes modifications to the employee salary column. An audit trail is essentially an automated, computer-generated journal that records the occurrence of events that modify a database table. In this scenario, the audit trail is useful for addressing employee complaints about unexpected changes in their salary level, or in the event that two employees should collude to attempt theft from the company by illegally altering salary levels.

CREATING THE AUDIT EMPLOYEE TABLE

One approach to creating an audit trail is through the use of a trigger. In this situation, a DBA or senior programmer or analyst can create a table to store audit trail information. We name this table *audit_employee* because this table name is descriptive of the information stored in the table. This table stores information about who makes changes to employee salaries and what changes were made.

Management at the Company directs you to keep track of the following information for employees who have their salary modified: employee SSN, old salary value, new salary value, name of the system user making the modification, and date and time of the modification. The *audit_employee* table is described in Table 10.1.

The CREATE TABLE statement for the *audit_employee* table is shown in SQL Example 10.12. Note the composite primary key for this table includes the *emp_ssn* and *datetime_changed* columns. This is necessary because individual employees may have their salary changed numerous times over the course of their tenure with a company.

```
/* SQL Example 10.12 */
CREATE TABLE audit_employee (
    emp_ssn           CHAR(9),
    old_salary        MONEY,
```

```
    new_salary          MONEY,
    system_user_name    CHAR(20),
    datetime_changed    DATETIME,
CONSTRAINT pk_audit_employee
    PRIMARY KEY (emp_ssn, datetime_changed) );
```

CREATING AND TESTING THE UPDATE SALARY TRIGGER

Your next task is to program a trigger that can store rows to the *audit_employee* table whenever an employee's salary is updated. The CREATE TRIGGER statement is shown in SQL Example 10.13. The trigger is named *update_salary*. This trigger only works for updates to one row at a time. Writing a trigger for multiple, simultaneous row updates is beyond the scope of this textbook.

```
/* SQL Example 10.13 */
CREATE TRIGGER update_salary
    ON employee AFTER UPDATE
    AS IF UPDATE(emp_salary)
        BEGIN
        DECLARE @emp_ssn CHAR(9)
        DECLARE @old_salary MONEY
        DECLARE @new_salary MONEY
        SELECT @old_salary = (SELECT emp_salary FROM deleted)
        SELECT @new_salary = (SELECT emp_salary FROM inserted)
        SELECT @emp_ssn = (SELECT emp_ssn FROM inserted)
        INSERT INTO audit_employee VALUES
            (@emp_ssn, @old_salary, @new_salary, USER_NAME(), GETDATE())
        END
```

The trigger in SQL Example 10.13 fires every time an UPDATE occurs to a row of the *employee* table as specified by the ON clause. The object of the AS clause is the IF UPDATE specification for the *emp_salary* column of the *employee* table. You may read this code as: *if an update occurs, execute the trigger code.*

The code that inserts a row in the *audit_employee* audit trail table is shown between the BEGIN and END statements. Three variables are declared that store the employee SSN, old salary, and new salary (*@emp_ssn @old_salary @new_salary*). The data types for these variables match their associated columns in the *employee* table.

Next SELECT statements store values to these three variables by selecting from two virtual tables in SQL Server named *deleted* and *inserted* (these two tables are described in the next section). Following this an INSERT statement inserts a row into the *audit_employee* table. Note that the USER_NAME( ) and GETDATE( ) functions are used to extract from the system tables and operating system the name of the system user who is making the row modification and the date and time at which the modification is made.

You can test the *update_salary* trigger by using the *individual_raise* procedure that you created earlier in this chapter. Let us give employee Bock with SSN 999-11-1111 a 5% raise. SQL Example 10.14 shows the execution of the *individual_raise* procedure.

Several *(1 row(s) affected)* messages are generated because the *individual_raise* procedure generates before and after output. These messages also reflect the application of the raise by the procedure as well as the execution of the trigger.

```
/* SQL Example 10.14 */
EXEC individual_raise @emp_ssn=999111111, @percent_raise=5.0

SSN          Last Name            Old Salary
---------    ------------------   ----------
999111111    Bock                 33,217.50

(1 row(s) affected)
(1 row(s) affected)
(1 row(s) affected)

SSN          Last Name            New Salary
---------    ------------------   ----------
999111111    Bock                 34,878.38
```

SQL Example 10.15 executes a SELECT statement to display the row that was inserted into the *audit_employee* table. The system user named **dbo** made the change to Bock's salary and at 1:48 A.M. in the early morning hours—a possible suspicious act because of the time of day that the UPDATE took place. Also, as you can see, the audit trail is invisible to any employee who makes a salary modification. This is because the firing of the trigger to record audit trail information does not cause the display of any message that would inform the system user as to the insertion of the row in the *audit_employee* table.

```
/* SQL Example 10.15 */
SELECT emp_ssn "SSN",
    CONVERT(CHAR(10), old_salary, 1) "Old Salary",
    CONVERT(CHAR(10), new_salary, 1) "New Salary",
    CAST(system_user_name AS CHAR(8)) "Who",
    CAST(datetime_changed AS CHAR(23)) "On DateTime"
FROM audit_employee;

SSN          Old Salary New Salary Who On DateTime
---------    ---------- ---------- --- --------------------
999111111    33,217.50  34,878.38  dbo May  9 2003   1:48AM

(1 row(s) affected)
```

Do you remember the stored procedure named *pay_raise* that was dropped earlier in the current chapter? If we had maintained the *pay_raise* stored procedure, it would no longer execute properly with the *update_salary* trigger because the trigger can only process updates for a single row at a time. However, this is not a problem because we dropped that procedure in favor of the *individual_raise* procedure.

DELETED AND INSERTED VIRTUAL TABLES

You may wonder about the virtual tables named *deleted* and *inserted* that were used in the SELECT statements of the *update_salary* trigger. The structure for these two virtual tables is automatically created by SQL Server. The *deleted* table is used to refer to values before the action that fires the trigger whereas the *inserted* table is used to refer to values after the action that fires the trigger.

As virtual tables, these tables do not actually exist in the database, but you can always treat them as if they exist because SQL Server automatically creates them whenever they are needed. You may wonder, what their structure is—what the column names and column data types are. These virtual tables both have a structure that is identical to the table to which a trigger refers. In the case of the *update_salary* trigger, the structure is identical to that of the *employee* table.

When data rows are inserted or deleted, these two virtual tables store copies of the rows that are deleted and inserted. When rows are updated, the *deleted* virtual table stores copies of the rows before an UPDATE statement executes and the *inserted* virtual table stores copies of the rows after an UPDATE statement executes.

TRIGGER EXAMPLE 2: ENFORCING A BUSINESS RULE

Management of the Company is concerned that employee salaries may be raised at a rate that exceeds company policy. You may recall that it is the policy of the Company that no employee may receive a raise that is greater than 10% of the base salary. This is an example of a business rule.

This business rule can be enforced by the *check_salary_raise* trigger shown in SQL Example 10.16. This particular trigger checks the percentage of a raise; and if the new employee salary figure is more than 10% larger than the old salary figure, the UPDATE transaction is canceled through use of a ROLLBACK TRANSACTION statement.

```
/* SQL Example 10.16 */
CREATE TRIGGER check_salary_raise
    ON employee AFTER UPDATE
    AS IF UPDATE(emp_salary)
        BEGIN
        DECLARE @old_salary MONEY
        DECLARE @new_salary MONEY
        SELECT @old_salary = (SELECT emp_salary FROM deleted)
        SELECT @new_salary = (SELECT emp_salary FROM inserted)
        IF @new_salary > @old_salary * 1.1
            BEGIN
                PRINT 'Salary Raise Exceeds Policy Limits'
                ROLLBACK TRANSACTION
            END
        ELSE
            BEGIN
                PRINT 'Salary Raise Approved'
            END
        END;
```

You can test the *check_salary_raise* trigger by again using the *individual_raise* procedure that was created earlier in the chapter. SQL Example 10.17 assigns a valid employee raise to Bock as shown by the *Salary Raise Approved* output message that is generated by the *check_salary_raise* trigger.

```
/* SQL Example 10.17 */
EXEC individual_raise @emp_ssn=999111111, @percent_raise=5.0

SSN          Last Name           Old Salary
---------    ----------------    ----------
999111111 Bock                   34,878.38

(1 row(s) affected)
(1 row(s) affected)

Salary Raise Approved

(1 row(s) affected)

SSN          Last Name           New Salary
---------    ----------------    ----------
999111111 Bock                   36,622.29

(1 row(s) affected)
```

SQL Example 10.18 shows the rows now stored in the *audit_employee* table. Bock is certainly doing well in terms of salary increases!

```
/* SQL Example 10.18 */
SELECT emp_ssn "SSN",
    CONVERT(CHAR(10), old_salary, 1) "Old Salary",
    CONVERT(CHAR(10), new_salary, 1) "New Salary",
    CAST(system_user_name AS CHAR(8)) "Who",
    CAST(datetime_changed AS CHAR(23)) "On DateTime"
FROM audit_employee;

SSN          Old Salary New Salary Who On DateTime
---------    ---------- ---------- --- -----------------------
999111111    33,217.50  34,878.38  dbo May  9 2003   1:48AM
999111111    34,878.38  36,622.29  dbo May  9 2003   4:36PM

(2 row(s) affected)
```

SQL Example 10.19 assigns an invalid raise of 11% to employee Bordoloi. The output of the *individual_raise* procedure shows Bordoloi's salary before the attempted raise. The *check_salary_raise* trigger caught the violation of policy and displayed the *Salary Raise Exceeds Policy Limits* message. Additionally, because the transaction was canceled by the ROLLBACK TRANSACTION statement, the *audit_employee* table cannot have any record of the modification. This is because a modification did not take place; thus, the *update_salary* trigger (an AFTER trigger) did not fire to store a row to the *audit_employee* table.

```
/* SQL Example 10.19 */
EXEC individual_raise @emp_ssn=999666666, @percent_raise=11.0

SSN         Last Name        Old Salary
---------   --------------   ----------
999666666   Bordoloi         60,898.75

(1 row(s) affected)
(1 row(s) affected)

Salary Raise Exceeds Policy Limits
```

DEFINING THE ORDER OF TRIGGER EXECUTION

Because SQL Server allows more than one trigger for a table or view, it is sometimes important to specify the order in which triggers execute. By definition, triggers execute in the order in which they are created. Thus, for our example thus far, the *update_salary trigger* fires before the *check_salary_raise* trigger.

Let us change the scenario a bit by dropping both of the triggers and then recreating them.

```
/* SQL Example 10.20 */
DROP TRIGGER update_salary;
DROP TRIGGER check_salary_raise;
```

Now, suppose that the *update_salary* trigger is rewritten as shown in SQL Example 10.21 to include a COMMIT statement (highlighted) as part of the trigger. Further, we recreate the *check_salary_trigger* by re-executing the CREATE TRIGGER statement in SQL Example 10.22.

```
/* SQL Example 10.21 */
CREATE TRIGGER update_salary
    ON employee AFTER UPDATE
    AS IF UPDATE(emp_salary)
        BEGIN
        DECLARE @emp_ssn CHAR(9)
        DECLARE @old_salary MONEY
        DECLARE @new_salary MONEY
        SELECT @old_salary = (SELECT emp_salary FROM deleted)
        SELECT @new_salary = (SELECT emp_salary FROM inserted)
        SELECT @emp_ssn = (SELECT emp_ssn FROM inserted)
        INSERT INTO audit_employee VALUES
            (@emp_ssn, @old_salary, @new_salary, USER_NAME(), GETDATE())
        COMMIT
        END
```

```
/* SQL Example 10.22 */
CREATE TRIGGER check_salary_raise
    ON employee AFTER UPDATE
    AS IF UPDATE(emp_salary)
        BEGIN
        DECLARE @old_salary MONEY
        DECLARE @new_salary MONEY
        SELECT @old_salary = (SELECT emp_salary FROM deleted)
        SELECT @new_salary = (SELECT emp_salary FROM inserted)
        IF @new_salary > @old_salary * 1.1
            BEGIN
                PRINT 'Salary Raise Exceeds Policy Limits'
                ROLLBACK TRANSACTION
            END
        ELSE
            BEGIN
                PRINT 'Salary Raise Approved'
            END
        END;
```

Now, SQL Example 10.23 again attempts to raise Bordoloi's salary by 11%. Clearly, this violates the business rule capping salary raises at 10%; however, if the *update_salary* trigger executes first and the update **commits**, then this renders the *check_salary_raise* trigger meaningless and Bordoloi receives the raise anyway. As you can see, Bordoloi's salary was raised to $67,597 and the *check_salary_raise* trigger had no effect.

```
/* SQL Example 10.23 */
EXEC individual_raise @emp_ssn=999666666, @percent_raise=11.0

SSN         Last Name           Old Salary
---------   ------------------  ---------
999666666 Bordoloi              60,898.75

(1 row(s) affected)
(1 row(s) affected)

SELECT emp_ssn, emp_last_name, emp_salary
FROM employee WHERE emp_ssn=999666666;

emp_ssn     emp_last_name       emp_salary
---------   ------------------  ----------------
999666666 Bordoloi              67597.6125
```

The *audit_employee* table also recorded the fact that Bordoloi (*emp_ssn* = 999-66-6666) received a salary increase along with the two earlier modifications made to Bock's salary.

```
/* SQL Example 10.24 */
SELECT emp_ssn "SSN",
    CONVERT(CHAR(10), old_salary, 1) "Old Salary",
```

```
      CONVERT(CHAR(10), new_salary, 1) "New Salary",
      CAST(system_user_name AS CHAR(8)) "Who",
      CAST(datetime_changed AS CHAR(23)) "On DateTime"
FROM audit_employee;


SSN        Old Salary New Salary Who On DateTime
---------- ---------- ---------- --- -----------------------
999111111  33,217.50  34,878.38  dbo May  9 2003  4:34PM
999111111  34,878.38  36,622.29  dbo May  9 2003  4:36PM
999666666  60,898.75  67,597.61  dbo May  9 2003  4:41PM
```

You can specify the order of trigger firing with a system stored procedure named *sp_settriggerorder* (read set trigger order) for an individual event such as an AFTER UPDATE transaction. The *sp_settriggerorder* procedure has a parameter named *@order* that allows you to specify values of either: (1) FIRST, (2) LAST, or (3) NONE. As you would expect from the value names, these specify whether a trigger is to fire FIRST or LAST as an AFTER trigger. The option NONE specifies no particular order for trigger firing. It also has a parameter named *@stmttype* that is used to specify the type of DML transaction. Example values would be: (1) update, (2) delete, or (3) insert.

SQL Example 10.25 shows the setting of a "first" specification for the *check_salary_raise* trigger for UPDATE transactions. We can test the order of the firing by again attempting to award an 11% pay increase to Bordoloi. As you can see, the *check_salary_raise* trigger fired first and rejected the pay raise. The update operation was rolled back.

```
/* SQL Example 10.25 */
EXEC sp_settriggerorder @triggername='check_salary_raise',
    @order='first', @stmttype='update'

The command(s) completed successfully.

EXEC individual_raise @emp_ssn=999666666, @percent_raise=11.0

SSN        Last Name        Old Salary
---------- ---------------- ----------
999666666  Bordoloi         67,597.61

(1 row(s) affected)
Salary Raise Exceeds Policy Limits
```

We know that the *check_salary_raise* trigger fired first, but can a row be inserted into the *audit_employee* table? The answer is no because row insertions would first be written to the *inserted* virtual table; however, the *check_salary_raise* trigger fired and rolled the transaction back. When the transaction was rolled back, this canceled the raise and no row was written to the *audit_employee* table to record the attempted update. SQL Example 10.26 verifies that the salary for Bordoloi did not actually change because there is no new record in the *audit_employee* table for a SSN of 999-66-6666. The only records listed are the earlier updates of Bock's salary and the single record for Bordoloi that was written before we established the new order for trigger execution.

```
/* SQL Example 10.26 */
SELECT emp_ssn "SSN",
    CONVERT(CHAR(10), old_salary, 1) "Old Salary",
    CONVERT(CHAR(10), new_salary, 1) "New Salary",
    CAST(system_user_name AS CHAR(8)) "Who",
    CAST(datetime_changed AS CHAR(23)) "On DateTime"
FROM audit_employee;

SSN        Old Salary New Salary Who On DateTime
---------- ---------- ---------- --- -------------------
999111111  33,217.50  34,878.38  dbo May  9 2003  1:48AM
999111111  34,878.38  36,622.29  dbo May  9 2003  4:36PM
999666666  60,898.75  67,597.61  dbo May  9 2003  4:41PM
```

INSTEAD OF TRIGGERS

An INSTEAD OF trigger fires in place of a triggering event such as an UPDATE or INSERT transaction. These triggers execute after SQL Server creates the *inserted* and *deleted* virtual tables, so the data rows for the triggering event are stored to these two virtual tables, but any existing integrity constraints and triggers checking business rules have not yet fired.

An advantage of INSTEAD OF triggers is that they can be created on views and tables, whereas AFTER triggers can only be created for tables. INSTEAD OF triggers use the data rows found in the *inserted* and *deleted* virtual tables for views that are in use to complete any required DML transaction. Let us examine the use of an INSTEAD OF trigger for a view named *project_equipment*. SQL Example 10.27 shows the CREATE VIEW statement for the *project_equipment* view.

```
/* SQL Example 10.27 */
CREATE VIEW project_equipment AS
    SELECT pro_number, pro_name, eqp_no, eqp_description, eqp_value,
        eqp_qty_on_hand, eqp_total_value
        FROM project JOIN equipment ON (eqp_pro_number = pro_number)
```

When a system user selects from this view, data rows for both the *project* and *equipment* tables display; specifically equipment assigned for use for the various projects the Company has undertaken. Note that the column named *eqp_total_value* is a computed (derived) column in the *equipment* base table (see the table definition in Appendix A).

Project 30 has one printer allocated (*eqp_number* = '5678'). Assume that another printer of the same type (printer type 5678) needs to be allocated to project 30. SQL Example 10.28 shows an UPDATE operation that attempts to use the *project_equipment* view to increase the number of printers from one to two. Attempting to execute the UPDATE based on the *project_equipment* view results in an error. The computed column *eqp_total_value* (referenced as derived in the error message) cannot be specified for update through use of a view. This is a limitation of views.

```
/* SQL Example 10.28 */
UPDATE project_equipment SET eqp_qty_on_hand = 2,
    eqp_value = 172.00, eqp_total_value = 344.00
    WHERE pro_number = 30 AND eqp_no='5678';

Server: Msg 4406, Level 16, State 2, Line 1
Update or insert of view or function 'project_equipment' failed because
it contains a derived or constant field.
```

SQL Example 10.29 shows a work-around for this problem by defining an INSTEAD OF trigger named *update_eqp_total_value* for the *project_equipment* view. Notice that the trigger is fired for the view; however, it updates the *equipment* base table directly based on values stored in the *inserted* virtual table. Two variables, *@pro_number* and *@eqp_no*, are defined and values for these variables are assigned by selecting them from the *inserted* virtual table. These variables are then used to specify the equipment item for a specific project that is to be updated. Additionally, only the quantity on hand (*eqp_qty_on_hand*) column value needs to be updated—you discover why as you continue to study this example.

```
/* SQL Example 10.29 */
CREATE TRIGGER update_eqp_total_value ON project_equipment
    INSTEAD OF UPDATE
    AS BEGIN
        DECLARE @pro_number SMALLINT
        DECLARE @eqp_no CHAR(4)
        SELECT @pro_number = (SELECT pro_number FROM inserted)
        SELECT @eqp_no = (SELECT eqp_no FROM inserted)
        UPDATE equipment SET eqp_qty_on_hand = 2
            WHERE eqp_pro_number = @pro_number AND eqp_no=@eqp_no
    END;
```

When the UPDATE transaction shown in SQL Example 10.25 is executed, the *equipment* base table was not updated. Now, after defining the INSTEAD OF trigger, the UPDATE transaction of SQL Example 10.28 can be re-executed. When you re-execute this transaction, the UPDATE transaction in Example 10.28 does not actually execute; instead, the UPDATE transaction specified as part of the INSTEAD OF trigger executes. Following re-execution of the update, SQL Example 10.30 shows a selection of rows from the *project_equipment* view to display the updated row information. The information about printer equipment 5678 for project 30 has been updated from one to two printers and the total value of the equipment item on hand is correct.

```
/* SQL Example 10.30 */
SELECT pro_number, eqp_no, eqp_value, eqp_qty_on_hand, eqp_total_value
FROM project_equipment
```

```
WHERE pro_number = 30 and eqp_no='5678';

pro_number eqp_no eqp_value     eqp_qty_on_hand eqp_total_value
---------- ------ ------------  --------------- ---------------
30          5678   172.0000     2                344.0000
```

Note that the value for *eqp_qty_on_hand* was updated to two printers. Also, the value stored in the *eqp_total_value* column was automatically updated to $344.00 because this column is derived by computing its value as the quantity on hand (*eqp_qty_on_hand*) times the value of an individual item (*eqp_value*).

SUMMARY

In this chapter you learned basic principles for creating stored procedures and triggers. Stored procedures are small programs that exist as database objects. They can automate batch processing for tasks such as audit trail creation. An advantage of stored procedures is that their execution plan is stored as part of a database; thus, the stored procedure executes very efficiently. The CREATE PROCEDURE statement allows the creation of procedures with parameters so that values can be passed to and from procedures. Procedures are executed with the EXEC statement.

Triggers are also database objects. They execute or "fire" whenever specific DML events for a database table or view occur. Triggers are used to enforce procedural integrity constraints called *business rules*. AFTER triggers can enforce integrity constraints for tables whereas INSTEAD OF triggers can enforce integrity constraints for both views and tables. The order of trigger execution where a table has multiple triggers can be specified by the *sp_settriggerorder* system procedure. After completing the review exercises provided in the next section, you will have the skills needed to write stored procedure and trigger program code.

REVIEW EXERCISES

LEARN THESE TERMS

AFTER clause. A clause that is synonymous with the FOR clause for defining triggers—specifies that a trigger fires after the triggering event.

CREATE PROCEDURE. The command used to create a stored procedure; also the permission required to create a stored procedure.

CREATE TRIGGER. The command used to create a trigger.

DEFAULT. The optional value specified for a parameter that is defined for a stored procedure.

EXEC. The statement used to execute a stored procedure when you are using SQL Query Analyzer.

Execution plan. The manner by which SQL Server plans to always execute a stored procedure. The execution plan is stored as part of a database, thereby ensuring efficient execution of the procedure.

FOR clause. A clause that is synonymous with the AFTER clause for defining triggers—specifies that a trigger fires after the triggering event.

INSTEAD OF clause. A clause that allows you to specify that a trigger should execute instead of the triggering event.

Parameter. Optional arguments that are part of a stored procedure definition used to pass values to a procedure and back to a calling program.

Procedural integrity. A new type of constraint that is enforced by triggers; this means to enforce what business managers refer to as *business rules*.

ROLLBACK TRANSACTION.   A statement used to cancel a DML transaction such as the UPDATE of a table.

Stored procedure.   A small computer program maintained as a database object, and used to automate batch processing, that is, tasks performed repetitively.

Trigger.   A small computer program that is maintained as a database object that is used to enforce procedural integrity.

CONCEPTS QUIZ

1. In general, what is the purpose of a stored procedure? Name some typical uses of stored procedures.
2. In addition to the ability to automate tasks, name an advantage of a stored procedure with respect to execution of a procedure.
3. How do stored procedures affect the granting of permissions with respect to modifying database objects?
4. What permission do you need as a system user to create a stored procedure?
5. What are three of the roles that individuals administering SQL Server may fill such that these individuals can grant you permission to create stored procedures?
6. Who is the owner of a stored procedure?
7. What is the purpose of a parameter in a stored procedure?
8. In the procedure shown here, what is the purpose of the "=3.0" clause?

```
CREATE PROCEDURE pay_raise (@percent_raise DECIMAL(3,1)=3.0)
    AS UPDATE employee
        SET emp_salary = emp_salary + (emp_salary * @percent_raise/100);
```

9. What statement is used to execute stored procedures when you are using the SQL Query Analyzer?
10. What is the purpose of specifying parameters with the EXEC statement that is used to execute a stored procedure?
11. The *pay_raise* stored procedure shown here processes a pay raise based on a percentage value supplied to the procedure. Write the EXEC statement that can award each employee a 2.5% raise.

```
CREATE PROCEDURE pay_raise (@percent_raise DECIMAL(3,1)=2.0)
    AS UPDATE employee
        SET emp_salary = emp_salary + (emp_salary * @percent_raise/100);
```

12. If no pay raise percentage is specified when using the procedure shown above, how much of a raise can employees receive, if any?
13. You are provided the first part of a CREATE PROCEDURE statement named *individual_raise*. A colleague of yours recommends that you attempt to execute the stored procedure with the EXEC statement shown below. What can happen?

```
CREATE PROCEDURE individual_raise (@emp_ssn CHAR(9),
        @percent_raise DECIMAL(3,1))
    AS   SELECT . . . (definition continues)

EXEC individual_raise @emp_ssn=999666666
```

14. What can happen if you attempt to execute the *individual_raise* procedure defined above with the following EXEC statement?

```
EXEC individual_raise 7.5, 999666666
```

15. Write the T-SQL statement to drop a stored procedure named *pay_overtime*.
16. When are triggers invoked? What type of action invokes them?
17. Give an example of procedural integrity.
18. Which clause should be used for a trigger that executes after the event that trigge the firing of the trigger?
19. Part of a CREATE TRIGGER statement is shown below. When can this trigg execute?

```
CREATE TRIGGER update_price
  ON product AFTER UPDATE
  AS IF UPDATE(pro_price)
     BEGIN . . . (more code is provided here)
```

20. What are the names of the virtual tables that are used to store information assoc ated with triggers? How are they created? How are they used?
21. How do the virtual tables mentioned in Question 20 store information during th processing of an UPDATE statement for a table that has a trigger?
22. What does a ROLLBACK TRANSACTION statement do? When would th statement be used?
23. How can you specify the order of trigger firing for a table that has two differe AFTER triggers?
24. What is an advantage associated with INSTEAD OF over AFTER triggers? Wh is a limitation?

SQL CODING EXERCISES AND QUESTIONS: COMPANY DATABASE

1. Management at the Company has been advised by the firm's primary vend supplying rental equipment that all equipment values are to be increased by 10 effective immediately. Write a procedure named *eqp_value_increase* with a paran eter named *percent_increase* that increases the value of equipment stored in tl equipment table by 10%—your procedure should affect the *eqp_value* colum Do not assign a default value to the *percent_increase* parameter.
2. Write the T-SQL code necessary to execute the *eqp_value_increase* procedure ar produce a result table that gives the new values for equipment.
3. Management has now learned that not all equipment values can increase by 10° Write a T-SQL statement that removes the *eqp_value_increase* stored procedu from the database.
4. Management now directs you to rewrite the *eqp_value_increase* stored procedu such that it accepts two parameters: the equipment number (*eqp_no*) and val increase (*eqp_value*). This enables changing the value of an individual equipme item by number.
5. Execute the query for equipment 5678 for an increase of 20%, and then display result table that shows the equipment number and new value for equipment 567
6. Modify the *eqp_value_increase* stored procedure to specify a default percenta increase in value of 3% for equipment if no increase is specified. You may accor plish the modification by removing the procedure from the database, and th creating it again.

7. Execute the revised *eqp_value_increase* procedure for equipment 4321 without specifying a percentage increase; then display a result table for that single item of equipment showing the new value.

8. Write a stored procedure named *replace_work_hours* that updates the *work_hours* column value in the *assignment* table. The procedure accepts three parameters corresponding to three columns in the table: *work_emp_ssn*, *work_pro_number*, and *work_hours*. For a given employee SSN and project number, the work hours value passed as a parameter to the procedure can replace the work hours currently stored in the table.

9. You have been notified by the manager of project 20 to update the hours worked for an employee on the project. Execute the procedure *replace_work_hours* to store a new *work_hours* column value of 15.5 for employee 999-55-5555 for project 20, and then display the new values in a result table.

10. Write a CREATE TABLE statement to create a table named *audit_assignment*. This table can store audit trail information about changes made to work hours information stored in the *assignment* table. The *audit_assignment* table must store the employee SSN (*work_emp_ssn*), project number (*work_pro_number*), old value for work hours (*work_hours*), and new value for work hours as well as the name of the system user making the modification and the date and time of the modification. You must define the table including appropriate data types and column sizes.

11. Write program code for a trigger named *update_work_hours* that stores a row to the *audit_assignment* table whenever a value for the *work_hours* column of the *assignment* table is modified.

12. Demonstrate that the trigger named *update_work_hours* functions as expected in terms of storing a row to the *audit_assignment* table, by executing the *replace_work_hours* stored procedure for employee SSN = 999555555, project number = 20, and new value for work hours of 17.8. Display the appropriate row from the *assignment* table and the rows in the *audit_assignment* table.

13. Write an AFTER trigger named *check_work_hours* that fires whenever an UPDATE transaction executes that updates the value stored to the *work_hours* column of the *assignment* table. The trigger should check the new value to be assigned for the hours worked to enforce a business rule that an employee cannot report working in excess of 250 hours on a project. If the new value to be inserted exceeds 250 hours, then the UPDATE transaction should roll back. Display an appropriate error message.

14. Test the *check_work_hours* trigger by attempting to store the value 250.5 for *work_hours* for the employee with SSN = 999555555 and project number 20. Display the *work_hours* column value for the appropriate row from the *assignment* table to prove that the trigger canceled the UPDATE transaction.

15. Execute the stored procedure that sets the *check_work_hours* trigger as the first AFTER trigger to fire for an UPDATE transaction for the *work_hours* column of the *assignment* table.

16. Create the view named *project_equipment* described in SQL Example 10.20. Create the *update_eqp_total_value* trigger described for this view. Execute the UPDATE transaction given in SQL Example 10.23 for project 2 and equipment number 1234 to increase the quantity on hand of the equipment to six units with an

individual unit value of $78.25, and a equipment total value of $469.50. Display the *pro_number*, *eqp_no*, *eqp_value*, *eqp_qty_on_hand*, and *eqp_total_value* columns in a result table from *project_equipment* view.

SQL Coding Exercises and Questions: Riverbend Database

1. After recent wage negotiations for hourly workers, the hospital's administration agreed to raise hourly wage rates (*wage_rate* column in the *staff* table) for staff members who are paid hourly by 3% effective immediately. Write a procedure named *wage_rate_increase* with a parameter named *percent_increase* that increases the wage rate as agreed. Do not assign a default value to the *percent_increase* parameter.

2. Write T-SQL code to display current wage rate values; then write T-SQL code to execute the *wage_rate_increase* procedure and produce a result table showing the new wage rate values. Sort the output by the last name of staff members who have a wage rate. Note that salaried staff members have a NULL value for the *wage_rate* column. The result tables should show the staff member's last and first names (limited to 20 characters), hospital title (limited to 25 characters), and wage rate formatted as $999.99.

3. You have been informed that some hourly workers receive wage rate increases that are different than the 3% that was previously thought to have been negotiated. Write T-SQL to remove the *wage_rate_increase* stored procedure from the database.

4. Now rewrite the stored procedure so that it accepts two parameters: the staff member identification number (*staff_id*) and percentage increase for the wage rate (*wage_rate*) increase.

5. Execute the revised *wage_rate_increase* stored procedure for the staff member with a *staff_id* value of '33358' and assign a wage rate of 10% to reward the employee for exceptional job performance. Write a SELECT statement to retrieve the modified row for this staff member to include the *staff_id*, *staff_last_name*, *staff_first_name*, *hospital_title*, and *wage_rate* with the output formatted to display on a single line. Format the *wage_rate* with a dollar sign ($).

6. Create a new stored procedure named *wage_rate_default* that works exactly like the *wage_rate_increase* stored procedure; however, if a percentage increase is not specified, the default percentage for the wage rate increase is 2%.

7. Execute the *wage_rate_default* procedure for the staff member with a *staff_id* of '33359' without specifying a wage rate percentage increase; then display a result table like that specified for Question 5 above showing the staff member's specified information.

8. The chief of accounting notifies you that a stored procedure is needed that updates values stored in the *treatment* table. The *treatment* table stores information about treatments received by patients by specific staff members for specific services. This includes the dollar amount charged for the treatment. Name the stored procedure *new_treatment_charge*. The procedure accepts three parameters corresponding to three columns in the table: *treatment_number*, *treatment_date*, and *actual_charge*. For a given set of values for the treatment number and date, replace the value stored in the *actual_charge* column with the new value of the parameter passed to the procedure.

9. Execute the *new_treatment_charge* stored procedure to store a new value of $55.55 for the treatment given on '6/10/2003 12:00 AM' with a *treatment_number* of 2. Display the new values in a result table.

10. Write a CREATE TABLE statement to create a table named *audit_treatment*. This table stores audit trail information about changes made to actual charges for treatments stored in the *treatment* table. The *audit_treatment* table must store the *treatment_number*, *treatment_date*, old value for the actual charge (*old_actual_charge*), and new value for actual charge (*new_actual_charge*) as well as the name of the system user making the modification and the date and time of the modification. Define the table including appropriate data types and column sizes. Only a primary key constraint is required.

11. Write program code for a trigger named *update_treatment_actual_charge* that stores a row to the *audit_treatment* table whenever a value for the *actual_charge* column of the *treatment* table is modified.

12. Demonstrate that the trigger *update_treatment_actual_charge* functions by executing the *new_treatment_charge* stored procedure for *treatment_number* 2 with a *treatment_date* of '6/10/2003 12:00 A.M.' and a new *actual_charge* value of $105.95. Display the appropriate row from the *treatment* table and the rows in the *audit_treatment* table.

13. Write an AFTER trigger named *check_service_charge* that fires whenever an UPDATE transaction executes, updating the value stored in the *service_charge* column of the *service* table. The trigger should check the new value to ensure that it is not more than 20% larger than the old value. If the new value for *service_charge* exceeds the 20% maximum increase, then the UPDATE transaction should roll back. Display an appropriate error message.

14. Test the *check_service_charge* trigger to execute an UPDATE statement that modifies the *service_charge* value for *service_id* = '10060' from the current value of $258.00 to a new value of $314.00—this would be an increase of about 22%, which would exceed the policy for increases in service charges. What output is displayed?

15. Test the *check_service_charge* trigger to execute an UPDATE statement that modifies the *service_charge* value for *service_id* = '10060' from the current value of $258.00 to a new value of $265.59. What output is displayed?

CHAPTER 11

SQL SERVER DATABASE ADMINISTRATION

As a Structured Query Language (SQL) programmer, you can expect to wor regularly with a database administrator (DBA) experienced in administerin the SQL Server database management system (DBMS). DBAs use the graphic use interface of SQL Server Enterprise Manager software to manage databases. You ca be a more effective SQL programmer if you have a basic understanding of databas administration principles, the Enterprise Manager software, and some of the mor commonly used database administration statements.

NOTE: To complete the majority of the tasks described in this chapter you must have a DBA or a privileged user account. Ordinary system users cannot execute statements described herein to create user accounts, create databases, and the like.

The examples shown in this chapter use the SQL Server 2000 version.

OBJECTIVES

In Chapter 2, you learned to create tables and indexes. These are basic database admi istration tasks. In this chapter, we extend your understanding of SQL Server databa administration by surveying topics with the following learning objectives:

- Develop a general understanding of database administration.
- Understand the duties of a DBA.
- Learn about the organization of an SQL Server database file structure.
- Create a database.
- Learn concepts concerning the SQL Server system catalog and database catalog
- Learn about the special *dbo* database user account.
- Become familiar with the Enterprise Manager software.
- Create system and database user accounts.

- Grant, deny, and revoke permissions.
- Create and allocate roles.

DATABASE ADMINISTRATION OVERVIEW

Database administration is a specialized area within a large information systems department that is separate from the application development area. Generally, application development includes systems analysis, systems design, programming, and systems testing. Database administration is concerned with administrative tasks that must be accomplished for application developers and information system users to access an organization's databases. A DBA is neither superior nor inferior to an application developer. DBAs and application developers must be both technically competent and capable of working closely with other professionals in a support type of relationship. One of the primary roles of a DBA is to provide the support needed by an application developer so the application developer can accomplish the task of building and maintaining information systems.

DATABASE ADMINISTRATOR DUTIES

A DBA is the individual assigned primary responsibility for administering a database. In addition to working closely with application developers, DBAs also work hand in hand with operating system administrators. Many of the tasks associated with administering an operating system and the associated computer servers are similar to the tasks of a DBA. Both system administrators and DBAs are concerned with issues such as system backup and recovery, system security, and user account allocation. A DBA's task list, however, focuses exclusively on organizational databases. A DBA must be able to do the following detailed tasks:

- Install DBMS software and upgrades.
- Design and create a database including the allocation of system disk storage for current and future database storage requirements.
- Start up and shut down database services.
- Create user accounts and monitor user activities.
- Grant database permissions to control data security and data access.
- Backup and recover a database in the event of system failure.
- Tune a database to optimize database performance.
- Manage database network connectivity.
- Migrate a database to a new version of the DBMS software.

Large organizations often have many DBAs. A DBA may be assigned responsibility for managing one or more individual databases or groups of databases. Large systems may require more than one DBA to manage an individual database.

ENTERPRISE MANAGER

The SQL Server 2000 Enterprise Manager is a Microsoft Management Console snap-in that provides a graphic user interface for administering SQL Server databases. It can be used to create databases, tables, and other database objects. You can also use it to create user accounts and allocate system and object permissions, manage security, schedule tasks, perform backups, and much more.

ENTERPRISE MANAGER GRAPHIC USER INTERFACE

Like the SQL Query Analyzer, the Enterprise Manager is accessed through the Windows Start button and Programs menu option. Figure 11.1 shows the initial Enterprise Manager window. The *Microsoft SQL Servers* option is highlighted in the Tree pane. Note the small plus [+] symbol to the left of this option, that can be selected to expand the Tree view.

Figure 11.2 shows the expanded Tree pane with the Company database selected. The pane to the right lists the various objects that can be managed for the Company database including diagrams, tables, views, and the like.

DATABASE TYPES

The databases listed in Figure 11.2 consist of two groups: (1) system databases and (2) user-defined or application databases. The system databases shown are Master, Model, MSDB, and Tempdb. The Pubs and Northwind databases are demonstration databases provided with many different Microsoft products, and these can be deleted if they are not of any use to you in business. The two user-defined, application databases named Company and Riverbend are those used with this textbook.

The Master system database stores information about other databases for an instance of SQL Server 2000. It also tracks disk space usage, the configuration of the DBMS, and information about database objects and source code.

The Model system database is, quite simply, a database template that is copied whenever you create a new database. You can configure database settings for the Model database and new databases inherit the settings of the Model database.

The Tempdb system database is used exactly as its name implies. It stores temporary objects and data, such as those created by an ORDER BY operation or a JOIN

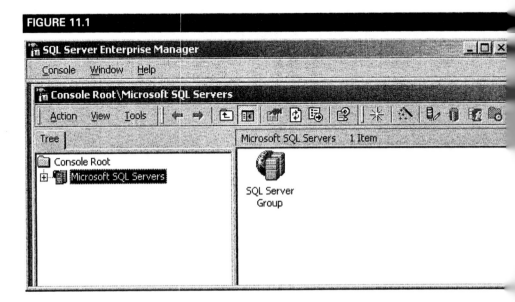

FIGURE 11.1

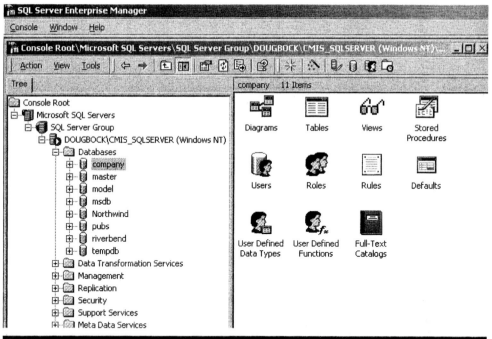

FIGURE 11.2

operation. When SQL Server 2000 is stopped and restarted as a Windows service, the data in Tempdb is not saved.

Finally, the MSDB system database is used by the SQL Server Agent service to schedule tasks such as database backup in system tables. As with other system databases and tables, you should not modify the data stored in the system tables. Microsoft recommends that you ignore the MSDB database other than to examine backup history information stored in it. A further discussion of the MSDB database is beyond the scope of this textbook.

You have seen examples of the Company and Riverbend databases used in this textbook. In fact, you can store all organizational tables and indexes in a single database, or you can separate tables according to business computer applications, such as payroll and inventory management. This means you can have a single or multiple databases managed by a single instance of SQL Server. Small companies tend to use a single database because this simplifies database administration tasks such as backup and recovery. Large companies may use multiple databases to assist in managing the complexity of the firm.

DATABASE FILES

The database files that comprise a database are physical Windows files. Every SQL Server database has at least two files—a primary data file and a transaction log file. The primary data file stores business application data as well as start-up information for the database. A database has only a single primary file.

Transaction log files store transaction log entries to support database recovery. Each database must have at least one transaction log file and may have more than one if activity in terms of row insertions, deletions, and updates for the database is high.

Secondary data files are used to store business application data that cannot fit into the primary data file. Small databases may not require secondary data files because all data may fit well into the primary data file. However, keep in mind that files are physical objects on a disk drive and files cannot span disk drives. So, if the primary data file grows so large as to consume most of the available space on a disk drive, then secondary data files are added on other disk drives to store the additional business application data that needs to be stored. The three file types are summarized in Table 11.1

The files that comprise a database can be examined using Windows Explorer, as shown in Figure 11.3. As we note earlier, each database has a single primary data file such

TABLE 11.1

File Type	Description
Primary data files	Used for data storage; also used to track the remaining user files in a database; filename extension is .mdf; each database has a single primary data file
Secondary data files	Used for storage; filename extension is .ndf; there can be numerous secondary data files or there may be none—their use is optional
Log files	Used to store transaction log entries to support database recovery; filename extension is .ldf

FIGURE 11.3

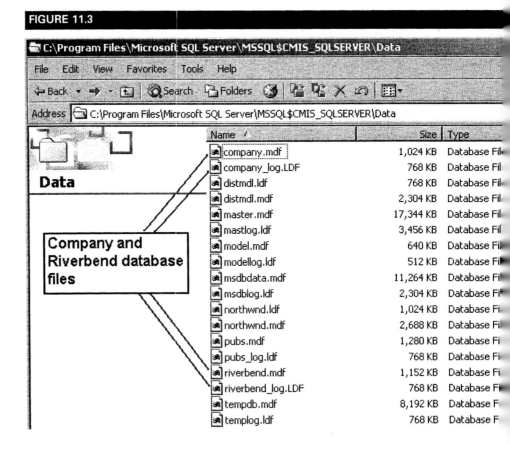

TABLE 11.2	
Page Type	**Description**
Data	Store pages of table row data
Index	Store pages of index values
Text/image	Stores data of type TEXT, NTEXT, and IMAGE; the table column for a column defined to store text or image data stores information that can be used to find the physical page address where the text or image data is stored

as the Company.mdf file, and a log file shown here as the Company_log.ldf file. Secondary data files are optional. In this diagram the primary data files (*.mdf*) and log files (*.ldf*) are stored on the same disk and directory because a single disk drive is available on the server. In practice with larger systems, you should store these files on different disk drives whenever possible to support database recovery efforts should they be necessary.

DISK STORAGE

SQL Server stores database objects in files by using two units of storage—the *page* and the *extent*. Database files are divided into pages as the main data storage unit whereas several pages grouped together in contiguous disk storage form an extent.

Pages are 8 KB in size. Pages contain a 96-byte header that stores system information. Data pages also store a row offset table. A row offset table contains information about the location of data rows within a page as well as each data row's identifying number. Most of the storage space in data pages is allocated to the storage of actual data rows.

A data row cannot span pages in SQL Server so the maximum row size is 8,060 bytes. This maximum does not apply to text or image data because that type of data is stored in separate files dedicated to the storage of text or image data. You may recall this discussion from Chapter 2. There are six different page types, but only three types concern you as the reader of this textbook, and these are summarized in Table 11.2.

Extents consist of contiguous pages. SQL Server allocates an extent of eight contiguous pages for a total of 64 KB when objects such as tables or indexes are created. Small tables and indexes are stored in mixed extents with a maximum of eight tables and indexes per mixed extent. When tables and indexes grow in size such that they cannot fit entirely within a mixed extent, they are allocated additional disk storage space in the form of 64 KB uniform size extents.

CREATING AN SQL SERVER DATABASE

An SQL Server relational database is typical of databases running on larger relational DBMS, and includes both memory and disk storage components. In fact, a single instance of SQL Server can support up to 32,767 individual databases. Each database can in turn, support hundreds, even thousands of tables and other database objects.

DATABASE CREATION

You may recall from Chapter 1 that a database can be created with the CREATE DATABASE statement while using the SQL Query Analyzer. However, the software tool of choice for creating and managing databases is the Enterprise Manager. It is a very easy to use software tool that can create, alter, and manage a database.

Figure 11.4 shows the first step in creating a new database with Enterprise Manager. Expand the Server node in the Tree pane until the Databases node is visible. You can either right-click the Databases node to display the pop-up menu shown in Figure 11.4, or select the Action menu and the New Database option to display the pop-up menu.

DATABASE PROPERTIES

Figure 11.5 shows the Database Properties dialog box with the General tab selected. The name for the new database is *TestDatabase*. The Collation name list box lists various language settings that can be selected for the collated display of data. We have used the default for the server (Server default) on which the database is to be stored.

Figure 11.6 shows the Database Properties dialog box with the Data Files tab selected. This dialog box is used to specify the physical file name for the primary data file. The file name is *TestDatabase_Data*, and the file is stored on drive C: in the folder named C:\Data. The data file has an initial file size of 1 MB. The file has been set to allow automatic growth in size in 10% increments. Optionally, you can control file growth by specifying the maximum size of a primary data file in kilobytes (KB), megabytes (MB), gigabytes (GB), or terabytes (TB).

Figure 11.7 shows the Database Properties dialog box with the Transaction Log tab selected. Similar to Figure 11.6, this form is used to specify the physical file name for the transaction log file storing information about transactions that process against the database. The transaction log is *TestDatabase_Log* and it is stored on drive C: in the folder named C:\DataLogs. Do you remember the Model database that we mentioned earlier in this chapter? Clicking the OK button causes SQL Server to create the files for the new database by copying the Model database template. Additionally, information about the new database is stored in the Master database.

FIGURE 11.4

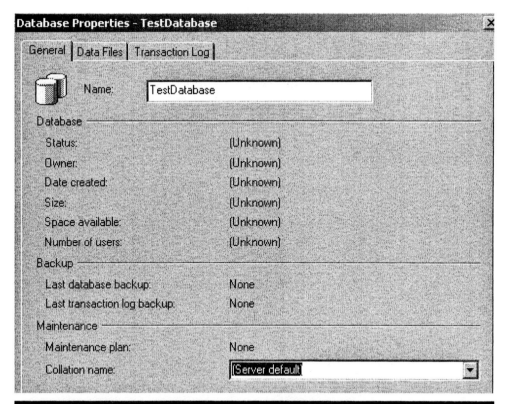

FIGURE 11.5

FILES AND FILEGROUPS

The management of larger databases that have several secondary data files can be made easier if the files are managed collectively as a unit. SQL Server provides this capability through the definition of a *filegroup* object type. You should think of a filegroup as a logical container object that holds files as a unit. One good use of filegroups is to simplify the task of database backup—a DBA can simply backup the filegroup instead of individual files, thereby ensuring that all files requiring backup are, in fact, written to backup media.

If you use the Enterprise Manager to create a database, the primary data file is assigned to a default filegroup named PRIMARY. Prior to adding secondary data files, use the Enterprise Manager to create a filegroup. You can then add secondary data files to the filegroup. To do this, right-click the name of the database in the Tree panel, and then select the Properties menu option. This displays the Properties dialog box shown in Figure 11.8. Select the Filegroups tab shown in the figure and enter the name of the filegroup to be created, and then click OK. The filegroup is named *TestDatabaseGroup1*. The next time you open the Properties dialog box, you can create new secondary files and assign them to the named filegroup.

You can alternatively create a filegroup while issuing a CREATE DATABASE statement. SQL Example 11.1 gives a sample CREATE DATABASE statement executed through use of the SQL Query Analyzer. In this example, the *TestDatabase* is

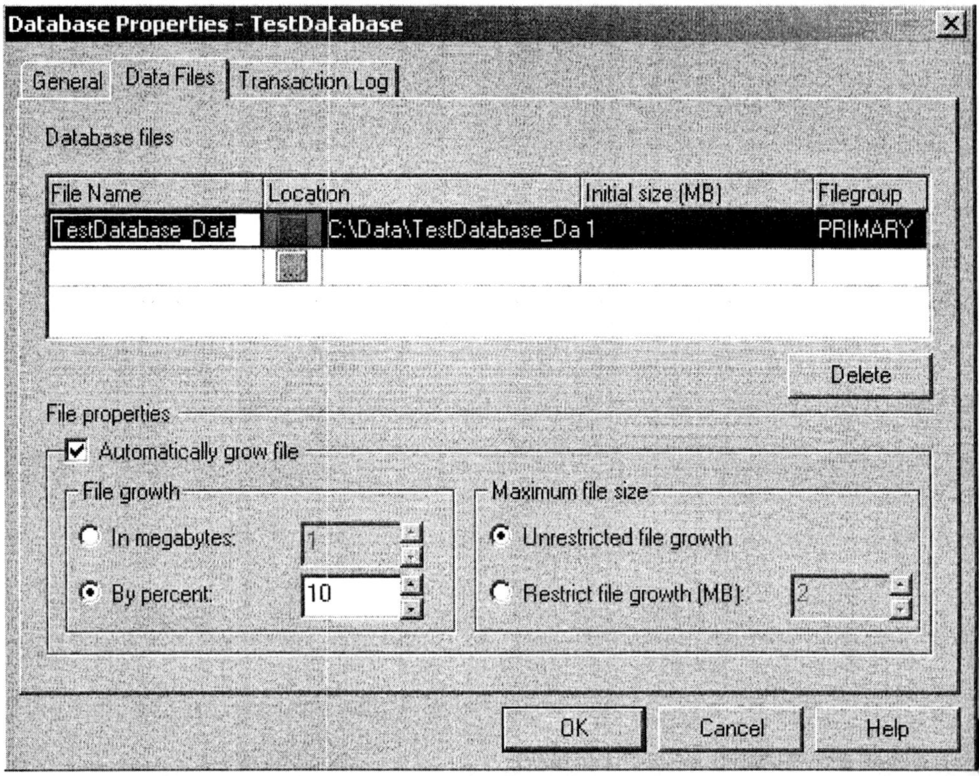

Database Properties - TestDatabase

General | Data Files | Transaction Log

Database files

File Name	Location	Initial size (MB)	Filegroup
TestDatabase_Data	C:\Data\TestDatabase_Da 1		PRIMARY

Delete

File properties

☑ Automatically grow file

File growth
- ○ In megabytes: 1
- ● By percent: 10

Maximum file size
- ● Unrestricted file growth
- ○ Restrict file growth (MB): 2

OK | Cancel | Help

FIGURE 11.6

created with a primary data file named *TestDatabase_Data*. The file is 10 MB in size with a maximum size of 50 MB. This statement also creates a filegroup named *TestDatabaseGroup1*; and creates two secondary data files that are assigned to the file group, one located on disk drive D:, and the second on disk drive E:. Additionally, the statement creates a transaction log file named *TestDatabase_Log* and assigns it to disk drive G:. The messages informing the DBA of the status of the CREATE DATABASE statement are shown at the end of the example.

```
/* SQL Example 11.1 */
CREATE DATABASE TestDatabase
ON PRIMARY
( NAME = TestDatabase_Data,
    FILENAME = 'C:\Data\TestDatabase_Data.Mdf',
    SIZE = 10,
    MAXSIZE = 50,
    FILEGROWTH = 25% ),
FILEGROUP TestDatabaseGroup1
( NAME = TestDatabaseSecondary1_Data,
    FILENAME = 'D:\Data\TestDatabaseSecondary1_Data.Ndf',
    SIZE = 20,
    MAXSIZE = 50,
    FILEGROWTH = 5% ),
```

```
( NAME = TestDatabaseSecondary2_Data,
   FILENAME = 'E:\Data\TestDatabaseSecondary2_Data.Ndf',
   SIZE = 10,
   MAXSIZE = 50,
   FILEGROWTH = 5% )
LOG ON
( NAME = 'TestDatabase_Log',
   FILENAME = 'G:\Datalogs\TestDatabase_Log.Ldf',
   SIZE = 5MB,
   MAXSIZE = 25MB,
   FILEGROWTH = 5MB );

The CREATE DATABASE process is allocating 10.00 MB on disk
'TestDatabase_Data'.
The CREATE DATABASE process is allocating 20.00 MB on disk
'TestDatabaseSecondary1_Data'.
The CREATE DATABASE process is allocating 10.00 MB on disk
'TestDatabaseSecondary2_Data'.
The CREATE DATABASE process is allocating 5.00 MB on disk
'TestDatabase_Log'.
```

FIGURE 11.7

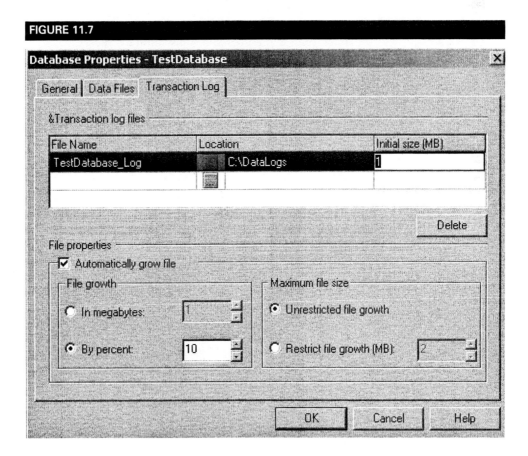

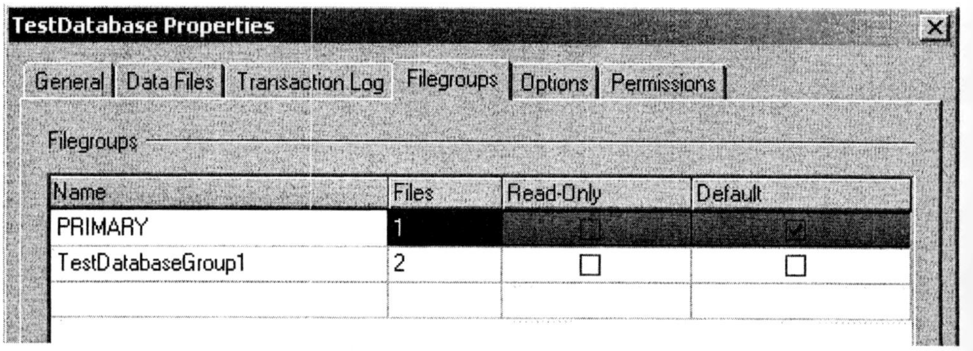

TestDatabase Properties

| General | Data Files | Transaction Log | Filegroups | Options | Permissions |

Filegroups

Name	Files	Read-Only	Default
PRIMARY	1		☑
TestDatabaseGroup1	2	☐	☐

FIGURE 11.8

There are some basic rules about filegroups that must be followed.

- A filegroup can only be used by one database—it cannot be spread across databases.
- A primary file is assigned to the primary filegroup and the filegroup cannot be changed once a file has been created.
- If you do not create a secondary filegroup to use, then secondary data files are automatically placed in the primary file group.
- Filegroups cannot contain transaction log files.

SQL SERVER SYSTEM CATALOG

The SQL Server *system catalog* consists of *system tables* that are stored in the Master database. System tables stored within individual databases are called the *database catalog*. Other database management systems and textbooks often use the term *data dictionary*—this is synonymous with *system catalog* and *database catalog*.

The system catalog stores information about the structure of objects in the system. These objects include databases, tables, views, indexes, and other objects. The most important system tables are summarized in Table 11.3.

Information stored in the system catalog is termed *metadata*, that is, data about data. When you create an object by using an SQL statement such as CREATE TABLE or CREATE INDEX, all the information about column names, column size, default values, constraints, index names, and other information is stored in the form of metadata in the system catalog.

System catalog tables are rarely accessed by system developers or system users. They are rarely modified by DBAs. Usually, only SQL Server processes access these tables for purposes of executing INSERT, UPDATE, and DELETE operations. If you access these tables as a DBA with the intent of modifying data stored in them, you risk destroying the integrity of the system catalog. In instances where you need to access system catalog table, you can use the SELECT statement to retrieve information. SQL Example 11.2 shows a query that retrieves the table identifying number and table type for the Company database *employee* table.

TABLE 11.3	
System Table Name	**Description**
Sysobjects	Stores 1 row for each object containing information such as the object identifying number, object name, object owner identifying number, object type, date created, and other information; this table is in every database
Syscolumns	This table of the master database and user-defined databases stores a row for every column of a base table, view, and stored procedure parameter including the table/procedure identifying number, column/parameter identifying number, column/parameter name, user identifying number, and other information
Sysindexes	This table of the master database and user-defined databases stores a row for every index and a row for tables that do not have clustered indexes including the index name, object identifying number from the Sysobjects table, index identifying number, and other information needed to describe the index structure
Sysusers	This table of the master database and user-defined databases stores a row for every Windows user, Windows group, SQL Server user, and SQL Server role including the user identifying number, database creator system identifier, and user or group name
Sysdatabases	This table of the master database stores a row for every system and user-defined database including the database identifying number, database name, database creator system identifier, creation date, and operating system path and name of the primary database file
Sysdepends	This table of the master database and user-defined databases stores a row for every relationship that exists between tables, views, and stored procedures including the table, view, or stored procedure identifying number and dependent object's identifying number
Sysconstraints	This table of the master database and user-defined databases stores a row for every integrity constraint including the integrity constraint identifying number, table identifying number, column identifying number on which the constraint is defined, and the type of integrity constraint

```
/* SQL Example 11.2 */
SELECT id "Table ID", type "Table Type"
FROM sysobjects
WHERE name = 'employee';


Table ID    Table Type
----------  ----------
2105058535 U

(1 row(s) affected)
```

SQL SERVER AND DATABASE ACCOUNTS

As you learned in Chapter 1, you can log into SQL Server through either a valid Windows user account or an SQL Server log-in account. The validation of your log-in information is termed authentication.

SQL SERVER AUTHENTICATION

If you work as a DBA, you can use either SQL Query Analyzer or Enterprise Manager to create SQL Server log-in accounts. Remember, you must be a privileged system user such as someone with DBA permissions to create log-in accounts and to perform the other activities covered throughout this section. When using Transact Structured Query Language (T-SQL), execute the *sp_addlogin* system procedure to create a log-in account. The general syntax is:

```
sp_addlogin 'login_name' [, 'password' [, 'database' [, 'language']]]
```

The password, database name, and language are all optional. The database name specifies the default database for the user on log-in. SQL Example 11.3 shows the creation of an SQL Server log-in account for Tom Thumb for the Company database with a password of *secret*.

```
/* SQL Example 11.3 */
EXEC sp_addlogin 'tthumb', 'secret', 'Company';
```

Passwords can be changed with the system procedure *sp_password*. The general syntax is shown along with SQL Example 11.4 that changes Tom Thumb's password of *secret* to *newsecret*.

```
sp_password 'old_password', 'new_password', 'login_name'
```

```
/* SQL Example 11.4 */
EXEC sp_password 'secret', 'newsecret', 'tthumb';
```

Access to existing databases can be revoked with the system procedure *sp_revokedaccess*. After access to databases is revoked, the SQL Server log-in account can be dropped with the *sp_droplogin* procedure. Using the Enterprise Manager to revoke user accounts is covered in detail later in this chapter.

Figure 11.9 shows the creation of an SQL Server log-in account by using the Enterprise Manager. Select the Tools menu, Wizards option to display the Select Wizard pop-up. Expand the Database tree and select the Create Login Wizard option, and then click OK. Click OK on the Welcome Screen that displays; then the next option asks for an authentication mode, as shown in Figure 11.10. Select the SQL Server log-in option, and then click Next.

Complete the log-in information required in Figure 11.11, and then click Next. Skip the Grant Access to Security Roles screen that appears next unless this system user is a DBA or privileged user. Figure 11.12 shows the database listing. Check the databases for which this user may have access, and then click Next followed by Finish on the last screen (not shown) to complete the account creation process.

FIGURE 11.9

DEFAULT DATABASE USER ACCOUNTS

Users who need to access a particular user-defined application database must have a valid *database user account* for that database. Each database has two default user accounts: **guest** and **dbo**. System users without a database user account for a specific database must use the **guest** account that exists, if such an account has been created.

FIGURE 11.10

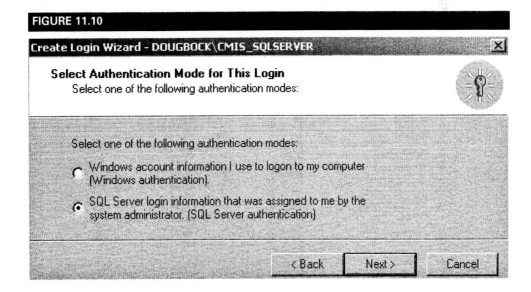

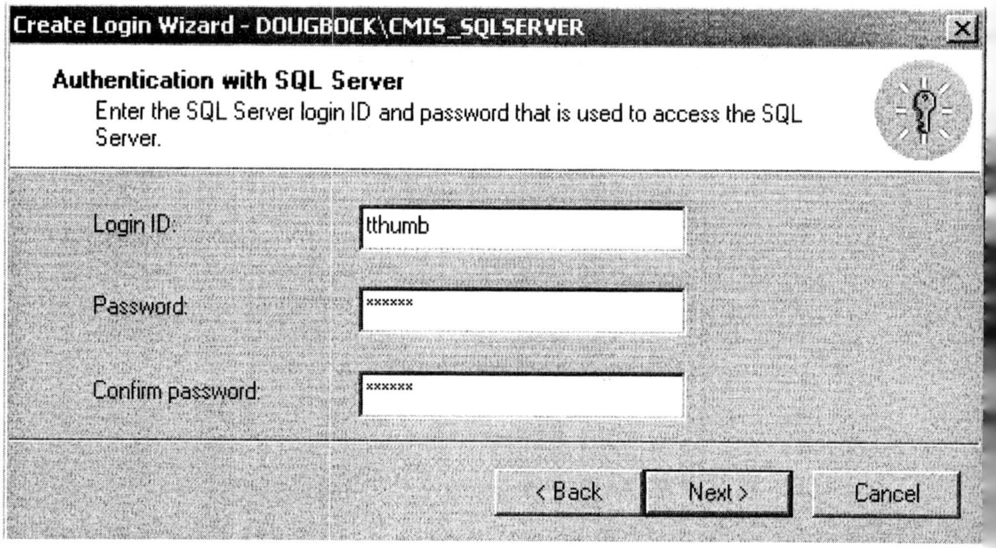

FIGURE 11.11

The **dbo** (database owner) account owns a database, and each database has this account. The account cannot be dropped. If you log in and create a database, the log-in is considered to be that of the database owner. Likewise, if you are a member of the *sysadmin* role, then when you log in, you are treated as the database owner. The *sysadmin* role is explained later in this chapter.

CREATING DATABASE USER ACCOUNTS

Database user accounts can be created with the Enterprise Manager or by executing a system procedure named *sp_grantdbaccess* within SQL Query Analyzer. This procedure associates the database user name with an existing Windows user account or an SQL Server security log-in account. SQL Example 11.5 shows the procedure used to create an account named *robertsmith* for a new Company employee named Robert Smith. Smith already has a Windows user account named *rsmith*.

```
/* SQL Example 11.5 */
EXEC sp_grantdbaccess 'rsmith', 'robertsmith'
```

If the DBA determines that Smith's database user account name should be identical to his Windows user account, the procedure is executed as shown in SQL Example 11.6. Some firms use database user account names that match Windows user account names. Other firms use different account names for Windows and SQL Server as a form of added security.

```
/* SQL Example 11.6 */
EXEC sp_grantdbaccess 'rsmith'
```

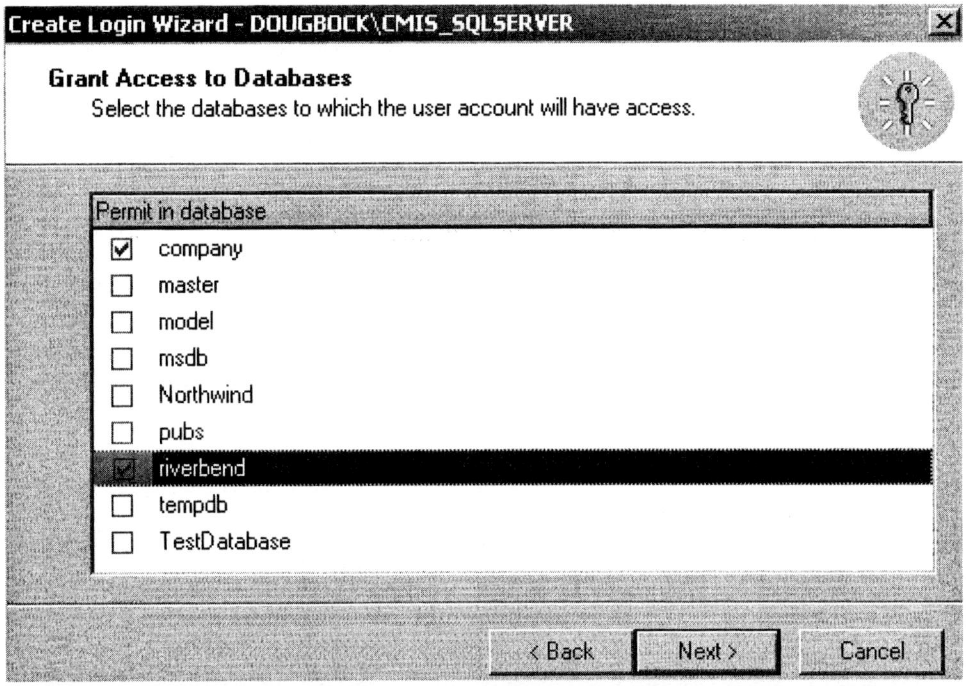

Create Login Wizard – DOUGBOCK\CMIS_SQLSERVER

Grant Access to Databases
Select the databases to which the user account will have access.

Permit in database

- ☑ company
- ☐ master
- ☐ model
- ☐ msdb
- ☐ Northwind
- ☐ pubs
- ☑ riverbend
- ☐ tempdb
- ☐ TestDatabase

< Back   Next >   Cancel

FIGURE 11.12

Figure 11.13 shows the creation of a Database user account with Enterprise Manager. Expand the server and folder named Databases as you have done in the past. Expand the database that the system user can access and right-click Users, and then select New Database User. In the Database User Properties dialog box, enter the login and user name and the permissions for the user. Permissions are explained in detail later in this chapter. Click OK to finish the process.

REVOKING DATABASE USER ACCOUNTS

The easiest way to revoke access permissions to SQL Server is through the Enterprise Manager. Select the Security folder, and then the Logins option, as shown in Figure 11.14. In the Logins pane to the right, select the user account to be revoked and right-click to display the pop-up menu. Click the Delete option and the system displays a warning that this can revoke the user's access to all databases. Click OK to complete the revocation.

A DBA can also revoke access to an individual database with the *sp_revokeddbaccess* system procedure. SQL Example 11.7 shows the use of this procedure to revoke access for the user named *rsmith*. Access is revoked for the database to which the DBA is currently connected.

```
/* SQL Example 11.7 */
EXEC sp_revokeddbaccess 'rsmith'
```

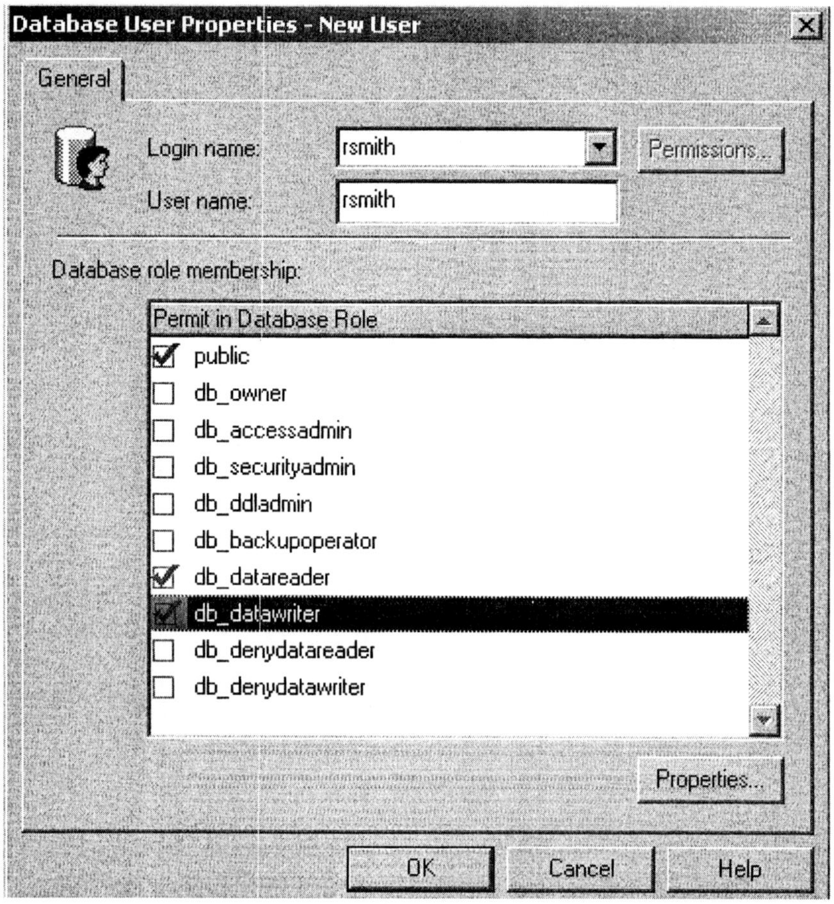

FIGURE 11.13

ROLES

The concept of a *role* is a simple one, and its purpose is to make it easier for a DBA to manage permissions. You should think of a role as a container of a group of permissions for a specific type of system user, such as an accountant. Each time we hire an accountant, we would assign the employee a new database user account and authorize that account all the permissions contained in the role called *Accountant*. Further, we can simplify the management of permissions because we can allocate a role to another role. Figure 11.15 depicts permissions (CREATE TABLE, SELECT ON ORDERS, UPDATE ON ORDERS) allocated to roles (Accountant and Clerk), and the roles allocated to system users (dbock, bbordoloi, tthumb, and rsmith).

From studying Figure 11.15, it should be apparent that if you add a new database user account for an employee who works as an accountant, then you can allocate almost all the permissions this user needs by simply allocating the role

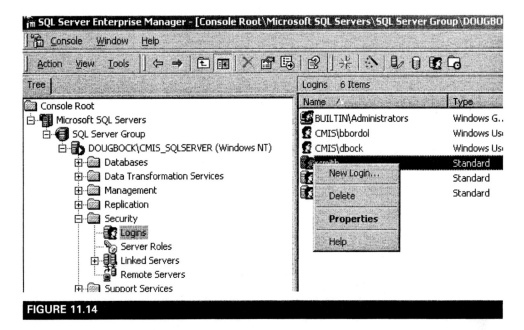

FIGURE 11.14

named *Accountant* to the new database user account. Further, if you determine that all accountants need an additional permission, such as INSERT ON ORDERS, that permission can be granted to the *Accountant* role, and all the database user accounts who are granted the role named *Accountant* can inherit the new permission. This considerably simplifies the management and allocation of database permissions.

A role name must be unique within a database. Additionally, a role can be allocated both statement (system) and object permissions. Roles can be created and managed by executing system procedures in the SQL Query Analyzer or through the Enterprise Manager.

FIGURE 11.15

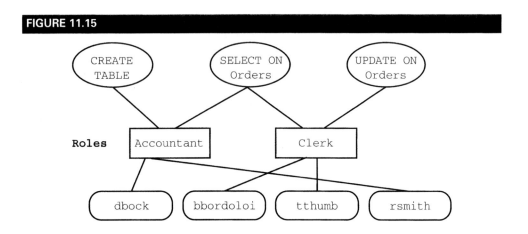

TABLE 11.4	
Fixed Server Role	*Description*
Sysadmin	Permission to perform any SQL Server activity
Dbcreator	Permission to create and modify databases with the CREATE DATABASE and ALTER DATABASE statements
Diskadmin	Permission to manage disk files
Processadmin	Permission to manage SQL Server processes such as those used to kill user processes
Securityadmin	Permission to manage log-ins; can manage the CREATE DATABASE permission
Serveradmin	Permission to configure SQL Server settings such as adding server log-ins and shutting down SQL Server
Setupadmin	Permission to install replication and manage extended procedures

FIXED SERVER ROLES

SQL Server has both fixed server and fixed database roles. Both of these role types have implicit permissions. Fixed server roles exist at the server level external to the databases. There are several of these roles and they are described and listed alphabetically (except for *sysadmin*) in Table 11.4. The *sysadmin* role is granted all permissions for SQL Server and is associated with the system administrator (**sa**) login and **dbo** user. The system administrator log-in always possesses the *sysadmin* role. Any system user allocated the *sysadmin* role is mapped to the **dbo** user when they are accessing a database.

Fixed server roles can be allocated through Enterprise Manager by expanding the Security folder, and then selecting the Server Roles option. In the Server Roles pane, right-click the role, as showed in Figure 11.16, and then select the Properties menu option.

FIGURE 11.16

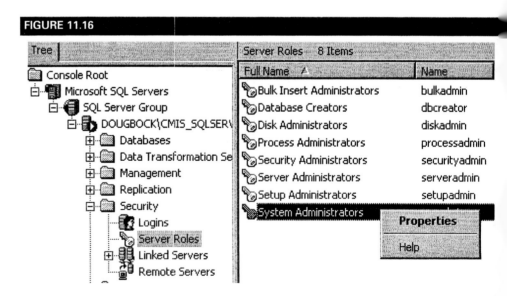

Figure 11.17 shows the Server Role Properties window. Click the Add button to display the Add Members window, select the members to add, click OK, and then OK again to close the Server Role Properties window.

FIXED DATABASE ROLES

These roles exist for each database running on SQL Server. Table 11.5 describes these roles. The roles are grouped according to purpose. The *db_owner* role is the most inclusive in terms of permissions. The *db_datareader* and *db_datawriter* roles must be granted judiciously—few user accounts should be authorized these roles. Can you tell why from your study of Table 11.5? It is because someone who is granted these two roles can take actions that can affect any database table or view. In fact, most of the roles listed in Table 11.5 should only be granted to DBAs and trusted senior systems analysts.

APPLICATION ROLES

As the name implies, application roles are used to specify permissions for computerized business database applications such as payroll or inventory management. These roles are substantially different from the roles listed above. Application roles are not allocated directly to database user accounts; instead, they are allocated to an application for a specific log-in session. The log-in session then loses all other permissions as long as the application is run. Additionally, an application role requires a password.

The system procedure *sp_addapprole* is used to create an application role and only database user accounts with the *db_owner*, *db_securityadmin*, and *sysadmin* fixed roles

FIGURE 11.17

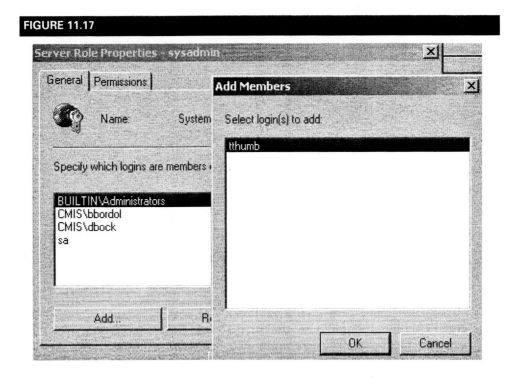

TABLE 11.5	
Fixed Database Role	**Description**
Db_owner	Users perform almost all database activities
Db_accessadmin	User can add and remove users
Db_datareader	Users have SELECT permissions on any database table or view
Db_datawriter	Users can run DML statements on any database table or view
Db_ddladmin	Users can run DDL statements as well as other privileges
Db_securityadmin	Users can execute T-SQL statements to GRANT, DENY, and REVOKE security permissions
Db_backupoperator	Users back up the database
Db_denydatareader	Users who cannot SELECT any database table or view—their SELECT permissions must be set at the object level
Db_denydatawriter	Users who cannot INSERT, UPDATE, or DELETE on any database table or view—their permissions must be set at the object level

can execute this procedure. SQL Example 11.8 shows an application role named *payroll* with the password *payemployees* being created.

```
/* SQL Example 11.8 */
EXEC sp_addapprole 'payroll', 'payemployees';
```

Any database user account can activate an application role if they know the password by using the *sp_setapprole* system procedure. If the application role is activated, it can only be deactivated by disconnecting your log-in session from the SQL Server. SQL Example 11.9 shows the *payroll* application role being activated.

```
/* SQL Example 11.9 */
EXEC sp_setapprole 'payroll', 'payemployees';
```

USER-DEFINED DATABASE ROLES

User-defined database roles are used to allocate common permissions to groups of database user accounts where the permissions are needed for employees to do their jobs. For example, you may create a role named *clerk* as noted at the beginning of this section, and then allocate various database permissions to *clerk*. Next you may allocate the role *clerk* to the database user accounts that require the group of permissions (e.g. everyone who works as a clerk). Again, you can use either SQL statements or Enterprise Manager to manage these roles. The SQL Server system procedures used to create user defined database roles are summarized in Table 11.6.

SQL Example 11.10 demonstrates the use of the *sp_addrole* procedure to create a role named *clerk* with an owner of *dbock*. If the owner is not specified, the role is owned by the **dbo** account. SQL Example 11.11 uses the *sp_addrolemember* procedure to add the database user account *rsmith* to the role *clerk*.

TABLE 11.6

User Defined Roles	Description
Sp_addrole	Creates a new user defined role in the database
Sp_droprole	Drops a user-defined role from the database, but only if all database user accounts have been removed from the role
Sp_addrolemember	Adds database user accounts to the role
Sp_droprolemember	Drops database user accounts from the role
Sp_helprole	Displays information about a specific role or about all roles if no role name is specified

```
/* SQL Example 11.10 */
EXEC sp_addrole 'clerk', 'dbock';
```

```
/* SQL Example 11.11 */
EXEC sp_addrolemember 'clerk', 'rsmith';
```

PERMISSIONS

The topic of permissions has to do with security as the name implies. Database users must have permission to perform various operations in a database or on a database object. Permissions are divided into two categories: statement and object.

GRANTING STATEMENT PERMISSIONS

Statement permissions are allocated through use of the GRANT statement, and represent the permission to execute a specific SQL statement, such as CREATE TABLE. The statement permissions include:

- CREATE DATABASE
- CREATE DEFAULT
- CREATE FUNCTION
- CREATE PROCEDURE
- CREATE RULE
- CREATE TABLE
- CREATE VIEW
- BACKUP DATABASE
- BACKUP LOG

The general form of the GRANT statement is:

```
GRANT [ALL | statement_list] TO account_list
```

The ALL keyword grants all existing statement permissions to database user accounts in the account list. Suppose you need to grant permission to create tables and

create views to two individual database user accounts: *tthumb* and *bbordol*.
SQL Example 11.12 shows this GRANT statement.

```
/* SQL Example 11.12 */
GRANT CREATE TABLE, CREATE VIEW TO tthumb, bbordol;
```

Further, suppose you have created a role named *clerk* and need to grant permission to create procedures and create functions to all employees working as clerks. SQL
Example 11.13 shows this GRANT statement.

```
/* SQL Example 11.13 */
GRANT CREATE PROCEDURE, CREATE FUNCTION TO clerk;
```

To use the Enterprise Manager to allocate statement permissions, expand the
Databases folder and right-click the name of the database for which permissions are to
be allocated. Next click the Properties option to display the Properties dialog box
shown in Figure 11.18. Select the user/role and simply check the statement permissions
to be allocated. Note that you can also use the Properties dialog box to revoke permissions previously allocated.

FIGURE 11.18

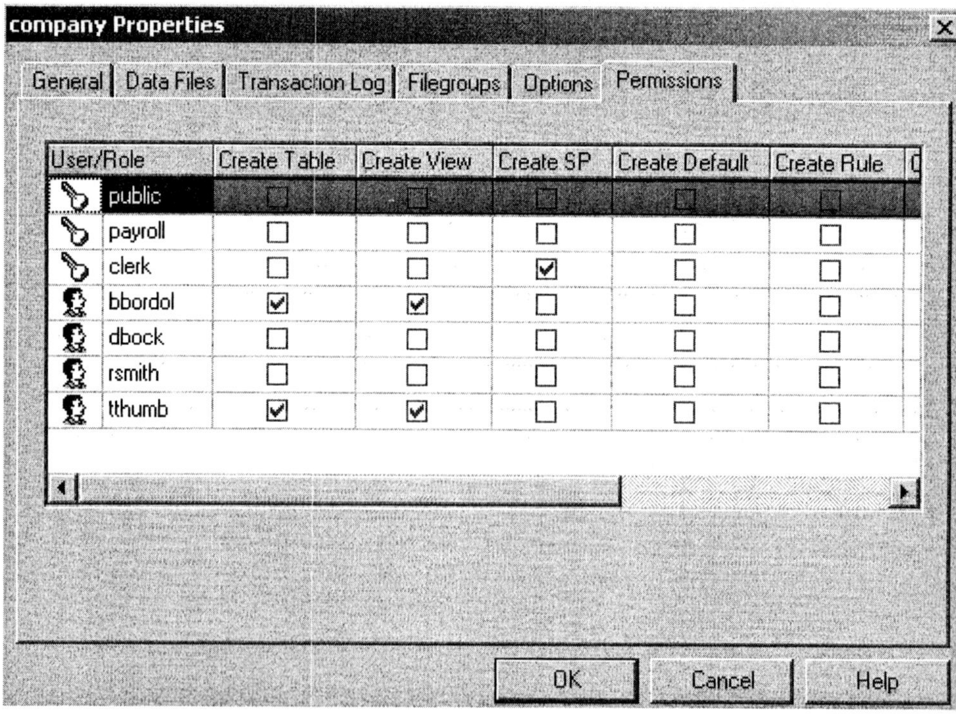

company Properties

User/Role	Create Table	Create View	Create SP	Create Default	Create Rule
public	☐	☐	☐	☐	☐
payroll	☐	☐	☐	☐	☐
clerk	☐	☐	☑	☐	☐
bbordol	☑	☑	☐	☐	☐
dbock	☐	☐	☐	☐	☐
rsmith	☐	☐	☐	☐	☐
tthumb	☑	☑	☐	☐	☐

GRANTING OBJECT PERMISSIONS

Object permissions apply to specific database objects and include the permission to SELECT, INSERT, UPDATE, DELETE, and perform other object manipulations. The GRANT statement is more complex and the general form is:

```
GRANT [ALL | permission_list] ON [table/view [column_list] | procedure]
TO account_list
[WITH GRANT OPTION] [AS {group_name | role_name}]
```

The keyword ALL and the account listing are used as with statement permissions. Permissions are granted on a specific table, view, or procedure with the ON clause. Within a table or view, specific columns may be designated, thereby allowing a database user to update selected columns while restricting the ability to modify other columns. This provides tremendous flexibility.

The WITH GRANT OPTION clause enables a database user to further grant the object permissions to other database users. Without this clause, a database user can use the permission, but cannot pass it to another database user.

The AS clause is required by any database user who is executing the GRANT statement who belongs to more than one group or role.

SQL Example 11.14 shows the granting of SELECT permissions on the *dependent* table of the Company database. SQL Example 11.15 shows granting multiple permissions to database user *dbock* for the *dependent* table with the grant option to grant these same permissions to other database user accounts. SQL Example 11.16 shows granting permission to update specific columns of the *dependent* table to the database user named *bbordol*. SQL Example 11.17 shows granting ALL permissions on the *dependent* table to database user *tthumb*. SQL Example 11.18 shows granting all permissions on the *assignment* table to everyone through use of the PUBLIC keyword.

```
/* SQL Example 11.14 */
GRANT SELECT ON dependent TO bbordol;
```

```
/* SQL Example 11.15 */
GRANT SELECT, DELETE ON dependent TO dbock
    WITH GRANT OPTION;
```

```
/* SQL Example 11.16 */
GRANT UPDATE ON dependent(dep_name, dep_gender) TO bbordol;
```

```
/* SQL Example 11.17 */
GRANT ALL ON dependent TO tthumb;
```

```
/* SQL Example 11.18 */
GRANT ALL ON assignment TO PUBLIC;
```

Figure 11.19 shows the use of Enterprise Manager to grant object permissions for a table. This same approach is used to grant object permissions for views and stored procedures. Expand the Database folder, select a database (Company), and then click the Tables object class. In the Tables pane to the right, right-click a table, such as *assignment* and select the All Tasks menu and Manage Permissions option. This displays the Object Properties dialog box. Simply check the object permissions to be granted to database user accounts. You can also revoke permissions by unchecking boxes.

DENYING PERMISSIONS

The ability to deny permissions simplifies security management by DBAs. The DENY statement both removes existing permissions from database user accounts and roles, and prevents the inadvertent granting of a permission to a database user account through a broadly defined role. For example, we might not want the database user *dbock* to have the permission to update the *dependent* table. However, we might grant this permission

FIGURE 11.19

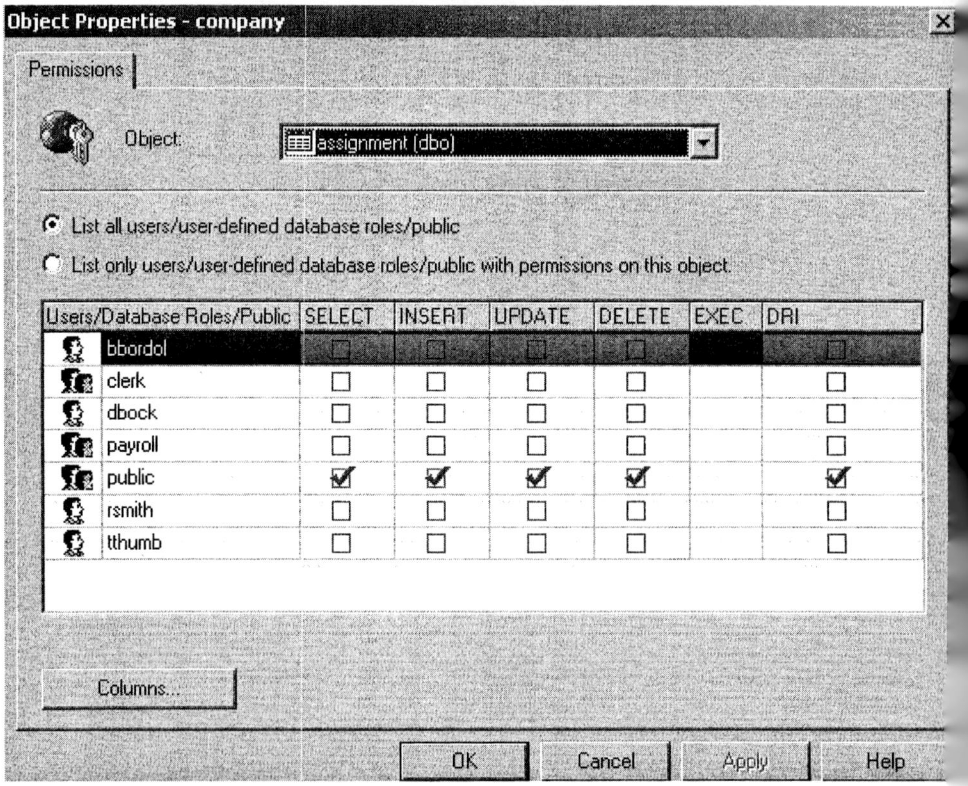

Users/Database Roles/Public	SELECT	INSERT	UPDATE	DELETE	EXEC	DRI
bbordol	☐	☐	☐	☐		☐
clerk	☐	☐	☐	☐		☐
dbock	☐	☐	☐	☐		☐
payroll	☐	☐	☐	☐		☐
public	☑	☑	☑	☑		☑
rsmith	☐	☐	☐	☐		☐
tthumb	☐	☐	☐	☐		☐

Object Properties - company

Permissions

Object: assignment (dbo)

● List all users/user-defined database roles/public
○ List only users/user-defined database roles/public with permissions on this object.

Columns...

OK   Cancel   Apply   Help

to the role named *clerk* as a permission for clerks in general and database user *dbock* might need the role *clerk*. You can restrict an individual permission for *dbock* from the role with the DENY statement. If we initially deny *dbock* a specific permission such as CREATE TABLE, and then later grant *dbock* a role that has the permission CREATE TABLE as part of the role, *dbock* still is denied permission to create tables.

The general forms of the DENY statement for statement and object permissions are shown below, respectively.

```
DENY [ALL | statement_list] TO account_list

DENY [ALL | permission_list] {[column_list] ON table/view |
   ON {table/view [column_list] | procedure}]
   TO account_list [CASCADE]
```

SQL Example 11.19 shows denying the CREATE TABLE permission for database user *tthumb*. SQL Example 11.20 shows denying the SELECT and UPDATE permission for database user *rsmith* for the *dependent* table.

```
/* SQL Example 11.19 */
DENY CREATE TABLE TO tthumb;
```

```
/* SQL Example 11.20 */
DENY SELECT, UPDATE ON dependent TO rsmith;
```

REVOKING PERMISSIONS

Earlier, we explained how to revoke both statement and object permissions by using the Enterprise Manager. You can also use the SQL REVOKE statement to permanently remove both statement and object permissions that have been granted. The PUBLIC keyword can also be used with the REVOKE statement. The general syntax of the REVOKE statement for both statement and object permissions is like that shown earlier for GRANT except that you replace GRANT with REVOKE and the keyword TO with the keyword FROM.

SQL Example 11.21 shows revoking permission to SELECT on the *dependent* table from all database user accounts through use of the PUBLIC keyword. SQL Example 11.22 shows revoking permission to UPDATE on the *dependent* table from database user *tthumb*.

```
/* SQL Example 11.21 */
REVOKE SELECT ON dependent FROM PUBLIC;
```

```
/* SQL Example 11.22 */
REVOKE UPDATE ON dependent FROM tthumb;
```

The REVOKE statement has an additional GRANT OPTION FOR clause that can be used to revoke the WITH GRANT OPTION permission without revoking the object permissions themselves from a database user account. SQL Example 11.23 shows revoking the WITH GRANT OPTION for the DELETE permission on the *dependent* table from database user *dbock*. The CASCADE clause causes database user account individuals who have been granted DELETE permissions by *dbock* to also lose their permission.

```
/* SQL Example 11.23 */
REVOKE GRANT OPTION FOR DELETE ON dependent FROM dbock CASCADE;
```

The REVOKE statement can also be used to revoke the denial of permissions so that a database user account once again has specific permissions. Earlier the database account *rsmith* was denied the SELECT permission for the *dependent* table. SQL Example 11.24 gives *rsmith* this permission again by using the TO clause.

```
/* SQL Example 11.24 */
REVOKE SELECT ON dependent TO rsmith;
```

SYSTEM PROCEDURES

The structure of the system tables in the system catalog changes frequently as Microsoft upgrades SQL Server. Accessing system tables via the SELECT statement is problematic whenever the SELECT statement is part of a stored procedure. This is because the SELECT statement can fail due to changes in column names in system tables. You can use system stored procedures to access information in system tables to manage an SQL Server database.

The system procedure *sp_help* displays information about database objects. The procedure takes as a parameter the name of any database object or data type. Executing *sp_help* with no parameter listing produces information on all objects in the current database. SQL Example 11.25 accesses information for the *dependent* table.

```
/* SQL Example 11.25 */
EXEC sp_help dependent

Name         Owner        Type          Created_datetime
-----------  -----------  ------------  ------------------------
dependent    dbo          user table    2003-01-27 15:24:06.030

Column_name        Type        Computed  Length    Prec   Scale
-----------------  ----------  --------  --------  -----  -----
dep_emp_ssn        char        no        9          no     no
dep_name           varchar     no        50         no     no
dep_gender         char        no        1          yes    no
```

```
dep_date_of_birth datetime   no      8      yes   (n/a)
dep_relationship  varchar    no      10     yes   no
other information is also listed . . .
```

The system procedure *sp_depends* displays dependency information among the various tables, views, and other database objects with dependencies. SQL Example 11.26 shows dependency information for the *employee* table.

```
/* SQL Example 11.26 */
EXEC sp_depends employee;
In the current database, the specified object is referenced by the
following:
Name                type
------------------  ------------
dbo.ck_emp_salary   check cns
```

There are a number of additional ways to display information about the system catalog including the use of system functions, property functions, and information schema. These mechanisms are beyond the scope of this book, but you may wish to investigate their use to increase your understanding of database administration.

SUMMARY

In this chapter you learned some basic principles of database administration. As you can see, SQL Server and the system catalog are complex. An SQL Server database includes both physical and logical objects. Files can be managed through the use of file groups.

The system catalog stores the metadata for an SQL Server instance and each database has a database catalog that stores metadata for all objects that exist within a database. You can access this metadata to learn more about various objects such as tables and indexes.

You have learned how to create both system user accounts, database user accounts, and roles; and how to allocate both system and object permissions to accounts and roles. Additionally, you have learned how to deny and revoke permissions that have been granted.

REVIEW EXERCISES

LEARN THESE TERMS

Application roles.   Used to specify permissions for computerized business database applications.

CREATE DATABASE.   A statement executed through use of the SQL Query Analyzer to create a database and all associated files.

CREATE TABLE privilege.   A type of privilege that includes the ability to create tables and indexes for those tables, as well as to drop the table and indexes.

CREATE USER.   A DBA statement used to create a user account.

Database administration. A specialized area within a large information systems department concerned with administrative tasks that must be accomplished for application developers and information system users to access an organization's databases.

Database catalog. Also stores system tables that track information about the structure of objects in a database.

DBA. The individual assigned primary responsibility for administering a database; also a prefix that added to all views that fall within the database administrator's schema of the database.

Dbo. A default database account that owns a database.

DENY <permission>. Removes existing permissions from database user accounts and roles and prevents the inadvertent granting of a permission to a database user account through a broadly defined role.

Enterprise Manager. A Microsoft Management Console snap-in that provides a graphic user interface for administering SQL Server databases.

Extent. Consists of contiguous pages allocated eight pages per extent for uniform size extents and eight pages per extent for mixed extents.

Filegroup. A logical container object that holds files as a unit.

Fixed server roles. These roles always exist at the server level outside of the databases.

Fixed database roles. These roles always exist for each database and are used to grant permissions needed for various database administrator activities.

GRANT <permission>. An SQL statement used to grant different permissions to database accounts and to roles.

Guest. A default database user account that allows guest access permissions to a database.

Master system database. Stores information about other databases for an instance of SQL Server 2000.

Metadata. Data stored in the data dictionary; data about data.

Model system database. A database template that is copied whenever you create a new database.

Object permissions. Allow a database account to perform a specific operation on a specific object such as a view, table, or index.

Page. A main data storage unit allocated in 8-KB sizes.

Primary data file. Stores business application data as well as start-up information for the database.

REVOKE <permission>. An SQL statement used to revoke statement and object permissions.

Role. A container type of object to which permissions can be allocated, and then the role can be allocated to a database account so that the account inherits the permissions associated with the role; simplifies management of permissions.

Secondary data files. Store business application data that cannot fit into the primary data file.

SQL Server authentication. A procedure for creating SQL Server log-in accounts that authenticate connection to SQL Server by a system user.

Statement permissions. Allow a user to perform specific types of operations such as creating, dropping, and altering objects.

Sysadmin role. Is granted all permissions for SQL Server 2000.

System Catalog. Consists of *system tables* that are stored in the Master database.

System databases. These databases are named Master, Model, MSDB, and Tempdb that are provided with all SQL Server installations.

System procedures. These procedures are used to access information in system tables to manage a SQL Server database.

Tempdb system database. Stores temporary objects and data such as that created by an ORDER BY operation or a JOIN operation.

Transaction log files. Store transaction log entries to support database recovery.

WITH GRANT OPTION. Used with the GRANT statement to enable a grantee of an object permission the ability to grant the object permission to another database account.

CONCEPTS QUIZ

1. Name three of the detailed tasks normally completed by DBAs.
2. What is the name of the pane in Enterprise Manager that is used to access Microsoft SQL Servers installed on a particular computer?
3. What are the two types of databases in an SQL Server 2000 installation?
4. Which database stores information about other databases for an instance of SQL Server 2000?
5. Which database is a template that is copied whenever you create a new database?

CHAPTER 11   SQL Server Database Administration   **299**

6. Which database stores temporary objects and data such as that created by an ORDER BY operation or a JOIN operation?
7. What are the names of the files that are always required in an SQL Server 2000 database?
8. What is the purpose of secondary data files?
9. What is the main data storage unit for an SQL Server 2000 database?
10. What is an extent?
11. What is the purpose of a filegroup?
12. What is a system catalog? What information is stored in a system catalog?
13. What are the two ways by which a system user can log into SQL Server 2000?
14. What are the two default user accounts that each database has? Which one owns the database?
15. What is a role?
16. Which fixed server role is granted all permissions for SQL Server 2000?
17. Which fixed database role is most inclusive in terms of permissions?
18. What are the two categories of permissions? Differentiate between these categories.
19. How do you take away specific permissions that have been previously granted to a database account?
20. What is the purpose of denying permissions with the DENY statement?

SQL Coding Exercises and Questions

In answering the SQL exercises and questions, submit a copy of each statement that you execute and any messages that SQL Server generates while executing your SQL statements. Also list the output for any result table that is generated by your SQL statements.

In this set of exercises, you can create a new database. To guarantee that your database name is unique for your installation of Microsoft SQL Server, your database name should consist of the first four letters of your last name and the four digits representing your day and month of birth. For example, if your last name is Bordoloi and if you were born on April 5, your database is to be named BORD0405 (where April = 04 and the fifth day of April = 05). If your last name is Bock and if you were born on December 12, then your database is to be named BOCK12.

1. Use SQL Query Analyzer to create a new database. Name the database as described above. Use the CREATE DATABASE statement or, if you elect, you may use the Enterprise Manager to create the database. The database should have a primary data named *DatabaseNamePri*, and two secondary data files named *DatabaseNameSec1* and *DatabaseNameSec2* where DatabaseName = the name of your database. These two secondary data files should be part of a filegroup named *DatabaseNameGroup1*. The transaction log file should be named *DatabaseNameLog*. Each file should be 1 MB in size. You should select the other file parameters.
2. Use SQL Query Analyzer or Enterprise Manager to create a user account using SQL Server 2000 authentication named *bob* that is identified by the password *wonderful*. Create two more accounts named *matilda* identified by *bootcamp* and *makita* identified by *swordfish*.
3. Use the *sp_grantdbaccess* system procedure to grant *bob*, *matilda*, and *makita* permission to access your database. Test your ability to connect to your database with SQL Query Analyzer for each of these three users.

4. Close SQL Query Analyzer for the user named *matilda*. Now use Enterprise Manager to revoke *matilda's* permission to connect to SQL Server. Do not forget to first remove *matilda* as a user within your database. Attempt to connect as *matilda* using SQL Query Analyzer. What error message is displayed?

5. Write the statement to grant *bob* the permission to create a table.

6. Bob needs to create a table named *books* that can be used to store information about books that the organization has in its library. The CREATE TABLE statement is shown below. Use SQL Query Analyzer connected as *bob* and execute this statement as part of this exercise. Which permission does system user *bob* need to create an index on the *books* table (you may need to research this permission)?

```
CREATE TABLE books (
Book_Id     CHAR(6),
Book_Title VARCHAR(50),
ISBN        CHAR(15),
Book_Price DECIMAL(6,2) );
```

7. *Bob* needs to insert two rows of data into the *books* table. Execute INSERT statements to store the following data into *books*.

Book_Id	Book_Title	ISBN	Book_Price
111111	My Favorite Book	1-111-11111111	149.95
222222	Another Good Book	2-222-22222222	18.50

8. System user *bob* wishes to grant system user *makita* the permission to query the *books* table. Write this statement. Demonstrate that *makita* can query the table by executing a SELECT statement. You have to qualify the name of the table a *bob.books*.

9. The *books* table is so popular that the head of our organization has directed *bob* to grant everyone in the organization the permission to query the *books* table. Write this statement.

10. System user *makita* is to be trusted by *bob* to insert rows into the *books* table. Further, this user is to be granted the right to grant the INSERT permission to other system users. Write the statement needed to grant this permission to *makita*. Next use SQL Query Analyzer to execute an INSERT statement to insert a new *books* row—you need to create your own data for this new row.

11. Write a statement that revokes all permissions that system user *makita* has on the *books* table. Be sure that you use the CASCADE option. Does this statement keep *makita* from querying the *books* table with a SELECT statement? Explain why or why not.

12. Connect to your database using your own user account. Use a system procedure to create a role named *books_mgr* (someone who manages books).

13. Use a system procedure to grant the role *books_mgr* to the system user named *makita*. Grant the role *books_mgr* to *bob*.

14. While connected as the user *bob* to SQL Query Analyzer, write a statement to grant the object privilege to DELETE rows from the *books* table to the role *books_mgr*. Also, grant UPDATE on the *book_price* column of the *books* table.

15. Demonstrate that the user *makita* now has the permission to delete rows from the *books* table by deleting the row with *book_id* = '111111'. Execute a SELECT statement to display the remaining rows in the table.

16. While connected as *bob*, write a statement to deny *makita* the permission to UPDATE the *books* table (any columns). Test the result of your statement by attempting to execute the following UPDATE statement. Attempt to update the *books* table while connected to SQL Query Analyzer as *bob*.

```
UPDATE bob.books SET book_price = 55.55 WHERE book_id = '222222';
```

17. If you wish to drop the role named *books_mgr*, what action must you first complete?

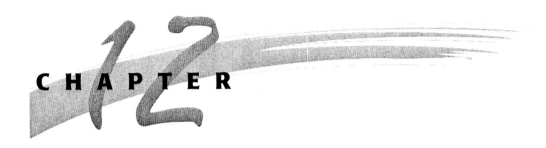

CHAPTER 12

EMBEDDED SQL

Did you know that the Structured Query Language (SQL) is used in conjunction with many different procedural and object-oriented programming host languages? This approach to programming is termed *embedded SQL*, and simply means that the host language includes the ability to use SQL statements to both retrieve and store records in a nonprocedural fashion while you are writing programming code with a procedural language. Does this sound confusing? Actually, it is quite simple for many languages. You can be a more effective SQL programmer if you have a basic understanding of the principles of embedding SQL commands.

OBJECTIVES

This chapter demonstrates methods for embedding SQL statements for Microsoft Visual Basic 6.0 and newer Visual Basic.NET languages. The Visual Basic language one of the most popular in the world and is used extensively to develop desktop systems that execute in a Microsoft Windows interface. We examine how SQL is embedded Visual Basic 6.0 programming code for both the retrieval and storage of table rows.

Visual Basic.NET is the latest evolution of the Visual Basic language Understanding how SQL is embedded in Visual Basic.NET is important because the object-oriented nature and powerful Web-coding capabilities of this language makes a likely language to be used for many years to come.

This chapter provides you with familiarity in using SQL with both Visual Basic and Visual Basic.NET in accessing data in Microsoft SQL Server databases. Your learning objectives for this chapter are:

- Learn the benefits of embedding SQL in a host language.
- Use ActiveX Data Object (ADO) control properties to specify an SQL statement in Visual Basic that retrieves data rows.
- Use ADO control properties to store (update) data rows.
- Use ADO.NET to connect a Visual Basic.NET program to a database.
- Use ADO.NET to execute a SELECT statement.

BENEFITS OF EMBEDDING SQL IN PROCEDURAL LANGUAGES

As you have learned from your studies thus far, SQL is a very powerful language for nonprocedural data processing. Recall that the term *nonprocedural* means a single SQL statement tells the information system *what* to do as opposed to *how* to accomplish the intended data processing task.

Transact Structured Query Language (T-SQL) is both a procedural and nonprocedural language. You have learned to use the nonprocedural statements of T-SQL quite well by this point. You also have gained limited experience with T-SQL procedural statements by learning some basic principles for writing Triggers and Procedures. As you have seen, procedural programming includes the ability to program iterative (loops) and decision coding (IF statements) structures as well as many other capabilities.

The study of embedded SQL statements in other languages adds a dimension to your understanding of the breadth of applicability of SQL. Modern programming emphasizes writing code procedures that "fire" based on "events" triggered by activities of both system users and the operating system. This is termed an event-driven, object-oriented approach. Computer applications are developed with this approach by programming in languages such as Visual C++, Visual Basic, Visual Basic.NET, and JAVA. These languages are often selected because they enable system developers to meet specialized or unique processing requirements.

As an example, consider how difficult it would be for a worker with no SQL training to extract information needed to support decision making. Such a worker might be a manager who is reviewing the status of employee personnel records, or a worker at a large retail store who needs to enter sales data for goods purchased by customers. These types of workers cannot be expected to formulate SQL commands to accomplish their work; still, we would often find these workers using computers to automate the record review or sales order processing tasks.

Programmers use procedural languages to build the computer interfaces that these workers use as part of their daily work. Procedural languages have the following advantages:

- A rich command set that provides the capability to program a graphic user interface to match unique system processing requirements.
- Language constructs such as iterative (WHILE and UNTIL loops) and decision structures (IF and SELECT CASE statements) that enable specialized record-at-a-time processing.
- The ability to program computer interfaces so that system users do not need specialized training in writing queries to use information systems coded with procedural languages.

EMBEDDING SQL IN VISUAL BASIC 6.0

ACTIVEX DATA OBJECTS CONTROL

Microsoft Visual Basic provides a visual programming language that is encased within an integrated development environment (IDE). The IDE enables computer programmers to develop information systems rapidly by dragging and dropping various control objects, such as text boxes and labels onto windows-like forms. As a programmer literally paints the information system user interface, Visual Basic writes the programming code behind the forms to implement the interface that is visually designed.

Visual Basic provides all the normal procedural programming constructs used by computer programmers including decision structures using IF statements and looping structures using both WHILE and UNTIL loops. Database processing is often accomplished through use of the ADO control. This specialized control enables a computer programmer to connect an application program written in Visual Basic to an existing database very quickly. Further, it is easy to create the database connection. Figure 12.1 shows an example employee processing form with an ADO control.

The ADO control is used to process *employee* table rows. The employee processing form displays a subset of the data columns from the *employee* table. This is a very common approach to visual programming with Visual Basic. The ADO control provides First, Previous, Next, and Last buttons (arrows) to make it easy to navigate from one row of data to the next. When one of the ADO control navigation buttons is clicked, the form displays the first, previous, next, or last row that is in the set of rows processed.

The ADO control also has properties that can be visually programmed to make database connection. The *ConnectionString* property stores a character string that specifies all the information needed to make a database connection. Part of the *ConnectionString* information specifies the use of the SQLOLEDB provider software

FIGURE 12.1

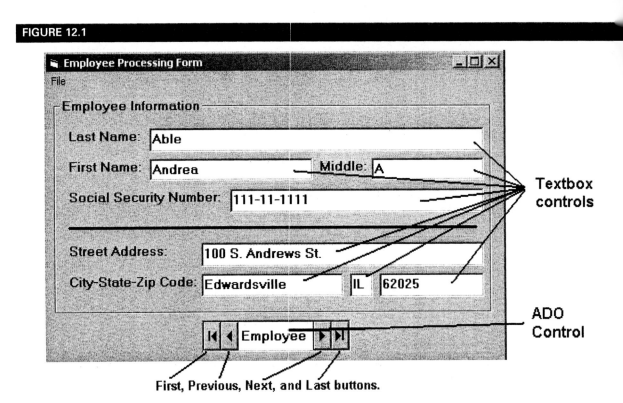

First, Previous, Next, and Last buttons.

(OLE DB) for the SQL Server database engine that is used to connect between the application program and the database, as well as the name of the server. The *ConnectionString* also specifies the database name, user identification, and password. In the coding segment shown in VB6 Example 12.1, a connection is made to a SQL Server database named *Company*.

```
REM VB6 Example 12.1
ConnectionString = "Provider=SQLOLEDB; Server=OurSQLServer;" &
    "Database=Company; User ID=dbock; Password=mypassword"

(Note: The ConnectionString value can be entered on a single coding
line-in that situation, the ampersand (&) is not used to concatenate the
two strings together.)
```

The *CommandType* property specifies how data rows are retrieved from a database. Data rows are retrieved from disk and stored in a memory object called a *recordset*. Although Visual Basic supports processing an entire table, the most common approach is to process a subset of table rows; thus, a record set usually consists of one or just a few table rows. This is because it is unwieldy to try to navigate through a large set of records where a table may store thousands and thousands of rows. Additionally, retrieving an entire table from a server over a network can cause network traffic to be unacceptably high. A programmer specifies a value for the *CommandType* property of "1-adCmdText," which means that an SQL statement will be used to retrieve the records for the recordset.

The *RecordSource* property stores the actual SQL statement used to create a recordset. For example, the records displayed for the record set in Figure 12.1 were retrieved with the SELECT statement shown in VB6 Example 12.2. As you can see, the SELECT statement is exactly like those you learned while studying earlier chapters of this textbook.

```
REM VB6 Example 12.2
SELECT emp_last_name, emp_first_name, emp_middle_name, emp_ssn,
    emp_address, emp_city, emp_state, emp_zip
FROM employee
WHERE emp_zip = '62025';
```

VB6 Example 12.2 creates a recordset that can have zero, one, or more data rows from the *employee* table depending on whether any employees have a zip code value of '62025.' Where there is more than one row in a recordset, the ADO control navigation buttons are used to move from one row to the next. You can also set an ADO control property that enables both reading and writing rows in a recordset. In this case, any changes made to a value displayed on the form while the system user navigates to another row causes the changed data to be saved automatically to the database.

There are two additional properties for each text box control that must be set for a Visual Basic form to display database data. These are the *DataSource* and *DataField*

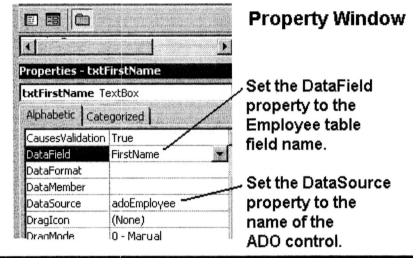

Property Window

Set the DataField property to the Employee table field name.

Set the DataSource property to the name of the ADO control.

FIGURE 12.2

properties. Figure 12.2 shows a Visual Basic property window associated with the text box control that displays the employee first name. The *DataSource* and *DataField* properties are indicated.

The *DataSource* property of each text box is set to the name of the ADO control. The ADO control for this specific form is named *adoEmployee*. Setting the *DataSource* property of a text box links the text box control to the appropriate ADO control because a form may have more than one ADO control. Next, the *DataField* property set to the appropriate column name from the *employee* table to specify the exact value to display in the text box. Each text box on the employee processing form usually has the same value for the *DataSource* property unless there is more than one database source for data. The *DataField* property for each text box must reflect the column data to be displayed in that particular text box. This same approach is used for other Visual Basic controls that display database rows—labels, list boxes, data combo boxes, data grids, and the like.

SELECTING SPECIFIC DATA ROWS

The SELECT statement in VB6 Example 12.2 has an obvious limitation. Can you find it? The SELECT statement has the zip code value "hard coded"—the statement always retrieves data rows in which the zip code equals '62025.' Hard coding data values such as a zip code may work well if managers often execute the same query over and over; however, a system user often needs to retrieve records based on values that are specified through some type of user input.

Figure 12.3 shows the use of an InputBox dialog box to allow a system user enter employee social security number (SSN) values. The SSN entered is used retrieve an individual *employee* table data row. The system user types an employee SSN into the InputBox text area, and clicks the OK button.

FIGURE 12.3

The SELECT statement in VB6 Example 12.3 is the command that we wish to execute for an employee SSN of '111-11-1111'; however, we need to avoid hard coding the SSN. Instead the query must use the SSN that is entered in the InputBox.

```
REM VB6 Example 12.3
SELECT emp_last_name, emp_first_name, emp_middle_name, emp_ssn,
    emp_address, emp_city, emp_state, emp_zip
FROM employee
WHERE emp_ssn = '111-11-1111';
```

It should be obvious that simply setting the *emp_ssn* column value in the WHERE clause to '111-11-1111' does not work. This problem is solved by storing the value entered into the InputBox to a Visual Basic memory variable that stores string or character data. The Visual Basic code to produce the InputBox and store the value is shown in VB6 Example 12.4. The value entered for the SSN is stored to the *strSSN* memory variable.

```
REM VB6 Example 12.4
Dim strSSN As String
strSSN = InputBox("Enter Employee SSN:", _
    "Employee SSN Search", vbOKCancel)
```

The program stores the SELECT statement to a second memory variable named *strSQL* in the code segment shown in VB6 Example 12.5. Note that the entire SELECT statement is stored inside double quote marks. Each piece of the SELECT statement is a string of characters that are concatenated together with the Visual Basic concatenation operator (the ampersand—&). The WHERE clause has the *emp_ssn* column name set equal to the value stored to the *strSSN* memory variable that was captured through use of the InputBox. Thus, at execution time, the SELECT statement stored to the *strSQL* memory variable includes the SSN stored to the *strSSN* memory variable.

```
REM VB6 Example 12.5
'Store SQL statement to a string variable
strSQL = "SELECT emp_last_name, emp_first_name, " & _
         "emp_middle_name, emp_ssn, emp_address, " & _
         "emp_city, emp_state, emp_zip" & _
         "FROM employee" & _
         "WHERE emp_ssn = " & strSSN
```

Finally, the *RecordSource* property of the ADO control is updated by storing the *strSQL* string variable to the *RecordSource* property, as shown in VB6 Example 12.6. The ADO control is refreshed with the *Refresh* method. The *Refresh* method automatically creates a new recordset, and the correct employee row is retrieved and displayed on the employee processing form.

```
REM VB6 Example 12.6
'Update the recordset retrieved by the ADO control
adoEmployee.RecordSource = strSQL
adoEmployee.Refresh
```

The code from these examples would typically be located within a compute mouse *Click* event procedure that is linked either to a menu option under the File menu shown on the employee processing form, or to a command button. The advantage of embedding SQL for a programmer is that the Visual Basic code is fairly simple to write, and the system can be developed rapidly by combining the power of the non-procedural SELECT statement with the versatility of the Visual Basic procedural programming language. Of course, additional code would be needed to handle the situation where an invalid employee SSN is entered or where the database connection lost due to some network failure; however, the basic code needed to retrieve and save data to and from a database table is fairly simple.

EMBEDDING SQL IN VISUAL BASIC.NET

WHY USE VISUAL BASIC.NET?

Microsoft's Visual Basic.NET language is one of the core programming languages Microsoft's new .NET framework. In fact, the programming language you elect to use within the .NET framework is not as critical as it has been in the past. This is because all the programming languages within the .NET framework compile to the same Microsoft Intermediate Language (MSIL), that executes under a Common Language Runtime environment that is part of the .NET framework. Visual Basic.NET continues to support the development of application program interfaces that are Windows based, but now it also provides powerful features for programming Web-based interfaces. This means that when you build a Web-based application program, the program can be run on a Web server and the information system data can be accessed by using any Web browser software. Thus, data can be retrieved and stored over the Internet

Visual Basic.NET can also be used to program a wide range of newer computing devices such as personal digital assistants and TV-based Internet terminals.

SYSTEM.DATA NAMESPACE

Within the .NET framework, all objects are members of *classes*. For example, Windows forms like that displayed in Figure 12.1 used to build an application interface are members of the *Forms* class. A *namespace* is an abstract object used to group classes together to make the classes easier to access. The *System.Data* namespace contains all the classes that you need to access almost any type of database. The *System.Data* namespace is divided into two sets of classes. One is termed **System.Data.SQLClient**, and is designed to connect to the Microsoft SQL Server database engine. The other is termed **System.Data.OleDB**, and is used to connect to any database with an Object Linking and Embedding Database (OLE DB)—a software driver used to connect to databases—such as an Oracle database or a Microsoft Access database.

ADO.NET

Visual Basic 6.0 uses the ADO approach to connect to databases through OLE DB providers (software drivers). ADO has evolved into ADO.NET in Visual Basic.NET. ADO.NET still uses OLE DB providers to connect to databases such as Microsoft SQL Server, Oracle, and Microsoft Access.

The major tasks facing a database programmer using VB.NET are:

- Configuring database components that create a connection and data set (data sets replace the recordsets used in VB 6.0);
- Executing SQL statements to add, delete, modify, or retrieve table rows;
- Working with data sets.

We examine the first two of these tasks. The third task, working with data sets, is beyond the scope of this text.

CONFIGURING DATABASE COMPONENTS

Although there are many ways to create database components used for an ADO.NET database connection, perhaps the simplest approach is to use the Data Adapter Configuration Wizard. In VB.NET, the Configuration Wizard automatically starts when you add a data adapter control to a VB.NET project. Figure 12.4 shows the selection of an SQLDataAdapter control from the Data tab of the development Toolbox, and the launching "welcome" screen for the Configuration Wizard. You may note that the OleDbDataAdapter control used for other types of databases such as Oracle and Microsoft Access can also be used to launch this same wizard.

Figure 12.5 shows the Choose Your Data Connection wizard window. This is used to select a data connection—we created a new connection by clicking the appropriate button. Existing connections can also be selected.

Choosing to create a new connection launches the Data Link Properties window shown in Figure 12.6. This window has several tabs. The Provider tab is used to select the Microsoft OLE DB Provider for SQL Server. The Connection tab is used to select

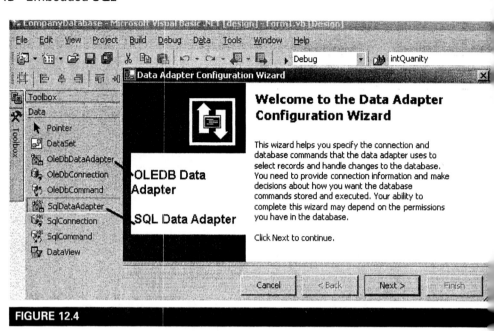

FIGURE 12.4

the computer server to which this particular VB.NET application should connect. Thi is also where you specify the method for secure connection described in Chapter 11 Here the system developer opted to use the trusted Windows integrated security pro vided by Windows login and password combinations. The database on the server is als specified—the Company database.

Clicking OK on the Data Link Properties page leads to additional windows wher you can specify to use SQL statements to process the data through the connectior Figure 12.7 shows a screen where you can either type an SQL statement directly int the window that is provided, or you can use the query builder interface to select th tables and table columns to be accessed. The query builder actually writes the SQ

FIGURE 12.5

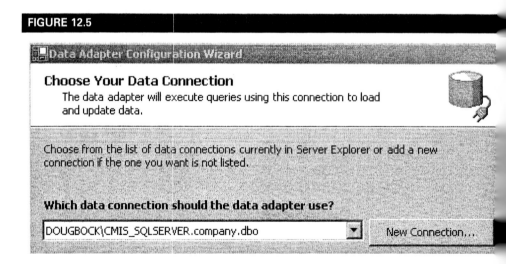

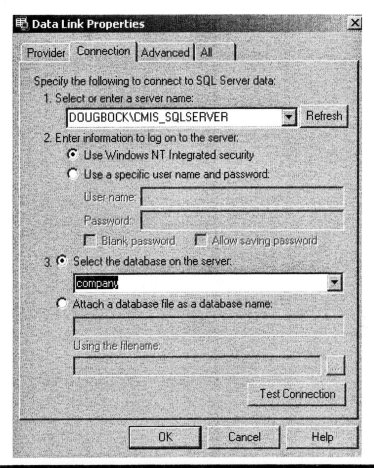

FIGURE 12.6

statement, as shown in Figure 12.7, including the specification of WHERE and ORDER BY clauses. This is a tremendous graphic user interface tool for writing SQL SELECT statements, especially if you have not written SQL in some time.

After you complete the creation of the data connection and data adapter controls, you are ready to generate a data set. The data set replaces the recordset of Visual Basic 6.0. This can again be generated by pointing and clicking the data adapter control and selecting an appropriate menu item. You can even preview the data set that is generated by the SQL SELECT statement, as shown in Figure 12.8.

The Data Adapter Configuration Wizard generates not only SELECT statements but also the corresponding INSERT, UPDATE, and DELETE statements for the specified data set. These statements are stored as properties of the SQLDataAdapter control. Figure 12.9 shows the final SQL Server database controls that were generated by the Data Adapter Configuration Wizard and through use of the data adapter menu. These include the SQLDataAdapter (*dbEmployee*), SQLConnection (*conEmployee*), and the generated data set (*DsEmployee1*), each renamed so that the control names are more meaningful to the programmer who writes any associated programming code.

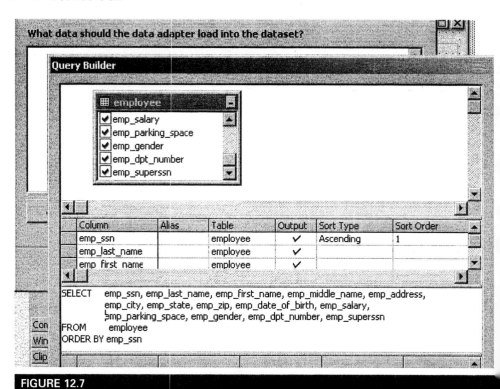

FIGURE 12.7

FIGURE 12.8

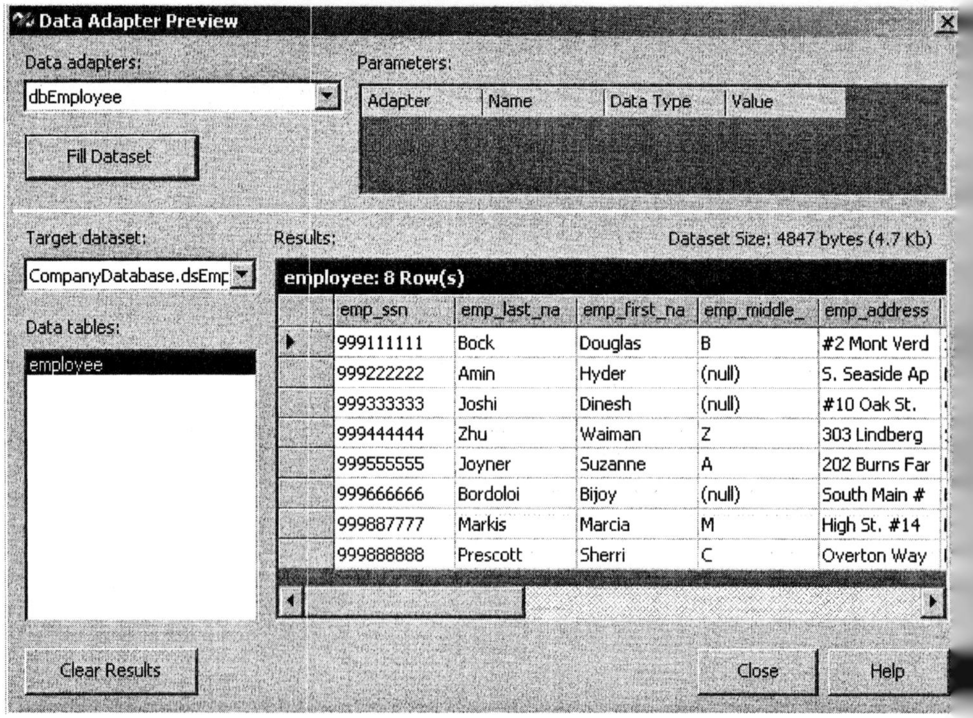

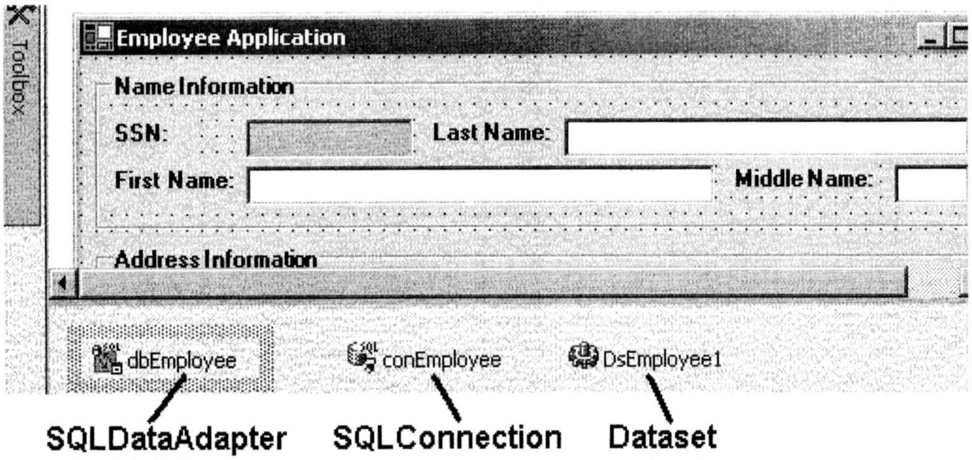

SQLDataAdapter   SQLConnection   Dataset

FIGURE 12.9

The only task that remains is to add controls such as labels and text boxes to the form that displays employee information. In fact, the controls used to display data can be added to the form either before or after the data adapter is configured. Figure 12.10 shows the completed form. This form uses text boxes to display data. The SSN is displayed to a text box, but the text box has been set to *read only* so that the SSN is not inadvertently changed. This causes the grey background for SSN shown on the form.

FIGURE 12.10

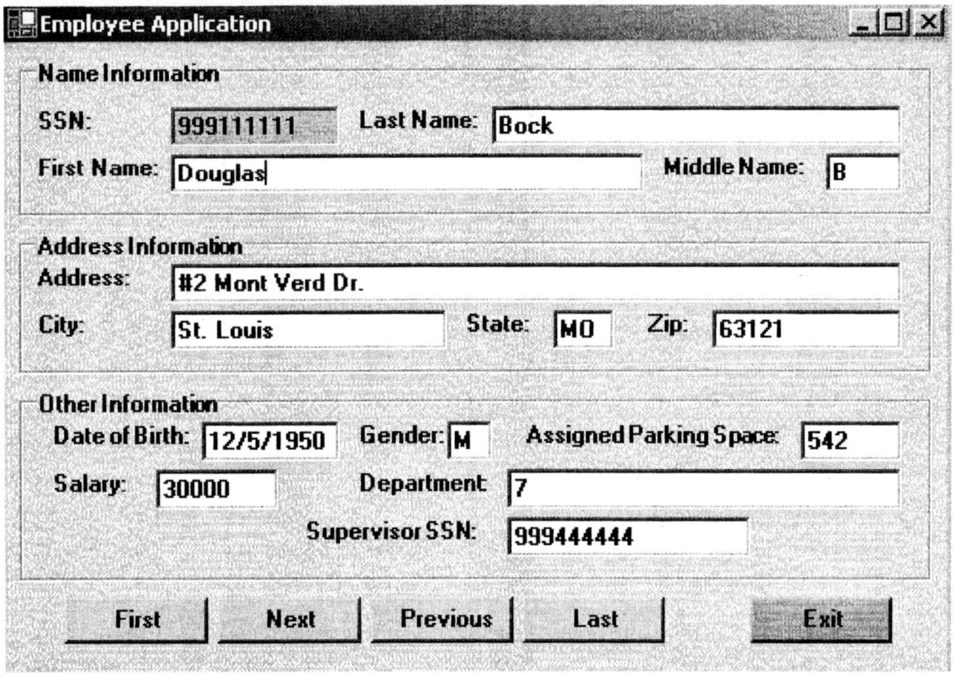

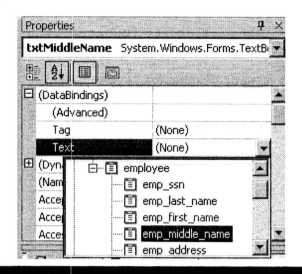

FIGURE 12.11

The form also has *navigation buttons* that are used to move around in the data set. A business manager can move to the first, next, previous, or last employee data row in the data set by simply pointing and clicking.

So, what makes the data from the data set display in the text boxes? Well, it is quite simple. Figure 12.11 shows the *DataBindings* property *Text* option. Simply select a text box, such as the one used to display data from the *emp_middle_name* column, and then select the column name from the listing displayed when you select the *Text* option. Do this for every control that displays employee data. The application programmer must write a simple procedure (not shown here) that will fill the data set when the application executes. The data displays, as in Figure 12.10.

As with Visual Basic 6.0, the SELECT statement can be modified to allow the system user to specify which rows to include in a data set based either on values captured through an InputBox or on values typed into a text box on a form. The Visual Basic.NET code used to insert, delete, and update data is beyond the scope of this textbook; however, the above example illustrates how SQL statements can be embedded within this visual programming language. Additionally, you need to understand that embedding SQL in this fashion simplifies the data retrieval task tremendously.

SUMMARY

In this chapter you learned that SQL statements can be embedded within procedural programming languages. The advantages of using embedded SQL for a computer programmer is an increase in work productivity because SQL statements add the power of a nonprocedural language to a procedural language. This simplifies data retrieval, manipulation, and storage. In both Visual Basic 6.0 and Visual Basic.NET database connections are created through the use of various types of Command and Connection objects. The use of various configuration wizards can greatly simplify the programming process.

REVIEW EXERCISES

LEARN THESE TERMS

ActiveX Data Objects (ADO).   An approach using a specialized control to enable the computer programmer to create database connections very rapidly.

Class.   In Visual Basic.NET, a class includes all object members that are grouped with similar characteristics. For example, the forms used to build an application interface are members of the *Forms class*.

CommandType.   An ADO control property that specifies how data is retrieved from a database.

ConnectionString.   An ADO control property used to specify how to connect to a database.

Data Adapter control.   Configured with the Data Adapter Configuration Wizard to create a data adapter that is used to store SQL statements and to create a database connection.

DataField.   A property of a control that is set to the actual column name from a table to be displayed in a form control such as a text box.

Data Set.   A memory object for VB.NET that includes all data rows retrieved to memory from a database for processing.

DataSource.   A property of a control such as a text box that specifies the name of the ADO control (recordset) that links the text box control to the database through the ADO control.

Embedded SQL.   The use of SQL commands in conjunction with procedural and object-oriented programming host languages where the SQL command is embedded within the host language.

OLE DB.   Object linking and embedding database provider.

Recordset.   A memory object for VB Version 6.0 that includes all data rows retrieved to memory from a database for processing.

RecordSource.   An ADO control property that stores the actual SQL statement used to create a recordset.

System.Data.OleDB.   One of the classes within the System.Data namespace that is used to connect to any database with an OLEDB provider such as Oracle or Microsoft Access.

System.Data.SQLClient.   One of the classes within the System.Data namespace that is used to connect to an SQL Server database.

CONCEPTS QUIZ

1. Why is it useful to embed SQL statements within a host language?
2. What is the purpose of an ADO control in Visual Basic 6.0?
3. How are controls on a Visual Basic form able to display data from relational database columns for Visual Basic 6.0?
4. What advantages does Visual Basic.NET have over Visual Basic 6.0?
5. What type of object is configured in Visual Basic.NET with a "wizard" to enable the embedding of SQL statements? What database controls are created as a result of the configuration process for an SQL Server database?

SQL CODING EXERCISES AND QUESTIONS: COMPANY DATABASE

In answering the SQL exercises and questions, submit a copy of each command that you execute and any messages that SQL Server generates while executing your SQL commands. Also list the output for any result table that is generated by your SQL statements.

1. Study the Company database in Appendix A. You plan to build a form in Visual Basic 6.0 to display all the columns for the *department* table. Write the SELECT statement to retrieve all rows from the table.

2. Suppose that in Question 1 only a single *department* table row should be retrieved to display on the Visual Basic form. The form has a text box named *txtDepartment* and the value of the department to display is referenced by the *txtDepartment.Text* property. Write an embedded SQL statement to retrieve the desired department. Store the SQL statement to a Visual Basic memory variable named *strSQL*.

3. The Visual Basic 6.0 ADO control used to process the *department* table referenced in Question 2 is named *adoDepartment*. Write the code necessary to store the *strSQL* memory variable to the appropriate property of the ADO control and to retrieve the desired department row.

4. Use VB.NET to build a form to display *employee* table information as was done in this chapter. Create a connection to a database provided by your instructor. Demonstrate that the form displays the data. As an option, you may wish to research the methods used to program the navigation buttons.

SQL Coding Exercises and Questions: Riverbend Database

1. Study the Riverbend database in Appendix B. You are building a form using Visual Basic 6.0 that can display all the columns for the *medical_specialty* table. Write the SELECT statement to retrieve all rows from the table.

2. You plan to revise the form design that displays *medical_specialty* information such that only a single row from the table can be retrieved for display on the form. The form has a text box named *txtSpecialtyCode*. The value displayed in the text box is referenced by the *txtSpecialtyCode.Text* property. Write an embedded SQL statement to retrieve the desired row. Store the SQL statement to a Visual Basic memory variable named *strSQL*.

3. The ADO control used to process the *medical_specialty* table referenced in Question 2 is named *adoMedSpec*. Write the code necessary to store the *strSQL* memory variable to the appropriate property of the ADO control and to retrieve the desired *medical_specialty* row by refreshing the *adoMedSpec* control.

4. Use VB.NET to build a form to display *medical_specialty* table information. Create a connection to the database named Riverbend that you created when you executed the CreateRiverbendDatabase.sql script described in Appendix B. Demonstrate that the form displays data rows from the table.

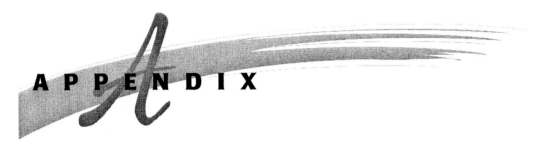

APPENDIX A

COMPANY DATABASE SCHEMA

Throughout the textbook SQL statements that query and modify information use example tables from the **Company** database. This is one of two databases used with this textbook; the second is the **Riverbend Hospital** database described in Appendix B.

DATABASE SCHEMA

Figure A.1 shows a diagram of the seven tables that comprise the company database, with the table names underlined in the figure (e.g., *employee*), and the column names shown inside the rectangles (e.g., *emp_ssn*).

Relationships between the tables are shown with connecting lines. Consider the line connecting the *employee* and *dependent* tables. Figure A.2 shows you how to interpret the relationship connecting lines.

Reading from the *employee* toward the *dependent* table, the line has a circle and three-legged "crow's foot," meaning this is an optional relationship (circle) such that each employee can optionally (circle) have no dependents. The three-legged crow's foot means an employee can have one or more dependents. Reading from the *dependent* toward the *employee* table, the line is crossed by two short lines indicating that this relationship is mandatory in this direction such that each dependent can belong to one and only one employee—a dependent cannot exist without an employee.

Figure A.2 shows two other symbol combinations. The first is the mandatory relationship with one or more *dependent* table rows per *employee* table row—this would be the situation if the company hired only employees who already had a dependent; however, this is not the case so this symbol was not used in Figure A.1. The other is the optional zero or one employee per dependent; and this also is not the case so this symbol was not used in Figure A.1. However, you may find other relationships that use these symbol combinations.

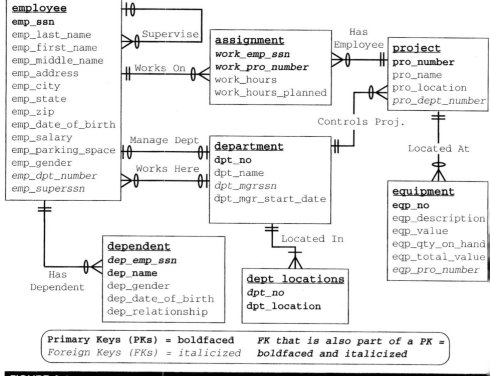

Primary Keys (PKs) = boldfaced   FK that is also part of a PK =
Foreign Keys (FKs) = italicized   boldfaced and italicized

FIGURE A.1

FIGURE A.2

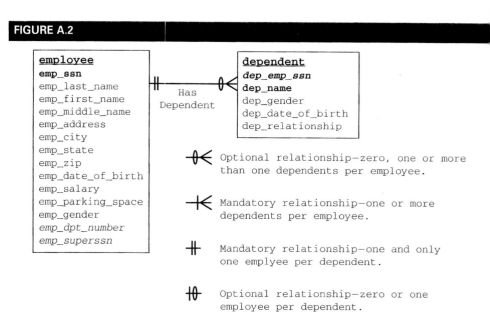

TABLE DEFINITIONS

DEPARTMENT TABLE

The company is organized into separate departments. Tables A.1 and A.2 describe the columns in the *department* table and show the test data stored for each department. Each department is identified by a unique department number (*dpt_no*) and has a department name. Each department has a manager and date on which the manager started managing the department. The manager's social security number (*dpt_mgrssn*) stored in the *department* table provides a FOREIGN KEY link to the specific employee that manages a department. Note that we have not *explicitly* defined *dpt_mgrssn* column to be a FOREIGN KEY referencing the table *employee* yet. This is because it is impossible for this column to reference the *employee* table which has not yet been created! As exemplified in the SQL script shown at the end of this Appendix, the ALTER command is used to redefine this column to be a FOREIGN KEY with appropriate integrity constraints—*after* creation of the *employee* table.

SQL Example A.1 gives the CREATE TABLE statement for the *department* table. Two constraints are named, one for the department primary key and the other to ensure that each department row must have a department name (NOT NULL).

```
/* SQL Example A.1 */
CREATE TABLE department (
    dpt_no                  SMALLINT
        CONSTRAINT pk_department PRIMARY KEY,
    dpt_name                VARCHAR(20)
        CONSTRAINT nn_dpt_name NOT NULL,
    dpt_mgrssn              CHAR(9) NULL,
    dpt_mgr_start_date      DATETIME NULL  );
```

TABLE A.1   TABLE NAME: department

Column Name	Data Type	Size	Comments
dpt_no	SMALLINT		**Primary Key.** Number assigned by the company
dpt_name	VARCHAR	20	Department name
dpt_mgrssn	CHAR	9	**Foreign Key** link to *employee* that manages this department
dpt_mgr_start_date	DATETIME		Date a manager was assigned to supervise the department

TABLE A.2   TABLE DATA: department

dpt_no	*dpt_name*	*dpt_mgrssn*	*dpt_mgr_start_date*
7	Production	999444444	05-22-1998
3	Admin and Records	999555555	01-01-2001
1	Headquarters	999666666	06-19-1981

DEPT_LOCATIONS TABLE

Each department may have multiple city locations within the company. To provide for normalized data maintenance, a separate *dept_locations* table stores location information. Tables A.3 and A.4 describe the columns and actual data stored in the *dept_locations* table. The primary key of the *dept_locations* table is a composite of *dpt_no* and *dpt_location*. There are no nonkey columns in the table. The *dpt_no* column also serves as a FOREIGN KEY link back to the *department* table.

SQL Example A.2 shows the CREATE TABLE statement to create *dept_locations*. Chapter 2 explains that the constraint specification to create the primary key is a special form of the PRIMARY KEY clause used to create composite keys for two or more columns. There is also a FOREIGN KEY clause to specify that the *dpt_no* column references the *department* table.

```
/* SQL Example A.2 */
CREATE TABLE dept_locations (
    dpt_no                SMALLINT,
    dpt_location          VARCHAR(20),
CONSTRAINT pk_dept_locations
    PRIMARY KEY (dpt_no, dpt_location),
CONSTRAINT fk_dept_loc_no FOREIGN KEY (dpt_no)
    REFERENCES department  );
```

TABLE A.3 TABLE NAME: dept_locations

Column Name	Data Type	Size	Comments
dpt_no	SMALLINT		**Primary key.** Number assigned by the company. Also **Foreign key** link to *department* table
dpt_location	VARCHAR	20	**Primary key.** One of many cities where department is located

TABLE A.4 TABLE DATA: dept_locations

dpt_no	dpt_location
1	Edwardsville
3	Marina
7	St. Louis
7	Collinsville
7	Edwardsville

EMPLOYEE TABLE

Employee information is stored in the *employee* table. Tables A.5 and A.6 describe the columns in the *employee* table and the data stored in the table. Individual employees are identified by their SSN (*emp_ssn*) as a primary key.

Employees work in departments. Some employees also manage departments. Figure A.1 shows these two relationships named *Manage-Dept* and *Works-Here*. The *Manage-Dept* relationship links each row in the *department* table to the *employee* table row for the employee who manages the department. The *Works-Here* relationship links the *employee* table to the *department* table for the department to which each employee is assigned to work.

You should interpret the *Works-Here* relationship as meaning that a department can have zero, one, or more than one assigned employees (crows foot), and that each employee is assigned to one and only one (mandatory) department. SQL Example A.3 shows the CREATE TABLE statement for the *employee* table. The *Works-Here* relationship is implemented by the FOREIGN KEY constraint named *fk_emp_dpt*.

The *Manage-Dept* relationship may confuse you. It simply means that each department has one and only one manager, and any given employee may optionally manage a department. Of course, most employees do not manage a department. The FOREIGN KEY constraint to enforce the *Manage-Dept* relationship is not specified in the CREATE TABLE statement for either the *employee* or *department* tables. This is because a constraint cannot be created for a nonexistent table and one of the two tables has to be created first. Instead, this constraint is added to the database after all the tables are created.

Employees are supervised by other employees. This is a unary or recursive relationship between rows within the *employee* table and is depicted as the *Supervise* relationship

TABLE A.5   TABLE NAME: employee

Column Name	Data Type	Size	Comments
emp_ssn	CHAR	9	**Primary key.** Employee SSN
emp_last_name	VARCHAR	25	Employee last name
emp_first_name	VARCHAR	25	Employee first name
emp_middle_name	VARCHAR	25	Employee middle name
emp_address	VARCHAR	50	Employee street address
emp_city	VARCHAR	25	City where employee resides
emp_state	CHAR	2	Two-character abbreviation of the state of residence
emp_zip	CHAR	9	Zip code for mailing
emp_date_of_birth	DATETIME		Employee date of birth
emp_salary	MONEY		Employee monthly salary
emp_parking_space	INT		Number of the parking space allocated to the employee
emp_gender	CHAR	1	Code — M = male; F = female
emp_dpt_number	SMALLINT		**Foreign key** link to department table; department to which an employee is assigned
emp_superssn	CHAR	9	**Foreign key** link to employee record supervising this employee

TABLE A.6

emp_ssn	emp_last _name	emp_first_ name	emp_middle_ name	emp_address	emp_city	emp_state
999666666	Bordoloi	Bijoy		South Main #12	Edwardsville	IL
999555555	Joyner	Suzanne	A	202 Burns Farm	Marina	CA
999444444	Zhu	Waiman	Z	303 Lindbergh	St. Louis	MO
999887777	Markis	Marcia	M	High St. #14	Monterey	CA
999222222	Amin	Hyder		S. Seaside Apt B	Marina	CA
999111111	Bock	Douglas	B	#2 Mont Verd Dr.	St. Louis	MO
999333333	Joshi	Dinesh		#10 Oak St	Collinsville	IL
999888888	Prescott	Sherri	C	Overton Way #4	Edwardsville	IL

emp_zip	emp_date _of_birth	emp_salary	emp_parking _space	emp_gender	emp_dpt _number	emp_superssn
62025	03-14-1954	55000	1	M	1	
93941	06-20-1971	43000	3	F	3	999666666
63121	12-08-1975	43000	32	M	7	999666666
93940	07-19-1978	25000	402	F	3	999555555
93941	03-29-1969	25000	422	M	3	999555555
63121	12-05-1950	30000	542	M	7	999444444
66234	09-15-1972	38000	332	M	7	999444444
62025	07-31-1972	25000	296	F	7	999444444

in Figure A.1. The *Supervise* relationship is enforced by the FOREIGN KEY constraint named *fk_emp_superssn* that links a given employee to that employee's supervisor; thus, the employee supervisor's SSN (*emp_superssn*) is stored as a column in the table. This relationship is covered in detail in Chapter 6.

```
/* SQL Example A.3 */
CREATE TABLE employee (
    emp_ssn                 CHAR(9)
        CONSTRAINT pk_employee PRIMARY KEY,
    emp_last_name           VARCHAR(25)
        CONSTRAINT nn_emp_last_name NOT NULL,
    emp_first_name          VARCHAR(25)
        CONSTRAINT nn_emp_first_name NOT NULL,
    emp_middle_name         VARCHAR(25) NULL,
    emp_address             VARCHAR(50) NULL,
    emp_city                VARCHAR(25) NULL,
    emp_state               CHAR(2) NULL,
    emp_zip                 CHAR(9) NULL,
    emp_date_of_birth       DATETIME NULL,
    emp_salary              MONEY
        CONSTRAINT ck_emp_salary
            CHECK (emp_salary <= 85000)
        CONSTRAINT nn_emp_salary NOT NULL,
    emp_parking_space       INT
```

```
        CONSTRAINT un_emp_parking_space UNIQUE,
    emp_gender                  CHAR(1) NULL,
    emp_dpt_number              SMALLINT,
    emp_superssn                CHAR(9),
CONSTRAINT fk_emp_dpt FOREIGN KEY (emp_dpt_number)
    REFERENCES department,
CONSTRAINT fk_emp_superssn FOREIGN KEY (emp_superssn)
    REFERENCES employee  );
```

PROJECTS TABLE

Projects for the company are controlled or supervised by departments. Each project is identified by a project number (*pro_number*) and the firm tracks each project by name and by location. Tables A.7 and A.8 show the columns in the table and data stored in the *project* table. Figure A.1 shows the *Controls-Proj* relationship. A department may have zero, one, or more active projects and a project belongs to one and only one department.

SQL Example A.4 gives the CREATE TABLE statement for the *project* table. The *fk_pro_dept_number* FOREIGN KEY constraint implements the *Controls-Proj* relationship.

```
/* SQL Example A.4 */
CREATE TABLE project (
    pro_number                  SMALLINT
        CONSTRAINT pk_project PRIMARY KEY,
    pro_name                    VARCHAR(25)
        CONSTRAINT nn_pro_name NOT NULL,
    pro_location                VARCHAR(25) NULL,
    pro_dept_number             SMALLINT,
CONSTRAINT fk_pro_dept_number FOREIGN KEY (pro_dept_number)
    REFERENCES department  );
```

ASSIGNMENT TABLE

Each employee is assigned to work on zero, one, or more projects. This is reflected in Figure A.1 by the *assignment* table and two relationships: *Works-On* and *Has-Employee*. The *assignment* table is an **association** table because it associates the *employee* and

TABLE A.7 TABLE NAME: project			
Column Name	*Data Type*	*Size*	*Comments*
pro_number	SMALLINT		**Primary key.** Identifying number assigned by the company
pro_name	VARCHAR	25	Project name
pro_location	VARCHAR	25	Project location
pro_dept_number	SMALLINT		**Foreign key** link to *department* controlling the project

TABLE A.8 TABLE DATA: project

pro_number	pro_name	pro_location	pro_dept_number
1	Order Entry	St. Louis	7
2	Payroll	Collinsville	7
3	Receivables	Edwardsville	7
10	Inventory	Marina	3
20	Personnel	Edwardsville	1
30	Pay Benefits	Marina	3

project tables. Tables A.9 and A.10 show the columns definitions and column data for the *assignment* table. The primary key for *assignment* is a composite of the primary key from the *employee* table combined with the primary key of the *project* table: *work_emp_ssn* and *work_pro_number* columns.

SQL Example A.5 gives the CREATE TABLE statement to create the *assignment* table. The PRIMARY KEY clause implements the primary key in the same fashion as was done earlier for the *dept_locations* table. Two FOREIGN KEY constraints, *fk_work_emp* and *fk_work_pro_number,* implement the *Works-On* and *Has-Employee* relationships by referencing back to the respective *employee* and *project* tables. You learn about the ON DELETE clauses when you study Chapter 2.

```
/* SQL Example A.5 */
CREATE TABLE assignment (
    work_emp_ssn              CHAR(9),
    work_pro_number           SMALLINT,
    work_hours                DECIMAL(5,1) NULL,
    work_hours_planned        DECIMAL(5,1) NULL,
CONSTRAINT pk_assignment
    PRIMARY KEY (work_emp_ssn, work_pro_number),
CONSTRAINT fk_work_emp
    FOREIGN KEY (work_emp_ssn) REFERENCES employee
        ON DELETE CASCADE,
CONSTRAINT fk_work_pro_number
    FOREIGN KEY (work_pro_number) REFERENCES project
        ON DELETE CASCADE  );
```

TABLE A.9 TABLE NAME: assignment

Column Name	Data Type	Size	Comments
work_emp_ssn	CHAR	9	**Primary key.** Employee SSN; also **Foreign key** link to *employee* table
work_pro_number	SMALLINT		**Primary key.** Project number; also **Foreign key** link to the *project* table
work_hours	DECIMAL	(5,1)	Number of hours an employee has worked on a project
work_hours_planned	DECIMAL	(5,1)	Number of planned (estimated) hours an employee may work on a project to complete the tasking

TABLE A.10   TABLE DATA: assignment

work_emp_ssn	work_pro_number	work_hours	work_hours_planned
999111111	1	31.4	35.0
999111111	2	8.5	10.2
999333333	3	42.1	65.0
999888888	1	21.0	20.0
999888888	2	22.0	20.0
999444444	2	12.2	15.5
999444444	3	10.5	30.0
999444444	1	NULL	NULL
999444444	10	10.1	10.5
999444444	20	11.8	10.2
999887777	30	30.8	25.5
999887777	10	10.2	15.0
999222222	10	34.5	42.3
999222222	30	5.1	11.8
999555555	30	19.2	18.3
999555555	20	14.8	NULL
999666666	20	NULL	15.5

DEPENDENT TABLE

Figure A.1 shows the *Has-Dependent* relationship between the *employee* and *dependent* tables. Tables A.11 and A.12 describe the columns and data for the *dependent* table. An employee may have zero, one, or more dependents; and a dependent belongs to one and only one employee. The firm only tracks minimal information about dependents to satisfy governmental reporting requirements for taxation and education purposes. Each *dependent* table row must reference an existing *employee* table row. The primary key of the *dependent* table is a composite of *dep_emp_ssn* and *dep_name*. The *dep_emp_ssn* column also serves to link *dependent* rows to the *employee* table.

SQL Example A.6 gives the CREATE TABLE statement for the *dependent* table. The PRIMARY KEY constraint named *pk_dependent* enforces the composite primary key. The FOREIGN KEY constraint named *fk_dep_emp_ssn* implements the *Has-Dependent* relationship.

TABLE A.11   TABLE NAME: dependent

Column Name	Data Type	Size	Comments
dep_emp_ssn	CHAR	9	**Primary key.** Employee SSN for this dependent; also **Foreign key** link to *employee* table
dep_name	VARCHAR	50	**Primary key.** Dependent name
dep_gender	CHAR	1	Dependent gender coded: M = male; F = female
dep_date_of_birth	DATETIME		Dependent date of birth
dep_relationship	VARCHAR	10	Relationship of dependent to employee (e.g., daughter, spouse, son)

TABLE A.12 TABLE DATA: dependent

dep_emp_ssn	dep_name	dep_gender	dep_date_of_birth	dep_relationship
999444444	Jo Ellen	F	04-05-1996	DAUGHTER
999444444	Andrew	M	10-25-1998	SON
999444444	Susan	F	05-03-1975	SPOUSE
999555555	Allen	M	02-29-1968	SPOUSE
999111111	Jeffery	M	12-31-1978	SON
999111111	Deanna	F	05-03-1981	DAUGHTER
999111111	Michelle	F	03-17-1984	SPOUSE
999111111	Rachael	F	10-04-1975	DAUGHTER
999111111	Mary Ellen	F	05-28-1956	SPOUSE
999666666	Mita	F	06-04-1956	SPOUSE
999666666	Anita	F	07-06-1984	DAUGHTER
999666666	Monica	F	12-30-1988	DAUGHTER
999666666	Rita	F	05-11-1994	DAUGHTER

```
/* SQL Example A.6 */
CREATE TABLE dependent (
    dep_emp_ssn             CHAR(9),
    dep_name                VARCHAR(50),
    dep_gender              CHAR(1) NULL,
    dep_date_of_birth       DATETIME NULL,
    dep_relationship        VARCHAR(10) NULL,
CONSTRAINT pk_dependent PRIMARY KEY (dep_emp_ssn, dep_name),
CONSTRAINT fk_dep_emp_ssn
    FOREIGN KEY (dep_emp_ssn) REFERENCES employee
        ON DELETE CASCADE );
```

EQUIPMENT TABLE

Equipment is acquired from a local equipment rental company for projects. When projects are completed, the equipment is returned; thus, the Company has no need to maintain a stock of equipment. A project can have zero, one, or more items of equipment as reflected by the *Located-At* relationship in Figure A.1. Equipment items are identified by an equipment number (*eqp_no*); and have a description, value, quantity on hand, and total value. The *eqp_pro_number* column in the table is a FOREIGN KEY link to the *project* table for the project that is using the equipment. Tables A.13 and A.14 describe the columns and data for the *equipment* table.

```
/* Create equipment table */
CREATE TABLE equipment (
    eqp_no                  CHAR(4)
        CONSTRAINT pk_equipment PRIMARY KEY,
    eqp_description         VARCHAR(15),
    eqp_value               MONEY,
    eqp_qty_on_hand         SMALLINT,
    eqp_total_value AS eqp_value * eqp_qty_on_hand,
    eqp_pro_number          SMALLINT,
```

```
CONSTRAINT fk_eqp_pro_number FOREIGN KEY (eqp_pro_number)
    REFERENCES project
        ON DELETE CASCADE );
```

TABLE A.13   TABLE NAME: equipment

Column Name	Data Type	Size	Comments
eqp_no	CHAR	4	**Primary key.** Equipment number
eqp_desc	VARCHAR	15	Equipment description
eqp_value	MONEY		Value of one equipment item
eqp_qty_on_hand	SMALLINT		Quantity of this item on hand for the project
eqp_total_value	MONEY		Total value of this equipment item on hand for the project = eqp_value * eqp_qty_on_hand
eqp_pro_number	SMALLINT		**Foreign key** link to project table

TABLE A.14   TABLE DATA: equipment

eqp_no	eqp_desc	eqp_value	eqp_qty_on_hand	eqp_total_value	eqp_pro_number
4321	Computer, PC	1100.00	2	2200.00	3
2323	Table, mobile	245.50	3	736.50	2
6987	Computer, PC	849.50	2	1699.00	1
1234	Chair, mobile	78.25	4	313.00	2
5678	Printer	172.00	1	172.00	30
9876	Computer, Ntpad	1400.23	2	2800.46	30

ADDITIONAL TABLE CONSTRAINTS

Earlier we discuss the *Manage-Dept* relationship between the *department* and *employee* tables. The FOREIGN KEY constraint for this relationship can be added to the *department* table definition by use of an ALTER TABLE statement now that the *employee* table has been created. You study how to alter tables to add constraints in Chapter 2.

```
/* SQL Example A.8 */
ALTER TABLE department ADD CONSTRAINT fk_dept_emp
    FOREIGN KEY (dpt_mgrssn)
        REFERENCES employee (emp_ssn);
```

CREATE COMPANY TABLES AND INDEXES

The **CreateCompanyDatabase.sql** script file contains the SQL statements shown above to create the tables and indexes for the Company database. The script also populates the tables with data. The script assigns explicit names to all table constraints and indexes. This script can be downloaded from the textbook website and is stored in a script file named **CreateCompanyDatabase.sql**. Chapter 1 provides you with a detailed explanation of the procedure you need to follow to create your own copy of the Company database.

A second script file named **RecreateCompanyDatabase.sql** contains the code needed to recreate the tables and indexes. You should only run this script if you have already created the Company database tables and need to recreate the tables for some reason; for example, you accidentally deleted some table rows. This script is also downloadable from the textbook website.

```sql
/* CreateCompanyDatabase.sql                       */
/*   7-23-2003                                      */
/* Script to create the Company database tables.   */
/* Script assumes the Company database has been    */
/*   created already.                              */

Use COMPANY
/* Create tables */
/* Create department table */
CREATE TABLE department (
    dpt_no                    SMALLINT
        CONSTRAINT pk_department PRIMARY KEY,
    dpt_name                  VARCHAR(20)
        CONSTRAINT nn_dpt_name NOT NULL,
    dpt_mgrssn                CHAR(9) NULL,
    dpt_mgr_start_date        DATETIME NULL  );

/* Create dept_locations table */
CREATE TABLE dept_locations (
    dpt_no                    SMALLINT,
    dpt_location              VARCHAR(20),
CONSTRAINT pk_dept_locations
    PRIMARY KEY (dpt_no, dpt_location),
CONSTRAINT fk_dept_loc_no FOREIGN KEY (dpt_no)
    REFERENCES department  );

/* Create project table */
CREATE TABLE project (
    pro_number                SMALLINT
        CONSTRAINT pk_project PRIMARY KEY,
    pro_name                  VARCHAR(25)
        CONSTRAINT nn_pro_name NOT NULL,
    pro_location              VARCHAR(25) NULL,
    pro_dept_number           SMALLINT,
CONSTRAINT fk_pro_dept_number FOREIGN KEY (pro_dept_number)
    REFERENCES department  );

/* Create employee table */
CREATE TABLE employee (
    emp_ssn                   CHAR(9)
        CONSTRAINT pk_employee PRIMARY KEY,
    emp_last_name             VARCHAR(25)
        CONSTRAINT nn_emp_last_name NOT NULL,
    emp_first_name            VARCHAR(25)
        CONSTRAINT nn_emp_first_name NOT NULL,
    emp_middle_name           VARCHAR(25) NULL,
```

```
    emp_address                 VARCHAR(50) NULL,
    emp_city                    VARCHAR(25) NULL,
    emp_state                   CHAR(2) NULL,
    emp_zip                     CHAR(9) NULL,
    emp_date_of_birth           DATETIME NULL,
    emp_salary                  MONEY
        CONSTRAINT ck_emp_salary
            CHECK (emp_salary <= 85000)
        CONSTRAINT nn_emp_salary NOT NULL,
    emp_parking_space           INT
        CONSTRAINT un_emp_parking_space UNIQUE,
    emp_gender                  CHAR(1) NULL,
    emp_dpt_number              SMALLINT,
    emp_superssn                CHAR(9),
CONSTRAINT fk_emp_dpt FOREIGN KEY (emp_dpt_number)
    REFERENCES department,
CONSTRAINT fk_emp_superssn FOREIGN KEY (emp_superssn)
    REFERENCES employee  );


/* Create assignment table */
CREATE TABLE assignment (
    work_emp_ssn                CHAR(9),
    work_pro_number             SMALLINT,
    work_hours                  DECIMAL(5,1) NULL,
    work_hours_planned          DECIMAL(5,1) NULL,
CONSTRAINT pk_assignment
    PRIMARY KEY (work_emp_ssn, work_pro_number),
CONSTRAINT fk_work_emp
    FOREIGN KEY (work_emp_ssn) REFERENCES employee
        ON DELETE CASCADE,
CONSTRAINT fk_work_pro_number
    FOREIGN KEY (work_pro_number) REFERENCES project
        ON DELETE CASCADE  );


/* Create dependent table */
CREATE TABLE dependent (
    dep_emp_ssn                 CHAR(9),
    dep_name                    VARCHAR(50),
    dep_gender                  CHAR(1) NULL,
    dep_date_of_birth           DATETIME NULL,
    dep_relationship            VARCHAR(10) NULL,
CONSTRAINT pk_dependent PRIMARY KEY (dep_emp_ssn, dep_name),
CONSTRAINT fk_dep_emp_ssn
    FOREIGN KEY (dep_emp_ssn) REFERENCES employee
        ON DELETE CASCADE  );


/* Create equipment table */
CREATE TABLE equipment (
    eqp_no                      CHAR(4)
        CONSTRAINT pk_equipment PRIMARY KEY,
    eqp_description             VARCHAR(15),
    eqp_value                   MONEY,
    eqp_qty_on_hand             SMALLINT,
    eqp_total_value AS eqp_value * eqp_qty_on_hand,
    eqp_pro_number              SMALLINT,
CONSTRAINT fk_eqp_pro_number FOREIGN KEY (eqp_pro_number)
```

```
                    REFERENCES project
                        ON DELETE CASCADE );

    /* POPULATE TABLES */
    /* Department rows.  Department manager SSN */
    /*   and date_mgr_startdate are null.        */
    INSERT INTO department VALUES (7, 'Production', NULL, NULL);
    INSERT INTO department VALUES (3, 'Admin and Records', NULL,
        NULL);
    INSERT INTO department VALUES (1, 'Headquarters', NULL, NULL);

    /* Dept_locations rows. */
    INSERT INTO dept_locations VALUES (1, 'Edwardsville');
    INSERT INTO dept_locations VALUES (3, 'Marina');
    INSERT INTO dept_locations VALUES (7, 'St. Louis');
    INSERT INTO dept_locations VALUES (7, 'Collinsville');
    INSERT INTO dept_locations VALUES (7, 'Edwardsville');

    /* Project rows. */
    INSERT INTO project VALUES (1, 'Order Entry', 'St. Louis', 7);
    INSERT INTO project VALUES (2, 'Payroll', 'Collinsville', 7);
    INSERT INTO project VALUES (3, 'Receivables', 'Edwardsville', 7);
    INSERT INTO project VALUES (10, 'Inventory', 'Marina', 3);
    INSERT INTO project VALUES (20, 'Personnel', 'Edwardsville', 1);
    INSERT INTO project VALUES (30, 'Pay Benefits', 'Marina', 3);

    /* Employee rows. */
    INSERT INTO employee VALUES('999666666', 'Bordoloi', 'Bijoy',
        NULL, 'South Main #12', 'Edwardsville', 'IL', 62025,
        '03-14-1954', 55000, 1, 'M', 1, NULL );
    INSERT INTO employee VALUES('999555555', 'Joyner', 'Suzanne',
        'A', '202 Burns Farm', 'Marina', 'CA', 93941,
        '06-20-1971', 43000, 3, 'F', 3, '999666666');
    INSERT INTO employee VALUES('999444444', 'Zhu', 'Waiman',
        'Z', '303 Lindbergh', 'St. Louis', 'MO', 63121,
        '12-08-1975', 43000, 32, 'M', 7, '999666666');
    INSERT INTO employee VALUES('999887777', 'Markis', 'Marcia',
        'M', 'High St. #14', 'Monterey', 'CA', 93940,
        '07-19-1978', 25000, 402, 'F', 3, '999555555');
    INSERT INTO employee VALUES('999222222', 'Amin', 'Hyder',
        NULL, 'S. Seaside Apt. B', 'Marina', 'CA', 93941,
        '03-29-1969', 25000, 422, 'M', 3, '999555555');
    INSERT INTO employee VALUES('999111111', 'Bock', 'Douglas',
        'B', '#2 Mont Verd Dr.', 'St. Louis', 'MO', 63121,
        '12-05-1950', 30000, 542, 'M', 7, '999444444');
    INSERT INTO employee VALUES('999333333', 'Joshi', 'Dinesh',
        NULL, '#10 Oak St.', 'Collinsville', 'IL', 66234,
        '09-15-1972', 38000, 332, 'M', 7, '999444444');
    INSERT INTO employee VALUES('999888888', 'Prescott', 'Sherri',
        'C', 'Overton Way #4', 'Edwardsville', 'IL', 62025,
        '07-31-1972', 25000, 296, 'F', 7, '999444444');

    /* Assignment rows. */
    INSERT INTO assignment VALUES ('999111111', 1, 31.4, 35.0);
    INSERT INTO assignment VALUES ('999111111', 2, 8.5, 10.2);
    INSERT INTO assignment VALUES ('999333333', 3, 42.1, 65.0);
```

```
INSERT INTO assignment VALUES ('999888888', 1, 21.0, 20.0);
INSERT INTO assignment VALUES ('999888888', 2, 22.0, 20.0);
INSERT INTO assignment VALUES ('999444444', 2, 12.2, 15.5);
INSERT INTO assignment VALUES ('999444444', 3, 10.5, 30.0);
INSERT INTO assignment VALUES ('999444444', 1, NULL, NULL);
INSERT INTO assignment VALUES ('999444444', 10, 10.1, 10.5);
INSERT INTO assignment VALUES ('999444444', 20, 11.8, 10.2);
INSERT INTO assignment VALUES ('999887777', 30, 30.8, 25.5);
INSERT INTO assignment VALUES ('999887777', 10, 10.2, 15.0);
INSERT INTO assignment VALUES ('999222222', 10, 34.5, 42.3);
INSERT INTO assignment VALUES ('999222222', 30, 5.1, 11.8);
INSERT INTO assignment VALUES ('999555555', 30, 19.2, 18.3);
INSERT INTO assignment VALUES ('999555555', 20, 14.8, NULL);
INSERT INTO assignment VALUES ('999666666', 20, NULL, 15.5);

/* Dependent rows. */
INSERT INTO dependent VALUES ('999444444', 'Jo Ellen', 'F',
    '04-05-1996', 'DAUGHTER');
INSERT INTO dependent VALUES ('999444444', 'Andrew', 'M',
    '10-25-1998', 'SON');
INSERT INTO dependent VALUES ('999444444', 'Susan', 'F',
    '05-03-1975', 'SPOUSE');
INSERT INTO dependent VALUES ('999555555', 'Allen', 'M',
    '02-29-1968', 'SPOUSE');
INSERT INTO dependent VALUES ('999111111', 'Jeffery', 'M',
    '12-31-1978', 'SON');
INSERT INTO dependent VALUES ('999111111', 'Deanna', 'F',
    '05-03-1981', 'DAUGHTER');
INSERT INTO dependent VALUES ('999111111', 'Rachael', 'F',
    '10-04-1975', 'DAUGHTER');
INSERT INTO dependent VALUES ('999111111', 'Michelle', 'F',
    '03-17-1984', 'DAUGHTER');
INSERT INTO dependent VALUES ('999111111', 'Mary Ellen', 'F',
    '05-28-1956', 'SPOUSE');
INSERT INTO dependent VALUES ('999666666', 'Mita', 'F',
    '06-04-1956', 'SPOUSE');
INSERT INTO dependent VALUES ('999666666', 'Anita', 'F',
    '07-06-1984', 'DAUGHTER');
INSERT INTO dependent VALUES ('999666666', 'Monica', 'F',
    '12-30-1988', 'DAUGHTER');
INSERT INTO dependent VALUES ('999666666', 'Rita', 'F',
    '05-11-1994', 'DAUGHTER');

/* equipment rows */
INSERT INTO equipment VALUES ('4321', 'Computer, PC', 1100.00, 2, 3);
INSERT INTO equipment VALUES ('2323', 'Table, mobile', 245.50, 3, 2);
INSERT INTO equipment VALUES ('6987', 'Computer, PC', 849.50, 2, 1);
INSERT INTO equipment VALUES ('1234', 'Chair, mobile', 78.25, 4, 2);
INSERT INTO equipment VALUES ('5678', 'Printer', 172.00, 1, 30);
INSERT INTO equipment VALUES ('9876', 'Computer, Ntpad', 1400.23, 2, 30);

/* Update department rows to add manager ssn and start date. */
UPDATE department SET dpt_mgrssn = '999444444',
    dpt_mgr_start_date = '5-22-1998'
    WHERE dpt_no = '7';
UPDATE department SET dpt_mgrssn = '999555555',
```

```
        dpt_mgr_start_date = '1-1-2001'
        WHERE dpt_no = '3';
UPDATE department SET dpt_mgrssn = '999666666',
        dpt_mgr_start_date = '6-19-1981'
        WHERE dpt_no = '1';

/* Add FOREIGN KEY constraint between the department */
/* and employee tables.                             */
 ALTER TABLE department ADD CONSTRAINT fk_dept_emp
    FOREIGN KEY (dpt_mgrssn)
        REFERENCES employee (emp_ssn);

/* Count table rows to ensure the script executed properly. */
SELECT COUNT(*) "Department Count should be 3" FROM department;
SELECT COUNT(*) "Dept Locations Count should be 5" FROM dept_locations;
SELECT COUNT(*) "Project Count should be 6" FROM project;
SELECT COUNT(*) "Employee Count should be 8" FROM employee;
SELECT COUNT(*) "Assignment Count should be 17" FROM assignment;
SELECT COUNT(*) "Dependent Count should be 13" FROM dependent;
SELECT COUNT(*) "Equipment Count should be 6" FROM equipment;

/* End of Script */
```

RIVERBEND HOSPITAL CASE

The Riverbend Hospital of Alton, Illinois, is a regional, acute care facility. The hospital maintains a moderate-sized information systems (IS) department that includes 20 to 25 employees. The IS department manager, Mr. John Blasé, directly supervises the senior employees in the department. The department has a senior database administrator, a senior network administrator, two senior operating systems administrators (one for UNIX and one for Windows), and two project managers. The IS staff also includes several senior programmer/ analysts, and approximately 10 junior programmer/analysts.

You have recently been hired as a junior programmer/analyst based on your collegiate training in Transact Structured Query Language (T-SQL). You have met with Ms. Juanita Benitez, the senior programmer/analyst in charge of the project team to which you are assigned. Ms. Benitez has assigned you responsibility for developing T-SQL queries to support a portion of the firm's database. She has directed you to study the entity-relationship diagram and database schema for the portion of the database that you can access.

ENTITY RELATIONSHIP DIAGRAM AND TABLE DEFINITIONS

Figure B.1 depicts the entity-relationship diagram. The Riverbend Hospital database is large. Many of the hospital's applications require access to data about patients. The central entity is the PATIENT.

PATIENT TABLE

Patient data is stored in the *patient* table described in Table B.1. Each patient is identified by a *patient_number* value that is assigned to the patient by the hospital.

PATIENT_NOTE TABLE

Each time a patient receives treatment or attention from a member of the nursing or physician medical staff at the hospital, an entry is made into the patient's automated

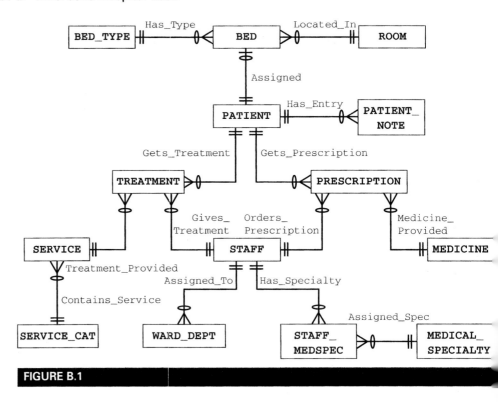

hospital record. This information is stored to the *patient_note* table in the *note_comme*
column. This table allows storage of individual note comments that are up to 40(
characters in size. The table allows for storage of an unlimited number of comments f•
a patient. The relationship between *patient* and *patient_note* is one-to-many, as shown
Figure B.1. Table B.2 describes the *patient_note* table.

BED, ROOM, AND BED_TYPE TABLES

When patients are admitted to the hospital, they are assigned to a specific bed. Patien▮
may request specific types of room accommodations (e.g., private, semiprivate, war▮
The hospital assigns each bed a unique identifier known simply as a *bed_numb*
A room may have zero, one, or more beds (some rooms do not contain beds, e.g., a ra▮
ology laboratory). The database has three additional tables, *bed*, *room*, and *bed_ty*
The *bed_type* table is used as a validation table. Tables B.3 to B.5 describe the colum▮
and structure of the *bed*, *room*, and *bed_type* tables.

STAFF AND WARD_DEPT TABLES

The hospital categorizes all personnel as *staff* members. Staff members include phy▮
cians, registered nurses (RNs), licensed practicing nurses (LPNs), various medi▮
technicians, administrative workers, and other personnel. All staff members are assign▮
to either a medical ward or to a hospital department. For example, an RN may ▮
assigned to General-Medical Surgical Ward 1 whereas a physician may be assigned to t▮

TABLE B.1   TABLE NAME: Patient

Column Name	Data Type	Size	Comments
pat_id	CHAR	6	**Primary key** patient identifier, value assigned by hospital; this value is also used to access patient account information
pat_ssn	CHAR	9	SSN, unique value
pat_last_name	VARCHAR	50	Last name
pat_first_name	VARCHAR	50	First name
pat_middle_name	VARCHAR	50	Middle name
pat_street_address	VARCHAR	50	Street address
pat_city	VARCHAR	50	City
pat_state	CHAR	2	State abbreviation
pat_zip	CHAR	9	Zip code
pat_date_of_birth	DATETIME		Date of birth
pat_telephone_number	CHAR	10	Telephone number
bed_number	SMALLINT		**Foreign key** link to the *bed* table

TABLE B.2   TABLE NAME: patient_note

Column Name	Data Type	Size	Comments
pat_id	CHAR	6	**Primary key**, patient identifier; also serves as a **Foreign key** link to the patient table
note_date	DATETIME		**Primary key**, date and time note posted
note_comment	VARCHAR	4000	Note on patient treatment or condition; physician comment; nurse comment

TABLE B.3   TABLE NAME: bed

Column Name	Data Type	Size	Comments
bed_number	SMALLINT		**Primary key**; number identifying each bed
room_id	CHAR	6	**Foreign key** link to *room* table; identifies the room where the bed is located
bed_type_id	CHAR	2	**Foreign key** link to *bed_type* table; two-digit code indicating the type of bed
bed_availability	CHAR	1	Coded column; N = bed is not occupied; Y = bed is occupied

TABLE B.4   TABLE NAME: bed_type

Column Name	Data Type	Size	Comments
bed_type_id	CHAR	2	**Primary key**; two-digit code indicating the type of bed
bed_description	VARCHAR	50	Description of the bed type

TABLE B.5 TABLE NAME: room			
Column Name	**Data Type**	**Size**	**Comments**
room_id	CHAR	6	**Primary key**; room identification value that identifies each hospital room
room_description	VARCHAR	25	Description of each room

Cardiology department. A staff member is assigned to one and only one ward or depart-ment whereas a ward or department may have many staff members assigned to it. Thus the relationship between the *ward_dept* and *staff* tables is one-to-many. Tables B.6 and B.7 describe the *staff* and *ward_dept* tables.

MEDICAL_SPECIALTY AND STAFF_MEDSPEC TABLES

There is a relationship between staff members with medical specialties and data stored in the *medical_specialty* table. Sometimes a physician or a medical technician has more than one specialty; thus, the relationship between the *staff* and *medical_specialty* tables

TABLE B.6 TABLE NAME: ward_dept			
Column Name	**Data Type**	**Size**	**Comments**
ward_id	CHAR	5	**Primary key**; coded value to identify ward or department
ward_dept_name	VARCHAR	50	Ward or department name
office_location	VARCHAR	25	Office location for the ward or department
telephone_number	CHAR	10	Office primary telephone number

TABLE B.7 TABLE NAME: staff			
Column Name	**Data Type**	**Size**	**Comments**
staff_id	CHAR	5	**Primary key**; value assigned by the hospital
staff_ssn	CHAR	9	SSN; unique value
staff_last_name	VARCHAR	50	Last name
staff_first_name	VARCHAR	50	First name
staff_middle_name	VARCHAR	50	Middle name
ward_dept_assigned	CHAR	5	**Foreign key** link to *ward_dept* table
office_location	VARCHAR	10	Office location
date_hired	DATETIME		Date employee staff member was hired
hospital_title	VARCHAR	50	Hospital title; examples: radiologist and RN
work_phone	CHAR	10	Work telephone number
phone_extension	CHAR	4	Work telephone number extension
license_number	CHAR	20	Medical licensure number assigned by the state medical board; NULL value for nonmedical staff members
salary	MONEY		Salary for salaried workers; NULL for hourly workers
wage_rate	SMALLMONEY		Hourly wage rate for hourly employees; NULL for salaried workers

is many-to-many and is implemented by the creation of a *staff_medspec* association table. The *staff_medspec* table decomposes the many-to-many relationship into two one-to-many relationships named *Has-Specialty* and *Assigned-Spec,* as shown in Figure B.1. The *staff_medspec* table has a composite primary key consisting of the primary key from *staff* and the primary key from *medical_specialty.* These tables are described in Tables B.8 and B.9.

SERVICE AND SERVICE_CAT TABLES

The hospital provides patients with various medical services. Services are categorized for insurance reporting purposes because insurance companies expect hospitals to use standard reporting categories and service codes. The hospital maintains data about services in a *service* table. Additionally, a *service_cat* (category) table stores validation data about service code categories. The relationship between a *service_cat* and *service* is one-to-many because each service falls into a single category. These two tables are described in Tables B.10 and B.11.

TREATMENT TABLE

The hospital keeps records of the services provided by a staff member to each patient. The rendering of a service is termed a *treatment* and is implemented by three relationships named *Gets-Treatment*, *Treatment-Provided*, and *Gives-Treatment* linking

TABLE B.8   TABLE NAME: medical_specialty

Column Name	Data Type	Size	Comments
specialty_code	CHAR	3	**Primary key**; medical specialty code
spec_title	VARCHAR	50	Title of the specialty
how_awarded	VARCHAR	100	How the specialty is awarded (e.g., by completion of medical board examination)

TABLE B.9   TABLE NAME: staff_medspec

Column Name	Data Type	Size	Comments
staff_id	CHAR	5	**Primary key**; also serves as **Foreign key** link to *staff* table; staff number
specialty_code	CHAR	3	**Primary key**; also serves as **Foreign key** link to *medical_specialty* table; medical specialty code
date_awarded	DATETIME		Date the specialty was awarded to the staff member

TABLE B.10   TABLE NAME: service_cat

Column Name	Data Type	Size	Comments
service_cat_id	CHAR	3	**Primary key**; service category identifier
service_cat_desc	VARCHAR	50	Service category description

TABLE B.11   TABLE NAME: service

Column Name	Data Type	Size	Comments
service_id	CHAR	5	**Primary key**; standard medical service identifier
service_description	VARCHAR	50	Description of service provided
service_charge	MONEY		Standard fee for a service; may be modified by the individual administering the service as required by the medical situation
service_comments	VARCHAR	2000	Comments concerning the service including how it should be administered, contraindications, etc.
service_cat_id	CHAR	3	**Foreign key** link to *service_cat* table; service category identifier

treatment to the *patient*, *service*, and *staff* tables, respectively, as shown in Figure B.1 Each *treatment* has a unique identifier, the *treatment_number*. Each table related to *treatment* is linked by storing a foreign key column (*pat_id*, *service_id*, and *staff_id*) i the *treatment* table. The hospital maintains information about treatments including th patient, staff member, and service as well as the date and time of the treatment an the treatment charge. Additional comments concerning each treatment are als recorded. These comments may include diagnosis information. Table B.12 describe the *treatment* table.

MEDICINE AND PRESCRIPTION TABLES

Physicians (staff members) prescribe medicines to be administered to patients by othe staff members. The hospital stores medicines in its internal pharmacy departmen Information about medicines that are stocked is stored in the *medicine* table. The pr scription of medicine is an association table that relates the *staff*, *patient*, and *medici* tables; and is implemented as the table named *prescription* with three one-to-ma relationships named *Orders-Prescription*, *Gets-Prescription*, and *Medicine-Provide* Only one medicine may be prescribed for each prescription. The *medicine* at *prescription* tables are described in Tables B.13 and B.14.

TABLE B.12   TABLE NAME: treatment

Column Name	Data Type	Size	Comments
treatment_number	INT		**Primary key**; unique for a treatment withi a given date
treatment_date	DATETIME		**Primary key**; required to ensure uniquene of the treatment_number column
pat_id	CHAR	6	**Foreign key** link to *patient* table
staff_id	CHAR	5	**Foreign key** link to *staff* table
service_id	CHAR	5	**Foreign key** link to *service* table
actual_charge	MONEY		Actual charge for the service provided
treatment_comments	VARCHAR	2000	Additional comments concerning the trea ment such as diagnosis information

TABLE B.13 TABLE NAME: medicine

Column Name	Data Type	Size	Comments
medicine_code	CHAR	7	**Primary key**; medicine standard code
med_name_sci	VARCHAR	50	Scientific name of the medicine
med_name_common	VARCHAR	50	Common name of the medicine
normal_dosage	VARCHAR	300	Normal dosage of the medicine for a prescription
medicine_comments	VARCHAR	500	Comments about the medicine
quantity_stock	INT		Quantity stocked
unit_measure	VARCHAR	20	Unit of measure (e.g., liters, grams, tablet, capsules)

TABLE B.14 TABLE NAME: prescription

Column Name	Data Type	Size	Comments
pre_number	INT		**Primary key**; prescription number system generated
pre_date	DATETIME		Prescription date
medicine_code	CHAR	7	**Foreign key** link to *medicine* table
pat_id	CHAR	6	**Foreign key** link to *patient* table
staff_id	CHAR	5	**Foreign key** link to *staff* table
dosage_prescribed	VARCHAR	50	Dosage prescribed (e.g., 50-mg tablet)
dosage_directions	VARCHAR	500	Directions for administering the medicine (e.g., two times daily)

CREATE RIVERBEND TABLES AND INDEXES

The *CreateRiverbendDatabase.sql* program script contains the T-SQL statements that create the Riverbend database tables and indexes. We provide the CREATE TABLE statements in this appendix to make it easy for you to understand the table and column names used in the end-of-chapter exercises. The complete script can be downloaded from the textbook Internet website. If you need to recreate the Riverbend database, you can also download the *RecreateRiverbendDatabase.sql* program script from the textbook Internet website.

```
/*  CreateRiverbendDatabase.sql script.
    7-23-03
    This script creates tables and indexes for the Riverbend
      Hospital database.  The script also populates tables with data. */

USE RIVERBEND

/* Create tables  */

/* Table room */
CREATE TABLE room (
    room_id            CHAR(6) CONSTRAINT pk_room PRIMARY KEY,
    room_description   VARCHAR(25) );

/* Table bed_type */
CREATE TABLE bed_type (
    bed_type_id        CHAR(2) CONSTRAINT pk_bed_type PRIMARY KEY,
    bed_description    VARCHAR(50) );
```

```
/* Table bed */
CREATE TABLE bed (
    bed_number              SMALLINT CONSTRAINT pk_bed PRIMARY KEY,
    room_id                 CHAR(6)  CONSTRAINT fk_bed_room
        REFERENCES room(room_id),
    bed_type_id             CHAR(2)  CONSTRAINT nn_bed_type_id NOT NULL
        CONSTRAINT fk_bed_bedtype REFERENCES bed_type(bed_type_id),
    bed_availability        CHAR(1) );

/* Table patient */
CREATE TABLE patient (
    pat_id                  CHAR(6) CONSTRAINT pk_patient PRIMARY KEY,
    pat_ssn                 CHAR(9) CONSTRAINT nn_pat_ssn NOT NULL,
    pat_last_name           VARCHAR(50) CONSTRAINT nn_pat_last_name NOT
                            NULL,
    pat_first_name          VARCHAR(50) CONSTRAINT nn_pat_first_name NOT
                            NULL,
    pat_middle_name         VARCHAR(50),
    pat_street_address      VARCHAR(50),
    pat_city                VARCHAR(50),
    pat_state               CHAR(2),
    pat_zip                 CHAR(9),
    pat_date_of_birth       DATETIME,
    pat_telephone_number    CHAR(10),
    bed_number              SMALLINT CONSTRAINT fk_pat_bed
        REFERENCES bed(bed_number) );

/* Table patient_note */
CREATE TABLE patient_note (
    pat_id                  CHAR(6),
    note_date               DATETIME,
    note_comment            VARCHAR(4000),
    CONSTRAINT pk_section PRIMARY KEY (pat_id, note_date),
    CONSTRAINT fk_pat_note_patient FOREIGN KEY (pat_id)
        REFERENCES patient ON DELETE CASCADE );

/* Table ward_dept */
CREATE TABLE ward_dept (
    ward_id                 CHAR(5) CONSTRAINT pk_ward_dept PRIMARY KEY,
    ward_dept_name          VARCHAR(50) CONSTRAINT nn_ward_dept_name NOT
                            NULL,
    office_location         VARCHAR(25) CONSTRAINT nn_ward_dept_location
                            NOT NULL,
    telephone_number        CHAR(10) );

/* Table staff */
CREATE TABLE staff (
    staff_id                CHAR(5) CONSTRAINT pk_staff PRIMARY KEY,
    staff_ssn               CHAR(9) CONSTRAINT nn_staff_ssn NOT NULL,
    staff_last_name         VARCHAR(50) CONSTRAINT nn_staff_last_name NOT
                            NULL,
    staff_first_name        VARCHAR(50) CONSTRAINT nn_staff_first_name NOT
                            NULL,
    staff_middle_name       VARCHAR(50),
    ward_dept_assigned      CHAR(5) CONSTRAINT fk_staff_ward_dept
        REFERENCES ward_dept(ward_id),
    office_location         VARCHAR(50),
```

```
    date_hired              DATETIME DEFAULT NULL,
    hospital_title          VARCHAR(50) CONSTRAINT nn_staff_title NOT
                            NULL,
    work_phone              CHAR(10),
    phone_extension         VARCHAR(4),
    license_number          VARCHAR(20),
    salary                  MONEY,
    wage_rate               SMALLMONEY );

/* Table medical_specialty */
CREATE TABLE medical_specialty (
    specialty_code          CHAR(3) CONSTRAINT pk_medical_specialty
                            PRIMARY KEY,
    spec_title              VARCHAR(50) CONSTRAINT nn_medical_spec_title
                            NOT NULL,
    how_awarded             VARCHAR(100) );

/* Table staff_medspec */
CREATE TABLE staff_medspec (
    staff_id                CHAR(5),
    specialty_code          CHAR(3),
    date_awarded            DATETIME DEFAULT GETDATE(),
    CONSTRAINT pk_staff_medspec PRIMARY KEY (staff_id, specialty_code),
    CONSTRAINT fk_staff_medspec FOREIGN KEY (staff_id) REFERENCES staff,
    CONSTRAINT fk_medspec_med_spec FOREIGN KEY (specialty_code)
        REFERENCES medical_specialty );

/* Table service_cat */
CREATE TABLE service_cat (
    service_cat_id          CHAR(3) CONSTRAINT pk_service_cat PRIMARY KEY,
    service_cat_desc        VARCHAR(50)
        CONSTRAINT nn_service_cat_desc NOT NULL );

/* Table service */
CREATE TABLE service (
    service_id              CHAR(5) CONSTRAINT pk_service PRIMARY KEY,
    service_description     VARCHAR(50) CONSTRAINT nn_service_description
                            NOT NULL,
    service_charge          MONEY CONSTRAINT ck_service_charge
        CHECK (service_charge >= 0),
    service_comments        VARCHAR(2000),
    service_cat_id          CHAR(3) CONSTRAINT fk_service_service_cat
        REFERENCES service_cat(service_cat_id) );

/* Table treatment */
CREATE TABLE treatment (
    treatment_number        INT,
    treatment_date          DATETIME,
    pat_id                  CHAR(6) CONSTRAINT nn_treatment_pat_id NOT
                            NULL,
    staff_id                CHAR(5) CONSTRAINT nn_treatment_staff_id NOT
                            NULL,
    service_id              CHAR(5) CONSTRAINT nn_treatment_service_id NOT
                            NULL,
    actual_charge           MONEY CONSTRAINT ck_treatment_actual_charge
        CHECK (actual_charge >= 0),
    treatment_comments      VARCHAR(2000),
```

```
        CONSTRAINT pk_treatment   PRIMARY KEY (treatment_number,
                                  treatment_date),
        CONSTRAINT fk_treatment_patient FOREIGN KEY (pat_id)
            REFERENCES patient,
        CONSTRAINT fk_treatment_staff FOREIGN KEY (staff_id)
            REFERENCES staff,
        CONSTRAINT fk_treatment_service FOREIGN KEY (service_id)
            REFERENCES service );

/* Table Medicine */
CREATE TABLE medicine (
        medicine_code           CHAR(7) CONSTRAINT pk_medicine PRIMARY KEY,
        med_name_sci            VARCHAR(50) CONSTRAINT nn_medicine_name_sci
                                NOT NULL,
        med_name_common         VARCHAR(50) CONSTRAINT nn_medicine_name_common
                                NOT NULL,
        normal_dosage           VARCHAR(300) CONSTRAINT nn_medicine_dosage NOT
                                NULL,
        medicine_comments       VARCHAR(500),
        quantity_stock          INT CONSTRAINT ck_medicine_qty_stock
            CHECK (quantity_stock >= 0),
        unit_measure            VARCHAR(20) );

/* Table prescription */
CREATE TABLE prescription (
        pre_number              INT CONSTRAINT pk_prescription PRIMARY KEY,
        pre_date                DATETIME,
        medicine_code           CHAR(7) CONSTRAINT
        nn_prescription_medicine_code NOT NULL,
        pat_id                  CHAR(6) CONSTRAINT nn_prescription_pat_id NOT
                                NULL,
        staff_id                CHAR(5) CONSTRAINT nn_prescription_staff_id
                                NOT NULL,
        dosage_prescribed   VARCHAR(50)
            CONSTRAINT nn_prescription_dosage_presc NOT NULL,
        dosage_directions   VARCHAR(500),
        CONSTRAINT fk_prescription_medicine FOREIGN KEY (medicine_code)
            REFERENCES medicine,
        CONSTRAINT fk_prescription_patient FOREIGN KEY (pat_id)
            REFERENCES patient,
        CONSTRAINT fk_prescription_staff FOREIGN KEY (staff_id)
            REFERENCES staff );

/* End of table and index definitions */
```

APPENDIX

SOLUTIONS TO ODD-NUMBERED EXERCISES

This appendix provides solutions to the odd-numbered end-of-chapter SQL coding exercises and questions for the Company and Riverbend database cases.

CHAPTER 1

SQL CODING EXERCISES AND QUESTIONS: COMPANY DATABASE

1. It is the primary statement in SQL used to query, or extract information from a database.

3. You simply list the columns from the table or tables to be displayed. The columns are listed in the order in which they are displayed.

5. A comma is used between column names as well as table names.

7. Using uppercase or lowercase commands has NO effect; however, by convention, we type commands and clauses such as SELECT, FROM, and WHERE in UPPER-case and column names, table names, and conditions in LOWER-case.

9. The ORDER BY clause.

SQL CODING EXERCISES AND QUESTIONS: RIVERBEND DATABASE

1. The relationship between the *patient* and *patient_note* tables is one-to-many, meaning each patient can have many different *patient_note* rows in the *patient_note* table.

3.
```
SELECT *
FROM patient
WHERE pat_id = '100306';
```

```
pat_id pat_ssn    pat_last_name
pat_first_name                              pat_middle_name
pat_street_address                          pat_city
pat_state pat_zip    pat_date_of_birth
```

```
pat_telephone_number bed_number
------ -------- ------------------ ----------------------------------
----------------------------------------------- --------------------
------------------ ----------------------------------------------
------- ----------------------------------------------------- -------- --
------- ----------------------------------------------------- --------
------------ --------------
100306 222333306 Santiago
Samuel                                                   Sampson
Southwest Drive #22                                      Edwardsville
IL        62025       1984-06-07 00:00:00.000
1005551039            36
```

5. SELECT *
   FROM bed_type;

   ```
   bed_type_id bed_description
   ----------- -------------------------------------------------
   E2          Emergency Room-Fixed
   E3          Emergency Room-Portable
   ER          Emergency Room-Rollaround
   P1          Pediatric-Age to 5
   P2          Pediatric-Age to 15
   R1          Regular Ward-Fixed
   R2          Regular Ward-Adjustable
   RA          Radiology Dept
   RE          Regular Ward-Elevated Leg
   SU          Surgery Room-Rollaround
   ```

7. SELECT ward_id, ward_dept_name
   FROM ward_dept;

   ```
   ward_id ward_dept_name
   ------- -----------------------------------------------
   ADMI2   Admissions and Records Department
   ADMIN   Administrative Processing Department
   CARD1   Cardiology Department
   CRITC   Critical Care Ward
   EMER1   Emergency Room Ward
   GYNO1   Gynecological Department
   MEDL1   Medical Laboratory Department 1
   MEDL2   Medical Laboratory Department 2
   MEDS1   Medical Surgical Ward 1
   MEDS2   Medical Surgical Ward 2
   NEWB1   New Born Nursery Ward
   ONCOL   Oncology Ward
   OUTP1   Outpatient Clinic Department
   PEDS1   Pediatrics Ward
   PHARM   Pharmacy Department
   RADI1   Radiology Dept
   SURG1   Surgical Ward
   SURRE   Surgical Recovery Ward
   ```

9. SELECT staff_id, specialty_code
   FROM staff_medspec
   WHERE specialty_code = 'RN1';

```
staff_id specialty_code
-------- --------------
66444    RN1
67555    RN1
```

11. The relationship is named *treatment*. Information is stored in four tables: *patient*, *staff*, *service*, and *treatment*.

12. The table is named *prescription*. The other tables with relationships are named *patient*, *staff*, and *medicine*.

CHAPTER 2

SQL CODING EXERCISES AND QUESTIONS: COMPANY DATABASE

1.
```
CREATE TABLE test_table (
     test_id             SMALLINT,
     test_description    VARCHAR(25) );
```

3.
```
SELECT * FROM test_table;
```

```
test_id test_description
------- ------------------------
1       Test row #1
2       Test row #2
```

5.
```
CREATE TABLE department (
     dpt_no                   SMALLINT
         CONSTRAINT pk_department PRIMARY KEY,
     dpt_name                 VARCHAR(20)
         CONSTRAINT nn_dpt_name NOT NULL,
     dpt_mgrssn               CHAR(9) NULL,
     dpt_mgr_start_date       DATETIME NULL  );
```

7.
```
BEGIN TRANSACTION;
INSERT INTO department VALUES (7, 'Production', NULL, NULL);
INSERT INTO department VALUES (3, 'Admin and Records', NULL, NULL);
INSERT INTO department VALUES (1, 'Headquarters', NULL, NULL);
COMMIT TRANSACTION;
```

9.
```
CREATE TABLE employee (
     emp_ssn                  CHAR(9)
         CONSTRAINT pk_employee PRIMARY KEY,
     emp_last_name            VARCHAR(25)
         CONSTRAINT nn_emp_last_name NOT NULL,
     emp_first_name           VARCHAR(25)
         CONSTRAINT nn_emp_first_name NOT NULL,
     emp_middle_name          VARCHAR(25) NULL,
     emp_address              VARCHAR(50) NULL,
     emp_city                 VARCHAR(25) NULL,
     emp_state                CHAR(2) NULL,
     emp_zip                  CHAR(9) NULL,
     emp_date_of_birth        DATETIME NULL,
     emp_salary               MONEY
         CONSTRAINT ck_emp_salary
             CHECK (emp_salary <= 85000)
```

```
                  CONSTRAINT nn_emp_salary NOT NULL,
         emp_parking_space        INT
              CONSTRAINT un_emp_parking_space UNIQUE,
         emp_gender               CHAR(1) NULL,
         emp_dpt_number           SMALLINT,
         emp_superssn             CHAR(9),
      CONSTRAINT fk_emp_dpt FOREIGN KEY (emp_dpt_number)
         REFERENCES department,
      CONSTRAINT fk_emp_superssn FOREIGN KEY (emp_superssn)
         REFERENCES employee );
```

11. The output should display nine rows of data including the row for the student.

13.
```
UPDATE employee
SET emp_address = '#6 Main St'
WHERE emp_last_name = 'Zhu';
```

15. `ALTER TABLE employee ADD salary_year_to_date MONEY;`

17.
```
CREATE INDEX employee_zip_last_name
ON employee (emp_zip, emp_last_name);
```

SQL Coding Exercises and Questions: Riverbend Database

1.
```
CREATE TABLE patient_archive (
     pat_id               CHAR(6)
        CONSTRAINT pk_patient_archive PRIMARY KEY,
     pat_ssn              CHAR(9)
        CONSTRAINT nn_pat_ssn_archive NOT NULL,
     pat_last_name        VARCHAR(50)
        CONSTRAINT nn_pat_last_name_archive NOT NULL,
     pat_first_name       VARCHAR(50)
        CONSTRAINT nn_pat_first_name_archive NOT NULL,
     pat_middle_name      VARCHAR(50),
     pat_street_address   VARCHAR(50),
     pat_city             VARCHAR(50),
     pat_state            CHAR(2),
     pat_zip              CHAR(9),
     pat_date_of_birth    DATETIME,
     pat_telephone_number CHAR(10)   );
```

3. `SELECT * FROM patient_archive;`

The information displayed will vary from student to student.

5.
```
CREATE TABLE ward_dept (
     ward_id        CHAR(5) CONSTRAINT pk_ward_dept PRIMARY KEY,
     ward_dept_name VARCHAR(50) CONSTRAINT nn_ward_dept_name NOT
        NULL,
     office_location VARCHAR(25)
        CONSTRAINT nn_ward_dept_location NOT NULL,
     telephone_number CHAR(10) );
```

7.
```
BEGIN TRANSACTION;
INSERT INTO ward_dept VALUES ('MEDS1', 'Medical Surgical Ward 1',
'SW1020', '1005559201');
```

```
INSERT INTO ward_dept VALUES ('MEDS2', 'Medical Surgical Ward 2',
'NW1018', '1005559202');
INSERT INTO ward_dept VALUES ('RADI1', 'Radiology Department',
'RA0070', '1005559203');
END TRANSACTION;
```

9.
```
CREATE TABLE staff2 (
      staff_id                CHAR(5) CONSTRAINT pk_staff2 PRIMARY KEY,
      staff_ssn               CHAR(9) CONSTRAINT nn_staff2_ssn NOT NULL,
      staff_last_name         VARCHAR(50)
         CONSTRAINT nn_staff2_last_name NOT NULL,
      staff_first_name        VARCHAR(50)
         CONSTRAINT nn_staff2_first_name NOT NULL,
      staff_middle_name       VARCHAR(50),
      ward_dept_assigned      CHAR(5) CONSTRAINT fk_staff2_ward_dept
         REFERENCES ward_dept(ward_id),
      office_location         VARCHAR(50),
      date_hired              DATETIME DEFAULT NULL,
      hospital_title          VARCHAR(50)
         CONSTRAINT nn_staff2_title NOT NULL,
      work_phone              CHAR(10),
      phone_extension         VARCHAR(4),
      license_number          VARCHAR(20),
      salary                  MONEY,
      wage_rate               SMALLMONEY );
```

11.
```
SELECT staff_id, staff_ssn, staff_last_name
FROM staff2;
```

   The output should be four rows of information.

13.
```
UPDATE staff2
SET office_location = 'SW4000'
WHERE staff_last_name = 'Webber';

SELECT staff_last_name, office_location
FROM staff2
WHERE staff_last_name = 'Webber';
```

```
staff_last_name                  office_location
------------------------------   ----------------
Webber                           SW4000
```

15.
```
ALTER TABLE medicine ADD med_unit_cost MONEY;
```

CHAPTER 3

1.
```
SELECT *
FROM assignment;
```

```
work_emp_ssn work_pro_number work_hours work_hours_planned
------------ --------------- ---------- ------------------
999111111    1               31.4       35.0
999111111    2               8.5        10.2
999222222    10              34.5       42.3

(17 row(s) affected)
```

3. SELECT work_emp_ssn, work_hours
   FROM assignment;

   ```
   work_emp_ssn work_hours
   ------------ ----------
   999111111    31.4
   999111111    8.5
   999222222    34.5
   ```

   (17 row(s) affected)

5. SELECT emp_last_name, emp_first_name, emp_date_of_birth,
          emp_gender "Gender"
   FROM employee
   ORDER BY emp_last_name;

   ```
   emp_last_name  emp_first_name  emp_date_of_birth         Gender
   -------------  --------------  -----------------------   ------
   Amin           Hyder           1969-03-29 00:00:00.000   M
   Bock           Douglas         1950-12-05 00:00:00.000   M
   Bordoloi       Bijoy           1954-03-14 00:00:00.000   M
   ```

   (8 row(s) affected)

7. SELECT CAST(emp_gender As CHAR(1)) "Gender",
          CAST(emp_last_name AS CHAR(12)) "Last Name",
          CAST(emp_first_name AS CHAR(12)) "First Name",
          CAST(emp_date_of_birth AS CHAR(12)) "Birth Date"
   FROM employee
   ORDER BY emp_gender, emp_last_name;

   ```
   Gender Last Name    First Name    Birth Date
   ------ ------------ ------------  ------------
   F      Joyner       Suzanne       Jun 20 1971
   F      Markis       Marcia        Jul 19 1978
   F      Prescott     Sherri        Jul 31 1972
   M      Amin         Hyder         Mar 29 1969
   M      Bock         Douglas       Dec  5 1950
   M      Bordoloi     Bijoy         Mar 14 1954
   M      Joshi        Dinesh        Sep 15 1972
   M      Zhu          Waiman        Dec  8 1975
   ```

   (8 row(s) affected)

9. SELECT dep_emp_ssn, CAST(dep_name AS CHAR(12)) "Dep Name",
          CAST(dep_date_of_birth AS CHAR(12)) "Birth Date",
          dep_relationship
   FROM dependent
   WHERE dep_relationship <> 'SPOUSE'
   ORDER BY dep_emp_ssn DESC;

   ```
   dep_emp_ssn Dep Name     Birth Date   dep_relationship
   ----------- ------------ ------------ ----------------
   999666666   Rita         May 11 1994  DAUGHTER
   999666666   Monica       Dec 30 1988  DAUGHTER
   999666666   Anita        Jul  6 1984  DAUGHTER
   999444444   Jo Ellen     Apr  5 1996  DAUGHTER
   ```

```
999444444    Andrew      Oct 25 1998   SON
999111111    Rachael     Oct  4 1975   DAUGHTER
999111111    Michelle    Mar 17 1984   DAUGHTER
999111111    Jeffery     Dec 31 1978   SON
999111111    Deanna      May  3 1981   DAUGHTER

(9 row(s) affected)
```

11. ```
    SELECT dpt_no, dpt_location
    FROM dept_locations
    ORDER BY dpt_no DESC;

    dpt_no dpt_location
    ------ --------------------
    7      St. Louis
    7      Edwardsville
    7      Collinsville
    3      Marina
    1      Edwardsville

    (5 row(s) affected)
    ```

13. ```
    SELECT TOP 10 PERCENT work_emp_ssn, work_hours
    FROM assignment
    ORDER BY work_hours DESC;

    work_emp_ssn work_hours
    ------------ ----------
    999333333    42.1
    999222222    34.5

    (2 row(s) affected)
    ```

SQL CODING EXERCISES AND QUESTIONS: RIVERBEND DATABASE

1. ```
   SELECT *
   FROM room;

   room_id room_description
   ------- -------------------------
   ER0001  Emergency Room Ward 1
   ER0002  Emergency Room Ward 2
   NW1001  General MedSurg, Single

   (61 row(s) affected)
   ```

3. ```
   SELECT CAST(service_id AS CHAR(10)) "Service ID",
       CAST(service_description AS CHAR(30)) "Description",
       service_charge
   FROM service;

   Service ID Description                    service_charge
   ---------- ------------------------------ --------------------
   10060      I and D Simple                 258.0000
   10061      I and D Comp. Multiple         320.0000
   10120      Cerumen-oval F.B.              230.0000

   (105 row(s) affected)
   ```

5. ```
   SELECT CAST(staff_last_name AS CHAR(15)) "Last Name",
       CAST(staff_first_name AS CHAR(15)) "First Name",
       CAST(date_hired AS CHAR(12)) "Date Hired", license_number
   FROM staff
   ORDER BY staff_last_name;
   ```

   ```
   Last Name       First Name       Date Hired    license_number
   --------------- ---------------  ------------  --------------------
   Adams           Adam             Jan 29 1985   NULL
   Barlow          William          May 16 2001   MO9873346
   Becker          Robert           Dec 14 1982   IL2398457

   (24 row(s) affected)
   ```

7. ```
   SELECT CAST(staff_first_name AS CHAR(15)) "First Name",
       CAST(staff_middle_name AS CHAR(1)) "Middle",
       CAST(staff_last_name AS CHAR(15)) "Last Name",
       CAST(date_hired AS CHAR(12)) "Date Hired", license_number
   FROM staff
   ORDER BY staff_first_name, staff_last_name;
   ```

   ```
   First Name      Middle Last Name       Date Hired    license_number
   --------------- ------ ---------------  ------------  --------------
   Adam            A      Adams            Jan 29 1985   NULL
   Alyssa          M      Smith            Jun 10 1999   IL98993455
   Betty           NULL   Boudreaux        Nov  5 2000   NULL

   (24 row(s) affected)
   ```

9. ```
   SELECT medicine_code, dosage_prescribed
   FROM prescription
   ORDER by medicine_code;
   ```

   ```
   medicine_code dosage_prescribed
   ------------- -------------------------------------------------------
   9999001       200 Mg. 4 times/day.
   9999001       50 Mg. IV every 4 hours.
   9999001       50 Mg. IV every 4 hours.

   (25 row(s) affected)
   ```

11. ```
    SELECT staff_id, specialty_code,
        CAST(date_awarded AS CHAR(12)) "Date Awarded"
    FROM staff_medspec
    WHERE specialty_code = 'RN1'
    ORDER BY staff_id;
    ```

    ```
    staff_id specialty_code Date Awarded
    -------- -------------- ------------
    66444    RN1            Mar  8 1988
    67555    RN1            Feb  4 1992

    (2 row(s) affected)
    ```

13. ```
    SELECT TOP 4 WITH TIES medicine_code,
        CAST(med_name_common AS CHAR(20)),
    ```
    ```

```
        quantity_stock
FROM medicine
ORDER BY quantity_stock DESC;


medicine_code                              quantity_stock
------------  --------------------         --------------
9999015       Nystatin                     45000000
9999016       Tagamet                      72050
9999003       Valium                       36000
9999005       PenVK                        34365


(4 row(s) affected)
```

15.
```
SELECT TOP 10 PERCENT WITH TIES medicine_code,
       CAST(med_name_common AS CHAR(20)) "Common Name",
       quantity_stock
INTO low_stock_medicine
FROM medicine
ORDER BY quantity_stock;


(3 row(s) affected)!
```

CHAPTER 4

SQL Coding Exercises and Questions: Company Database

1.
```
SELECT CAST(emp_first_name AS CHAR(12)) "First Name",
       CAST(emp_last_name AS CHAR(12)) "Last Name",
     emp_gender "Gender", emp_dpt_number "Dept"
FROM employee
WHERE emp_gender = 'M' AND emp_dpt_number = 7;


First Name    Last Name     Gender Dept
------------  ------------  ------ ------
Douglas       Bock          M      7
Dinesh        Joshi         M      7
Waiman        Zhu           M      7


(3 row(s) affected)
```

3.
```
SELECT CAST(emp_first_name AS CHAR(12)) "First Name",
       CAST(emp_last_name AS CHAR(12)) "Last Name",
       CONVERT(CHAR(10), emp_salary, 1) "Salary"
FROM employee
WHERE emp_salary IN (43000, 55000);


First Name    Last Name     Salary
------------  ------------  ----------
Waiman        Zhu           43,000.00
Suzanne       Joyner        43,000.00
Bijoy         Bordoloi      55,000.00


(3 row(s) affected)
```

5. SELECT CAST(emp_first_name AS CHAR(12)) "First Name",
          CAST(emp_last_name AS CHAR(12)) "Last Name",
          CONVERT (CHAR (10), emp_salary, 1) "Salary"
   FROM employee
   WHERE emp_salary BETWEEN 35000 AND 45000
   ORDER BY emp_salary;

```
First Name    Last Name     Salary
------------  ------------  ---------
Dinesh        Joshi          38,000.00
Waiman        Zhu            43,000.00
Suzanne       Joyner         43,000.00
```

(3 row(s) affected)

7. SELECT CAST(emp_first_name AS CHAR(12)) "First Name",
          CAST(emp_last_name AS CHAR(12)) "Last Name"
   FROM employee
   WHERE emp_first_name LIKE 'D%';

```
First Name    Last Name
------------  ------------
Douglas       Bock
Dinesh        Joshi
```

(2 row(s) affected)

9. SELECT CAST(emp_first_name AS CHAR(12)) "First Name",
          CAST(emp_last_name AS CHAR(12)) "Last Name",
          '$' + CONVERT(CHAR(10), emp_salary, 1) "Annual",
          '$' + CONVERT(CHAR(10), emp_salary/12, 1) "Monthly",
        '$' + CONVERT(CHAR(10), emp_salary/52, 1) "Weekly"
   FROM employee
   ORDER BY emp_last_name;

```
First Name    Last Name     Annual       Monthly      Weekly
------------  ------------  -----------  -----------  ------------
Hyder         Amin          $ 25,000.00 $  2,083.33 $     480.77
Douglas       Bock          $ 30,000.00 $  2,500.00 $     576.92
Bijoy         Bordoloi      $ 55,000.00 $  4,583.33 $   1,057.69
Dinesh        Joshi         $ 38,000.00 $  3,166.67 $     730.77
Suzanne       Joyner        $ 43,000.00 $  3,583.33 $     826.92
Marcia        Markis        $ 25,000.00 $  2,083.33 $     480.77
Sherri        Prescott      $ 25,000.00 $  2,083.33 $     480.77
Waiman        Zhu           $ 43,000.00 $  3,583.33 $     826.92
```

(8 row(s) affected)

11. SELECT emp_last_name "Last Name", emp_superssn "SSN",
         emp_gender "Gender", CAST(emp_state AS CHAR(5)) "State"
    FROM employee
    WHERE emp_gender = 'F' AND emp_state = 'CA';

```
Last Name                   SSN        Gender State
--------------------------  ---------  ------ -----
Joyner                      999666666  F      CA
Markis                      999555555  F      CA
```

(2 row(s) affected)

13.
```
SELECT work_emp_ssn, work_pro_number, work_hours
FROM assignment
WHERE work_pro_number IN (1, 15, 20, 22, 25, 28, 30);

work_emp_ssn work_pro_number work_hours
------------ --------------- ----------
999111111    1               31.4
999222222    30              5.1
999444444    1               NULL
999444444    20              11.8
999555555    20              14.8
999555555    30              19.2
999666666    20              NULL
999887777    30              30.8
999888888    1               21.0

(9 row(s) affected)
```

15.
```
CREATE TABLE contract_employee (
       emp_id     CHAR(2),
       emp_job    VARCHAR(12),
       emp_salary DECIMAL(8,2),
       emp_bonus  DECIMAL(6,2));

INSERT INTO contract_employee
    VALUES ('10', 'BIG BOSS', 100000, NULL);
INSERT INTO contract_employee
    VALUES ('20', 'LITTLE BOSS', 50000, NULL);
INSERT INTO contract_employee
    VALUES ('30', 'WORKER', 10000, 2000);
INSERT INTO contract_employee
    VALUES ('40', 'WORKER', 11000, 3000);

SELECT emp_id, emp_job, emp_salary + emp_bonus "Total Comp"
FROM contract_employee;

emp_id    emp_job          Total Comp
--------- ---------------- --------------------
10        BIG BOSS         NULL
20        LITTLE BOSS      NULL
30        WORKER           12000.0000
40        WORKER           14000.0000

(4 row(s) affected)
```

SQL CODING EXERCISES AND QUESTIONS: RIVERBEND DATABASE

1.
```
SELECT CAST(pat_last_name AS CHAR(15)) "Last Name",
    CAST(pat_first_name AS CHAR(15)) "First Name",
    CAST(pat_city AS CHAR(15)) "City",
    pat_state "State", pat_zip "Zip Code"
FROM patient
WHERE pat_zip = '62025';

Last Name        First Name       City             State Zip Code
---------------  ---------------  ---------------  ----- --------
Earnhardt        Earnest          Edwardsville     IL    62025
Franken          Frank            Edwardsville     IL    62025
```

```
Monday          Mandy           Edwardsville   IL    62025
. . .

(25 row(s) affected)
```

3. ```
SELECT CAST(staff_last_name AS CHAR(15)) "Last Name",
       CAST(staff_first_name AS CHAR(15)) "First Name",
       CAST(hospital_title AS CHAR(5)) "Title",
       CAST(ward_dept_assigned AS CHAR(10)) "Ward-Dept"
FROM staff
WHERE (ward_dept_assigned = 'ONCOL' OR ward_dept_assigned = 'MEDS1')
      AND hospital_title = 'M.D.';
```

```
Last Name       First Name      Title Ward-Dept
--------------- --------------- ----- ----------
Bock            Douglas         M.D.  MEDS1
Eakin           Maxwell         M.D.  MEDS1
Klepper         Robert          M.D.  ONCOL

(3 row(s) affected)
```

5. ```
SELECT CAST(staff_last_name AS CHAR(15)) "Last Name",
       CAST(staff_first_name AS CHAR(15)) "First Name",
       CAST(hospital_title AS CHAR(5)) "Title",
       CAST(ward_dept_assigned AS CHAR(10)) "Ward-Dept"
FROM staff
WHERE ward_dept_assigned NOT IN ('ONCOL', 'MEDS1', 'CARD1', 'RADI1')
      AND hospital_title = 'M.D.'
ORDER BY ward_dept_assigned;
```

```
Last Name       First Name      Title Ward-Dept
--------------- --------------- ----- ----------
Sumner          Elizabeth       M.D.  EMER1
Schultheis      Robert          M.D.  OUTP1
Becker          Robert          M.D.  SURG1
Becker          Roberta         M.D.  SURG1
Jones           Quincey         M.D.  SURG1
Barlow          William         M.D.  SURG1
Smith           Susan           M.D.  SURG1

(7 row(s) affected)
```

7. ```
SELECT CAST(medicine_code AS CHAR(8)) "Med Code",
       CAST(med_name_common AS CHAR(25)) "Medicine Name",
       CONVERT(CHAR(8), quantity_stock, 1) "Quantity"
FROM medicine
WHERE quantity_stock NOT BETWEEN 500 AND 25000;
```

```
Med Code Medicine Name   Quantity
-------- ------------------------- --------
9999003 Valium   36000
9999005 PenVK   34365
9999015 Nystatin   45000000
9999016 Tagamet   72050
9999018 Bactroban Ung. Ointment   367

(5 row(s) affected)
```
```

9.
```
SELECT CAST(staff_last_name AS CHAR(15)) "Last Name",
     CAST(staff_first_name AS CHAR(15)) "First Name",
     CAST(hospital_title AS CHAR(15)) "Title"
FROM staff
WHERE staff_last_name LIKE '%o%' AND hospital_title = 'M.D.'
ORDER BY staff_last_name, staff_first_name;
```

```
Last Name          First Name         Title
---------------    ---------------    ---------------
Barlow             William            M.D.
Bock               Douglas            M.D.
Bordoloi           Bijoy              M.D.
Jones              Quincey            M.D.
Quattromani        Toni               M.D.

(5 row(s) affected)
```

11.
```
SELECT CAST(pat_last_name AS CHAR(15)) "Last Name",
bed_number "Bed"
FROM patient
WHERE bed_number IS NULL;
```

```
Last Name          Bed
---------------    ------
North              NULL
Overstreet         NULL
Howard             NULL
Mullins            NULL

(4 row(s) affected)
```

CHAPTER 5

SQL CODING EXERCISES AND QUESTIONS: COMPANY DATABASE

1.
```
SELECT COUNT(*) "Number of Dependents"
FROM dependent;
```

```
Number of Dependents
--------------------
13

(1 row(s) affected)
```

3.
```
SELECT MIN(dpt_mgr_start_date) "Longest Working Manager"
FROM department;
```

```
Longest Working Manager
-----------------------------------------------------
1981-06-19 00:00:00.000
```

5.
```
SELECT COUNT(dep_gender) "Number Male Dependents"
FROM dependent
WHERE dep_gender = 'M';
```

```
Number Male Dependents
----------------------
3
      ●

(1 row(s) affected)
```

7. ```
   SELECT dep_relationship "Dependent Type",
         COUNT(dep_relationship) "Dependent Count"
   FROM dependent
   GROUP BY dep_relationship;

   Dependent Type Dependent Count
   -------------- ---------------
   DAUGHTER            7
   SON                 2
   SPOUSE              4

   (3 row(s) affected)
   ```

9. ```
   SELECT dep_relationship "Dependent Type",
         COUNT(dep_relationship) "Dependent Count"
   FROM dependent
   GROUP BY dep_relationship
   ORDER BY COUNT(dep_relationship) DESC;

   Dependent Type Dependent Count
   -------------- ---------------
   DAUGHTER            7
   SPOUSE              4
   SON                 2

   (3 row(s) affected)
   ```

11. ```
    SELECT pro_dept_number "Department",
          COUNT(pro_number) "Project Count"
    FROM project
    GROUP BY pro_dept_number;

    Department Project Count
    ---------- -------------
    1              1
    3              2
    7              3

    (3 row(s) affected)
    ```

13. ```
    SELECT pro_dept_number "Department",
          COUNT(pro_number) "Project Count"
    FROM project
    GROUP BY pro_dept_number
    HAVING COUNT(pro_number) >= 2;

    Department Project Count
    ---------- -------------
    3              2
    7              3

    (2 row(s) affected)
    ```

15. ```
SELECT work_pro_number "Project Number",
     SUM(work_hours) "Total Hours"
FROM assignment
GROUP BY work_pro_number
HAVING AVG(work_hours) >= 15
ORDER BY SUM(work_hours);
```

```
Project Number Total Hours
-------------- ----------------------------------------
1              52.4
3              52.6
10             54.8
30             55.1

(4 row(s) affected)
```

Warning: Null value is eliminated by an aggregate or other SET operation.

SQL CODING EXERCISES AND QUESTIONS: RIVERBEND DATABASE

1. ```
SELECT COUNT(*) "Number of Staff Members"
FROM staff;
```

```
Number of Staff Members
-----------------------
24

(1 row(s) affected)
```

3. ```
SELECT MAX(date_hired) "Newest Staff Member"
FROM staff;
```

```
Newest Staff Member
-------------------------------------------------------
2001-10-15 00:00:00.000

(1 row(s) affected)
```

5. ```
SELECT '$' + CONVERT(CHAR(10), AVG(wage_rate), 1) "Average Wage",
     '$' + CONVERT(CHAR(10), SUM(wage_rate), 1) "Total Wage"
FROM staff;
```

```
Average Wage Total Wage
------------ ----------
$     7.82 $     15.63

(1 row(s) affected)
```

Warning: Null value is eliminated by an aggregate or other SET operation.

7. ```
SELECT bed_type_id "Bed Type", COUNT(bed_type_id) "Number Counted"
FROM bed
GROUP BY bed_type_id;
```

```
Bed Type Number Counted
-------- --------------
E2   4
E3   2
```
```

```
ER      4
P1      6
P2      7
R1      24
R2      28
RA      8
RE      11
SU      4

(10 row(s) affected)
```

9.
```
SELECT service_cat_id "Service Category",
       COUNT(service_cat_id) "Number of Services"
FROM service
WHERE service_cat_id NOT IN ('LAB','INJ')
GROUP BY service_cat_id;

Service Category Number of Services
---------------- ------------------
CAR              1
OLA              18
PRO              9
RAD              19
SUR              20

(5 row(s) affected)
```

11.
```
SELECT staff_id "Staff Member ID",
       COUNT(service_id) "Treatment Count"
FROM treatment
GROUP BY staff_id;

Staff Member ID Treatment Count
--------------- ---------------
01885           14
10044           8
23100           8
. . .

(16 row(s) affected)
```

13.
```
SELECT staff_id "Staff Member ID",
       COUNT(service_id) "Treatment Count"
FROM treatment
WHERE staff_id NOT IN ('66432', '66444')
GROUP BY staff_id
HAVING COUNT(service_id) >= 10;

Staff Member ID Treatment Count
--------------- ---------------
01885           14
23232           13
66427           12
66532           16
67555           12

(5 row(s) affected)
```

15.
```
SELECT service_id "Service",
     '$' + CONVERT(CHAR(10), AVG(actual_charge), 1) "Average Charge"
FROM treatment
GROUP BY service_id
HAVING AVG(actual_charge) >= 1000
ORDER BY AVG(actual_charge);
```

```
Service Average Charge
------- --------------
12010   $  1,480.00
12001   $  3,325.00
12002   $  6,500.00
12005   $  6,500.00
12009   $  7,800.00
12007   $  8,500.00

(6 row(s) affected)
```

CHAPTER 6

SQL CODING EXERCISES AND QUESTIONS: COMPANY DATABASE

1.
```
SELECT d.dpt_no, dpt_name, dpt_location
FROM department d, dept_locations;
```

```
dpt_no dpt_name             dpt_location
------ -------------------- --------------------
1      Headquarters         Edwardsville
1      Headquarters         Marina
1      Headquarters         Collinsville
1      Headquarters         Edwardsville
1      Headquarters         St. Louis
3      Admin and Records    Edwardsville
3      Admin and Records    Marina
3      Admin and Records    Collinsville
3      Admin and Records    Edwardsville
3      Admin and Records    St. Louis
7      Production           Edwardsville
7      Production           Marina
7      Production           Collinsville
7      Production           Edwardsville
7      Production           St. Louis

(15 row(s) affected)
```

3.
```
SELECT CAST(dpt_no As CHAR(6)) "Dept#",
     CAST(dpt_name As CHAR(17)) "Department",
     CAST(emp_last_name + ', '+ emp_first_name As CHAR(16))
     "Employee",
     '$' + CONVERT (CHAR (10), emp_salary, 1),
     CAST(emp_parking_space As CHAR(7)) "Parking"
FROM department JOIN employee ON (dpt_mgrssn = emp_ssn);
```

```
Dept#  Department        Employee           Parking
------ ----------------- ----------------- ----------- -------
1      Headquarters      Bordoloi, Bijoy   $ 55,000.00 1
3      Admin and Records Joyner, Suzanne   $ 43,000.00 3
7      Production        Zhu, Waiman       $ 43,000.00 32
```

(3 row(s) affected)

5. SELECT dpt_name "Department", pro_number "Proj#",
       CAST(pro_name AS CHAR(16)) "Project",
       CAST(pro_location AS CHAR(16)) "Location"
   FROM department JOIN project ON (dpt_no = pro_dept_number)
   WHERE dpt_name = 'Production' OR pro_location = 'Edwardsville';

```
Department          Proj#  Project          Location
------------------- ------ ---------------- ----------------
Production          1      Order Entry      St. Louis
Production          2      Payroll          Collinsville
Production          3      Receivables      Edwardsville
Headquarters        20     Personnel        Edwardsville
```

(4 row(s) affected)

7. SELECT CAST(e.emp_last_name + ', '+ e.emp_first_name As CHAR(16))
       "Employee",
       a.work_pro_number "Proj#", a.work_hours "Hours"
   FROM employee e LEFT OUTER JOIN assignment a ON (e.emp_ssn =
       a.work_emp_ssn)
   WHERE a.work_hours IS NULL
   ORDER BY emp_last_name, emp_first_name;

```
Employee         Proj#  Hours
---------------- ------ -------
Bordoloi, Bijoy  20     NULL
Zhu, Waiman      1      NULL
```

(2 row(s) affected)

9. SELECT CAST(e.emp_last_name As CHAR(12)) "Employee",
       CAST(d.dep_name As CHAR(12)) "Dependent",
       CAST(d.dep_date_of_birth As CHAR(12)) "Birth Date"
   FROM employee e JOIN dependent d ON (e.emp_ssn = d.dep_emp_ssn)
   ORDER BY e.emp_last_name;

```
Employee     Dependent     Birth Date
------------ ------------ ------------
Bock         Deanna       May  3 1981
Bock         Jeffery      Dec 31 1978
Bock         Mary Ellen   May 28 1956
Bock         Michelle     Mar 17 1984
Bock         Rachael      Oct  4 1975
Bordoloi     Anita        Jul  6 1984
Bordoloi     Mita         Jun  4 1956
Bordoloi     Monica       Dec 30 1988
Bordoloi     Rita         May 11 1994
Joyner       Allen        Feb 29 1968
Zhu          Andrew       Oct 25 1998
```

```
Zhu          Jo Ellen     Apr  5 1996
Zhu          Susan        May  3 1975
```

(13 row(s) affected)

11.
```
SELECT CAST(m.emp_last_name As CHAR(12))"Supervisor",
      CAST(d.dpt_name As CHAR(12))"Department",
      CAST(e.emp_last_name As CHAR(12)) "Employee Supervised"
FROM employee m, employee e, department d
WHERE m.emp_ssn = e.emp_superssn AND
    m.emp_ssn = d.dpt_mgrssn AND
    d.dpt_no = 7;
```

```
Supervisor    Department    Employee Supervised
------------  ------------  --------------------
Zhu           Production    Bock
Zhu           Production    Joshi
Zhu           Production    Prescott
```

(3 row(s) affected)

13.
```
SELECT CAST(emp_last_name As CHAR(10)) "Last Name",
      CAST(dep_name As CHAR(10)) "Dependent",
      CAST(dep_relationship As CHAR(8)) "Relationship"
FROM employee, dependent
WHERE emp_ssn = dep_emp_ssn AND
    emp_gender <> dep_gender
ORDER BY emp_last_name;
```

```
Last Name   Dependent   Relationship
----------  ----------  ------------
Bock        Deanna      DAUGHTER
Bock        Mary Ellen  SPOUSE
Bock        Michelle    DAUGHTER
Bock        Rachael     DAUGHTER
Bordoloi    Anita       DAUGHTER
Bordoloi    Mita        SPOUSE
Bordoloi    Monica      DAUGHTER
Bordoloi    Rita        DAUGHTER
Joyner      Allen       SPOUSE
Zhu         Jo Ellen    DAUGHTER
Zhu         Susan       SPOUSE
```

(11 row(s) affected)

SQL Coding Exercises and Questions: Riverbend Database

1.
```
SELECT p.pat_id,
      CAST(pat_last_name as CHAR(12)) "Patient Name",
      note_comment
FROM patient p JOIN patient_note pn
    ON (p.pat_id = pn.pat_id);
```

```
pat_id Patient Name note_comment
------ ------------ ---------------------------------------------
100001 Able         Patient admitted from surgery at 1715 hours
100001 Able         Abdominal dressing dry and intact following liver
```

surgery. Biliary drainage tube with moderate amount (50cc) of dark
greenish drainage noted this shift.
100002 Benton   Patient admitted from surgery at 0810 hours

(174 row(s) affected)

3. SELECT CAST(staff_last_name + ', ' + staff_first_name AS CHAR(25))
        "Staff Member",
        CAST(ward_dept_name AS CHAR(36)) "Ward or Dept"
   FROM ward_dept wd JOIN staff s ON (wd.ward_id =
        s.ward_dept_assigned)
   ORDER BY ward_dept_name, staff_last_name, staff_first_name;

```
Staff Member                Ward or Dept
------------------------    ------------------------------------
Adams, Adam                 Administrative Processing Department
Boudreaux, Beverly          Administrative Processing Department
Clinton, William            Administrative Processing Department
Thornton, Billy             Administrative Processing Department
Boudreaux, Betty            Admissions and Records Department
Quattromani, Toni           Cardiology Department
Sumner, Elizabeth           Emergency Room Ward
Brockwell, Mary Ellen       Gynecological Department
Bock, Douglas               Medical Surgical Ward 1
Eakin, Maxwell              Medical Surgical Ward 1
Simmons, Leslie             New Born Nursery Ward
Young, Yvonne               New Born Nursery Ward
Klepper, Robert             Oncology Ward
Zumwalt, Mary               Oncology Ward
Schultheis, Robert          Outpatient Clinic Department
Bordoloi, Bijoy             Radiology Dept
Smith, Alyssa               Radiology Dept
Webber, Eugene              Radiology Dept
Simmons, Lester             Surgical Recovery Ward
Barlow, William             Surgical Ward
Becker, Robert              Surgical Ward
Becker, Roberta             Surgical Ward
Jones, Quincey              Surgical Ward
Smith, Susan                Surgical Ward
```

(24 row(s) affected)

5. SELECT sc.service_cat_id "Category",
        CAST(service_cat_desc AS CHAR(28)) "Category Description",
        service_id "Service",
        CAST(service_description AS CHAR(25)) "Service Description"
   FROM service_cat sc JOIN service s
        ON (sc.service_cat_id = s.service_cat_id)
   WHERE sc.service_cat_id IN ('CAR','LAB')
   ORDER BY sc.service_cat_id, service_id;

```
Category Category Description          Service Service Description
-------- ----------------------------  ------- ---------------------
CAR      Cardiology                    93000   EKG/Interp
LAB      Laboratory-General            80048   Basic Metabolic
LAB      Laboratory-General            80050   General Panel
```

```
LAB        Laboratory-General        80053    Complete Metabolic
LAB        Laboratory-General        80055    Prenatal Panel
LAB        Laboratory-General        80061    Lipid Panel
LAB        Laboratory-General        80072    Arthritis Panel (RA, ANA,
LAB        Laboratory-General        80076    Hepatic Function
LAB        Laboratory-General        83036    Hgb A1C
LAB        Laboratory-General        84152    PSA
LAB        Laboratory-General        84443    TSH
LAB        Laboratory-General        84450    SGOT
LAB        Laboratory-General        85022    CBC
LAB        Laboratory-General        85610    Protime/INR
LAB        Laboratory-General        87060    Throat Culture
LAB        Laboratory-General        87088    Urine Culture
LAB        Laboratory-General        88142    Pap Smear
LAB        Laboratory-General        88304    Pathology-General

(18 row(s) affected)
```

7.
```
SELECT CAST(pat_last_name + ', ' + pat_first_name AS CHAR(25))
    "Patient",
    p.bed_number "Bed", CAST(bed_description AS CHAR(27)) "Bed Desc"
FROM patient p JOIN bed b ON (p.bed_number = b.bed_number)
    JOIN bed_type bt ON (b.bed_type_id = bt.bed_type_id)
ORDER BY p.bed_number;

Patient                    Bed    Bed Desc
------------------------   ----   ---------------------------
Benton, Barbara            1      Regular Ward-Fixed
Chen, Rue                  4      Regular Ward-Fixed
Davis, David               6      Regular Ward-Fixed
. . .

(56 row(s) affected)
```

9.
```
COLUMN "Patient" FORMAT A25;
COLUMN "Bed" FORMAT 9999;

SELECT CAST(pat_last_name + ', ' + pat_first_name AS CHAR(25))
    "Patient",
    p.bed_number "Bed"
FROM patient p LEFT OUTER JOIN bed b
    ON (p.bed_number = b.bed_number)
WHERE p.bed_number IS NULL
ORDER BY pat_last_name, pat_first_name;

Patient                    Bed
------------------------   ------
Howard, Ronald             NULL
Mullins, Mildred           NULL
North, Norbert             NULL
Overstreet, Orville        NULL

(4 row(s) affected)
```

11.
```
SELECT CAST(pat_last_name + ', ' + pat_first_name AS CHAR(20))
    "Patient",
    CAST(s.service_description AS CHAR(20)) "Treatment Svc",
```

```
        CAST(staff_last_name + ', ' + staff_first_name AS CHAR(20))
        "Staff Member"
FROM patient p, treatment t, staff st, service s
WHERE p.pat_id = t.pat_id AND
      st.staff_id = t.staff_id AND
      s.service_id = t.service_id
ORDER BY pat_last_name, pat_first_name;
```

The result table is the same as for chapter 6, Riverbend question 10 and is not given here.

13.
```
SELECT CAST(pat_last_name + ', ' + pat_first_name AS CHAR(20))
       "Patient",
       CAST(m.med_name_common AS CHAR(20)) "Prescription",
       CAST(staff_last_name + ', ' + staff_first_name AS CHAR(20))
       "Staff Member"
FROM patient p, prescription pr, medicine m, staff st
WHERE p.pat_id = pr.pat_id AND
      m.medicine_code = pr.medicine_code AND
      st.staff_id = pr.staff_id
ORDER BY pat_last_name, pat_first_name;
```

Patient	Prescription	Staff Member
Algebra, Albert	Rocephin	Sumner, Elizabeth
Ashcroft, Arthur	Lanoxin	Brockwell, Mary Elle
Boudreaux, Billy	Lanoxin	Bock, Douglas
. . .		

(25 row(s) affected)

15.
```
SELECT CAST(pat_last_name + ', ' + pat_first_name AS CHAR(20))
       "Patient",
       CAST(m.med_name_common AS CHAR(20)) "Prescription",
       CAST(staff_last_name + ', ' + staff_first_name AS CHAR(20))
       "Staff Member"
FROM patient p JOIN prescription pr ON (p.pat_id = pr.pat_id)
     JOIN medicine m ON (m.medicine_code = pr.medicine_code)
     JOIN staff st ON (st.staff_id = pr.staff_id)
WHERE st.staff_id = '66425'
ORDER BY pat_last_name, pat_first_name;
```

Patient	Prescription	Staff Member
Chang, Charlie	Lanoxin	Quattromani, Toni
Chang, Charlie	Alupent	Quattromani, Toni
Pauley, Paul	Alupent	Quattromani, Toni
Ridgeway, Ricardo	Lanoxin	Quattromani, Toni
Ridgeway, Ricardo	Valium	Quattromani, Toni

(5 row(s) affected)

CHAPTER 7

SQL CODING EXERCISES AND QUESTIONS: COMPANY DATABASE

1.
```
SELECT CAST(emp_last_name As CHAR(12)) "Last Name",
       CAST(emp_first_name As CHAR(12)) "First Name"
```

```
FROM employee
WHERE emp_ssn IN
    (SELECT work_emp_ssn
     FROM assignment
     WHERE work_pro_number IN (10, 20, 30) );
```

```
Last Name    First Name
------------ ------------
Amin         Hyder
Zhu          Waiman
Joyner       Suzanne
Bordoloi     Bijoy
Markis       Marcia
```

```
(5 row(s) affected)
```

3.
```
SELECT CAST(emp_last_name As CHAR(12)) "Last Name",
       CAST(emp_first_name As CHAR(12)) "First Name"
FROM employee
WHERE emp_ssn IN
    (SELECT work_emp_ssn
     FROM assignment
     WHERE work_pro_number NOT IN (10, 20, 30) )
ORDER BY emp_last_name;
```

```
Last Name    First Name
------------ ------------
Bock         Douglas
Joshi        Dinesh
Prescott     Sherri
Zhu          Waiman
```

```
(4 row(s) affected)
```

5.
```
SELECT CAST(emp_last_name AS CHAR(12)) "Last Name",
       CAST(emp_first_name AS CHAR(12)) "First Name",
       CAST(emp_date_of_birth AS CHAR(12)) "Birth Date"
FROM employee
WHERE emp_date_of_birth <
    (SELECT MIN(emp_date_of_birth)
     FROM employee
     WHERE emp_dpt_number = 3);
```

```
Last Name    First Name   Birth Date
------------ ------------ ------------
Bock         Douglas      Dec  5 1950
Bordoloi     Bijoy        Mar 14 1954
```

```
(2 row(s) affected)
```

7.
```
SELECT work_emp_ssn "Emp SSN", work_hours "Hours Worked",
       work_pro_number "Project"
FROM assignment a1
WHERE work_hours =
    (SELECT MIN(work_hours)
     FROM assignment
     WHERE a1.work_pro_number = work_pro_number)
ORDER BY work_pro_number;
```

```
Emp SSN   Hours Worked Project
--------- ------------ -------
999888888 21.0         1
999111111 8.5          2
999444444 10.5         3
999444444 10.1         10
999444444 11.8         20
999222222 5.1          30

(6 row(s) affected)
```

9. ```
SELECT emp_ssn "Emp SSN",
      CAST(emp_last_name As CHAR(10)) "Last Name",
      CAST(emp_first_name As CHAR(10)) "First Name",
      emp_dpt_number "Dept",
      '$' + CONVERT (CHAR (10), emp_salary, 1) "Salary",
      CAST(emp_date_of_birth As CHAR(11)) "Birth Date"
FROM employee e1
WHERE emp_date_of_birth =
      (SELECT MAX(emp_date_of_birth)
       FROM employee
       WHERE e1.emp_dpt_number = emp_dpt_number)
ORDER BY emp_dpt_number;
```

```
Emp SSN   Last Name  First Name Dept   Salary       Birth Date
--------- ---------- ---------- ------ ------------ -----------
999666666 Bordoloi   Bijoy      1      $ 55,000.00 Mar 14 1954
999887777 Markis     Marcia     3      $ 25,000.00 Jul 19 1978
999444444 Zhu        Waiman     7      $ 43,000.00 Dec  8 1975

(3 row(s) affected)
```

11. ```
SELECT CAST(emp_last_name As CHAR(12)) "Last Name",
      CAST(emp_first_name As CHAR(12)) "First Name"
FROM employee e1
WHERE EXISTS
      (SELECT dpt_mgrssn
       FROM department
       WHERE e1.emp_ssn = dpt_mgrssn);
```

```
Last Name    First Name
------------ ------------
Zhu          Waiman
Joyner       Suzanne
Bordoloi     Bijoy

(3 row(s) affected)
```

SQL CODING EXERCISES AND QUESTIONS: RIVERBEND DATABASE

1. ```
SELECT CAST(pat_last_name AS CHAR(12)) "Last Name",
      CAST(pat_first_name AS CHAR(12)) "First Name"
FROM patient
WHERE pat_id IN
      (SELECT pat_id
       FROM treatment
```
```

```
           WHERE service_id IN ('82947', '90788'));


    Last Name    First Name
    ------------ ------------
    Davis        David
    Quentin      Quincy
    Mousseau     Mickey
    . . .

    (13 row(s) affected)
```

3.
```
   SELECT CAST(pat_last_name AS CHAR(12)) "Last Name",
          CAST(pat_first_name AS CHAR(12)) "First Name"
   FROM patient
   WHERE pat_id IN
        (SELECT pat_id
          FROM treatment
          WHERE service_id NOT IN ('82947', '90788'))
   ORDER BY pat_last_name, pat_first_name;


   Last Name    First Name
   ------------ ------------
   Able         Andrew
   Algebra      Albert
   Ashcroft     Arthur
   . . .

   (54 row(s) affected)
```

5.
```
   SELECT CAST(pat_last_name AS CHAR(12)) "Last Name",
          CAST(pat_first_name AS CHAR(12)) "First Name"
   FROM patient
   WHERE pat_id IN
        (SELECT pat_id
          FROM prescription
          WHERE medicine_code IN ('9999003', '9999002'))
   ORDER BY pat_last_name, pat_first_name;


   Last Name    First Name
   ------------ ------------
   Howard       Ronald
   Quentin      Quincy
   . . .

   (8 row(s) affected)
```

7.
```
   SELECT CAST(staff_last_name AS CHAR(15)) "Last Name",
          CAST(staff_first_name AS CHAR(15)) "First Name",
          CAST(hospital_title AS CHAR(20)) "Title",
          CAST(date_hired AS CHAR(12)) "Date Hired"
   FROM staff
   WHERE date_hired <
        (SELECT Min(date_hired)
          FROM staff
          WHERE hospital_title = 'R.N.');
```

```
Last Name        First Name       Title                 Date Hired
---------------  ---------------  --------------------  ------------
Bock             Douglas          M.D.                  Aug 11 1987
Webber           Eugene           M.D.                  Feb 16 1995
Adams            Adam             Records Clerk         Jan 29 1985
Quattromani      Toni             M.D.                  Nov 10 1989
Schultheis       Robert           M.D.                  Dec 14 1979
Klepper          Robert           M.D.                  Feb  1 1984
Becker           Robert           M.D.                  Dec 14 1982
Becker           Roberta          M.D.                  Dec 14 1982
Jones            Quincey          M.D.                  Jan  1 1990

(9 row(s) affected)
```

9.
```
SELECT CAST(s.service_id AS CHAR(10)) "Service ID",
       CAST(s.service_description AS CHAR(40)) "Description"
FROM service s
WHERE service_id IN
    (SELECT s2.service_id
     FROM service s2 JOIN treatment t2 ON
        (s2.service_id=t2.service_id)
     WHERE service_charge - actual_charge >
        (SELECT AVG(service_charge - actual_charge)
         FROM service s3 JOIN treatment t3 ON
             (s3.service_id=t3.service_id)
         WHERE service_cat_id = 'SUR'));
```

```
Service ID Description
---------- ----------------------------------------
12001      Thoracic-General Exploratory
12007      Cranial
12010      Spinal-Exploratory

(3 row(s) affected)
```

11.
```
SELECT CAST(staff_last_name + ', ' + staff_first_name AS CHAR(30))
       "Name",
       CAST(ward_dept_assigned AS CHAR(20)) "Ward-Dept",
       '$' + CONVERT(CHAR(12), salary, 1) "Salary"
FROM staff s1
WHERE salary =
    (SELECT MIN(salary)
     FROM staff s2
     WHERE s1.ward_dept_assigned = s2.ward_dept_assigned AND
         hospital_title = 'M.D.')
ORDER BY ward_dept_assigned;
```

```
Name                            Ward-Dept             Salary
------------------------------  --------------------  ------------
Quattromani, Toni               CARD1                 $  225,325.00
Sumner, Elizabeth               EMER1                 $  165,000.00
Eakin, Maxwell                  MEDS1                 $  150,000.00
Klepper, Robert                 ONCOL                 $  150,655.00
Schultheis, Robert              OUTP1                 $  175,425.00
Webber, Eugene                  RADI1                 $  175,000.00
Becker, Roberta                 SURG1                 $  230,000.00

(7 row(s) affected)
```

13.
```
SELECT CAST(staff_last_name + ', ' + staff_first_name AS CHAR(25))
     "Name",
     CAST(ward_dept_assigned AS CHAR(10)) "Ward-Dept",
     '$' + CONVERT(CHAR(12), salary, 1) "Salary",
     CAST(date_hired AS CHAR(12)) "Date Hired"
FROM staff s1
WHERE date_hired =
   (SELECT MAX(date_hired)
    FROM staff s2
    WHERE s1.ward_dept_assigned = s2.ward_dept_assigned AND
        salary IS NOT NULL)
ORDER BY ward_dept_assigned;
```

Name	Ward-Dept	Salary	Date Hired
Boudreaux, Betty	ADMI2	$ 32,895.00	Nov 5 2000
Boudreaux, Beverly	ADMIN	$ 37,520.00	Oct 15 2001
Quattromani, Toni	CARD1	$ 225,325.00	Nov 10 1989
Sumner, Elizabeth	EMER1	$ 165,000.00	Feb 16 2001
Brockwell, Mary Ellen	GYNO1	$ 68,000.00	Feb 23 1996
Eakin, Maxwell	MEDS1	$ 150,000.00	Jan 6 1998
Young, Yvonne	NEWB1	$ 42,000.00	Feb 26 2000
Zumwalt, Mary	ONCOL	$ 69,500.00	Jan 3 1996
Schultheis, Robert	OUTP1	$ 175,425.00	Dec 14 1979
Bordoloi, Bijoy	RADI1	$ 178,500.00	Aug 23 1999
Barlow, William	SURG1	$ 275,000.00	May 16 2001
Simmons, Lester	SURRE	$ 62,000.00	Mar 3 1998

(12 row(s) affected)

CHAPTER 8

SQL Coding Exercises and Questions: Company Database

1.
```
CREATE VIEW salary_view (ssn, last_name, first_name, salary) AS
    SELECT emp_ssn, emp_last_name, emp_first_name, emp_salary
    FROM employee

SELECT *
FROM salary_view
WHERE salary >= 30000;
```

ssn	last_name	first_name	salary
999111111	Bock	Douglas	30000.0000
999333333	Joshi	Dinesh	38000.0000
999444444	Zhu	Waiman	43000.0000
999555555	Joyner	Suzanne	43000.0000
999666666	Bordoloi	Bijoy	55000.0000

(5 row(s) affected

3.
```
CREATE VIEW dependent_view (Employee_SSN, Name, Gender,
    Birth_Date, Relationship) AS
SELECT *
FROM dependent
```

5.
```
CREATE VIEW department_projects (dept_no, department,
     project, location) AS
SELECT dpt_no, CAST(dpt_name AS CHAR(17)),
     CAST(pro_name AS CHAR(15)), CAST(pro_location AS CHAR(15))
FROM department d JOIN project p ON (d.dpt_no = p.pro_dept_number)
WHERE (pro_location = 'Edwardsville' OR pro_location = 'Marina')
GO
SELECT dept_no, department, project, location
FROM department_projects;
```

```
dept_no department          project          location
------- ------------------  ---------------  ---------------
7       Production          Receivables      Edwardsville
3       Admin and Records   Inventory        Marina
1       Headquarters        Personnel        Edwardsville
3       Admin and Records   Pay Benefits     Marina

(4 row(s) affected)
```

7.
```
SELECT *
FROM department_projects
WHERE dept_no = 3;
```

```
dept_no department          project          location          pro_no
------- ------------------  ---------------  ---------------   ------
3       Admin and Records   Inventory        Marina            10
3       Admin and Records   Pay Benefits     Marina            30

(2 row(s) affected)
```

9.
```
CREATE TABLE sales_order (
     so_number              INTEGER IDENTITY(100,1)
          CONSTRAINT pk_sales_order PRIMARY KEY,
     so_value               DECIMAL(9,2),
     so_emp_ssn             CHAR(9),
CONSTRAINT fk_so_emp_ssn
     FOREIGN KEY (so_emp_ssn) REFERENCES employee );
GO
INSERT INTO sales_order VALUES (155.59, '999111111');
INSERT INTO sales_order VALUES (450.00, '999444444');
INSERT INTO sales_order VALUES (16.95,  '999444444');
INSERT INTO sales_order VALUES (15.95,  '999111111');
GO
SELECT *
FROM sales_order;
```

```
so_number   so_value    so_emp_ssn
----------- ----------- ----------
100         155.59      999111111
101         450.00      999444444
102         16.95       999444444
103         15.95       999111111

(4 row(s) affected)
```

NOTE: so_number values may vary depending on how many times a student executes the INSERT statements attempting to solve this exercise.

11.
```
CREATE VIEW sales (SO_Number, Value, Emp_SSN, Description,
Quantity, Price) AS
    SELECT so_number, so_value, so_emp_ssn, od_product_desc,
        od_quantity_ordered, od_product_price
    FROM sales_order s JOIN order_details o
        ON (s.so_number = o.od_number)
GO
SELECT *
FROM sales;
```

SO_Number	Value	Emp_SSN	Description	Quantity	Price
104	200.00	999111111	End Table	1	100.00
104	200.00	999111111	Table Lamp	2	50.00

(2 row(s) affected)

SQL CODING EXERCISES AND QUESTIONS: RIVERBEND DATABASE

1.
```
CREATE VIEW medicine_view (med_code, common_name,
    scientific_name, quantity, units) AS
SELECT medicine_code, CAST(med_name_common AS CHAR(18)),
    CAST(med_name_sci AS CHAR(16)),
    quantity_stock, CAST(unit_measure AS CHAR(20))
FROM medicine
GO
SELECT *
FROM medicine_view
WHERE quantity <= 1000;
```

med_code	common_name	scientific_name	quantity	units
9999004	Dalmane	Flurazepam	855	Milligram
9999007	Atarax	Hydroxyzine	855	M.Gram/C.Centimeter
9999018	Bactroban Ung. Oin	Mupirocin	367	Tube

(3 row(s) affected)

3.
```
CREATE VIEW patient_view (Patient_ID, Last_Name, First_name,
    Birth_Date) AS
SELECT pat_id, CAST(pat_last_name AS CHAR(15)),
    CAST(pat_first_name AS CHAR(15)),
    CAST(pat_date_of_birth AS CHAR(12))
FROM patient
GO
SELECT *
FROM patient_view
WHERE Patient_ID >= '60000';
```

Patient_ID	Last_Name	First_name	Birth_Date
666117	Teal	Thomas	Sep 2 1966
666118	Vanquish	Vanna	Oct 3 2046
666119	Uniform	Uley	Aug 13 2035

```
666120     Youngman        Yvonne          Oct  3 2046
666121     Zenna           Zina            Oct 31 2042

(5 row(s) affected)
```

5. ```
CREATE VIEW prescription_view (prescription, pre_date,
     dosage, directions, medicine, patient, staff_id, staff) AS
SELECT pr.pre_number, CAST(pr.pre_date AS CHAR(12)),
     pr.dosage_prescribed,
     pr.dosage_directions, m.med_name_common,
     CAST(pa.pat_last_name + ' ' + pa.pat_first_name AS CHAR(20)),
     pr.staff_id, s.staff_last_name
FROM prescription pr, patient pa, staff s, medicine m
WHERE pr.pat_id = pa.pat_id AND
     pr.staff_id = s.staff_id AND
     pr.medicine_code = m.medicine_code
GO
SELECT *
FROM prescription_view
WHERE prescription = '755444020';
```

```
prescription pre_date      dosage
directions
medicine                                        patient
staff_id staff
----------- ------------ -------------------------------------
----- ---------------------------------------------------------
---------------------------------------------------------------
---------------------------------------------------------------
--------------------------------------------- ----------------
--------------------------- ------------------ ------ ---------
--------------------------------------
755444020   Jun 10 2003  2 G. daily in IV.
NULL
Rocephin                                        Algebra Albert
10044    Sumner

(1 row(s) affected)
```

7. ```
CREATE VIEW staff_location_view (staff_member, staff_id,
     ward_dept_id, ward_department, telephone, exten) AS
SELECT CAST(s.staff_last_name + ' ' + s.staff_first_name AS
CHAR(20)),
     s.staff_id, w.ward_id, w.ward_dept_name, s.work_phone,
     s.phone_extension
FROM staff s, ward_dept w
WHERE w.ward_id = s.ward_dept_assigned
GO
SELECT *
FROM staff_location_view
WHERE ward_dept_id = 'MEDS1';
```

```
staff_member           staff_id ward_dept_id ward_department
telephone   exten
-------------------- -------- ------------ -----------------------
---------------------- ---------- -----
Bock Douglas           01885    MEDS1        Medical Surgical Ward 1
1005559268 0011
```

```
Eakin Maxwell        23232    MEDS1      Medical Surgical Ward 1
1005559268 0001
```

```
(2 row(s) affected)
```

9.
```
DROP VIEW staff_location_view;
DROP VIEW treatment_view;
```

```
The command(s) completed successfully.
```

11.
```
INSERT INTO patient2 (pat_ssn, pat_last_name, pat_first_name)
    VALUES ('900000000','Zucker','Zina');
INSERT INTO patient2 (pat_ssn, pat_last_name, pat_first_name)
    VALUES ('900000001','Zucker','Zachary');
GO
SELECT pat_id, pat_ssn, pat_last_name, pat_first_name
FROM patient2;
```

```
pat_id      pat_ssn    pat_last_name
pat_first_name
----------- ---------- --------------------------------------------
-----------------------------------------
700000      900000000 Zucker
Zina
700001      900000001 Zucker
Zachary
```

```
(2 row(s) affected)
```

CHAPTER 9

SQL CODING EXERCISES AND QUESTIONS: COMPANY DATABASE

1.
```
SELECT UPPER(emp_last_name)+ ', ' + emp_first_name + ' '
    + LEFT(IsNull(emp_middle_name, ''), 1) "Employee Name"
FROM employee;
```

```
Employee Name
--------------------------------
BOCK, Douglas B
AMIN, Hyder
JOSHI, Dinesh
ZHU, Waiman Z
JOYNER, Suzanne A
BORDOLOI, Bijoy
MARKIS, Marcia M
PRESCOTT, Sherri C
```

```
(8 row(s) affected)
```

3.
```
SELECT emp_last_name + STR(emp_salary, 8, 0) "Name and Salary"
FROM employee
ORDER BY emp_last_name;
```

```
Name and Salary
--------------------------------
Amin    25000
Bock    30000
Bordoloi    55000
Joshi    38000
Joyner    43000
Markis    25000
Prescott    25000
Zhu    43000


(8 row(s) affected)
```

5. ```
   SELECT UPPER(emp_last_name)+ ', ' + emp_first_name + ' '
       + LEFT(IsNull(emp_middle_name, ''), 1) "Employee Name"
   FROM employee
   WHERE CHARINDEX('oy', emp_last_name+emp_first_name) != 0
   ORDER BY emp_last_name, emp_first_name;
   ```

```
Employee Name
------------------
BORDOLOI, Bijoy
JOYNER, Suzanne A

(2 row(s) affected)
```

7. ```
   SELECT SUBSTRING(emp_last_name,1,4) "Name",
       SUBSTRING(emp_ssn,6,4) "SSN"
   FROM employee
   ORDER BY emp_last_name;
   ```

```
Name SSN
---- ----
Amin 2222
Bock 1111
Bord 6666
Josh 3333
Joyn 5555
Mark 7777
Pres 8888
Zhu  4444


(8 row(s) affected)
```

9. ```
   SELECT emp_last_name "Last Name",
       CONVERT(CHAR(15), ISNULL(emp_superssn, 'Top Dog')) "Supervisor SSN"
   FROM employee
   ORDER BY emp_last_name;
   ```

```
Last Name                 Supervisor SSN
------------------------- ---------------
Amin                      999555555
Bock                      999444444
Bordoloi                  Top Dog
```
```

```
Joshi                       999444444
Joyner                      999666666
Markis                      999555555
Prescott                    999444444
Zhu                         999666666

(8 row(s) affected)
```

11. ```
SELECT emp_last_name "Last Name", work_pro_number "Project",
      ROUND(work_hours,0) "Hours"
FROM assignment a, employee e
WHERE e.emp_ssn = a.work_emp_ssn AND
    work_pro_number IN (2,10)
ORDER BY work_pro_number, emp_last_name;
```

```
Last Name                   Project Hours
------------------------    ------- -------
Bock                        2       9.0
Prescott                    2       22.0
Zhu                         2       12.0
Amin                        10      35.0
Markis                      10      10.0
Zhu                         10      10.0

(6 row(s) affected)
```

13. ```
SELECT CONVERT(CHAR(15), dep_name) "Name",
      CONVERT(CHAR(15),dep_date_of_birth, 106) "Birthday",
      CONVERT(CHAR(15),DATEADD(year, 65, dep_date_of_birth), 106)
      "Date 65"
FROM dependent;
```

```
Name            Birthday        Date 65
--------------- --------------- ---------------
Deanna          03 May 1981     03 May 2046
Jeffery         31 Dec 1978     31 Dec 2043
Mary Ellen      28 May 1956     28 May 2021
. . .

(13 row(s) affected)
```

15. ```
SELECT CONVERT(CHAR(12), dep_name) "Name",
      CONVERT(CHAR(6), REPLACE(dep_gender,'F','Female')) "Gender"
FROM dependent
WHERE dep_gender = 'F'
ORDER BY dep_name;
```

```
Name   Gender
------------ ------
Anita   Female
Deanna   Female
Jo Ellen   Female
. . .

(10 row(s) affected)
```
```

SQL Coding Exercises and Questions: Riverbend Database

1. SELECT UPPER(staff_last_name)+ ', ' + staff_first_name + ' '
       + LEFT(IsNull(staff_middle_name, "), 1) "Staff Name"
    FROM staff
    ORDER BY staff_last_name, staff_first_name, staff_middle_name;

```
Staff Name
----------------------
ADAMS, Adam A
BARLOW, William A
BECKER, Robert B
. . .

(24 row(s) affected)
```

3. SELECT UPPER(staff_last_name)+ ', ' + staff_first_name + ' '
       + LEFT(IsNull(staff_middle_name, "), 1) "Staff Name"
    FROM staff
    WHERE CHARINDEX('ou', staff_last_name+staff_first_name, 1) != 0
    ORDER BY staff_last_name, staff_first_name, staff_middle_name;

```
Staff Name
--------------------------
BOCK, Douglas B
BOUDREAUX, Betty
BOUDREAUX, Beverly
YOUNG, Yvonne E

(4 row(s) affected)
```

5. SELECT CAST(room_id+' '+STR(bed_number) AS CHAR(25)) "Rooms/Beds"
    FROM bed
    ORDER BY room_id;

```
Rooms/Beds
-----------------------
ER0001          50
ER0001          51
ER0001          52
. . .

(98 row(s) affected)
```

7. SELECT CAST(staff_last_name+', '+staff_first_name AS CHAR(25)) "Name",
       '$' + CONVERT(CHAR(11), salary, 1) "Salary Amount"
    FROM staff
    ORDER BY staff_last_name;

```
Name                       Salary Amount
-------------------------- -------------
Adams, Adam                $  35,500.00
Barlow, William            $ 275,000.00
Becker, Robert             $ 235,450.00
. . .

(24 row(s) affected)
```

9. SELECT s.service_id "Service",
       '$'+CONVERT(CHAR(10), s.service_charge, 1) "Service Charge",
       '$'+CONVERT(CHAR(10), t.actual_charge, 1) "Actual Charge",
       '$'+CONVERT(CHAR(10), ABS(s.service_charge - t.actual_charge),1)
       "Difference"
   FROM service s JOIN treatment t ON (s.service_id = t.service_id)
   WHERE s.service_charge - t.actual_charge > 0
   ORDER BY ABS(s.service_charge - t.actual_charge) DESC;

```
Service Service Charge Actual Charge Difference
------- -------------- ------------- -----------
12001   $  6,200.00    $    450.00   $  5,750.00
12010   $  3,500.00    $  1,480.00   $  2,020.00
12007   $ 10,000.00    $  8,500.00   $  1,500.00
99203   $     95.00    $     75.00   $     20.00
99203   $     95.00    $     75.00   $     20.00
99058   $    155.00    $    150.00   $      5.00
90782   $     75.00    $     70.00   $      5.00

(7 row(s) affected)
```

11. SELECT CAST(staff_last_name+', '+staff_first_name AS CHAR(30))
        "Staff Name", CAST(hospital_title AS CHAR(20)) "Hospital Title",
        CONVERT(CHAR(12), date_hired, 107) "Date Hired"
    FROM staff
    ORDER BY date_hired;

```
Staff Name                        Hospital Title        Date Hired
-------------------------------   --------------------  --------------
Schultheis, Robert                M.D.                  Dec 14, 1979
Becker, Robert                    M.D.                  Dec 14, 1982
Becker, Roberta                   M.D.                  Dec 14, 1982
. . .

(24 row(s) affected)
```

13. SELECT CAST(pat_last_name+', '+pat_first_name AS CHAR(30))
        "Patient Name",
        CONVERT(CHAR(14), pat_date_of_birth, 107) "Birth Date",
        CONVERT(CHAR(14), DATEADD(YEAR,60,pat_date_of_birth), 107)
        "60th Birthday"
    FROM patient
    ORDER BY pat_date_of_birth;

```
Patient Name                      Birth Date      60th Birthday
-------------------------------   --------------  --------------
Grant, Gregory                    Dec 05, 1951    Dec 05, 2011
Monday, Mandy                     May 21, 1952    May 21, 2012
North, Norbert                    Jan 15, 1956    Jan 15, 2016
. . .

(60 row(s) affected)
```

15. SELECT b.room_id "Room #", b.bed_number "Bed",
        CAST(bt.bed_description AS CHAR(30)) "Bed Description",
        CAST(REPLACE(bed_availability,'Y','Occupied') AS CHAR(10))

```
              "Availability"
       FROM bed b JOIN bed_type bt ON (bt.bed_type_id = b.bed_type_id)
       ORDER BY b.room_id, b.bed_number;


       Room # Bed    Bed Description                 Availability
       ------ ------ ------------------------------- ------------
       ER0001 50     Emergency Room-Rollaround       Occupied
       ER0001 51     Emergency Room-Rollaround       N
       ER0001 52     Emergency Room-Fixed            Occupied
       . . .


       (98 row(s) affected)
```

CHAPTER 10

SQL CODING EXERCISES AND QUESTIONS: COMPANY DATABASE

1. CREATE PROCEDURE eqp_value_increase (@percent_increase DECIMAL(3,1))
      AS UPDATE equipment
         SET eqp_value = eqp_value + (eqp_value *
            @percent_increase/100);

   The command(s) completed successfully.

3. DROP PROCEDURE eqp_value_increase;
   The command(s) completed successfully.

5. EXEC eqp_value_increase '5678', 20.0

   ```
   SELECT eqp_no, eqp_description, eqp_value
   FROM equipment
   WHERE eqp_no = '5678';


   eqp_no eqp_description eqp_value
   ------ --------------- --------------------
   5678   Printer         227.0400
   ```

7. EXEC eqp_value_increase '4321'

   (1 row(s) affected)

   ```
   SELECT eqp_no, eqp_description, eqp_value
   FROM equipment
   WHERE eqp_no = '4321';


   eqp_no eqp_description eqp_value
   ------ --------------- --------------------
   4321   Computer, PC    1246.3000
   ```

9. EXEC replace_work_hours '999555555', 20, 15.5;

   (1 row(s) affected)

   ```
   SELECT work_emp_ssn, work_pro_number, work_hours
   FROM assignment
   WHERE work_emp_ssn = '999555555' AND work_pro_number = 20;
   ```

```
work_emp_ssn work_pro_number work_hours
------------ --------------- ----------
999555555    20              15.5
```

11. ```
    CREATE TRIGGER update_work_hours
        ON assignment AFTER UPDATE
        AS IF UPDATE(work_hours)
            BEGIN
            DECLARE @work_emp_ssn CHAR(9)
            DECLARE @old_work_hours DECIMAL(5,1)
            DECLARE @new_work_hours DECIMAL(5,1)
            SELECT @old_work_hours = (SELECT work_hours FROM deleted)
            SELECT @new_work_hours = (SELECT work_hours FROM inserted)
            SELECT @work_emp_ssn = (SELECT work_emp_ssn FROM inserted)
            INSERT INTO audit_assignment VALUES
                (@work_emp_ssn, @old_work_hours, @new_work_hours,
                 USER_NAME(), GETDATE())
            END
    ```

    The command(s) completed successfully.

13. ```
    CREATE TRIGGER check_work_hours
        ON assignment AFTER UPDATE
        AS IF UPDATE(work_hours)
            BEGIN
            DECLARE @new_work_hours DECIMAL(5,1)
            SELECT @new_work_hours = (SELECT work_hours FROM inserted)
            IF @new_work_hours > 250
                BEGIN
                    PRINT 'Work Hours Reported Exceeds Policy'
                    PRINT 'Transaction Was Canceled'
                    ROLLBACK TRANSACTION
                END
            ELSE
                BEGIN
                    PRINT 'New Work Hours Value Recorded'
                END
            END;
    ```

    The command(s) completed successfully.

15. ```
    EXEC sp_settriggerorder @triggername='check_work_hours',
        @order='first', @stmttype='update'
    ```

    The command(s) completed successfully.

SQL CODING EXERCISES AND QUESTIONS: RIVERBEND DATABASE

1. ```
   CREATE PROCEDURE wage_rate_increase (@percent_increase DECIMAL(3,1))
       AS UPDATE staff
           SET wage_rate = wage_rate + (wage_rate *
               @percent_increase/100)
           WHERE wage_RATE IS NOT NULL;
   ```

   The command(s) completed successfully.

3. `DROP PROCEDURE wage_rate_increase;`

   ```
   The command(s) completed successfully.
   ```

5. `EXEC wage_rate_increase '33358', 10.0`

   ```
   (1 row(s) affected)
   ```

   ```sql
   SELECT staff_id "Staff Id",
       CAST(staff_last_name + ', ' + staff_first_name AS CHAR(20))
       "Staff Name",
       CAST(hospital_title AS CHAR(25)) "Hospital Title",
       '$' + CONVERT(CHAR(7), wage_rate, 1) "Wage Rate"
   FROM staff
   WHERE staff_id = '33358';
   ```

   ```
   Staff Id Staff Name           Hospital Title            Wage Rate
   -------- -------------------- ------------------------- ---------
   33358    Thornton, Billy      Building Custodian        $   9.38

   (1 row(s) affected)
   ```

7. `EXEC wage_rate_default '33359'`

   ```
   (1 row(s) affected)
   ```

   ```sql
   SELECT staff_id "Staff Id",
       CAST(staff_last_name + ', ' + staff_first_name AS CHAR(20))
       "Staff Name",
       CAST(hospital_title AS CHAR(25)) "Hospital Title",
       '$' + CONVERT(CHAR(7), wage_rate, 1) "Wage Rate"
   FROM staff
   WHERE staff_id = '33359';
   ```

   ```
   Staff Id Staff Name           Hospital Title            Wage Rate
   -------- -------------------- ------------------------- ---------
   33359    Clinton, William     Building Custodian        $   7.72

   (1 row(s) affected)
   ```

9. `EXEC new_treatment_charge 2, '6/10/2003 12:00 AM', 55.55`

   ```
   (1 row(s) affected)
   ```

   ```sql
   SELECT treatment_number "Treatment No",
       CAST(treatment_date AS CHAR(12)) "Treatment Date",
       '$' + CONVERT(CHAR(12), actual_charge, 1) "New Actual Charge"
   FROM treatment
   WHERE treatment_date = '6/10/2003' AND  treatment_number= 2;
   ```

   ```
   Treatment No Treatment Date New Actual Charge
   ------------ -------------- -----------------
   2            Jun 10 2003    $        55.55

   (1 row(s) affected)
   ```

11. ```sql
    CREATE TRIGGER update_treatment_actual_charge
      ON treatment AFTER UPDATE
      AS IF UPDATE(actual_charge)
        BEGIN
    ```
    ```

```
DECLARE @treatment_number INT
DECLARE @treatment_date DATETIME
DECLARE @old_actual_charge MONEY
DECLARE @new_actual_charge MONEY
SELECT @treatment_number = (SELECT treatment_number FROM deleted)
SELECT @treatment_date = (SELECT treatment_date FROM deleted)
SELECT @old_actual_charge = (SELECT actual_charge FROM deleted)
SELECT @new_actual_charge = (SELECT actual_charge FROM inserted)
INSERT INTO audit_treatment VALUES
    (@treatment_number, @treatment_date, @old_actual_charge,
    @new_actual_charge, USER_NAME(), GETDATE() )
END

The command(s) completed successfully.
```

13.
```
CREATE TRIGGER check_service_charge
ON service AFTER UPDATE
AS IF UPDATE(service_charge)
BEGIN
DECLARE @old_service_charge MONEY
DECLARE @new_service_charge MONEY
SELECT @old_service_charge = (SELECT service_charge FROM deleted)
SELECT @new_service_charge = (SELECT service_charge FROM inserted)
IF @new_service_charge > (@old_service_charge * 1.2)
    BEGIN
        PRINT 'New Service Charge Exceeds 20% Policy'
        PRINT 'Transaction Was Canceled'
        ROLLBACK TRANSACTION
    END
ELSE
    BEGIN
        PRINT 'New Service Charge Value Recorded'
    END
END;

The command(s) completed successfully.
```

15.
```
UPDATE service SET service_charge = 265.59
    WHERE service_id = '10060';

New Service Charge Value Recorded

(1 row(s) affected)
```

CHAPTER 11

SQL Coding Exercises and Questions

Note: These exercises require you to select an appropriate database name based on your last name, birth day, and birth month. This is to ensure that each of you has a unique, individual database to use for your exercises. In the solutions presented we have elected to name the database Ch 11.

1. ```sql
   CREATE DATABASE Ch11
   ON PRIMARY
   ( NAME = Ch11Pri,
       FILENAME = 'C:\Data\Ch11Pri.Mdf',
       SIZE = 1,
       MAXSIZE = 50,
       FILEGROWTH = 25% ),
   FILEGROUP Ch11Group1
   ( NAME = Ch11Sec1,
       FILENAME = 'C:\Data\Ch11Sec1.Ndf',
       SIZE = 1,
       MAXSIZE = 50,
       FILEGROWTH = 5 ),
   ( NAME = Ch11Sec2,
       FILENAME = 'C:\Data\Ch11Sec2',
       SIZE = 1,
       MAXSIZE = 50,
       FILEGROWTH = 5 )
   LOG ON
   ( NAME = 'Ch11Log',
       FILENAME = 'C:\Datalogs\Ch11Log.Ldf',
       SIZE = 1MB,
       MAXSIZE = 25MB,
       FILEGROWTH = 5MB );
   ```

3. ```sql
   EXEC sp_grantdbaccess 'bob';
   EXEC sp_grantdbaccess 'matilda';
   EXEC sp_grantdbaccess 'makita';
   ```

5. ```sql
   GRANT CREATE TABLE TO bob;
   ```

7. ```sql
   INSERT INTO books VALUES('111111','My Favorite Book',
   '1-111-11111111', 149.95);
   INSERT INTO books VALUES('222222','Another Good Book',
   '2-222-22222222',18.50);
   ```

   ```
   SELECT * FROM books;
   Book_Id Book_Title              ISBN             Book_Price
   ------- ------------------- --------------- ----------
   111111  My Favorite Book    1-111-11111111  149.95
   222222  Another Good Book   2-222-22222222  18.50
   ```

9. ```sql
   GRANT SELECT ON books TO PUBLIC;
   ```

11. ```sql
    REVOKE ALL ON books FROM makita CASCADE;
    ```
    No, Makita can still query the books table because bob granted SELECT to PUBLIC.

13. ```sql
    EXEC sp_addrolemember 'books_mgr', 'makita';
    EXEC sp_addrolemember 'books_mgr', 'bob';
    ```

15. ```sql
    DELETE FROM books WHERE book_id = '111111';
    (1 row(s) affected)
    ```

```
SELECT * FROM books;
Book_Id Book_Title                    ISBN              Book_Price
------- ----------------------------- ----------------  ----------
222222  Another Good Book             2-222-22222222    18.50
333333  Makita Book                   3-333-33333333    8.55

(2 row(s) affected)
```

17. Drop all the database users from the role.

CHAPTER 12

SQL CODING EXERCISES AND QUESTIONS: COMPANY DATABASE

1. SELECT * from department;

3. adoDepartment.RecordSource = strSQL
   adoDepartment.Refresh

SQL CODING EXERCISES AND QUESTIONS: RIVERBEND DATABASE

1. SELECT * from medical_specialty;

3. adoMedSpec.RecordSource = strSQL
   adoMedSpec.Refresh

INDEX